THE FIRST WORLD WAR

OSPREY
PUBLISHING

THE FIRST WORLD WAR

THE WAR TO END ALL WARS

Peter Simkins, Geoffrey Jukes and Michael Hickey

Foreword by Hew Strachan

First published in Great Britain in 2003 by Osprey Publishing,
Midland House, West Way, Botley, Oxford OX2 0PH, UK
4301 21st Street, Suite 220B, Long Island City, NY 11101, USA
Email: info@ospreypublishing.com

OSPREY PUBLISHING IS PART OF THE OSPREY GROUP

Previously published as: Essential Histories 13: *The First World War (1) The Eastern Front 1914–1918*; Essential Histories 14: *The First World War (2) The Western Front 1914–1916*; Essential Histories 22: *The First World War (3) The Western Front 1917–1918*; Essential Histories 23: *The First World War (4) The Mediterranean Front 1914–1923*.

This new edition was first published in 2014.

A CIP catalogue record for this book is available from the British Library
ISBN: 978-1-4728-0830-1

Cartography by The Map Studio
Index by Sandra Shotter
Typeset in ITC New Baskerville & Bodoni
Origination by PDQ Media, Bungay, UK
Printed and bound through Worldprint Ltd in China

14 15 16 17 18 10 9 8 7 6 5 4 3 2 1

Osprey Publishing is supporting the Woodland Trust, the UK's leading woodland conservation charity, by funding the dedication of trees.

www.ospreypublishing.com

Front cover image: poppy fields. (Corbis)
Back cover image: British stretcher bearers battle with the mud. (IWM Q 5935)

IMPERIAL WAR MUSEUMS COLLECTIONS
Many of the photos in this book come from the Imperial War Museums' huge collections which cover all aspects of conflict involving Britain and the Commonwealth since the start of the twentieth century. These rich resources are available online to search, browse and buy at www.iwmcollections.org.uk. In addition to Collections Online, you can visit the visitor rooms where you can explore over 8 million photographs, thousands of hours of moving images, the largest sound archive of its kind in the world, thousands of diaries and letters written by people in wartime and a huge reference library. www.iwm.org.uk

CONTENTS

Chapter 3: The Eastern Front 1914–1918

Chapter 4: The Mediterranean Front 1914–1923

FOREWORD
By Professor Hew Strachan

The First World War was fought on many fronts intensively and simultaneously. In this respect it bears direct comparison with the Second World War. In the Second World War, the relationship between fronts, and the co-ordination of their efforts, would be called grand strategy. But this was not a phrase known or used in 1914–1918. Most of the campaigns described in this volume were self-contained in their origins and even in their conduct. They represented national efforts made in pursuit of national goals.

In this respect the First World War became a world war because it conflated wars that had lives and directions of their own. It began in the Balkans. As such it was the third Balkan war fought in rapid succession since 1912, and in most respects the interests of the principal Balkan states in the war never ranged beyond the Balkan peninsula. Serbia, Bulgaria and Romania all sought local objectives. The exception was the most reluctant of the Balkan belligerents, Greece, which had eyes on territory in Asia Minor. But that conflict – the one fought over the Ottoman Empire – makes the same point: it too began before 1914 and it did not end in 1918. In fact its conclusion was reached with the establishment of modern Turkey in 1923.

Only two powers, one on each side, fully confronted the fact that they were fighting a multi-front war. Britain was of Europe but not in it; moreover it had sprawling and vulnerable global interests. These included India and a network of colonial bases between Delhi and London. Their sizeable Muslim populations were intimately affected by the fate of Islam's Holy Cities, which lay within the Ottoman Empire. The pursuit of grand strategy therefore found its most coherent form in the debates of the British cabinet as it weighed the priorities of competing commitments. These went to the most basic issues of war and peace. Should Britain introduce conscription in order to raise a mass army? Should it not concentrate on what it could do best, providing the arms and money for other powers on the European mainland to fight? The resulting discussions were frequently acrimonious, and after the war the memoirs of the participants flung accusations that made 'easterners' and 'westerners', 'frocks' and 'brasshats' terms of abuse rather than precise descriptions. In reality the categories were never that neat, and the vigour with which the various options were canvassed bore testimony to the strength, not the weakness, of democracies in effective decision-making.

Germany was more genuinely divided between 'easterners' and 'westerners', but here the casualty was strategy itself. It stood at the physical heart of Europe, and it was the mainstay of the Central Powers' alliance. Its armies could go east or west with comparable facility, but it never found a consistent policy with which to determine their deployment. Moreover, as Peter Simkins makes clear in his contribution to this volume, by 1918 Germany's most important voice in the war's direction, Erich Ludendorff, had lost his way. By then its allies were critically dependent on Berlin not only for weapons and money, but also for military advice and leadership. Germany could not stretch its resources that far.

The First World War may in some respects have begun before 1914 and continued after 1918, but this does not mean that fighting was continuous in this period, however defined. Even in the middle of the war two fronts enjoyed periods of comparative quiet. Both fall within the purview of Michael Hickey's section of this book. In the autumn of 1915 Serbia, the country for whose defence the Entente powers of Russia, France and Britain had – at least nominally – gone to war, was overrun. Confronted by Austria-Hungary and Germany from the north and Bulgaria from the east, its army fell back through Albania to the Adriatic Sea. From here it was evacuated via Corfu to Thessalonika. Throughout 1916, 1917, and much of 1918, the Macedonian front was quiet enough for the British troops there to be known as 'the gardeners of Salonika'. Then in mid-September 1918 it roared into life, and the Allied forces, led by the Serbs, knocked Bulgaria out of the war and threatened what Churchill saw as the soft underbelly of Europe.

Six months after the collapse of Serbia, in April 1916, a British division, besieged at Kut-el-Amara on the River Tigris in Mesopotamia, surrendered to the Turks. Here too the front went quiet. The British did not resume their advance on Baghdad until the following winter, taking the city on 11 March 1917. On the Turks' other southern front, in greater Syria, there were similar pauses, the product not only of different priorities but also of the weather and of supply problems.

Serbia, Macedonia, Mesopotamia and Palestine are all treated here as part of the Mediterranean theatre. And so they were for a power like Britain that waged economic war through its mastery of the world's oceans and used the sea to project its forces overseas. But that was not how it seemed to Turkey. It had one front, in the Caucasus, which determined the forces available for its other fronts, including in 1915 Gallipoli. However, here the Caucasus is treated by Geoffrey Jukes as part of the Eastern Front. That was precisely the context into which it fitted for Germany: a Turkish thrust into Georgia and Azerbaijan could draw Russian troops away from the Eastern Front. The latter ran from the Baltic states in the north, through Poland, to Galicia in the south. When Romania entered the war on the side of the Entente in 1916, the Eastern Front extended yet further, as Russia found to its cost. Romania managed to divert German and Austro-Hungarian troops from Russia, but then required Russia to send troops to help it. Geoffrey Jukes concludes that by the winter of 1916–1917 the defence of Romania had become the principal preoccupation of Stavka, the Russian high command.

The message here is that no one theatre of war could in reality be treated in isolation from its neighbour. Romania was a Balkan power; the fighting in Serbia had implications for Russia; the frontiers of both Germany and Austria-Hungary straddled the compartments into which this book is logically divided. Much of Vienna's war effort was directed against Italy, and so undermined its conduct of the war against Russia. But when in October 1917 it achieved one of the most spectacular victories of the war, at Caporetto on the River Isonzo, the response of Italy's allies had repercussions for the war in the west, not the east. French and British divisions were despatched to Italy, and the Supreme War Council was created to coordinate the Allies' efforts – a process which would culminate with the appointment of Ferdinand Foch as Allied Supreme Commander in March 1918.

Peter Simkins acknowledges this interdependence, but still argues that the Western Front was the heart of the war. The fact that others agree with him is recognised by his being allowed twice as much space to discuss a smaller theatre of war (in geographical terms) as is each of his fellow contributors. And he is probably right. Germany was the mainstay of the Central Powers, and however many divisions they sent to other fronts, the total never exceeded that on the Western Front. Moreover, for Britain too the Western Front was an irreducible minimum, for two sensible strategic reasons. First, it had entered the war to secure the neutrality of Belgium. It could not afford to have an over-mighty continental power threatening its principal sea-lanes and imperial communications. Secondly, its chief ally in this endeavour was France. France had been invaded. The need to drive the Boche from its homeland, to recover its industries, to restore its frontiers and to liberate its peoples gave a dynamism and intensity to the Western Front probably unequalled elsewhere. There were no long pauses here, and when armistice came it meant victory for one side and defeat for the other.

Hew Strachan

INTRODUCTION
By Professor Robert O'Neill

The focus of our authors moves from the origins of the war to the battles of the Western Front, then to the Eastern Front including the Russian Revolution, and finally to the war across the Mediterranean from Italy and the Balkans to the Dardanelles, Sinai, Palestine and Mesopotamia.

The First World War challenged political and military leaders in a way in which no other conflict had since the Napoleonic Wars of a century earlier. It was the first truly global conflict among several major powers, ranging across Europe, Africa, the Middle East and East Asia, and hence over the Atlantic, Indian and Pacific oceans. Of course the principal instigators, Germany and Austria-Hungary, did not intend the war to be anything other than a European conflict, with later consequences for the wider world. But in threatening the interests of Great Britain in August 1914, the Central Powers brought into immediate play not only the full resources of the British Empire, but also those of Britain's East Asian ally, Japan. Only one hour after hostilities had begun for Britain, the Royal Australian Navy was firing on and capturing the first of 24 German ships seized in Australian waters. On 23 August Japan declared war on Germany and began to eliminate the German presence in China and the northern Pacific.

The German colonial empire in Africa soon became the theatre for a protracted struggle. The Ottoman Empire, despite its strong naval links with Britain, chose to side with the Central Powers, whose armies the Turks rated the more highly. For Britain, whose navy was converting from coal to oil as its principal fuel, control of the Persian Gulf region at the south-eastern end of the Ottoman Empire was vital and this need set a wider dimension to the conflict. The fact that France's principal ally, Russia, shared a border with the Ottoman Empire meant that soon the armies of both Russia and Turkey were engaged in and around the Caucasus. Thus the direct clashes of the German and French armies in Western Europe, and of the German, Austrian and Russian armies in Eastern Europe, while being potentially of decisive importance, have to be understood as two campaigns in a global engagement.

Because success eluded the Central Powers on these two key European fronts, the resources of the world beyond Europe became increasingly important in inclining the balance of force in Europe in favour of Britain, France, Russia and their allies. The opening of the war did not directly touch the United States, and the US Government attempted to remain aloof from what it saw as a war between European powers. But American commerce needed the freedom of the seas and from 1915 this liberty came into jeopardy. Also the balance of American interests made its technological and industrial resources more readily available to Britain and France than to Germany. It was only a matter of time before the increasingly hard-pressed Germans were to attack American shipping and draw the United States into the war on their opponents' side.

By 1914 the technological revolution in armaments, and hence in tactics and strategy, had reached the point at which the total resources of the belligerent powers became essential elements in the conflict. Human resources in Europe soon became fully stretched. Political leaders, where they were wise, paid heed to the needs, aspirations and opinions of their citizens and subjects. Societies which had moved towards becoming representative democracies had more effective ways of bearing the strains of the conflict than had the more autocratic structures of Germany, Austria-Hungary, Russia and the Ottoman Empire. Britain and France endured the war much more cohesively than did the other four, all of whose empires were to collapse either during the war or as immediate consequences of it.

When Russia was plunged into revolution in 1917, it withdrew from the war and virtually allowed the Central Powers to command resources and territory from the Baltic to Ukraine. The German high command drew fresh hope for a decisive victory in Western Europe in 1918. While Lenin consolidated his authority in the Russian heartland, General Ludendorff moved forces to the west for his great gamble, Operation *Michael*. But the strain of war was telling on every German family and when *Michael* failed, a crisis of morale at home and in the trenches set a limit on what German soldiers, workers and women were prepared to tolerate. Acceptance of defeat in 1918 brought with it the end of the German monarchy and initiated the experiment in democracy that we now call the Weimar era, which in turn was to collapse under the impact of Nazism.

The role of women was extended into new domains by the pressures of war. They played an increasing part in industrial production. Their responsibilities as carers for families and homes became heavier under

The opposing sides, 1914–1918.

the impact of war-induced shortages, the absence of their men and the burden of bereavement. Their demands for political power through having the right to vote could no longer be resisted by those democracies that had refused it in the face of the Suffragette movement of the pre-war years. While women in even the most advanced democracies did not gain equality with men in the sense that we now understand the term, the First World War was a powerful catalyst of the social change which was to lead to an era in which women now share the highest political (but not military) offices with men.

The period of the First World War was one of the most fruitful in terms of technological development and application. Aviation, developed only just before the war, became a major asset for the belligerents. Tens of thousands of aircraft were produced by the major powers. Strategic bombing began and civilians learned to recognise warning alarms and the 'all clear' signal. Chemical warfare was introduced to the battlefield in a major way. The submarine became a potent threat to the mercantile and naval shipping of the powers that controlled the surface of the sea. The range and destructive power of artillery increased immensely. The development of radio communications allowed senior commanders to control their forces directly and immediately over distances unimagined before, from the continental theatres of action in Europe to the oceans of the world. The firepower of the machine gun and the now more accurately made rifle increased the defensive capabilities of infantry in trenches.

The challenge to the feasibility of attacking such defences forced military leaders to develop new tactics and new ways of devolving initiative to front-line commanders when in action. It took all too long before these new approaches were developed and tested to the point at which they began husbanding the lives of the hapless infantry who had to make attacks across open ground. Both sides proved adept in inventing new methods of combat, so lengthening the war and adding to its huge costs in human life and resources. But finally the weight of Allied numbers and firepower eroded the capacity of the armies of the Central Powers to hold their ground, and their collapse followed shortly.

The length and heavy human toll of the war inclined both mass opinion and practically minded politicians towards placing a ban on the offensive use of military power and requiring nations to settle matters in dispute by negotiation or arbitration. President Woodrow Wilson of the United States took the lead in drawing up the Covenant of an association to achieve these ends: the League of Nations. Although it was to fail and be discarded in the 1930s, the League did much good work in the 1920s and provided many lessons, positive and negative, which influenced the foundation and shaping of its successor, the United Nations. The scope of this conflict, the new developments it fostered and its costs and consequences have made the First World War one of the most rewarding passages in human history for study and contemplation.

This study of that war is brought to you by three authors who know their fields well, have studied and written about them with distinction over many years, and most importantly have interesting and important new things to say about their respective topics. Peter Simkins, formerly Senior Historian at the Imperial War Museum, London, has pioneered new approaches to the history of events on the Western Front, especially the ingenuity and intelligence of the men involved, leavened by their sense of humour and the capacity to care for their comrades. Geoffrey Jukes, a modern Russian historian and linguist, was a Senior Fellow in International Relations at the Australian National University, Canberra. He has studied his subject deeply, walked the key battlefields and visited Russia many times to draw on and appraise the work of its scholars. Michael Hickey has seen war as a soldier in Korea, in East Africa, at Suez and in Aden in the 1950s and 60s. His books include a major study of the Dardanelles Campaign. He has also walked many a mile over the battlefields of Europe and the Middle East, testing his ideas in terms of what the war was like for the men on the ground there in 1914–1918. This book is but an introduction to a vast and fascinating topic. Knowledge of the problems men and women faced during the First World War, and of the solutions they developed, from the tank to the League of Nations, is a good foundation for the understanding of international events, especially wars, in the 21st century and how their destructive effects might be avoided or minimised.

CHRONOLOGY

1908	Austria-Hungary annexes Bosnia-Herzegovina
1912–1913	Balkan Wars
	Loss of Turkish North African provinces to Italy

1914

28 June	Assassination of Archduke Franz Ferdinand and his wife at Sarajevo
5/6 July	Germany gives Austria-Hungary blank cheque of support against Serbia
23 July	Austro-Hungary issues ultimatum to Serbia
25 July	Serbia mobilises
26 July	Austro-Hungarian mobilises against Serbia; Russia enters 'period preparatory to war'
28 July	Austrian Emperor Franz Josef signs declaration of war against Serbia
29 July	Germany demands immediate cessation of Russian mobilisation preparations
30 July	Russia decrees full mobilisation in support of Serbia
31 July	Russian mobilisation begins; Germany

	proclaims 'threatening danger of war' and issues ultimatum to Russia
1 August	Germany declares war on Russia and orders general mobilisation; France orders general mobilisation
2 August	Germany issues ultimatum to Belgium demanding right of passage through its territory; German troops invade Luxembourg
3 August	Germany declares war on France; Germany invades Belgium; Turkey declares 'armed neutrality'; Italy declares neutrality
4 August	Britain declares war on Germany; United States declares neutrality
5 August	France asks Russia to attack Germany; Montenegro declares war on Austria
6 August	Austria-Hungary declares war on Russia; Serbia declares war on Germany; French troops move into Upper Alsace
7 August	Germany captures citadel at Liège
10 August	France declares war on Austria-Hungary
12 August	Austria-Hungary invades Serbia; Britain declares war on Austria-Hungary
12–13 August	Russia invades East Prussia
14 August	Battle of the Frontiers begins
17 August	Battle of Stallupönen
20 August	Battle of Gumbinnen
23 August	Battle of Mons; British Expeditionary Force begins retreat
26 August	Battle of Le Cateau
26 August–2 September	Battle of Komarów
27–31 August	Battle of Tannenberg
31 August	Greece formally declares neutrality

3 September	Battle of Lemberg
5–10 September	Battle of the Marne
7–17 September	Battle of the Masurian Lakes
11 September	Battle of Grodek
13–27 September	Battle of the Aisne
14 September	Falkenhayn takes over control of German operations from Moltke
17 September	'Race to the sea' begins
1 October	Turkey closes Dardanelles
10 October	Antwerp falls to Germany
18–30 October	Battle of the Yser
19–30 October	First battle of Warsaw
20 October–22 November	First Battle of Ypres
1 November	Turkey declares war on Anglo-French Entente
2 November	Russia and Serbia declare war on Turkey
3 November	Falkenhayn succeeds Moltke as Chief of the German General Staff
5 November	Britain and France declare war on Turkey
7–17 November	Second battle of Warsaw
11 November	Ottoman Sultan, as Caliph of Islam, proclaims *jihad* against Britain and France
11–12 November	Battle of Wloclawek
13–16 November	Battle of Kutno
19–25 November	Battle of Lódz
3–12 December	Battle of Limanowa-Lapanów
8 December	Austrian Third Army retakes Carpathian passes
17 December	French winter offensive begins in Artois

20 December	French winter offensive begins in Champagne
29 December	Battle of Sarikamis begins

1915

2 January	Russia appeals to London for a diversionary attack to be made against Turkey
4 January	French offensive in Artois ends
17 January	Russians finish mopping up operations at Sarikamis
3 February	Turks fail to cross Suez Canal
19 February	Allied fleet begins bombardment of outer forts at the Dardanelles
10–12 March	Battle of Neuve Chapelle
18 March	Anglo-French naval attack on the Chanak Narrows repulsed with loss of three battleships
22 March	Russians capture Przemysl, taking 100,000 prisoners
22 April	Germans use poison gas for the first time on the Western Front
22 April–25 May	Second battle of Ypres
25 April	Allied attack on Gallipoli begins
2–10 May	Battle of Gorlice-Tarnów
9 May	Allied offensive begins in Artois; battle of Aubers Ridge
9–10 May	Battle of Sanok
13–18 May	Battle of Jaroslaw
15–27 May	Battle of Festubert
23 May	Italian Government declares war on Austria-Hungary

25–26 May	Formation of a coalition cabinet and creation of Ministry of Munitions announced in Britain
20–22 June	Austrians retake Lemberg
July	Russians withdraw from Galicia
4 August	Allied reconnaissance party arrives at Salonika to assess port and railway facilities
5 August	Third battle of Warsaw; Germans take Warsaw
6 August	Allied landings made at Anzac and Suvla Bay
7 August	Tsar appoints himself Commander-in-Chief of the Russian Army
10 August	Turkish counter-attack at Gallipoli drives British and New Zealanders off high ground
20 August	Italy declares war on Turkey
September	Zimmerwald conference of Socialist Internationals; Germans capture Vilnius
21 September	Greek premier Venizelos calls for massive Allied reinforcement of Salonika as condition for Greek entry into war
25 September	Allied offensive in Artois and Champagne; first use of poison gas by British at battle of Loos
27 September	Greek King Constantine consents to Allied force landing at Salonika
October	Battle of Dunaburg
1 October	British advance party arrives at Salonika
5 October	Combined German-Austrian attack on Serbia begins; British and French forces land at Salonika
9 October	Belgrade falls; Austrians invade Montenegro
11 October	Bulgarian troops invade Serbia
14 October	Mutual declaration of war between Serbia and Bulgaria

19 December	Evacuation of the Anzac and Suvla beach heads at Gallipoli in one night without casualties; Haig replaces Sir John French as Commander-in-Chief of the British Expeditionary Force

1916

8 January	Successful completion of Gallipoli evacuation at Helles
10 January	Completion of Allied 'Entrenched Camp' at Salonika
14 January	Battle of Köprüköy; Russians advance on Erzerum
27 January	First Military Service Act becomes law in Britain, introducing conscription for men aged between 18 and 41
11–16 February	Battle of Erzerum; Russians take Erzerum and Mus
21 February	Battle of Verdun begins
25 February	Germans capture Fort Douaumont at Verdun
18 March	Unsuccessful Russian Vilnius offensive begins; ends 14 April
April	International Socialist Conference held at Kienthal (Second Zimmerwald Conference)
24 April	Easter Rising in Dublin
29 April	In Mesopotamia, Kut falls with 13,309 British and Indian prisoners plus over 3,000 non-combatants
25 May	Second Military Service Act becomes law in Britain, extending conscription to married men
31 May/1 June	Naval battle of Jutland
4 June	Opening of Brusilov's offensive

5 June	Sherif Hussein starts Arab revolt at Medina, proclaims independence of Hedjaz
1 July	Battle of the Somme begins
3–9 July	Unsuccessful offensive by Russian West Front
7 July	Lloyd George succeeds Kitchener (drowned en route to Russia) as War Minister
28 July	Opening of second phase of Brusilov's offensive
27 August	Romania declares war on Austria-Hungary, invades Transylvania
29 August	Hindenburg succeeds Falkenhayn as Chief of German General Staff, with Ludendorff as 'First Quartermaster General'
1 September	Britain and France secretly sign the Sykes–Picot agreement on post-war partition of the Ottoman Empire
6 September	Romanians complete occupation of Transylvania
15 September	British use tanks for the first time at Flers-Courcelette on the Somme
19 September	German-led forces invade Transylvania
3 October	German victories in Transylvania and Dobrudja
10 October	Tsar terminates Brusilov's offensive
11 October	Allies disarm Greek forces; riots in Athens in protest at Allied action
16–17 October	Final unsuccessful Russian effort to take Vladmir-Volynski
24 October	French counter-attack at Verdun; Fort Douaumont recaptured
21 November	Emperor Franz Josef dies, aged 86; succeeded by his great-nephew Charles
23 November	Greek Provisional Government at Salonika declares war on Germany and Bulgaria

25 November	Battle of the Somme ends
1 December	Fighting in Athens between royalist troops and Anglo-French detachments
7 December	Lloyd George becomes Prime Minister, succeeds Asquith
12 December	Nivelle replaces Joffre as French Commander-in-Chief

1917

5–7 January	Allied conference in Rome to discuss priorities for campaigns in Italy and Salonika
February	Cold weather disrupts food and fuel supplies to Russian cities
1 February	Germany begins unrestricted submarine warfare
18–22 February	German forces commence preliminary withdrawal from Ancre sector
20 February	First attack on Hedjaz railway by Arab irregulars
8–12 March	Food riots in Petrograd; garrison troops mutiny
11 March	Baghdad falls to General Maude
12 March	Russian Revolution begins; Provisional Government and Petrograd Soviet formed
14 March	Petrograd Soviet Order No. 1 claims control over garrison
15 March	Tsar abdicates
16 March	Germans begin main withdrawal to the Hindenburg Line
26 March	First battle of Gaza
6 April	United States declares war on Germany

9 April	Opening of British Arras offensive; Canadians storm Vimy Ridge
16 April	Lenin arrives in Petrograd; French spring offensive begins on the Aisne
17 April	Second battle of Gaza; despite use of tanks, momentum is lost and attack stalls
5 May	Allies launch major offensive in Serbia but fail to get Serb co-operation
15 May	Pétain succeeds Nivelle as French Commander-in-Chief
16 May	Kerensky becomes Russian Minister of War
22 May	Kerensky appoints Brusilov as Commander-in-Chief
7 June	British attack on Messines Ridge
12 June	King Constantine of Greece abdicates after Allied ultimatum, succeeded by younger son Alexander; British and French troops arrive at Piraeus
18 June	Russian South–West Front offensive begins
26 June	Venizelos confirmed by Allies as Greek Prime Minister
2 July	Russian South–West Front offensive stalls; Greece declares war on Central Powers; in Arabia, Colonel Lawrence and Arab irregulars attack Turkish garrisons
6 July	Central Powers counter-attack on Eastern Front; South–West Front retires to River Seret
10 July	North and West Front troops refuse to attack
13 July	Kornilov replaces Brusilov, calls off offensives
31 July	Third battle of Ypres begins
27 August	Failure of Kornilov's attempt to seize power
1–5 September	German Riga campaign

12 September	In Italy new German Fourteenth Army under General von Below deploys on Isonzo front
24 October	Battle of Caporetto; Austro-German attack breaks Italian Second Army
29 October	General Cadorno orders retreat to line of River Piave
31 October	Italians back behind River Tagliamento; in Palestine, Allenby opens third battle of Gaza
5 November	Allies confer at Rapallo as Italians ask for 15 Allied divisions
6 November	Passchendaele captured by Canadians
7 November	Bolsheviks seize power
8 November	Lenin proposes peace: 'no annexation and no indemnities'
9 November	General Diaz replaces Cadorna as Italian Commander-in-Chief
16 November	Allenby resumes advance on Jerusalem; Clemenceau becomes French Prime Minister
20 November	Battle of Cambrai begins
9 December	Jerusalem falls to Allenby
10 December	Armistice between Romania and Central Powers
17 December	Armistice between Russia and Central Powers
22 December	Russo–German peace negotiations begin at Brest-Litovsk; in Salonika, General Guillaumat replaces Sarrail as Allied Commander-in-Chief; Austrians fail to break through River Piave as astonishing revival in Italian national morale takes place

1918

1 February	Austrian Navy mutinies at Cattaro
9 February	Germany signs separate peace with Ukraine

10 February	Trotsky ends negotiations
19 February	Germans advance to within 80 miles of Petrograd
3 March	Treaty of Brest-Litovsk; Russia leaves the war
21 March	German Operation *Michael* offensive begins in Picardy
26 March	Foch appointed to co-ordinate Allied operations on Western Front
9 April	German *Georgette* offensive begins in Flanders
27 May	German *Blücher* offensive begins on the Aisne
9 June	German *Gneisenau* offensive begins
15 July	Last German offensive begins near Reims
18 July	Allied counterstroke on the Marne
8 August	Battle of Amiens begins
14 September	Final Allied offensive starts in Macedonia with battle of the River Vardar; mutinies break out in Bulgarian Army
19 September	Allenby fights and wins battle of Megiddo
20 September	RAF aircraft destroy the Turkish Seventh Army in defiles of Wadi Fara
23 September	British capture Acre and Haifa
26 September	Start of Franco-American offensive in Meuse–Argonne sector; Bulgaria seeks peace terms as mutinous troops March on Sofia to declare a republic
28 September	Start of Allied offensive in Flanders
29 September	British, Australian and American troops open main offensive on Hindenburg Line; Bulgaria signs armistice after talks at Salonika
1 October	Allenby and Lawrence arrive simultaneously at Damascus

24 October	Allies attack on wide front and win battle of Vittorio Veneto, followed by rout of Austrian Army with mass desertions of Czech, Serb, Croat and Polish troops
26 October	General Ludendorff resigns
30 October	Ottoman Empire sues for peace
3 November	Austria-Hungary signs armistice
9 November	Kaiser Wilhelm II abdicates
11 November	Armistice between Allies and Germany ends hostilities on the Western Front

1919

8 January	General Milne appointed Commander-in-Chief at Constantinople with garrison of 35,000 troops
3 February	Venizelos outlines Greek claims to Smyrna at Versailles
13 May	Greek troops land at Smyrna
22 May	In Turkey Kemal issues his 'Amasya Decisions', calling for new national government
28 June	Treaty of Versailles signed
11 July	Ottoman Government outlaws Kemal, who is elected President by new Turkish National Congress on 23 July
27 November	Kemal sets up National Council of Representatives at Angora (renamed Ankara)

1920

16 March	Allies tighten occupation of Constantinople; massacres of Armenians by Turks continue
18 March	Last meeting of Imperial Ottoman Parliament

23 April	In Turkey, the Grand National Assembly convenes at Ankara and forms new government
25 April	League of Nations mandates for Palestine and Mesopotamia announced; Palestinian Arabs attack British troops and Jewish settlers
22 June	Greeks launch offensive in Anatolia against Turkish Nationalist forces and advance to Usak, 120 miles east of Smyrna
25 July	Greek forces occupy Adrianople in Turkish Thrace
10 August	Treaty of Sèvres; Turkish nationalists refuse to accept it and go to war with Greece

1923

23 August	Following the Treaty of Lausanne, replacing the Treaty of Sevres, Allies evacuate Constantinople

Chapter 1

THE WESTERN FRONT 1914–1916

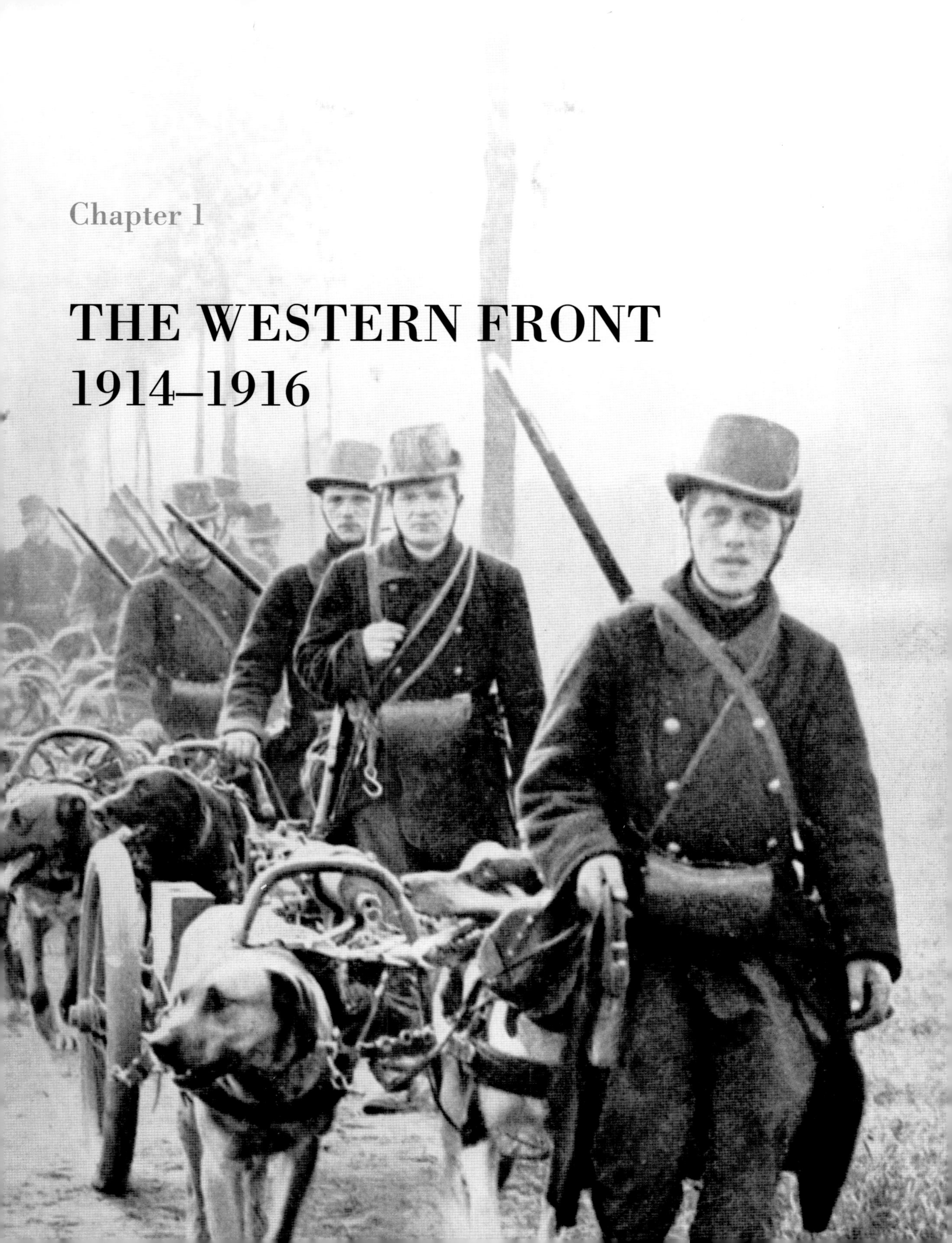

BACKGROUND TO WAR: THE ROAD TO WAR

The route which led the major powers of Europe to war in 1914 was long and tortuous, with many complex and interwoven factors eventually combining to drive them into a protracted and cataclysmic struggle. Among these factors were new naval and military technology, colonial rivalries, economic competition and irreconcilable national ambitions. However, perhaps the most important and obvious turning point towards a general European conflict was the Franco-Prussian War of 1870–1871. That limited confrontation had seen the humiliating defeat of France and the unification of Germany under Prussian leadership. The sudden emergence of the German Empire, which as part of the spoils of victory took the provinces of Alsace and Lorraine from France, brought about a fundamental shift in the European balance of power. Germany's subsequent and accelerating progress towards economic ascendancy only intensified the anxieties of her neighbours and competitors.

For the best part of two decades, between 1871 and 1890, the new European status quo was not seriously challenged, thanks to the diplomatic dexterity and deviousness of Otto von Bismarck, the German Chancellor,

Previous page:
Belgian troops during the withdrawal to Antwerp, 20 August 1914. Note the dog-drawn machine guns. (IWM Q81728)

Below:
British recruits at Aldershot in 1914. Many of those who volunteered at the outbreak of war would not see action until 1915 or 1916.

in keeping France isolated. When Bismarck left office in 1890 it was not long before a fresh series of unpredictable currents began to erode the foundations of his carefully constructed Continental system. A rapid deterioration in Russo-German relations and a rapprochement between Tsarist Russia and Republican France compelled Germany to strengthen its existing links with the Austro-Hungarian Dual Monarchy, so ensuring that it possessed an ally to the east. While Germany was undeniably the dominant partner in this particular alliance, it would pay a heavy price for a policy that tied it more closely to a dilapidated empire that was itself finding it increasingly difficult to curb the nationalist aspirations of its diverse subject peoples in south-eastern Europe. The potentially explosive situation in the Balkans was made more dangerous by the decline of Turkish influence there, offering both Austria and Russia (the self-proclaimed protector of the southern Slavs) tempting territorial and political prizes in the region. In seeking to exploit such opportunities, Austria and Russia each embarked upon a course which could only end in confrontation. The rise of Serbia added yet another hazardous element to an unstable regional mixture. Serbia had been infuriated by Austria's annexation of Bosnia and Herzegovina in 1908 but had itself gained influence and territory as a result of the Balkan Wars of 1912 and 1913, giving Austria, in turn, mounting cause for disquiet and irritation.

Kaiser Wilhelm II, Emperor of Germany 1888–1918. (Topfoto)

With the departure of Bismarck, the belligerent and erratic Wilhelm II – who had become *Kaiser* (Emperor) in 1888 – soon spurred Germany to follow a more aggressive path in international relations. France, already determined to avenge the disaster of 1870–1871 and win back its lost provinces, was further alarmed by Germany's developing industrial and military muscle; Russia too had grounds for concern about an Austro-German alliance that not only threw an ominous shadow along its western frontier but was likely to counteract Russian interests in the Balkans.

The first, and probably the most significant, crack in the edifice erected by Bismarckian diplomacy came in 1892 with the removal of its cornerstone – the isolation of France. That year, Russia and France concluded a military agreement – reinforced by additional talks in 1893 and 1894 – under which each promised to come to the other's aid if either were attacked by Germany.

Moreover, the change from Bismarck's *Realpolitik* (politics of realism) to the *Weltpolitik* (world policy or politics) of Kaiser Wilhelm II ultimately forced Britain to review its relations with other leading players on the European and world stage. Admittedly, Germany was not the only power that made Britain uneasy. Recurrent tension in its relations with France and Russia, previously its chief naval competitors, had caused Britain to pass the Naval Defence Act in 1889 in order to safeguard the supremacy on which its national security and prosperity rested. The Act embraced the doctrine that the Royal Navy's establishment should, at any given time, match the combined naval strength of any two other countries. The maintenance of this 'Two Power Standard' became more difficult as the United States and Japan also began to overtake Britain industrially and to build ocean-going fleets. Britain was, however, content to stick largely to its policy of 'splendid isolation' so long as the balance of power in Europe was not imperilled and no single nation became too dominant or threatened Britain's security by making a hostile move into the Low Countries towards the Channel ports.

Britain was, in fact, relatively friendly with Germany for much of the last quarter of the 19th century, not least because Queen Victoria's eldest daughter was married to the German Crown Prince, Frederick, who succeeded to the imperial throne in March 1888. Frederick died from cancer after reigning for barely three months, and the accession of his estranged and impulsive son, Wilhelm II, heralded fresh competition with Britain for colonies and overseas markets as the new Kaiser sought world power status for Germany. Even so, it was the German Navy Laws of 1898 and 1900 that did most to alienate Britain. Shaped by the German Naval Secretary, Rear Admiral Alfred von Tirpitz, with the Kaiser's enthusiastic support, these measures disclosed Germany's intention to construct a fleet, including 38 battleships, within 20 years. Regarding Britain as Germany's 'most dangerous naval enemy', Tirpitz envisaged the German fleet as a political pawn which would strengthen his country's hand in world affairs. To this end he wished to provide Germany with sufficient capital ships to mount a genuine challenge in the North Sea and give it the capability of inflicting such damage on the Royal Navy that the latter would fall below the 'Two Power Standard'. The launching of 14 battleships in Germany between 1900 and 1905 inaugurated a naval arms race that would enter an even more menacing phase when Britain launched the revolutionary turbine-driven 'all-big-gun' battleship HMS *Dreadnought* in 1906.

German backing for the Boers during the South African War of 1899–1902 hastened the demise of Britain's earlier isolationist policy. Since the United States Navy was not obviously aimed *directly* at its interests, Britain, in 1901, deliberately abandoned any attempts to compete with growing

American naval power. The following year an Anglo-Japanese treaty was signed, considerably reducing British anxieties in the Far East and enabling Britain to concentrate more warships in home waters. In 1904 the *Entente Cordiale* greatly strengthened British diplomatic and, later, military ties with its traditional rival, France. A similar understanding was reached with Russia in 1907, once Japan's victory in the Russo-Japanese War of 1904–1905 had all but removed the long-standing Russian threat to India. Thus before the end of the first decade of the 20th century Britain had swung noticeably towards the Franco-Russian alliance.

The understandings with France and Russia did not constitute formal agreements and neither did they commit Britain irrevocably to go to war in support of either power, but it was now at least morally bound to France and Russia in opposition to the Central Powers, Germany and Austria. Any unforeseen incident involving one or more of these countries might well ignite a general conflagration which, because of the rival alliance systems, could engulf them all. In these circumstances it would certainly not have served Britain's interests to stand aside and allow Germany to conquer France and occupy the Channel ports. Therefore, despite all the contradictions in Britain's new international stance, the possibility of its participation in a European war on the side of France and Russia was – as Germany should have been well aware – far from remote.

Diplomatic manoeuvres, opposing alliances and naval rivalries were not the only ingredients which rendered the European powder keg more explosive and conditioned nations and peoples for armed conflict. The spread of education and adult literacy in the decades before 1914 also saw the rise of a popular press ready to glamorise deeds of military valour or take an unashamedly jingoistic line when reporting foreign affairs. Chauvinism and aggressive imperialism were similarly encouraged by capitalism. Fashionable ideas about 'national efficiency' and concepts such as 'Social Darwinism' emphasised the survival of the fittest and fostered the belief that war was a purifying ordeal necessary to counter any signs of national decadence and moral degeneration. As most political and military leaders erroneously thought that should war come, it would be short, statesmen were generally more willing to solve international disputes by military rather than diplomatic means.

All the individual national motives for conflict and collective failures to halt the slide into the abyss cannot, however, conceal the primacy of Germany's responsibility for war in 1914. In the often savage debate that has raged since the work of Professor Fritz Fischer in the 1960s, historians have disagreed about the extent to which Germany positively sought and planned the conflict in advance; but few have denied that Germany was its

European alliances before and during the First World War.

mainspring. For Prussian aristocrats, the officer class and industrialists, war held great attraction as a means of negating or diverting attention from the increasing internal influence of the Social Democratic Party. It would also enable Germany to forestall the modernisation and improvement of the Russian Army, expected to be complete by 1916–1917. Since Germany's impressive economic expansion had not yet been rewarded by world power status, a successful war would simultaneously end its diplomatic and military encirclement and bring it the geopolitical influence it felt it deserved.

On 8 December 1912, the Kaiser summoned his senior military advisers to a war council. The fact that some of the conclusions reached on this occasion coincided with the actual events of 1914 has led Fischer and other historians to view the meeting as evidence that Germany's leaders took a conscious decision there and then to go to war within 18 months. The importance of the meeting in this respect may have been exaggerated, but there is no doubt that the Kaiser and the military-political-industrial élite wanted hegemony in Europe and were fully prepared to contemplate war, with all its attendant risks, as the quickest way of realising their ambitions. This in itself represented a serious enough threat to European peace but the situation was made infinitely more hazardous by the iron grip which the Kaiser and his circle maintained on the reins of power in Germany. Whereas considerable checks and balances were imposed upon the political and military leaders of Britain and France by their respective parliamentary systems, the German Army was essentially beyond civilian control. Its senior officers were directly responsible to the Kaiser, and neither the Chancellor nor the state secretaries (or 'ministers') were ultimately answerable to the Reichstag, the German parliament. In other words, those in Germany who were most willing to plunge Europe into war in order to deal with their own internal and external difficulties, and to assure Germany's standing in the world, were subject to the fewest effective restraints.

WARRING SIDES: THE OPPOSING ARMIES

Germany's strategic ambitions and the unique status its armed forces enjoyed within society helped to ensure that, until 1916 at least, the Imperial German Army would be the dynamo of the First World War. It was Germany's war plan that did most to determine the course, if not the nature, of the conflict. The plan itself had been shaped originally, between 1897 and 1905, by Count Alfred von Schlieffen, then Chief of the German General Staff. Schlieffen's overriding aim had been to enable Germany to deal successfully with the strategic nightmare of a two-front war against Russia and France, should such a situation arise. However, by appearing to offer a feasible solution to this problem, the plan reduced the army's fears of a two-front war and, correspondingly, strengthened its willingness to accept the risks of such a conflict. In these respects, one could argue that the Schlieffen Plan, instead of being a mere precautionary measure, actually increased the likelihood of a general European struggle.

Schlieffen estimated that, should Germany have to face both France and Russia, the latter would be slower to mobilise and deploy, giving Germany a vital margin of some six weeks in which to overcome France by means of

Count Alfred von Schlieffen, Chief of the German General Staff 1891–1905. His war plan, with modifications, largely shaped German strategy in 1914. (Mary Evans Picture Library)

a massive and rapid campaign in the west. As soon as France was defeated, Germany could then transfer the bulk of its forces to the east to tackle Russia. There was a danger, nonetheless, that the fortresses along France's north-eastern frontier might fatally delay the German Army's lightning western offensive. Accordingly Schlieffen resolved that German forces must cross a narrow strip of Dutch territory known as the 'Maastricht Appendix', then sweep through neutral Belgium before driving into north-western France. The pivotal role in the campaign was given to five armies deployed between Metz and Holland, totalling 35 corps in all. The most powerful forces were allocated to the extreme right wing of the offensive. One army here was expected to swing round to the west of Paris, on the outer flank of a colossal wheeling movement which was intended to take the opposing French armies in the rear before trapping them up against their own frontier. It was anticipated that, on the outbreak of war, the French would advance immediately into Lorraine, so two weaker German armies were assigned to the left, or eastern, wing. Their task was to contain the French movement and even fall back slowly, if required, in the hope of luring the enemy forces beyond any point from which they could seriously interfere with the planned German encirclement.

Helmuth von Moltke, Schlieffen's successor, made several key alterations to the original plan between 1906 and 1914. Though a diligent and painstaking officer, Moltke was also introspective and suffered from bouts of low self-confidence. He was especially anxious about the potential threat to German communications which the expected French thrust into Lorraine would pose. Consequently, most new divisions created after 1906 were assigned to the German left wing rather than the crucial right. Once seven times stronger than the left, the right wing became only three times stronger as a result of Moltke's changes. Of equal significance was his decision to abandon the projected movement through Holland while sticking with the planned advance through Belgium. This decision was doubly unfortunate for it not only complicated the problems of deployment – squeezing the right-wing armies into a tighter initial bottleneck – but also failed to eliminate the considerable diplomatic and strategic disadvantages almost certain to ensue from any German violation of Belgium's neutrality. Historians have rightly observed that, even as originally conceived, the Schlieffen Plan was unworkable, as it paid insufficient heed to the problems of over-extended supply lines, inadequate communications systems, the fatigue of troops and the unpredictability of battle. It also miscalculated the speed of Russian mobilisation and the level of resistance that Belgian forces and civilians would offer. However, it is equally true to say that the changes wrought by Moltke did little or nothing to improve it and further undermined its already tenuous prospects of success.

Conscription, the bedrock of the German military system, permitted Germany to increase the size of its army swiftly, from a peacetime strength of around 840,000 to more than 4,000,000 trained soldiers when war was declared. Able-bodied young German males first joined the Landsturm at the age of 17; at the age of 20 they were called to the colours for full-time military training, which lasted two or three years, depending upon their arm of service. Thereafter they would pass into the reserve for four or five years and then carry out additional spells of service with the Landwehr and Landsturm until they reached 45. The Landwehr and

German infantry photographed on manoeuvres before the First World War. (Getty Images)

Opposite:
The rival war plans.

Landsturm, upon mobilisation, would undertake defensive duties on lines of communication, and the reservists were alternatively recalled to regular units or formed new reserve corps and divisions that could confidently be used as front-line formations. The system, especially the employment of reservists, was to give the Germans a significant advantage over the French Army in some critical sectors along the front in the opening weeks of the war.

In the summer of 1914 German infantry training was in the midst of a transition from close-order to open-order tactics – a factor that would cost their infantry dear. However, the army as a whole was excellently trained, had a solid nucleus of highly capable non-commissioned officers and could claim a clear superiority in its light, medium and heavy howitzers – weapons which would quickly prove their worth in the operations to come.

The French military system was likewise based upon conscription. In 1913 compulsory service had been extended to three years with the colours, then 14 in the reserve. Because its population was smaller, France had to call up a bigger proportion of the nation's men, including colonial recruits, to attain even a semblance of parity with Germany. At the outbreak of war, France was able to muster approximately 3,680,000 trained soldiers but had fewer reserve formations than the Germans mobilised.

In the wake of the humiliation of the Franco-Prussian War French military doctrine had been recast. The most important figure in this process was Lieutenant-Colonel (later Marshal) Ferdinand Foch. His teachings as Chief Instructor (1896–1901) and Commandant (1908–1911) of the *Ecole Supérieure de Guerre* placed the 'will to conquer' firmly at the core of the French Army's creed and inspired an almost mystical faith in the primacy of the *offensive à l'outrance* (attack to the limit). The same gospel was preached by one of Foch's disciples, Colonel Louis de Grandmaison, who between 1908 and 1911 headed the War Ministry's important Operations Branch. It was reflected too in the army's superb, quick-firing 75mm field gun, which more than matched its German 77mm equivalent, although medium and heavy artillery were given a lower priority.

The plan with which the French went to war – known as Plan XVII – was prepared under the guidance of General Joseph Joffre, the Chief of the French General Staff from 1911 and the Commander-in-Chief designate in the event of hostilities. The imperturbable Joffre, a follower of the Foch–Grandmaison philosophy, rejected a previous scheme for a defensive concentration along the Belgian border and instead announced his intention to 'advance with all forces united to attack the German armies'. Five French field armies would be deployed under Plan XVII. Of these, the First and

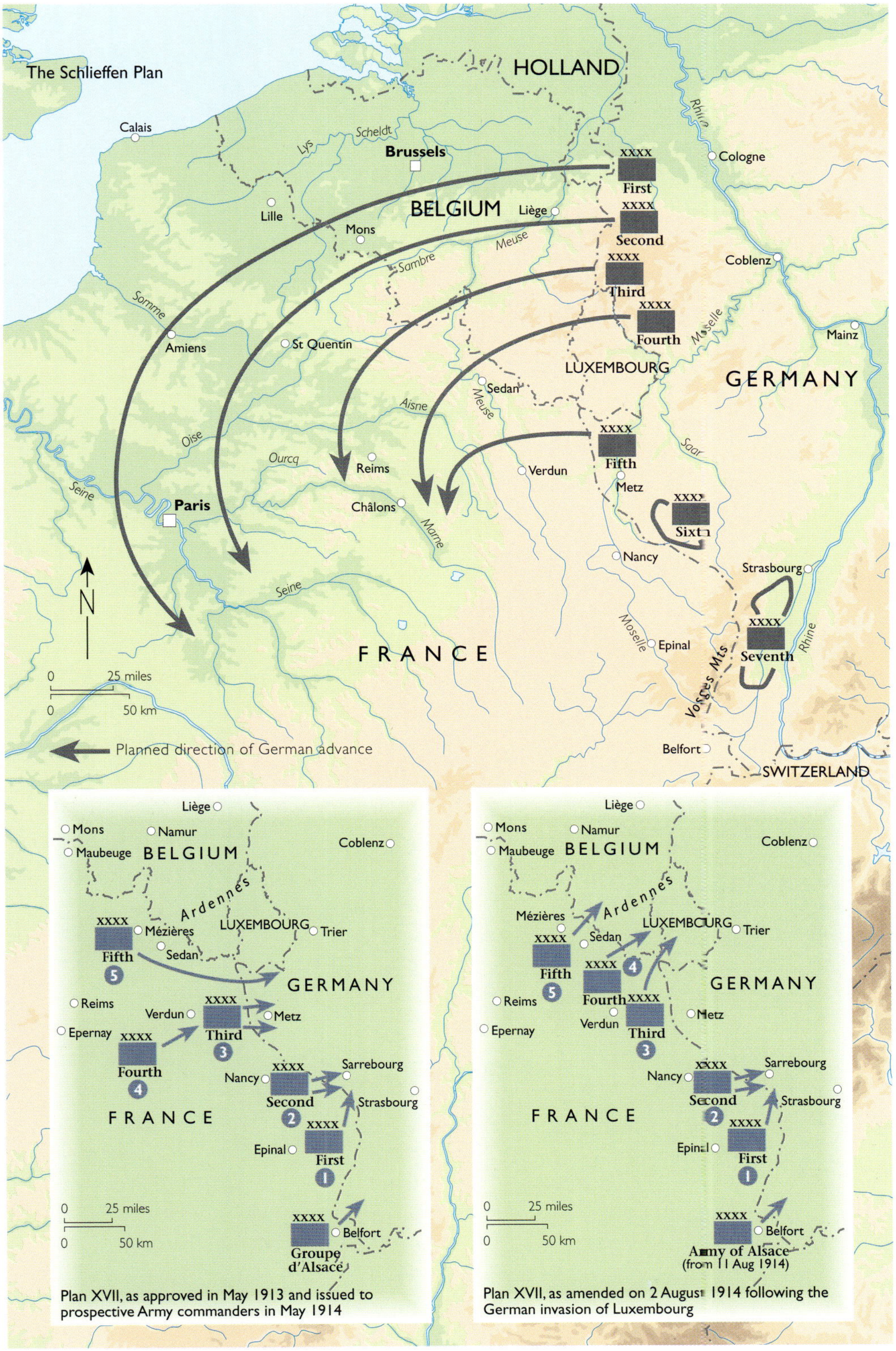

Plan XVII, as approved in May 1913 and issued to prospective Army commanders in May 1914

Plan XVII, as amended on 2 August 1914 following the German invasion of Luxembourg

Second Armies on the right wing were to advance into Lorraine, exactly as Schlieffen had hoped. In the centre, the Third Army would attack towards Thionville and Metz. The Fifth Army, situated on the left between Mézières and Montmédy, had a more flexible role and, depending upon the route the Germans took, would either follow the Third Army's general direction or thrust north-east through the Belgian Ardennes and Luxembourg. The Fourth Army would be kept in semi-reserve, ready to reinforce the left or centre as required.

While more adaptable than the Schlieffen Plan, the French Plan XVII had a fundamental weakness. In grossly underestimating the extent to which German reserve troops would be employed alongside regular formations, the French, from the outset, were badly wrong-footed by the breadth and strength of the German sweep through Belgium. The Belgian Field Army was not expected to be a major player in the unfolding drama. Belgium had introduced conscription in 1913 but, when the crisis came, mobilised only 117,000 officers and men. The outbreak of war also found the Field Army divided by strategic disputes and in the middle of reorganisation.

Recruits from Bermondsey line up for an inspection. (Corbis)

Joffre also accorded relatively little weight to a possible British contribution when drawing up Plan XVII. Traditionally shielded from invasion by the Royal Navy, Britain still had a small, long-service professional army, raised by voluntary enlistment and regarded as sufficient to police and garrison its world-wide empire and protect British interests overseas. Five separate compulsory-service Bills had been placed before Parliament between 1908 and 1914 but all had been defeated. The underlying problem was that, in peacetime, no political party was prepared to risk the wrath of the taxpayer or commit electoral suicide by shedding the voluntary system and supporting a financially costly expansion of the army. The reforms of R. B. Haldane, as Secretary of State for War from 1905 to 1912, had thus to be achieved within an agreed military budget which, during most of his term of office, was limited to around £28,000,000. Even after Haldane's reforms – and including its Regular Reserve, Special Reserve and part-time Territorial Force – the British Army, on mobilisation, only totalled some 733,000. There was the possibility of receiving reinforcements from India and the Dominions, although India's security could not be jeopardised and Dominion manpower was as yet of uncertain quantity and quality.

A battery of French 75mm quick-firing field guns in action in 1914. The barrel of the gun nearest the camera is at full recoil. (Mary Evans Picture Library)

The principal offensive component of the army was the British Expeditionary Force (BEF) of six infantry divisions and one cavalry division, numbering approximately 120,000. Behind this were the 'Saturday Afternoon Soldiers' of the Territorial Force, formed from the old Volunteer Force in 1908. Some 269,000 strong in July 1914, the Territorial Force had been created chiefly for home defence but could provide a framework for future army expansion if necessary. Both the Regular Army and the Territorial Force lacked heavy artillery in 1914 and were below strength. However, individually the men of the BEF were better trained than any of their European counterparts and had unrivalled standards of rifle-shooting, with many infantrymen capable of firing 15 aimed rounds per minute.

No agreement existed which irreversibly bound the BEF to fight on the European mainland if war came. However, Anglo-French staff talks since 1906 made this probable. As no one – least of all the Admiralty – had succeeded in putting forward a compelling and realistic alternative, the only cogent plan for the deployment of the BEF likely to be implemented, if only by default, was one that had been prepared after 1910 by the Director of Military Operations, Brigadier-General Henry Wilson, an ardent Francophile and friend of Foch. Under this scheme the BEF, on mobilisation, would assemble on the French left, in the Hirson–Maubeuge–Le Cateau area. Minimal consideration had been given to the long-term ramifications of this deployment. The logical corollaries to any meaningful continental commitment were the possible need to raise a mass army and the related necessity for industrial mobilisation to ensure that these much larger forces would be properly supplied. Britain's experiences in the first half of the coming war would be all the more painful because the country was permitted to enter a major conflict without any blueprint for military or industrial expansion or, indeed, any clear idea of the scale of effort that might be required.

OUTBREAK: COUNTDOWN TO WAR

The incident that finally ignited the flames of war in Europe occurred on 28 June 1914, when, during an official visit to Sarajevo, capital of the newly annexed Austrian province of Bosnia, Archduke Franz Ferdinand, the heir to the Austrian throne, was assassinated with his wife. The assassin, Gavrilo Princip, was one of a group of conspirators recruited and despatched to Sarajevo by the Black Hand, a Serbian terrorist group, with the connivance of the chief of Serbian military intelligence. The Serbian Government itself did not inspire the assassination but certainly knew of the plot and made well intentioned, if feeble, attempts to warn Austria about it. Austria eagerly exploited the opportunity to humble Serbia and thereby snuff out its challenge to Austro-Hungarian authority in the Balkans. First, however, Austria sought Germany's backing for its proposed course of action. Germany, in turn, saw in the Austro-Serbian confrontation a golden chance of securing hegemony in Europe, achieving world status while splitting the encircling Entente powers, forestalling Russian modernisation, eradicating the dangers to Austria-Hungary and suffocating domestic opposition. Even though it might drag the whole of Europe into armed conflict, Germany was prepared to take this calculated risk to achieve its ends. Therefore, on 5 and 6 July Germany gave Austria a 'blank cheque' of unconditional support against Serbia.

Having obtained Germany's endorsement, on 23 July Austria issued a ten-point ultimatum to Serbia. The latter accepted nine of the points but rejected, in part, the demand that Austrian officials should be involved in the investigation of the assassination, regarding such interference as a challenge to its sovereignty. On 25 July Serbia mobilised its army; Russia also confirmed partial mobilisation before entering, on 26 July, a 'period

German conscripts are given a rousing send-off as they leave Berlin by train for the front, August 1914. (Topfoto)

preparatory to war'. Austria reciprocated by mobilising the same day and then, on 28 July, declared war on Serbia. Up to this point it might still have been possible to isolate the problem, but Germany continued to act in an uncompromising manner which only served to heighten tensions and gave the crisis international dimensions. On 29 July Germany demanded an immediate cessation of Russian preparations, failing which Germany would be forced to mobilise. Russia could not afford to acquiesce meekly in the destruction of Serbian sovereignty, or increased Austrian influence in eastern and south-eastern Europe. Consequently, on 30 July Russia ordered general mobilisation in support of Serbia.

Russian mobilisation began the following day but was not the inevitable precursor to war: its forces could, if necessary, have stayed on their own territory for weeks while negotiations proceeded. Germany, however, proclaimed a *Kriegsgefahrzustand* (threatening danger of war) on 31 July and presented Russia with an ultimatum. Russia's failure to respond led Germany to order general mobilisation and declare war on Russia on 1 August. This action caused France to mobilise and set in motion the remaining cogs in the intricate machinery of European alliances and understandings, for the Schlieffen Plan required, from the outset, a violation of neutral Belgium and an attack on France, quite independent of any action the Russians might take. On 2 August Germany handed Belgium an ultimatum insisting on the right of passage through its territory. This was firmly rejected and the next day Germany declared war on France. Early on 4 August German forces crossed the frontier into Belgium. The strength of the German armies on this flank was awesome. Colonel-General Alexander von Kluck's First Army, on the extreme right, numbered 320,000 troops. The neighbouring Second Army, under Colonel-General Karl von Bülow, and the Third Army, commanded by General Max von Hausen, respectively totalled 260,000 and 180,000. The invasion of Belgian territory brought Britain into the conflict. Though it had no formal agreements with France and Russia, Britain was committed in principle, by a treaty concluded in 1839, to guarantee Belgian independence and neutrality. In 1906 the Foreign Office had observed that this pledge did not oblige Britain to aid Belgium 'in any circumstances and at whatever risk' but, realistically, the huge threat posed by Germany to the balance of power and the Channel ports had to be resisted. Moreover, it proved much easier for Britain's Liberal Cabinet to rally the nation behind a war for 'gallant little Belgium' than behind an abstract concept such as the preservation of the status quo or the balance of power. Britain's own ultimatum expired without reply at 11pm (London time) on 4 August and she declared war on Germany.

THE FIGHTING: WAR ON THE WESTERN FRONT 1914–1916

The invasion of Belgium

The changes to the Schlieffen Plan wrought by Moltke dictated that the German right-wing armies must pass through the Meuse Gap between Holland and the Ardennes, a narrow corridor dominated by Liège. Failure to capture Liège and its ring of 12 forts quickly would wreck the complex German timetable at the start. A force of six brigades had the task of reducing Liège. Attached to this force was Erich Ludendorff, who as head of the General Staff's mobilisation and deployment section from 1908 to 1913 had been largely instrumental in planning the operation. The forts could withstand 21cm shells but the Skoda works at Pilsen and the Krupp works at Essen had produced huge 30.5cm and 42cm 'Big Bertha' howitzers capable of firing armour-piercing shells over 7 miles.

A German 42cm 'Big Bertha' howitzer of the type used to bombard Liège in August 1914. (Mary Evans Picture Library)

A flawed deployment also impaired the Belgian defence. King Albert, as Commander-in-Chief, advocated a concentration on the Meuse, between Namur and Liège, so that the Belgian Army could delay the Germans further forward until Franco-British support arrived. However, the Chief of Staff, General de Selliers de Moranville, cautiously stationed most of his forces centrally behind the River Gette, where they could cover Brussels and, if necessary, fall back on Antwerp. Consequently, when the crisis came King Albert barely had time to send one division to Namur and another, plus one brigade, to reinforce Liège.

The assault on 5 August began badly for the Germans. As casualties grew, Ludendorff himself assumed command of the attack in the centre. By 7 August the Germans had penetrated the ring of forts and entered Liège, where Ludendorff audaciously secured the surrender of the citadel. The forts held out until the huge howitzers materialised on 12 August, then within four days all were battered into submission, allowing the German right-wing armies to advance. Ludendorff, now a national hero, went to the Eastern Front as Chief of Staff of General Paul von Hindenburg's Eighth Army.

German reservists travelling to the Western Front, August 1914. The train bears the inscription 'A trip to Paris – see you again on the boulevard'. (Topfoto)

The non-appearance of French and British forces persuaded the Belgian Field Army to withdraw towards Antwerp on 18 August. Two days later the Germans entered Brussels. Bombarded by the German super-heavy howitzers, the city of Namur fell on 23 August, followed swiftly by the last of its forts. To maintain their schedule and avoid leaving substantial rearguards, the Germans implemented a policy of *Schrecklichkeit* ('frightfulness'), attempting to subdue the population by executing civilians or destroying property. Alleged civilian resistance against the rearguard of the First Army led, for example, to the burning of Louvain and its library of irreplaceable medieval manuscripts.

One can question whether the defence of Liège and subsequent resistance did much to delay the German advance. The Germans might actually have *gained* four or five days if Belgian opposition had been weaker but they still managed to cross Belgium more or less on time. What really harmed their plan was the need to detach some five corps from their right wing to invest Namur, Maubeuge and Antwerp.

Battle of the Frontiers

The French Plan XVII was first put to the test on 6 August, when Bonneau's VII Corps advanced into Upper Alsace. Bonneau was soon obliged, by German troops from Strasbourg, to retire but the Army of Alsace, under General Pau, tried again on 14 August, retaking Mulhouse. However, as threats to the Allied left and centre developed, Joffre had to withdraw Pau's formations for use elsewhere along the front. These opening moves left the French with only a small corner of Alsace in the eastern foothills of the Vosges.

The principal thrust into Lorraine by Dubail's First Army and de Castelnau's Second Army also began on 14 August. Schlieffen had intended the German left-wing armies to give ground, enticing the French forces away from the decisive right wing, but when Crown Prince Rupprecht of Bavaria proposed a counter-attack by his own Sixth Army and Heeringen's Seventh Army, Moltke – seduced by the prospect of enveloping both French flanks – let them proceed.

The subsequent actions at Sarrebourg and Morhange on 20 August rapidly revealed that, for the French infantry, offensive spirit would not by itself triumph over modern artillery and machine guns. The French, suffering enormous losses, were pushed back on their own frontier fortifications. Here, however, they mustered sufficient strength and resolve to organise a successful defence of Nancy and the Moselle line. The modifications to their original plan had not, in the event, enabled the Germans to deal the French right a mortal blow, and as the fighting in this region became less intense Joffre could again transfer troops to buttress the Allied centre and left. On the other hand, having vastly underestimated the extent to which the Germans would employ reservists, and still unaware of the real width of the German drive through Belgium, Joffre misjudged the strength of the German centre. On being ordered to advance north-east into the Ardennes, Ruffey's Third Army and de Langle de Cary's Fourth Army blundered into German forces around Neufchâteau and Virton on 21–22 August and were bloodily repulsed.

Moltke's overall handling of operations was even less certain than that of the French. On 17 August he made a misguided effort to improve the co-ordination of the German right wing, placing Kluck under the orders of the more cautious Bülow. This irritated the pugnacious Kluck and also inhibited him from swinging the First Army as far west as was necessary to turn the Allied left. Nevertheless, the true scale of German strength and movements began to dawn upon Lanrezac, the French Fifth Army commander, as he approached the Sambre and Meuse between Charleroi and Givet and found the German Second and Third Armies advancing towards him from the north and east through Belgium. His warnings caused some at French General Headquarters to brand him a defeatist, but as Bülow's forces crossed the Sambre on 21 August and French

Crowds gather to cheer on ANZAC troops as they march to Westminster Abbey in London. The photograph illustrates public enthusiasm for the war at that time. (Corbis)

counter-attacks failed the next day, all hopes of a French offensive to the north-east evaporated. On 22 August, displaying untypical impetuosity and without waiting for Hausen's Third Army, Bülow pressed the French back an additional 5 miles. This counteracted the planned effect of Hausen's Meuse crossing on 23 August for, with the French Fifth Army further south than expected, it was correspondingly harder to attack its rear. Even so, when Hausen appeared on his right, Lanrezac felt that he must act immediately to avert disaster.

Battle of Mons

By this time the BEF, under Field-Marshal Sir John French, had reached the Maubeuge–Le Cateau area, on the Allied left. Field-Marshal Lord Kitchener – who had been appointed Secretary of State for War on 5 August – feared that this forward concentration might lead to the BEF being overwhelmed by the German forces massing north of the Meuse. He could not change the assembly area but the perceived threat of a German invasion caused him to delay the embarkation of two Regular divisions. Thus at the start of the campaign the volatile Sir John French only had four infantry divisions and one cavalry division to hand. His problems, and his temper, worsened when the commander of II Corps, Grierson, suffered a fatal heart attack and Kitchener chose to replace him with General Sir Horace Smith-Dorrien, whose relations with French had long been tense. Nevertheless, after an otherwise smooth assembly, the BEF moved up into the industrial region near Mons on 22 August, expecting to participate in an Allied offensive into Belgium.

Instead it speedily became evident that the BEF was directly in the path of the German First Army sweeping down from the north-east, Lanrezac having failed to stop the Germans on the Sambre. Despite his exposed position, Sir John promised to cover Lanrezac's left by standing at Mons for 24 hours. II Corps manned the line of the Mons-Condé Canal and a small salient around the town, while Lieutenant-General Sir Douglas Haig's I Corps was to its right. For a time Kluck was ignorant of the British deployment across his axis of advance. During the morning of 23 August his leading corps – running headlong into the BEF – made a succession of piecemeal, badly co-ordinated assaults against Smith-Dorrien's positions in the salient and along the canal. The BEF's incomparable musketry exacted a terrible toll from the dense German formations but the British quickly became acquainted with the power and accuracy of the German artillery. Although Haig's I Corps was not heavily engaged, Smith-Dorrien's troops largely held on until the late afternoon, when relentless German pressure and numerical superiority finally told. Accordingly II Corps fell back about 2 miles to pre-selected positions.

The BEF had performed well in its first important battle, keeping Kluck's First Army at bay for the best part of a day. Most of the 1,600 British casualties were in II Corps. That night, however, the threat to the French Fifth Army's right near Dinant prompted Lanrezac to withdraw without consulting Joffre or the British. The BEF had no alternative but to conform with Lanrezac. In some respects this proved a blessing in disguise, as the rearward move coincided with renewed German efforts to turn the vulnerable British left flank.

Allied retreat

In the last week of August, the Allied armies everywhere were in retreat, though they retained enough resilience to organise determined rearguard operations. It was at this point, with Plan XVII in tatters and the truth about the German use of reservists becoming frighteningly apparent, that the impassive Joffre displayed his best qualities. Refusing to abandon all thoughts of an offensive, he created a new Sixth Army, commanded by General Maunoury, on the endangered Allied left, having coolly taken troops from his own reserves and the French right for this purpose. Joffre's calmness under pressure was in total contrast to the increasing nervousness of his opponent, Moltke. As Falkenhayn and Ludendorff would show in years to come, the German General Staff often allowed fleeting operational opportunities to obscure its original strategic aim. Moltke was no different in this regard. The dazzling prospect of achieving a double envelopment

Men of the 4th Battalion, Royal Fusiliers, resting in the Grand Place, Mons, on 23 August 1914. (IWM Q70071)

of the Allied armies had already persuaded him to give the commanders of his left-wing armies their head, and on 25 August he further dismantled the Schlieffen Plan by releasing two corps from the key right wing to help block the Russian advance in East Prussia. Given that formations had also been detached to deal with various fortresses, the three German right-wing armies had by now lost more than a quarter of their strength and had still not fulfilled their principal task.

The battle of the frontiers and the Allied retreat to the Marne, 22 August–5 September 1914.

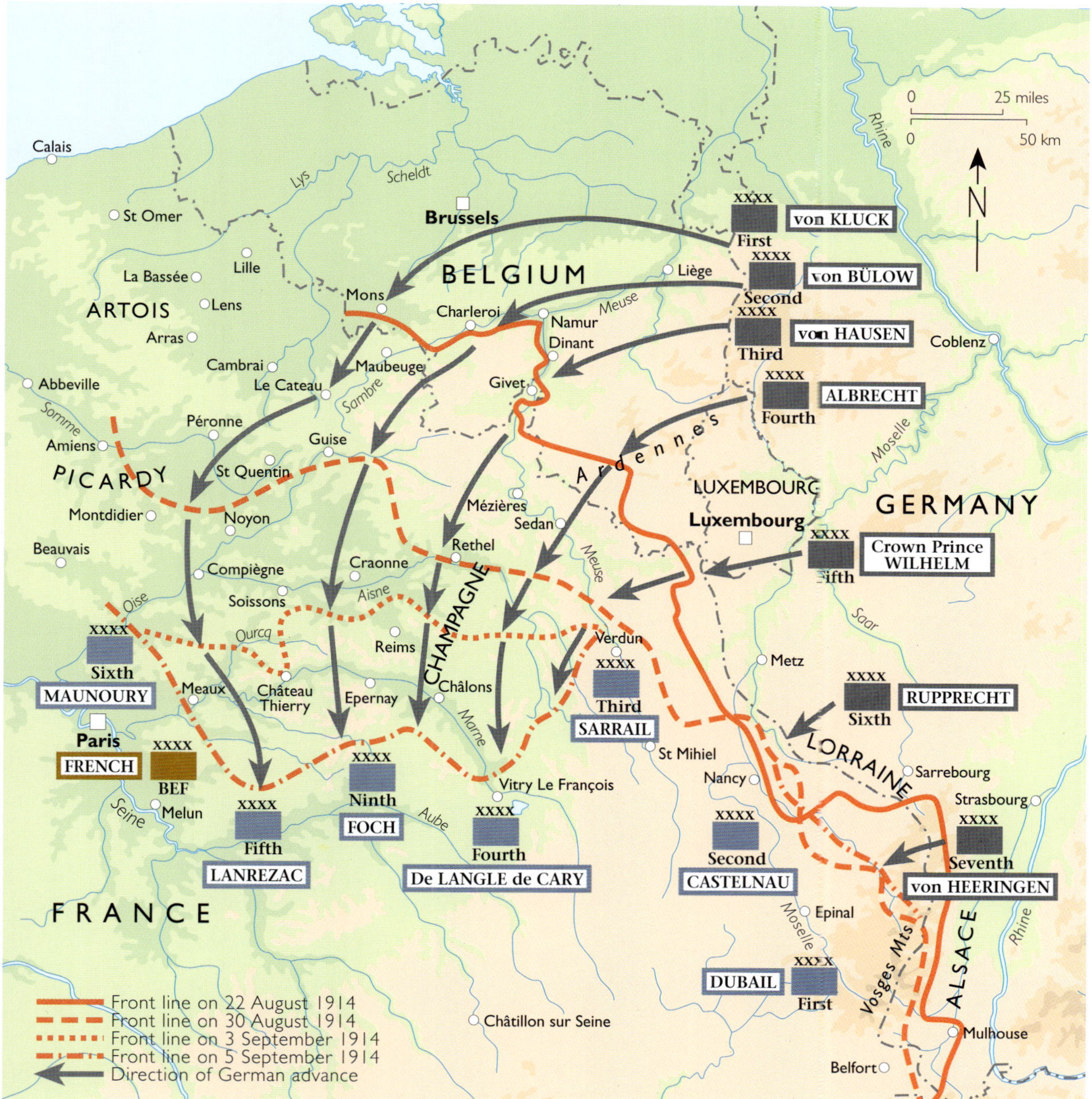

For the Allied and German troops who had to march some 20 miles a day in the searing late August heat, thirst, fatigue, hunger and blistered feet were of much greater concern than the grand designs of their commanders. After the battle of Mons, the BEF's two corps had become separated by the Forest of Mormal. On 26 August, Smith-Dorrien judged that the Germans were so close to II Corps that he could not disengage without fighting another battle. Contrary to the wishes of Sir John French, he conducted a determined holding action at Le Cateau, where the Germans again suffered severely in the face of the BEF's musketry. II Corps itself lost 7,182 officers and men, but because of its timely stand was able to continue its retreat in relatively good order.

Smith-Dorrien's strained relations with Sir John French deteriorated beyond repair after Le Cateau. However, the stand by II Corps achieved its objective, for it not only led the Germans to overestimate British strength but also deterred Kluck from immediate pursuit. Moreover, Kluck's mistaken conclusion that the BEF was falling back south-west rather than to the south gave the British formations an unexpected breathing space, permitting them to retreat comparatively unmolested over the next few days. Yet the respite did not dispel Sir John French's gloom. Feeling let down by the French and disheartened by the BEF's casualties, he now believed that he could only save the BEF by taking it out of the Allied line of battle and retiring behind the Seine. It took the personal intervention of Kitchener, in a hastily arranged visit to France on 1 September, to prevent Sir John from following this course.

The Marne miracle

After the BEF had escaped his clutches, Kluck was freed from Bülow's direct command on 27 August and at first headed south-west towards Amiens. By 28 August the BEF was less of a priority to him as he began to consider wheeling inwards, a move which might enable him to push Lanrezac away from Paris and to roll up the French Fifth Army's left. At this juncture Joffre ordered an unenthusiastic Lanrezac to turn his face to the west and counter-attack between Guise and St Quentin. Lanrezac, in fact, handled the operation with great skill. On 29 August, the prestigious Guard Corps of the German Second Army was checked at Guise by the French I Corps, commanded by the energetic Franchet d'Esperey. This blow caused an apprehensive Bülow to call for Kluck's support, so presenting the latter with the pretext he required to change direction. Without seeking Moltke's prior agreement, on 30 August Kluck ordered his First Army to execute the wheel inwards. Instead of passing west of the French capital as planned, First Army would move north-east of it, exposing Kluck's flank to attack by Maunoury's French Sixth Army, now positioned north of Paris. With both events and his subordinates rapidly slipping beyond his control, Moltke tamely gave his blessing to Kluck's manoeuvre.

The glittering opportunity offered by Kluck's swerve inwards was not immediately appreciated by the Allies. One effect of the move, however, was to bring Kluck back into contact with the BEF. Some spirited rearguard actions ensued, such as that at Néry on 1 September, when 'L' Battery, Royal Horse Artillery, won three Victoria Crosses while helping to hold off the German 4th Cavalry Division for four hours. Having retreated 200 miles, the BEF crossed the Marne on 3 September but aerial reconnaissance revealed the vulnerability of Kluck's left flank. On 4 September, as Kluck drew ahead of Bülow across the Marne, the Military Governor of Paris, General Galliéni, persuaded Joffre to halt the retreat and order the Allied left to deliver a general counter-attack. At almost the same time Moltke tacitly acknowledged the failure of the German right wing's offensive by stopping Kluck and Bülow and directing them to swing round to face the eastern side of Paris.

On 6 and 7 September Kluck coped brilliantly with the French Sixth Army's initial attacks against his flank and communications, reversing his own First Army, pivoting to the west and sending three corps by forced marches to confront Maunoury along the Ourcq. Troops rushed from Paris in taxicabs could not prevent Maunoury's units from being pushed back, but Kluck's further movement westwards again extended the gap between the German First and Second Armies. Bülow too had responded capably to the pressure exerted by the French Fifth Army (now commanded by Franchet d'Esperey) and the newly created Ninth Army, under Foch. By its third day the Allied counterstroke was faltering; in several places it had been repulsed with heavy losses. At the crisis of the battle, on 9 September, it was the Germans who lost their nerve. As the BEF recrossed the Marne and advanced cautiously into the gap between the two German right-wing armies, an anxious and exhausted Bülow ordered a retreat. His decision was endorsed by Lieutenant-Colonel Hentsch, a hard-working but impressionable staff officer sent to the front to represent the utterly demoralised Moltke. Kluck was left with no option but to retire northwards to the Aisne, with Bülow.

The 'Miracle of the Marne' saved Paris and dealt the final blow to German plans for a swift victory in the west. In many respects the Marne fighting had boiled down to a battle of wills between the opposing commanders. While the nerves of Moltke and Bülow had given way, the stolid Joffre had retained his grip; his reputation and his authority, as the saviour of France, would become unshakeable in the following months. Moltke, on the other hand, did not survive long in office. On 14 September General Erich von Falkenhayn was given control of operations, although to preserve appearances and morale Moltke kept his post, in name only, until 3 November. However, if the Allies had gained a momentous strategic success on the Marne, they were still a very long way from defeating the German armies.

Deadlock

Despite their reverse on the Marne, the German right-wing armies fell back to strong positions, especially the Chemin des Dames ridge, some 4 miles north of the River Aisne between Craonne and Soissons. Deriving its name from a road built along its crest for Louis XV's daughters, this steep, wooded ridge had a series of finger-like spurs extending down towards the Aisne. It was here, on the BEF's line of advance, that a significant gap remained between the German First and Second Armies, but unhappily for the Allies, neither the BEF nor neighbouring French formations could push on quickly enough to exploit the situation. The BEF's commanders have since been criticised for lack of drive and unnecessary concern about their flanks, yet the troops were tired after three weeks of marching and fighting. Moreover, the BEF was advancing through countryside intersected by rivers; many bridges had been demolished by the Germans; poor weather restricted aerial reconnaissance; and a shift of front on 11 September increased congestion on roads. Upon reaching the Aisne, the BEF again found that most bridges had been destroyed and that the Germans had a considerable concentration of artillery on its northern side. Nonetheless, the bulk of the BEF's three corps – the third having been formed on 30 August – managed to cross the river on 13 September and probe forward up the valleys and spurs.

The delays cost the Allies dear, for the British were just too late in assaulting the heights north of the Aisne. The fall of Maubeuge on 7–8 September released German troops for other tasks and the VII Reserve Corps, under Zwehl, rushed to plug the gap on the German right. Following a forced march of 40 miles in 24 hours, during which almost a quarter of its infantry dropped out, leading elements of the corps reached positions along the Chemin des Dames by 2pm on 13 September, two hours before the vanguard of Haig's I Corps, on the British right, approached the crest. Though few recognised it at the time, this was one of the defining moments of the war.

The next day, in a true 'soldier's battle' of confused, close-quarter fighting, British attempts to take the ridge met heavy artillery fire and entrenched German infantry. Some battalions of I Corps managed to pierce the German line and cross the Chemin des Dames to look down into the Ailette valley beyond. They were subsequently forced back but gallantly maintained a foothold near the crest. II and III Corps to their left had failed to make much progress, with the result that by dusk the British line stretched south-west from the Chemin des Dames on the right, down towards the Aisne near Missy and Chivres and thence westward to Crouy near Soissons. Over the following fortnight German efforts to drive the British back across the Aisne were thwarted by the BEF's superior musketry, and a defensive stand-off – dominated by machine guns, rifles and artillery – descended on the Aisne battlefield as both sides dug in. The stalemate of trench warfare had arrived on the Western Front.

Race to the sea

With deadlock gripping the front from the Aisne eastwards, each side tried to turn the other's open flank to the west and north in what became known as the 'race to the sea'. Maunoury's French Sixth Army struck first astride the Oise on 17 September but was blocked near Noyon by the German IX Reserve Corps, moving down from Antwerp. Two days later another German corps, coming from Reims, stopped an advance over the Avre by de Castelnau's Second Army, itself brought from Lorraine to bolster the Allied left. Joffre formed a new French Tenth Army, under General de Maud'huy, which attempted to get round the German right flank further north but subsequently struggled, early in October, to hold Arras against a thrust by three German corps. These operations between the Aisne and Belgium did not, however, lead to a cessation of fighting elsewhere. In late September the French beat off repeated assaults at Verdun, although the German Fifth Army, under Crown Prince Wilhelm, gained ground in the Argonne forest and a troublesome German salient was established on the western bank of the Meuse, at St Mihiel. The shape which the Western Front would largely retain until 1918 was fast being moulded.

Worried about becoming enmeshed in the Aisne stalemate, Sir John French urged Joffre to allow the BEF to disengage and resume its former position on the Allied left. Tactically the BEF – lacking heavy artillery but possessing effective cavalry – would be of greater value on the open left flank while, strategically, it seemed sensible to shorten its lines of communication with the Channel ports. Despite the problems which would arise from the passage of British divisions across French lines of communication, Joffre sanctioned the move. On 1 October the BEF began a side-step to the Flanders plain, a region which would become one of its main fields of sacrifice for the remainder of the conflict.

In the first three weeks of October Smith-Dorrien's II Corps pushed towards La Bassée while, to the north, Major-General Pulteney's III Corps advanced towards Lille. The Cavalry Corps, commanded by Lieutenant-General Edmund Allenby and operating on Pulteney's left, occupied Messines and Wytschaete, linking with the recently formed IV Corps which, after the surrender of Antwerp, was ordered to Ypres. The co-ordination of operations between the Oise and the sea was entrusted by Joffre to Foch, who was appointed to head a new Northern Army Group. There were no formal arrangements for unity of command and Foch had no direct powers over the British and Belgians, but in practice his allies

– wherever possible – acted upon his proposals rapidly and without friction at this stage of the war.

Such co-operation was essential, for Falkenhayn was currently displaying a deft strategic touch, using railways cleverly to gain a vital edge in redeploying and reinforcing his armies. With the Germans setting the pace, the Allies were at greater risk of being outflanked in late October and early November. The German Sixth Army, which had moved across the front from Lorraine, strove to dislodge the Allies from their positions between La Bassée and Menin, and a reconstituted Fourth Army, under Duke Albrecht of Württemberg, closed in on Ypres. The latter formation included four new reserve corps with a large proportion of highly motivated young volunteers from universities and technical colleges who, although hurriedly trained, offered Falkenhayn a potentially decisive advantage as he sought to outflank the Allied left and drive down the Channel coast.

Antwerp falls

Once the 'race to the sea' gathered speed, the Germans knew that they must finally deal with the problem posed by Antwerp, to which the Belgian Field Army had withdrawn in August. The Belgians had made sorties from Antwerp on 24 August and 9 September, trying to disrupt German communications, but these efforts had merely exacerbated the exhaustion and low morale of their own troops. King Albert's objections notwithstanding, Joffre spurred him into ordering a third sortie. This had hardly begun when, on 28 September, the Germans opened a bombardment against Antwerp's outer forts.

The Germans had few spare formations available and the force they assembled, under General von Beseler, mostly comprised Reserve, Landwehr or Ersatz units. However, the 80,000 garrison troops supplementing the Belgian Field Army were of indifferent quality and Antwerp's 48 forts and redoubts were obsolete and outgunned. Hence, although numerical weakness restricted Beseler to an assault on the city's south-eastern defences, five days of infantry attacks and bombardment by super-heavy siege artillery were enough to breach the outer ring of forts.

The Belgians were now convinced of the need to evacuate Antwerp. Warned of their intentions by the British Minister in Belgium, the British Government belatedly intervened. In a personal visit to Antwerp on 3 October the First Lord of the Admiralty, Winston Churchill, persuaded the Belgians to continue their resistance provided that, within three days, the British could guarantee relief forces would be sent. The French offered the 87th Territorial Division and a Marine Brigade while the British promised a contingent, commanded by Lieutenant-General Sir Henry Rawlinson, which contained the Regular 7th Division and 3rd Cavalry Division.

In actuality the only reinforcements to arrive were from the newly formed Royal Naval Division, which reached Antwerp between 4 and 6 October. Their presence did not prevent the Germans from extending a bridgehead across the River Nethe, thereby hastening the city's fall.

The greater part of the Belgian Field Army duly carried out a further retirement to the Nieuport–Dixmude line along the River Yser. Rearguards, including the Royal Naval Division, left Antwerp during the night of 8–9 October and on 10 October the city formally surrendered. Rawlinson's force, designated IV Corps, had landed at Zeebrugge and Ostend but could do no more than concentrate at Ghent to cover the withdrawal of the Royal Naval Division and Belgians before moving south-west to join the French 87th Division in protecting Ypres. The eleventh-hour British contribution to Antwerp's defence had been too small to save the city; however, it did help to delay the surrender for some five days, winning precious time for the main BEF to reach Flanders. The true value of British intervention at Antwerp, within the wider context of the whole 1914 campaign, would become clear over the next six weeks.

The 2nd Battalion, Royal Scots Fusiliers, digging trenches north of the Menin Road, near Ypres, on 20 October 1914. (IWM)

Fighting on the Yser

Having abandoned Antwerp, the Belgian Field Army, with the French Marine Brigade, consolidated its positions between Dixmude and the coast near Nieuport. King Albert's decision to stand there, rather than help his allies inland, proved sensible. On 14 October Falkenhayn ordered the German Sixth Army to remain temporarily on the defensive south of Ypres while the Fourth Army – incorporating the four Reserve Corps of young volunteers – made the potentially decisive thrust between Menin and the sea, towards Calais. Its right, on the coast, would be covered by Beseler's III Reserve Corps, including units from the Antwerp operations.

Beseler's attack on 18 October – augmented the following day by XXII Reserve Corps – pushed back Belgian outposts east of the Yser, but further assaults on 19–20 October were repulsed at Dixmude and at Nieuport, where the Germans were shelled by Allied warships. Foch sent the French 42nd Division to stiffen the Nieuport sector, but on 22 October the Germans established a bridgehead across the Yser, at Tervaete. Once again employing their super-heavy guns, the Germans delivered repeated blows at Dixmude – now perilously close to being outflanked. As their losses grew it became progressively more difficult for the Belgians to continue their stubborn defence. Consequently, on 28 October they opened the gates of the Furnes lock at Nieuport and flooded the low ground east of the embankment carrying the Nieuport–Dixmude railway.

At first this desperate measure did not stop the Germans who, by noon on 30 October, had seized Ramscapelle and reached Pervyse. However, that night the rising water forced Beseler to pull III Reserve Corps back across the Yser, followed, two days later, by XXII Reserve Corps. Frustrated near the coast, Falkenhayn and Duke Albrecht were obliged to turn their attention inland again and launch their next major attack in the Ypres area.

First battle of Ypres

While the struggle on the Yser raged, the BEF had largely clung to its positions at Messines, Ploegsteert and La Bassée. The farmland surrounding the Belgian town of Ypres was now the only sector where either side had a real chance of outflanking the enemy. Arriving from the Aisne on 20 October, Haig's I Corps advanced north of Ypres, near Langemarck, but ran head-on into the German XXIV and XXVI Reserve Corps approaching from the north-east. Far from striking a decisive blow, the Allies became embroiled in a fluctuating encounter battle during which they were compelled to feed in units piecemeal simply to hold their ground. On the German side, the patriotism of the young volunteers could not disguise their limited training and they fell in thousands at Langemarck, attacking in dense skirmish lines. Remembered by the Germans as the *Kindermord von Ypern* (Massacre of the Innocents at Ypres), their sacrifice was later accorded a special place in Nazi mythology.

Although the front remained fluid, trenches were now snaking across the flat farmland. Aware, by the evening of 24 October, that the Reserve Corps assaults would probably fail, the Germans decided to make a fresh attack a few miles further south, between Gheluvelt and Messines. There, on 29 October, a task force under General von Fabeck renewed German efforts to achieve a breakthrough. The Allies experienced a major crisis on 31 October when the British positions at Gheluvelt were overrun but, as at Langemarck, the Germans lost cohesion after the initial breach, again exposing weaknesses in their training, and a bold counter-attack by 357 officers and men of the 2nd Worcestershires drove them from Gheluvelt.

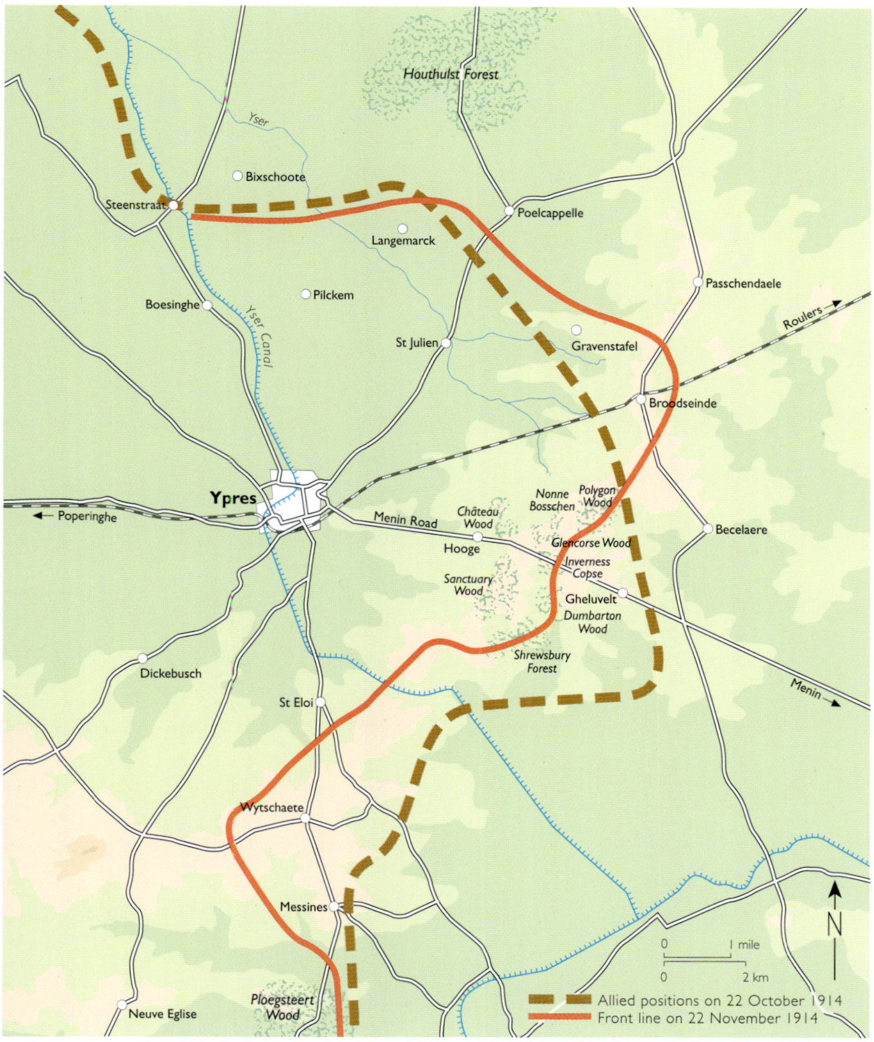

The first battle of Ypres, October–November 1914.

Over the next few days, however, Allenby's cavalry and the French were pushed off Messines Ridge. The situation was stabilised with the deployment of extra French troops on the BEF's flanks but the respite was brief. Another German assault on 11 November saw a composite Prussian Guard Division break through the British lines just north of the Menin Road. Once more employing obsolete tightly packed formations, the Germans were halted by a combination of point-blank British artillery fire and a scratch force which included cooks, brigade headquarters clerks and engineers. Not knowing that this represented the last line of British resistance, the Prussian Guard faltered and were then cleared from the *Nonne Bosschen* (Nun's Wood) by a vigorous counter-attack by the 2nd Oxfordshire and Buckinghamshire Light Infantry.

The Cloth Hall at Ypres, showing the damage caused by German artillery fire in October and November 1914. (Mary Evans Picture Library)

The Allies had survived the last crisis of 1914. Within a week or so snow cloaked the battlefield and the grandiose plans of the belligerents lay in ruins. The transfer of four German cavalry and eight infantry divisions to the Eastern Front by early December underlined Falkenhayn's acknowledgement of that fact. Despite gaining a great deal of valuable territory in Belgium and northern France, the Germans now faced their ultimate nightmare: a prolonged two-front war, the very scenario they had sought to avoid. The original, highly trained, professional BEF had also gone beyond recall. It had done much to halt the German drive on the Channel ports but suffered 58,000 additional casualties between 14 October and 30 November. The forces of the British Empire had begun their long and bloody association with Ypres, where the Allies occupied a hazardous salient dominated by German-held ridges to the south and east.

The winter of 1914–1915

With the onset of winter, the deadlock became total. Continuous trench lines now extended from the Belgian coast to the Swiss frontier. The Germans had not yet constructed the formidable defensive systems which, for most of the war, their overall strategy in the west would dictate. Believing, in late 1914, that the building of a second position might weaken the resolve of troops in the front defences, the Germans depended at first on a single line, to be held at all costs. However, during the winter they revised this policy, adding depth to these defences with concrete machine-gun posts 1,000 yards to the rear of the front line. The 21 miles of front then held by the BEF, between Wytschaete and the La Bassée Canal, ran through the low-lying Flanders plain, where the shallow trenches often flooded.

Having prepared for siege operations at the outset of the war, the Germans were comparatively well endowed with weapons suitable for trench warfare, including mortars, grenades, heavy guns and howitzers. The BEF, however, was compelled to fashion improvised mortars from drainpipes and grenades from jam tins. All the armies were experiencing shell shortages. Falkenhayn later stated that the failure of just one ammunition train that winter 'threatened to render whole sections of the front defenceless'. The French, requiring 50,000 rounds of 75mm ammunition daily, were producing only 11,000 rounds per day in mid-November 1914, while by January some British 18-pounder guns were restricted to firing just four rounds a day. Steps were taken at home to increase munitions production, but British industry could not be transformed overnight to meet the war's unprecedented demands.

Casualty rates in 1914 hit the BEF particularly hard. As a small, professional volunteer force it could ill afford the loss of 3,627 officers and 86,237 men between August and December 1914, most casualties being among the Regulars of its first seven divisions. To compensate for the losses, the Indian Corps reached the Western Front in October, followed, between November and January, by the 8th, 27th and 28th Divisions – all formed from Regulars drawn from overseas garrisons. Twenty-three Territorial battalions also reinforced the BEF in 1914, and in February the next year the 1st Canadian Division arrived. On 26 December the BEF was reorganised into two armies: the First Army under Haig and the Second Army under Smith-Dorrien. In Britain, Kitchener, who foresaw a long and costly war, had begun a vast expansion of Britain's military forces, forming a series of 'New Armies', each of which duplicated the six divisions of the original BEF. More than 1,186,000 volunteers enlisted in the first five months, but they would take time to train.

Men of the London Rifle Brigade fraternise with Saxon troops, near Ploegsteert, Christmas 1914. (Mary Evans Picture Library)

Meanwhile the British soldiers at the front were struggling to hold the line. Musketry standards had already declined and morale had slumped as the Germans made gains in minor operations at Givenchy in December and near Cuinchy in January. Christmas 1914 was marked by a spontaneous unofficial truce in Flanders, where German and British soldiers fraternised in No Man's Land, taking photographs, swapping souvenirs and even playing football. Hardening attitudes, as the war became increasingly bloody and impersonal, ensured that such incidents on this scale would not recur, but 'live and let live' understandings – accepted by both sides – frequently prevailed in quiet sectors until the Armistice.

Falkenhayn's decision in November 1914 to stand temporarily on the defensive in the west – where he believed the war would ultimately be won – proved a huge mistake. A weakened and now inexperienced BEF might not have withstood further heavy blows during the winter, but the respite granted by the Germans allowed the Allies to reorganise, giving Britain, in particular, the chance to train Kitchener's New Armies and strengthen the BEF with additional Territorial and Dominion contingents. Falkenhayn hoped that once the Russians had been pushed back over the Vistula he would resume the offensive in the west. However, a combination of factors forced him to continue with a predominantly defensive strategy there in 1915.

Austria needed a major victory to deter neighbouring Romania and Italy from joining the Allies, and without extra German assistance, especially in the Carpathians, it was feared that Austria might even seek a separate peace. Hindenburg and Ludendorff could claim that all the titanic efforts in the west had resulted only in deadlock, whereas they – with fewer resources – had twice frustrated Russian attempts to invade Germany and had also won territory in Russian Poland. Since both the Kaiser and his Chancellor, Bethmann-Hollweg, agreed that the Eastern Front should be given priority, Falkenhayn found it necessary to stifle his own immediate strategic inclinations.

For the French the options were far simpler. The Germans occupied large areas of Belgium and northern France – including regions rich in raw materials or heavy industry. These could only be liberated through an offensive policy. Joffre remained convinced that a breakthrough was possible, but conceded that a succession of preliminary attacks might be required to devour German reserves before the enemy line finally ruptured. In a phrase attributed to Joffre – *Je les grignote* ('I keep nibbling at them') – lay the embryo of three years of attrition. But where should the French strike? Joffre decided to pinch out the German-held salient between Reims and Arras, the snout of which, at Noyon, pointed towards Paris. He would attack it from two directions. One thrust eastwards, from Artois, might drive the Germans back across the Douai plain and menace their supply lines to Cambrai and St Quentin, while another advance northwards, from Champagne, could sever railway links feeding the German centre. A third offensive, launched from the Verdun–Nancy front, might also cut the Thionville–Hirson railway communications and loosen the German grip in this sector, as the routes north of the Ardennes could not, by themselves, sustain the whole German front in the west.

Joffre's strategy, which shaped Franco-British operations throughout 1915, was essentially sound. In an amended form it would produce decisive results in the second half of 1918. However, during the war's first winter, the Allies had neither the means nor the tactical skills to apply it successfully and, lacking appropriate equipment and fresh troops, Joffre could only mount significant attacks on the fronts of the Fourth Army in Champagne and the Tenth Army in Artois.

Directed by Foch, the left-hand blow of Joffre's winter offensives was struck on 17 December in Artois. De Maud'huy's Tenth Army attempted to pierce the German defences around Souchez, north of Arras, and seize Vimy Ridge, which offered excellent observation over the Lens coalfield and the Douai plain. Pétain's XXXIII Corps was ordered to secure Carency, guarding the western approaches to Souchez, and Maistre's XXI Corps would press towards the Notre Dame de Lorette spur, situated on the other side of the Souchez valley, opposite the north-western end of Vimy Ridge. Since they were short of heavy artillery, the French had to stagger their attacks, allowing the Germans to concentrate their defensive firepower. Fog, rain and thick mud hampered operations and forced the French to end the Artois attacks early in January 1915; they had incurred nearly 8,000 casualties for meagre gains on the southern edge of Carency and north of Notre Dame de Lorette.

On 20 December the Fourth Army had attacked on a 20-mile front in Champagne. The XVII and Colonial Corps, on the right, achieved early successes, taking important strongpoints in the enemy front line, but XXII Corps, on the left, made little headway against flanking machine-gun fire.

Operations ran on into January, when, as in Artois, miserable weather and the exhaustion of the troops forced the French to suspend the offensive. The Germans exploited this lull to strengthen their support positions where the front line had been breached or imperilled. The second phase of this battle began on 16 February and lasted until 17 March, with limited attacks continuing for another fortnight. The Germans experienced the full horrors of rapid 'drum fire' from French 75mm guns yet only yielded a few scattered villages on the forward slopes of the hills. The Champagne offensive cost the French some 240,000 casualties and failed to disrupt the railway communications supplying the German centre.

Diversionary attacks in support of the main offensives did not alleviate the gloom. On the Aisne, ground was won by Maunoury's Sixth Army at Vauxrot and Crouy, but the French were pushed back to the left bank in January by a brutal German counterstroke. Assaults by Sarrail's Third Army between the Meuse and Argonne, intended to cover the right of the Champagne offensive, led to a further 12,000 French casualties. The eastern flank bore witness to a savage struggle for the Hartmannsweilerkopf. This peak, dominating the Alsace plain, was in French possession by 26 April, though the Army of the Vosges (later the French Seventh Army) lost 20,000 men in the four-month battle.

Despite Joffre's assurances in March 1915 that French soldiers had 'an obvious superiority in morale', his winter offensives had been expensive failures. Given his previous service as an engineer officer, his inability to adapt to what were basically siege warfare conditions was as disappointing as his want of tactical flair. Even Foch, the arch-apostle of *élan*, reviewed his tactical principles as the need for sufficient heavy artillery to destroy enemy trenches and strongpoints became increasingly apparent.

Neuve Chapelle

The BEF, after a wretched winter in the trenches, was in no state to support the French offensives until the early spring of 1915. However, knowing that the War Council in London was considering operations in the Dardanelles and Balkans, its senior commanders feared that unless the BEF made a positive contribution soon, resources might be diverted away from the Western Front. The appointment of Lieutenant-General Sir William Robertson as the BEF's Chief of Staff in January also brought a more robust approach to the work of General Headquarters (GHQ). By mid-February a plan was approved for an attack by Haig's First Army on a narrow, 2,000-yard front in Flanders. The aim was to eliminate the German salient around Neuve Chapelle, secure Aubers Ridge and threaten Lille, an important road and rail junction. The despatch of the Regular 29th Division to the Dardanelles prevented the BEF from relieving the French IX Corps at Ypres and precluded a simultaneous French attack in Artois. Rather than postpone Haig's operation indefinitely, Sir John French decided that it should go ahead independently, if only to demonstrate that the BEF could do more than merely hold the line.

The First Army's thorough planning provided the BEF with a valuable template for future set-piece trench assaults. Photographic reconnaissance by the Royal Flying Corps facilitated the production and distribution of detailed trench maps and enabled the assaulting units to rehearse the initial phase of the attack, while precise artillery timetables were issued for the first

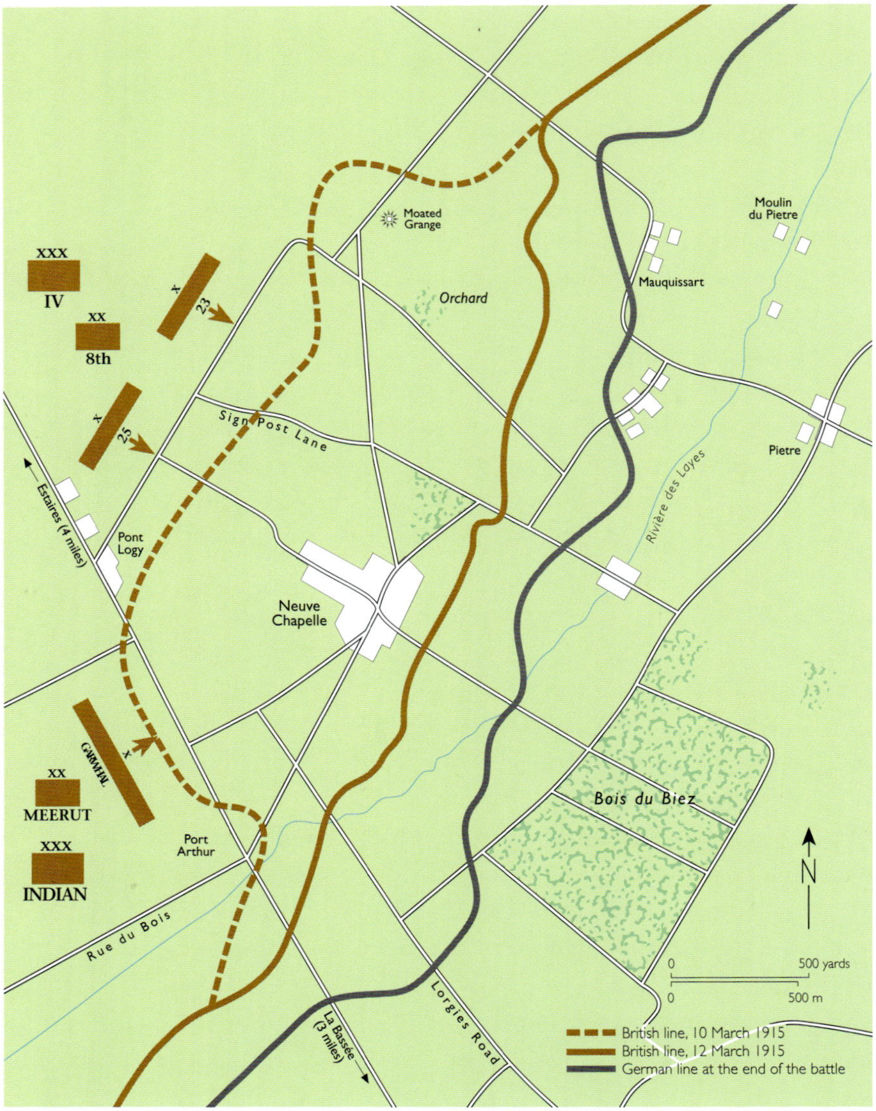

The battle of Neuve Chapelle, 10–12 March 1915.

time. The artillery was allocated 100,000 rounds – one-sixth of the BEF's total stocks – and was limited to a 35-minute hurricane bombardment, following which fire would be lifted from the enemy front trenches and a barrage laid down to impede German reinforcements.

On 10 March, the day of the assault, the surprised German defenders were numbed by the hurricane bombardment. The attacking brigades of the Indian Corps and Rawlinson's IV Corps swiftly took the front trenches. Thereafter delays on the flanks caused congestion in the centre, and German strongpoints also held up the advance – robbing the attack of its impetus. British and Indian troops had seized the German defences on a frontage of

4,000 yards, penetrated to a maximum depth of 1,200 yards, captured Neuve Chapelle and flattened the salient west of the village, but they could not exploit their early gains. Haig therefore suspended the attack late on 12 March. The British had suffered nearly 13,000 casualties, the Germans about 12,000. The BEF could now be taken seriously as an attacking force, yet Neuve Chapelle also highlighted several intrinsic problems of trench assaults. Careful preparation would generally help attackers to break into enemy positions but it was much harder to move artillery and reserves forward quickly enough to *break out* of those defences before enemy reinforcements arrived. The absence of adequate means of communication also rendered it extremely difficult for commanders to control operations once shells had destroyed forward telephone cables and runners had been killed or wounded. However, the effectiveness of the short hurricane bombardment was one lesson which the BEF, to its cost, largely ignored or discounted over the next two years.

'Papa' Joffre, the French Commander-in-Chief, 1914–1916. (Mary Evans Picture Library)

Second battle of Ypres

Before the Allies could launch their next offensive operations the Germans – employing poison gas for the first time on the Western Front – attacked the northern flank of the Ypres Salient. This blow reflected all the confusion of strategic purpose that characterised Falkenhayn's term as Chief of the German General Staff. The Salient was important to both sides, but because Falkenhayn still accorded priority to the Eastern Front, the use of gas at Ypres was largely experimental. Thus the objectives of XXIII and XXVI Reserve Corps were confined to Langemarck, Pilckem Ridge and the Yser canal line up to Ypres itself, while the Fourth Army was denied fresh reserves. However, the Germans hoped that the capture of the higher ground near Pilckem might render it impossible for the Allies to hold the Salient.

The French 45th (Algerian) and 87th Territorial Divisions occupied the sector between the Yser canal and Poelcappelle which the Germans were to attack. Just after 5pm on 22 April, following a short but ferocious bombardment, the Germans released clouds of chlorine gas from 5,730 cylinders. With no protection against the gas, the French divisions retreated in panic, opening a 5-mile gap to the left of the 1st Canadian Division's positions. Langemarck and Pilckem fell and at dusk the Germans were only 2 miles from Ypres. Fortunately for the Allies, the German troops were unwilling to pursue the gas too closely and, lacking reserves, failed to grasp their sole opportunity to effect a breakthrough in the west. During the night a new defensive line was patched together by the British and Canadians. When a second gas attack came at St Julien on 24 April, the Canadians – using towels, bandages and handkerchiefs soaked in urine or water as improvised respirators – courageously prevented further erosion of the front.

Foch, co-ordinating Allied operations in Flanders, did not enjoy his finest hour at Ypres in April–May 1915. However, his faith in the infallibility of the offensive unshaken, and ignoring the loss of guns during the German advance, he ordered the local French commander to undertake counter-attacks that were plainly impractical. Various assaults by the BEF between 23 and 26 April, made with inadequate artillery support and negligible French assistance, failed to regain the lost ground. On 27 April, painfully aware that German gunners could now shell the Salient from the left rear, Smith-Dorrien urged withdrawal to a more defensible 'GHQ Line' to the east of Potijze and Wieltje and within 2,000 yards of Ypres. The suggestion was rejected by the mercurial Sir John French, who was in optimistic mood following a promise of extra divisions from Foch. With his doubts about Smith-Dorrien re-awakened, French immediately transferred responsibility for all British troops around Ypres to the V Corps commander, Herbert Plumer.

This incident precipitated Smith-Dorrien's resignation and he was succeeded in command of Second Army by Plumer on 6 May. The loss of the able Smith-Dorrien did not ultimately prove as calamitous to the BEF as it might have done, since Plumer displayed an almost unrivalled understanding and mastery of the new tactical conditions on the Western Front, particularly at Ypres. It is ironic that between 1 and 3 May, when the demands of the imminent Artois offensive ended hopes of French reserves being sent to Ypres, Plumer was permitted to draw back his forces, much as Smith-Dorrien had proposed, though – partly to allow room for possible future movements – Plumer's line was slightly further east, about 3 miles from Ypres.

In May the Germans made four more gas attacks, seizing additional ground on the Bellewaarde and Frezenberg ridges. When the battle ended, on 25 May, the Ypres Salient – now less than 3 miles deep – had assumed the basic form it would keep for the next two years. For the second time in seven months the BEF had halted a German drive on Ypres; this latest defence had cost another 58,000 casualties, compared with nearly 38,000 German losses. Furthermore, with the Germans positioned on three sides and holding the key ridges to the east and south, there was no relief from the enemy guns and no foreseeable end to the suffering of BEF units occupying the Salient.

Artois and Flanders

Events on the Eastern Front, where the Central Powers had launched a devastating offensive between Gorlice and Tarnów on 2 May, made the projected Allied spring offensive in Artois even more significant as a means of giving indirect help to the Russians (see chapter 3). Joffre and Foch proposed that in Artois, after a prodigious six-day preliminary bombardment by 1,252 guns, the French Tenth Army, now commanded by General d'Urbal, would assault Vimy Ridge to open the way for an advance into the Douai plain.

When the offensive began, on 9 May, Pétain's XXXIII Corps – attacking in the crucial central sector – achieved early successes beyond expectations. In 90 minutes his troops moved forward 2½ miles on a 4-mile front and the 77th and Moroccan Divisions reached the crest of Vimy Ridge between Souchez and La Folie Farm. The drawback was that because d'Urbal had not anticipated such a swift advance, his nearest reserves were over 7 miles away and could not be brought up in time to exploit these successes. Inevitably, by nightfall the Germans had counter-attacked and pushed Pétain's troops off the crest. From now on, the offensive degenerated into a bitter close-quarter struggle in the labyrinth of German strongpoints and trenches on or below the ridge. As the grisly spectre of attrition re-imposed itself, the French made a few extra gains, securing much of the vital neighbouring spur of Notre Dame de Lorette. On 16 June the impressive Moroccan Division again reached the top of Vimy Ridge, but as before could not hold on to all its gains. Five weeks of fighting had cost an additional 100,000 French casualties while German losses totalled some 60,000. All that Joffre and Foch could show for this sacrifice was the recapture of 5 more miles of French soil and a precarious toe-hold on Vimy Ridge.

The BEF's part in the offensive operations of 9 May was a larger-scale version of its own March assault, with Haig's First Army attacking either side of Neuve Chapelle in a fresh effort to secure Aubers Ridge. The success of the short bombardment in March was borne in mind, but the BEF's worrying shortage of heavy guns and ammunition limited the preliminary bombardment to 45 minutes. As the German defences in this sector had been strengthened since March, the bombardment was simply not heavy enough. With plenty of time to emerge from their dug-outs and man their trench parapets relatively unscathed, the defenders inflicted 11,000 casualties for only tiny British gains, compelling Haig to terminate the attack early on 10 May.

Overleaf:
A trench scene showing German soldiers posed with a captured Maxim gun. Other details include the use of a loophole plate, and right, a trench periscope. The shaft of the periscope has been shrouded in fabric to blend more effectively with the sandbag parapet. The troops carry slung gas mask tins. (Courtesy of Stephen Bull)

Bowing to Joffre's calls to maintain the pressure, Sir John French approved a further First Army attack for 15 May at Festubert, about 2 miles north of the La Bassée Canal. A notable shift towards an attrition policy was signalled by GHQ's guidance to Haig that the enemy should be relentlessly 'worn down by exhaustion and loss until his defence collapses'. The preceding bombardment, lasting 60 hours, had been much longer than on 9 May and the objective line was deliberately less ambitious, being only 1,000 yards away. Between 15 and 27 May the BEF incurred 16,000 casualties for a maximum advance of some 1,300 yards – just enough to encourage future reliance on longer artillery bombardments before infantry attacks. In coming to believe that wearing-out fights, longer and heavier bombardments and wider attack frontages would be needed for any breakthrough, the French and British alike had drawn several misleading conclusions from the May battles and would then follow a series of costly and false tactical trails over the next two years.

Of much greater long-term significance, however, was the fact that the 'Shells Scandal' – generated in Britain by disclosures of ammunition shortages at Aubers Ridge – contributed directly to the creation of a Ministry of Munitions and to the formation of a coalition government. The new systematic policy of munitions production was far better tailored to the demands of modern war, even though the real benefits of this were not fully evident until mid-1917.

During the spring and summer of 1915 the expansion of the BEF gained impetus. From February to September the BEF was augmented by 15 New Army and six Territorial divisions. The 2nd Canadian Division also arrived in September, permitting the formation of the Canadian Corps. As its strength grew, the BEF took over more of the Allied line, including a 5-mile stretch between the La Bassée Canal and Lens in May and an additional 15 miles on the Somme in August. The latter sector became the responsibility of a new Third Army, under General Sir Charles Monro. In June the French created three Army Groups – the Northern, Central and Eastern – commanded respectively by Foch, de Castelnau and Dubail. Pétain's efforts in Artois were rewarded by promotion to the command of the French Second Army.

Even when no big offensives were in prospect, the Western Front was by no means quiet. In April the French made an abortive attempt to eradicate the potential threat posed to the eastern flank of Verdun by the German-held St Mihiel salient, incurring 64,000 casualties in the process. Another 32,000 French officers and men fell in the Argonne sector from 20 June to 14 July. Meanwhile the Germans continued to experiment with new weapons. After first using flamethrowers near Verdun in February, they subjected the raw British 14th (Light) Division to a terrifying 'liquid fire' attack at Hooge, near Ypres, on 30 July. In this sector, the short distance between the opposing trenches favoured the employment of flamethrowers;

henceforth such conditions would rarely recur. Moreover, the British 6th Division, in a well-prepared minor attack on 9 August, recovered all the ground they had lost at Hooge a few days earlier.

Allied plans for the autumn

Early in June Joffre revealed his plans for a combined autumn offensive. Like those of the previous winter, they envisaged convergent attacks from Artois and Champagne to isolate and eliminate the German-held Noyon salient and its communications. Initially Joffre intended to make the principal effort in Artois, but later he decided to shift the main weight of the offensive to Champagne, where the French Second and Fourth Armies would face fewer fortified villages than the Tenth Army did in Artois. The latter would again assault Vimy Ridge supported, north of Lens, by the British.

Both Sir John French and Haig, keenly aware of their weaknesses in heavy artillery, were unhappy about the role assigned to the BEF. In particular, the First Army was expected to advance across a difficult area of villages, mines and slag heaps – precisely the sort of terrain that had persuaded Joffre to switch the main blow from Artois to Champagne. Throughout June and July Joffre and Foch refused to be swayed by the protests of the British commanders. Then, in mid-August, the deteriorating strategic situation – following Allied setbacks in Italy and Gallipoli and on the Eastern Front – prompted Kitchener to modify his own views and order French and Haig to accept Joffre's plan, 'even though by so doing we may suffer very heavy losses'.

To deliver the principal blow in the more thinly populated Champagne region, the French had to construct additional light railways and roads, causing the postponement of the offensive until 25 September. The Germans, however, were not idle and hastened to build a new second defensive position 2–4 miles behind the first, employing prisoners of war and French civilians to speed up the work. Despite a series of alarmist reports from the German Third Army commander, Einem, concerning French preparations in Champagne, Falkenhayn remained sufficiently unruffled to undertake a tour of the front with the Kaiser as late as 21 September. Joffre was similarly optimistic. 'Your *élan* will be irresistible,' he assured his troops on the eve of the offensive.

Second battle of Champagne

The autumn offensive in Champagne began in a downpour on 25 September. Advancing with colours held aloft and bands playing the *Marseillaise*, the infantry of de Castelnau's Central Army Group made heartening initial progress. The German front trenches were badly damaged and their defensive barbed wire had been cut in many places by the four-day preliminary bombardment; this helped the French infantry arrive at the

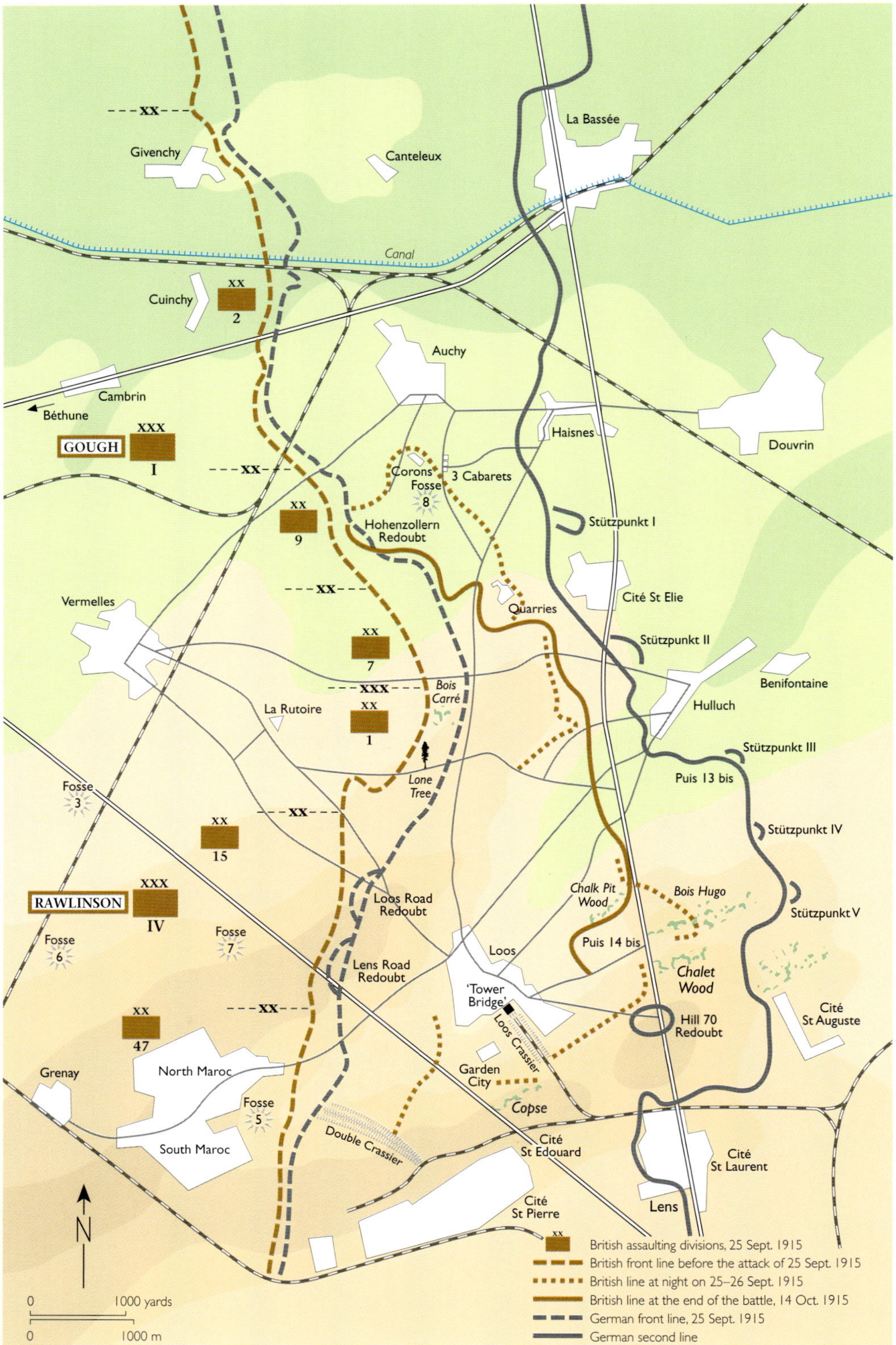

La Bassée
Givenchy
Canteleux
Canal
Cuinchy
2
Auchy
Cambrin
Béthune
GOUGH
I
Haisnes
Douvrin
Corons
Fosse 8
3 Cabarets
Stützpunkt I
9
Hohenzollern Redoubt
Cité St Elie
Vermelles
Quarries
7
Stützpunkt II
Benifontaine
Bois Carré
Hulluch
La Rutoire
1
Stützpunkt III
Lone Tree
Puis 13 bis
Fosse 3
15
Stützpunkt IV
RAWLINSON
IV
Loos Road Redoubt
Chalk Pit Wood
Bois Hugo
Stützpunkt V
Fosse 6
Fosse 7
Loos
Puis 14 bis
Lens Road Redoubt
Chalet Wood
'Tower Bridge'
Loos Crassier
Hill 70 Redoubt
Cité St Auguste
47
Grenay
North Maroc
Garden City
Copse
Fosse 5
South Maroc
Double Crassier
Cité St Edouard
Cité St Laurent
Lens
Cité St Pierre
N
0 1000 yards
0 1000 m
British assaulting divisions, 25 Sept. 1915
British front line before the attack of 25 Sept. 1915
British line at night on 25–26 Sept. 1915
British line at the end of the battle, 14 Oct. 1915
German front line, 25 Sept. 1915
German second line

Opposite:
The battle of Loos, September–October 1915.

enemy first position in reasonably good order. They broke through in four places. Although the Moroccan Division was halted around the heights of the Bois de Perthes, in the centre of the 20-division attack frontage, the 10th Colonial Division, on its left, penetrated up to 3,000 yards in under 60 minutes and reached the German second position. To the right of the Moroccans, the 28th Division was similarly successful, and ground was also won on the extreme flanks, but most of the assaulting divisions of the French Second and Fourth Armies failed to match the gains near the Bois de Perthes.

At noon Falkenhayn – still touring the front – reached the German Fifth Army headquarters and was briefed on the situation. He reacted by switching a division from the Vosges to the German Third Army and directed units of X Corps, recently transferred from the Eastern Front, towards Einem's battle area. The early French successes encouraged Joffre to give the Central Army Group two extra reserve divisions and to order the Eastern Army Group to pass on to it as much 75mm ammunition as could be spared. In fact, the German positions in Champagne were not seriously threatened. Having clearly seen the preparations for the offensive, the Germans had withdrawn most of their artillery behind their second position where, protected by relatively uncut wire, they intended to base their main defence.

Closing up to the German second position along a front of about 8 miles on 26 September, the French won only a shallow foothold in the defences and the offensive lost momentum. The French artillery lacked direct observation over the next series of German trenches, which were sited on reverse slopes. From 27 to 29 September a succession of desperate French attacks secured just a few small lodgements in the second position. As ammunition ran low and casualties grew, Pétain, commanding the French Second Army, had the moral courage to halt operations on his own initiative, obliging Joffre, in turn, to stop the offensive. A resumption of attacks on 6 October had no better outcome. The Champagne offensive had obviously fallen short of Joffre's promises, and since French losses were nearly 144,000 – against 85,000 German casualties – its slender gains could scarcely be justified, even by the grim standards of a long-term policy of attrition.

Loos

Haig's fears about the shortage of heavy artillery for his First Army's part in the Artois offensive were eased by the distribution of around 5,000 cylinders of chlorine gas to Lieutenant-General Hubert Gough's I Corps and Rawlinson's IV Corps. Rawlinson advocated 'bite and hold' tactics, drawing the Germans into expensive counter-attacks, but Haig – visualising the possibility of something more than a subsidiary success – hoped to break through the

German first and second positions between Loos and Haisnes, then advance east to the Haute Deule Canal. To this end Haig would deploy all six divisions of I and IV Corps in the main assault, on the understanding that XI Corps, in general reserve, would be transferred to him as soon as it was needed. Sir John French, who remained nervous about the coming operations, wanted to retain the reserves under GHQ's control until the attack developed, although he did accede to Haig's request that the heads of the two leading divisions of XI Corps should be within 4–6 miles of the start line on the morning of the assault. The choice of XI Corps for this role was in itself curious, since two of its three divisions had been in France less than a month.

Following a four-day bombardment the gas was released at 5.50am on 25 September, 40 minutes before the infantry assault. The gas largely failed in the centre and on the left, drifting back over the British trenches in places. Nevertheless, the 9th (Scottish) Division overcame the daunting defences of the Hohenzollern Redoubt and Fosse 8, while the 15th (Scottish) Division captured Loos village. Receiving Haig's request for the reserves at 8.45am, Sir John French freed the inexperienced 21st and 24th Divisions by 9.30. However, the slow transmission of orders and congestion in the rear – partly the fault of Haig's staff – delayed their arrival. They were forced to march at night, over unknown and debris-strewn terrain, for an attack the next morning, without artillery support and against the uncut wire of the German second position between Lens and Hulluch. It is small wonder that their attack dissolved into a disorganised retirement. The Germans soon recaptured many of the earlier British gains, including the Hohenzollern Redoubt.

The French, anxious not to repeat their mistakes of May, placed *their* own reserves too far forward on this occasion and suffered severe casualties from artillery fire. Even so, their Tenth Army finally seized Souchez on 26 September. The Germans kept possession of Vimy Ridge but the French took an important knoll – later called 'The Pimple' – at its northern end, and held this feature for nearly five months. A further British attack on the Hohenzollern Redoubt on 13 October only secured its western face.

These scattered tactical prizes were trifling rewards for the Allies, the Artois offensive having cost over 50,000 British casualties and approximately 48,000 French. German losses overall totalled about 56,000. In the BEF, Sir John French can rightly be censured for keeping the reserves too far back and retaining control of them too long. That said, the tactical handling of those reserves by Haig and his staff, once they came under First Army's direct orders, was unimpressive. Clearly the BEF – not least its senior commanders – had much still to learn, although the combat performance of the Scottish New Army divisions – 9th and 15th – offered some encouragement for the future.

Haig takes command of the BEF

Sir John French was swept away by the recriminations over the handling of the reserves at Loos and was succeeded as Commander-in-Chief of the BEF by Douglas Haig on 19 December 1915. Historians disagree about the extent to which Haig manipulated the situation to his own advantage. Increasingly disenchanted with his superior since Mons, Haig had certainly taken care to ensure that his feelings about French were known in the corridors of power. One should note, however, that, within a few months Haig's blend of single-minded professionalism and growing pragmatism had helped to generate fundamental improvements in the infrastructure, organisation, equipment and tactics of the BEF. His influence was also apparent in the appointment of Lieutenant-General Sir William Robertson as Chief of the Imperial General Staff (CIGS) on 23 December. Before accepting that post, Robertson insisted that the CIGS should be the Cabinet's only authoritative source of advice on operations. Though not uncritical of Haig, Robertson broadly supported the latter's opinion that the war would be won in France. The decision to evacuate Gallipoli having already been reached, the elevation of Haig and Robertson virtually guaranteed the primacy of the Western Front in British strategic policy in 1916.

General Sir Douglas Haig, Commander-in-Chief of the British Expeditionary Force from December 1915. He was promoted to Field Marshal at the end of 1916. (IWM Q23659)

It was now evident to Allied generals that protracted operations were the prerequisite of decisive victory. The battles of 1915 had established that methodical planning, intense bombardments and furious infantry assaults would usually lead to the capture of enemy front positions but the problems of exploiting the 'break-in' seemed intractable. With the German positions becoming stronger and deeper, the Allies had yet to surmount the difficulties of launching a series of attacks on successive positions, with each requiring fresh reserves and artillery preparation. Furthermore, while acknowledging the necessity of attrition, Allied commanders had not relinquished all hopes of a breakthrough and did not entirely appreciate that attrition worked best when the ground seized was not itself of great importance except as bait to lure in and eliminate as many enemy troops as possible. Indeed, many senior Allied commanders remained wedded to the idea of seizing particular objectives rather than conceiving limited offensives to kill the maximum number of Germans.

There had been some new developments in tactics during 1915. By the end of the year the Germans were moving away from the columns and skirmish lines of 1914 and were training special assault detachments, or 'storm troops', which

had their own flamethrowers, light artillery and mortars for close fire support and advanced independently to deal with enemy strongpoints. In France, flexible infantry tactics were similarly promoted by Captain André Laffargue, who wrote a seminal pamphlet entitled *The Attack in Trench Warfare.* The British – struggling to cope with the huge influx of citizen soldiers in the expanding BEF – were currently less progressive in tactical thinking, but the appearance of the Stokes mortar and Mills grenade, as well as a conspicuous rise in munitions production, indicated that they would shortly begin to win the vital war of matériel.

Bombers of the 1st Battalion, Scots Guards, priming Mills grenades in Big Willie Trench, near Loos, in October 1915. (Mary Evans Picture Library)

At an inter-Allied conference at Chantilly from 6 to 8 December it was concluded that to counter the Central Powers' ability to shift reserves rapidly from theatre to theatre on interior lines of communication the Allies should launch simultaneous offensives in 1916 on the Italian, Eastern and Western fronts. Joffre proposed to Haig, at the end of December, that the main Franco-British blow might be struck astride the River Somme. On 23 January 1916 he suggested that, prior to the offensive, the BEF should engage the Germans in 'wearing-out fights' in April and May. Haig saw such actions as a key preliminary phase of the main battle, not as separate operations. Determined to avoid squandering the under-trained BEF prematurely, he resisted this aspect of Joffre's proposals. While personally favouring a Flanders offensive, Haig was nonetheless sharply aware that Britain was still the junior partner in the military alliance. Consequently, on 14 February, he agreed with Joffre that the BEF would play its part in a joint offensive on the Somme around 1 July 1916.

The Western Front 1914–1918.

Attrition in the ascendant

Even as the Allies were formulating their plans for 1916, the Germans were preparing to beat them to the punch. There were currently no serious threats to the Central Powers in the east, so Falkenhayn could at last think again about attacking in the west, where a major victory was clearly required to nullify the growing Allied superiority in men and matériel. Britain, seen by Falkenhayn as the 'arch-enemy', might eventually be brought to heel by unrestricted submarine warfare, but attacks on neutral shipping also risked causing a wrathful United States to join the Allies.

Another solution, on land, might be to convince France that further sacrifice was futile, thereby knocking Britain's 'best sword' from its hand. The events of 1915 had shown that a mass breakthrough was unlikely, so Falkenhayn decided instead to order a limited offensive in a specially selected sector which the French would defend at any cost. In such an action, Falkenhayn reasoned, 'the forces of France will bleed to death' as successive waves of French reinforcements were lured within range of a gigantic concentration of German artillery.

Falkenhayn's chosen killing ground was the fortress-city of Verdun, a symbol of French national pride located in a salient which German guns could bombard from three sides. The offensive would be conducted by the German Fifth Army under Crown Prince Wilhelm, the heir to the throne, thus ensuring the Kaiser's support. (In fact, the real authority in the Fifth Army lay with its Chief of Staff, Knobelsdorf, the Kaiser's own appointee. 'Whatever he advises you, you must do,' the Kaiser pointedly informed his son.)

Almost encircled by ridges and hills on both banks of the Meuse, Verdun was also protected by rings of forts. The strongest, in theory, was Fort Douaumont, perched on a 1,200-foot height north-east of the city, on the right bank. However, the strength of the forts was illusory, many of their guns having been removed to provide extra firepower for the French autumn operations. A member of the Chamber of Deputies, Emile Driant, had infuriated Joffre by disclosing Verdun's weaknesses to fellow Deputies. By a remarkable twist of fate, Driant, in February 1916, was commanding two battalions of *Chasseurs* in the Bois des Caures – a feature at the epicentre of the German attack.

It is open to debate whether Falkenhayn actually meant to seize Verdun. His decisions to strike the initial blow with only nine divisions, to keep reserves under his own control and to restrict the assault to the right bank all indicate that this was not his principal aim. On the other hand, Crown Prince Wilhelm was encouraged to proceed with planning on the assumption that the objective was to capture Verdun 'by precipitate methods'. Not for the first time, nor indeed the last, confusion about strategic purpose infected German offensive operations. The immediate task of secretly massing over 1,220 artillery pieces behind the German front was meticulously carried out but nobody could influence the weather. Gales, rain and blizzards forced Falkenhayn to delay the assault – scheduled to start on 12 February – for nine days.

Attack at Verdun

The battle opened at dawn on 21 February. A single 38cm naval gun, 20 miles from the city, fired the first round at a bridge spanning the Meuse. This shell, which missed its target, was the prelude to a nine-hour bombardment of unprecedented savagery. More than 80,000 shells fell in the Bois des Caures alone. With their rearward communications severed, the bewildered defenders were in no condition to repel a major assault. Fortunately for the French, the German planners had been too cautious, limiting infantry operations on the first day to strong fighting patrols which would employ infiltration tactics to seek out weak spots in the French line. Only the VII Reserve Corps commander, Zwehl, disregarded these orders and showed what might have been achieved. He deployed storm troops just behind the fighting patrols and, in five hours, secured the Bois d'Haumont. In the Bois des Caures, however, Driant's shrewd use of strongpoints instead of continuous trench lines enabled the surviving *Chasseurs* to defend that position obstinately against the German XVIII Corps.

On 22 February Zwehl was again the pace-setter, bursting through a regiment of Territorials on the French 72nd Division's left at the Bois de Consenvoye and then seizing Haumont to tear open a gap in the French first line and expose the left flank of the Bois des Caures. During the late afternoon the heroic Driant was killed whilst endeavouring to withdraw his shattered battalions to Beaumont. Much of the French front line had crumbled but despite terrible casualties the defenders were inflicting increasing losses on the Germans, especially among their key storm troops. The next day the

Soldiers of the French 68th Infantry Regiment in a dug-out in the Ravin de Souchez, October 1915. (IWM Q49296)

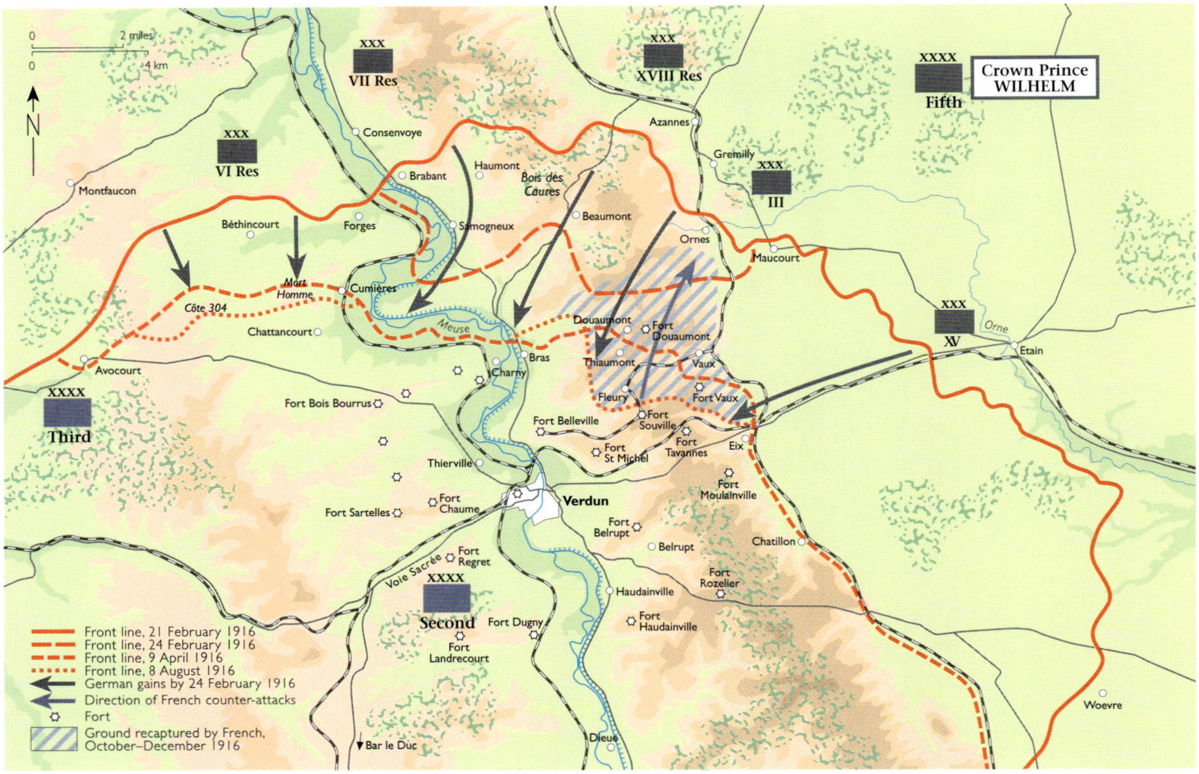

The battle of Verdun, February–December 1916.

Germans came up against an intermediate line that had only recently been created on de Castelnau's orders and so was not marked on German maps. The dogged defence of Herbebois by the French 51st Division was overcome that evening but overall German gains were disappointing on 23 February. The 37th African Division began to reach the battlefield to shore up the depleted units of the French XXX Corps and, ominously for the Germans, powerful French artillery was massing on the left bank of the Meuse.

In the short term these developments were of scant comfort to the French. Before dawn on 24 February Samogneux was in German hands. The French 51st and 72nd Divisions were close to collapse. Beaumont then fell and in barely three hours the French second position broke apart. Algerian Zouaves and Moroccan *Tirailleurs* of the 37th Division were committed piecemeal to the battle but, with no protection from the bitter cold or the fury of the German guns, they could not stabilise the situation. Indeed, the 3rd Zouaves – facing the Brandenburgers of the German III Corps – melted away, so uncovering Fort Douaumont, a pivotal point in the defences. As darkness descended, the leading elements of Balfourier's French XX Corps arrived to relieve the battered XXX Corps but there was no guarantee that these fresh troops could repair the disintegrating front.

Fort Douaumont is captured

On 25 February the 24th Brandenburg Regiment entered the gap left by the 3rd Zouaves. Some detachments pushed beyond the stipulated objectives as far as Fort Douaumont. Here, partly because of a French staff and command muddle, the garrison numbered less than 60. Emboldened by the curious inactivity of the fort, a few pioneers, under a sergeant named Kunze, pressed through the outer defences to the dry moat. Still undetected, they climbed through a gun embrasure in to one of the fort's galleries. Though German 42cm shells had not inflicted critical damage on the fort, the shock waves and fumes they produced had driven the defenders to shelter in the bowels of the fort. Kunze was followed in by three more small groups of Brandenburgers and the dejected garrison surrendered by 4.30pm.

The capture of such a prize at minimal cost sparked national rejoicing in Germany. The attackers appeared to have a clear route into Verdun and the commander of the French Central Army Group, de Langle de Cary, had already advocated withdrawal to the heights to the east and south-east. However, the combative de Castelnau, at French General Headquarters, opposed this policy. Having ensured that Pétain's Second Army would be brought out of reserve to hold the left bank of the Meuse, he travelled to Verdun on 25 February and scotched all thoughts of retirement. He also called for Pétain's area of responsibility to embrace the right bank of the

A German MG08 machine-gun crew in action. (IWM Q87923)

Meuse, which was to be defended at all costs. To some extent these measures were playing into Falkenhayn's hands, yet, as de Castelnau knew, French doctrine and national sentiment made it inconceivable to abandon Verdun.

Like Plumer at Ypres in 1915, the pragmatic Pétain's preference would probably have been controlled withdrawal. However, as an unambitious officer who shunned intrigue and ostentation, Pétain was ideally suited to the role in which he was now cast. Again like Plumer, he understood modern firepower and was trusted by his troops. His very presence at Verdun lifted morale and he inspired renewed confidence in the Verdun forts as the backbone of a 'Line of Resistance'. French artillery was concentrated to give the Germans a taste of attrition. Above all, Pétain grasped the importance of logistics. As rail links to Verdun were cut by German long-range artillery, he took pains to ensure that supplies were maintained along the single viable route south – a road which became known as the *Voie Sacrée* (Sacred Way). By June vehicles were moving up and down this lifeline at the rate of one every 14 seconds.

Spring and summer fighting at Verdun

The German advance was, in truth, already losing impetus before Pétain's measures began to take effect. Falkenhayn had made few reserves available and Fifth Army now rued its earlier caution in deferring the main infantry attack until the second day. As fire increased from French artillery on the left bank of the Meuse – particularly from guns near the Bois Bourrus ridge and a hill known as *Le Mort Homme* (The Dead Man) – the Germans also regretted confining their first attack to the right bank. Persuaded by the Crown Prince and Knobelsdorf that this flanking fire must be suppressed, Falkenhayn provided more troops so that the offensive could be extended to the left bank. A major attack, centred on *Le Mort Homme*, would be made on 6 March, followed quickly by a renewed push on the right bank towards Fort Vaux. The Crown Prince, for one, wanted the battle to be terminated once German casualties exceeded French losses.

The sombre pattern of the Verdun fighting for months to come was firmly established in March. All German attempts to seize *Le Mort Homme* failed, and each assault invariably prompted a French counter-attack. Artillery fire from both sides was unrelenting. By the end of March German casualties totalled 81,607, only 7,000 fewer than the French.

To improve the morale and freshness of French units, Pétain introduced the 'Noria' system, rotating them more frequently in and out of the line, whereas the Germans kept formations at the front for longer periods. The BEF's relief of the French Tenth Army at Arras further ameliorated French manpower difficulties.

The Germans too adjusted their command structure at Verdun, giving General von Gallwitz responsibility for the left bank and entrusting the right bank to General von Mudra, but April passed with *Le Mort Homme* and the neighbouring height, *Côte 304*, still beyond their clutches.

Wavering between ruthlessness and self-doubt, Falkenhayn started to ponder the possible need to 'seek a decision elsewhere', and the Crown Prince harboured even greater reservations about prolonging the battle. Knobelsdorf, however, had no such misgivings, and exploited his unique position to gain Falkenhayn's backing for further attacks. He also succeeded in getting the pessimistic Mudra replaced with the aggressive Lochow. After a heavier bombardment than that of 21 February the Germans took *Côte 304* early in May and had seized the whole of *Le Mort Homme* by the end of the month, albeit at frightful cost.

Pétain's achievements in slowing the Germans were hardly extolled by Joffre, who wished him to adopt a more offensive stance and was worried that the 'Noria' system was soaking up reserves required for the Somme. Joffre's solution was to elevate Pétain to the command of the Central Army Group and appoint Robert Nivelle as Pétain's successor at Second Army. Nivelle, a fervent disciple of the Foch–Grandmaison philosophy, took direct control of the battle on 1 May. Another officer who now strode to centre stage was Charles Mangin, a divisional commander nicknamed 'The Butcher' or 'Eater of Men' because of his belief in attacking regardless of losses. Rejecting Pétain's wise advice to wait until he had enough men to strike on a broader front, Mangin – with the approval of Joffre and Nivelle – hurled his 5th Division into a murderous yet vain attempt to recapture Fort Douaumont on 22–23 May.

The battle now created its own momentum, resembling an all-consuming monster impossible to control. Attack-minded commanders on both sides ensured that there would be no pause in the slaughter. Disappointed at the negligible progress on the right bank, Knobelsdorf won Falkenhayn's endorsement for a new five-division assault in this sector. The attack, codenamed *May Cup*, commenced on 1 June with the objectives of capturing Fort Vaux, Fort Souville and the strongpoint called the *Ouvrage de Thiaumont* – seen as the final obstacle shielding Verdun.

At Fort Vaux the garrison fought valiantly, disputing every yard of the dark underground passages against grenade, gas and flamethrower attacks before extreme thirst forced them to capitulate on 7 June. The next day the Germans took hold of the *Ouvrage de Thiaumont*, only to lose it again almost immediately. In a miniature version of the whole battle, this feature would change hands 14 times between then and 24 October. Pétain's 'Line of Resistance' was cracking, and he was becoming ever more irritated by British inaction on the Somme. Joffre's marshalling of reserves for the Somme offensive, combined with Nivelle's profligacy with troops in incessant counter-attacks at Verdun, undermined the benefits of the 'Noria' system. By 12 June the Second Army had just one fresh brigade in reserve.

The Germans, however, were hamstrung by their own manpower problems at the critical moment, since Brusilov's offensive against the Austrians on 4 June had forced Falkenhayn to release three divisions from the west for the Eastern Front. Undeterred, Knobelsdorf brushed aside the Crown Prince's objections to further assaults and assembled sufficient troops, including the splendid Alpine Corps, to attack Fort Souville, less than 3 miles from Verdun.

By mid-1916 the German Army, like its opponents, was exploring the potential of the 'creeping barrage', which helped infantry advance towards objectives behind a moving curtain of fire. At the same time the Germans were placing greater emphasis on infiltration tactics, whereby specialist assault teams and storm troops were trained to bypass strongpoints and drive deep into enemy positions before striking them from the rear and flanks. When Fort Souville was attacked on 23 June the Germans used 'Green Cross' shells filled with deadly phosgene gas – principally to silence the French gunners – and took Fleury. This success roused Nivelle to issue an Order of

Kaiser Wilhelm II (centre) with Ludendorff (right) and Hindenburg (left). (IWM Q23746)

the Day which ended with the immortal phrase: *Ils ne passeront pas!* (They shall not pass!). The Germans were indeed halted and contributed to their own failure by attacking on a narrow frontage with inadequate reserves.

While the original aim of the Verdun offensive had long since been obscured, the cost in blood had been too high for either side to risk national dishonour by becoming the first to terminate the battle. The intransigent Knobelsdorf ordered one more assault on Fort Souville on 11 July and some 30 soldiers reached its glacis, within sight of Verdun, before they were pushed back, captured or killed.

This was the nearest the Germans came to Verdun. The opening of the Somme offensive on 1 July changed the whole strategic picture and Falkenhayn directed the Fifth Army to 'adopt a defensive attitude'. The Crown Prince's wishes were finally granted on 23 August, when the Kaiser sanctioned Knobelsdorf's transfer to the Eastern Front. Romania's entry into the war on the Allied side four days later precipitated the downfall of Falkenhayn, who had insisted this would not occur. He was succeeded as Chief of the General Staff by Field Marshal von Hindenburg, who brought with him his own Chief of Staff – Ludendorff, the hero of Liège – whose impact on the Western Front would be immense.

The French counterstroke

Ludendorff, who had helped mastermind most of the German victories in the east, knew how important he was to Hindenburg and demanded the title 'First Quartermaster General' rather than 'Second Chief of the General Staff'. He was also given joint responsibility for all decisions, and from then on Hindenburg's leadership became largely symbolic. Ludendorff assumed almost dictatorial powers, wielding enormous influence over German political affairs, the economy and foreign policy as well as on military operations.

After visiting the Western Front in early September Hindenburg and Ludendorff made crucial changes in German tactics and strategy. On 2 September a strict defensive posture at Verdun was decreed. Falkenhayn's rigid linear defence tactics – holding ground at all costs and, when lost, recapturing it by instant counter-attack – was superseded by a flexible zonal defence system, as recommended by the First Army's Chief of Staff, Colonel von Lossberg. This included a thinly held outpost zone in front of the main battle or defence zone and strong counter-attack formations kept close at hand but beyond enemy artillery range. Hindenburg and Ludendorff also ordered the construction of new defensive positions behind the existing lines. These rear positions, embodying the latest principles of elastic defence, were built in great depth but reduced the overall length of front, enabling the Germans to achieve economies in manpower.

To the German soldiers facing the inevitable French counterstroke at Verdun, these changes were of little immediate assistance. With Pétain ensuring that there would be sufficient artillery and infantry to attack on a broad front, the French blow was planned by Nivelle but would be delivered by Mangin, now commanding the French forces on the right bank. More than 650 artillery pieces were assembled, including two 40cm railway guns for use against Fort Douaumont. As one of its leading champions, Nivelle relied heavily upon the creeping barrage, although this time the artillery supporting the infantry concentrated more on suppressing German troops than on destroying particular targets and field fortifications. These tactics would prove highly effective when the initial counterstroke was made on 24 October: the *Ouvrage de Thiaumont* and Fleury were rapidly retaken that day, as was Fort Douaumont, which fell to Moroccan troops. Fort Vaux was recaptured on 2 November, much of the ground lost between February and July was regained, and on 15 December another attack carried the French lines 2 miles beyond Douaumont. The Germans, however, clung on to *Le Mort Homme.*

This last convulsion brought the agony of Verdun to an end. French casualties tallied 377,000 against 357,000 German. Nobody had secured any discernible advantage from the slaughter. Falkenhayn's irresolution and failure to reconcile the means to the end had caused his original strategy to backfire; in the process he drained the lifeblood from the German Army as well as from the French. Indeed, neither side would completely recover from the battle before the Armistice.

Preparing for the Somme

By June 1916 the BEF comprised well over a million men. Its 48 divisions were organised into five armies and included formations from Australia, Canada, India, New Zealand, Newfoundland and South Africa. This expansion was the product of colossal feats of improvisation in Britain and its Dominions since August 1914. The decline of voluntary recruiting had forced Britain to introduce conscription for single men in January 1916 and married men in May that year. However, compulsory service had not yet made an impact on the BEF, which, alone among the major armies in mid-1916, was still composed of volunteers. Many of these were in Territorial units or in the divisions of the 'New Armies' recruited in response to Kitchener's appeals. The BEF's highly localised character was typified by its 'Pals' battalions, raised by civilian committees and made up of workmates, friends or men with a common social or geographical background. As the Territorials too were recruited from comparatively narrow geographical areas, in 1916 the BEF embraced many units which had close links with particular communities.

A captured German gun is shown here as a war prize for some British troops, who are all smiles as a result. (Corbis)

Of the 247 infantry battalions that would be in the front line or immediate reserve on the Somme on 1 July, 141 were New Army formations. Though full of confident and enthusiastic volunteers, relatively few of these units had participated in a major battle. However, the New Zealand Division and the four Australian divisions that reached France by June did contain a fair nucleus of men who had seen action at Gallipoli.

The choice of the Somme region in Picardy for the Franco-British offensive in 1916 was largely determined by the fact that it marked the junction of the French and British forces. Its drawbacks were that no great strategic objectives, such as rail centres, lay close behind the German front and also that, because the sector had long been quiet, the Germans had constructed formidable defences in the Somme chalk, including dug-outs up to 40ft below ground. Between February and June the demands of Verdun had reduced the French contribution to the Somme assault to only 11 divisions. For the first time in the war the British would therefore play the leading role in an Allied offensive on the Western Front.

Haig's intention was that, on the first day, Rawlinson's Fourth Army – created on 1 March – should take the German front defences from Serre

Opposite:
The British Fourth Army's zone of operations, Somme offensive, 1 July 1916.

to Montauban, then the German second position from Pozières to the Ancre and the slopes in front of Miraumont. The 46th and 56th Divisions, on the northern flank, would attempt to pinch out the German salient at Gommecourt in a diversionary operation. To their right, the 31st, 4th and 29th Divisions (VIII Corps) would attack between Serre and Beaumont Hamel. On the other side of the Ancre, the 36th (Ulster) and 32nd Divisions (X Corps) were to assault the daunting Thiepval defences, including the Schwaben and Leipzig Redoubts. The 8th and 34th Divisions (III Corps) would attack Ovillers and La Boisselle, astride the Albert–Bapaume road; XV Corps, with the 21st, 17th and 7th Divisions, was to secure Fricourt and Mametz; and on Rawlinson's right, next to the French, the 18th and 30th Divisions (XIII Corps) would capture Montauban. North and south of the River Somme itself, General Fayolle's French Sixth Army would assist the British advance by attacking towards the German second position opposite Péronne, between Maurepas and Flaucourt. Should the initial assault gain its objectives, Haig aimed to burst through the German second position on the higher ground between Pozières and Ginchy and, in due course, capture the enemy third position in the Le Sars–Flers sector, thus threatening Bapaume. This might, in turn, clear the way for Hubert Gough's Reserve Army, formed on 23 May, to swing northwards, in the direction of Arras.

British planning for the Somme was muddled by fundamental differences between the operational ideas of Haig and Rawlinson. As at Loos, Haig hoped for a breakthrough; Rawlinson favoured 'bite and hold' tactics, whereby the advancing troops would consolidate gains and shatter German counter-attacks as the artillery was brought forward for the next bound. Rawlinson's object was 'to kill as many Germans as possible with the least loss to ourselves'. As Haig's subordinate, he strove to follow his chief's general directive but because Haig entrusted the detailed planning to Rawlinson – and since their differences in operational approach were neither adequately discussed nor settled – the final scheme for the assault was riddled with contradictions, faulty assumptions and misunderstandings. Rawlinson's tactical guidance to his own subordinates was equally open to different interpretations. His lingering reservations about the ability of New Army divisions to execute complicated manoeuvres were reflected in the *Fourth Army Tactical Notes*, issued in May 1916. Rawlinson observed that his relatively inexperienced citizen-soldiers had 'become accustomed to deliberate action based on precise and detailed orders' and recommended that the assaulting troops 'must push forward at a steady pace in successive lines', though he also stressed 'celerity of movement' and, later in the *Notes*, suggested that small columns making use of natural cover, 'are preferable during the preliminary stages of the advance'. He did not, however,

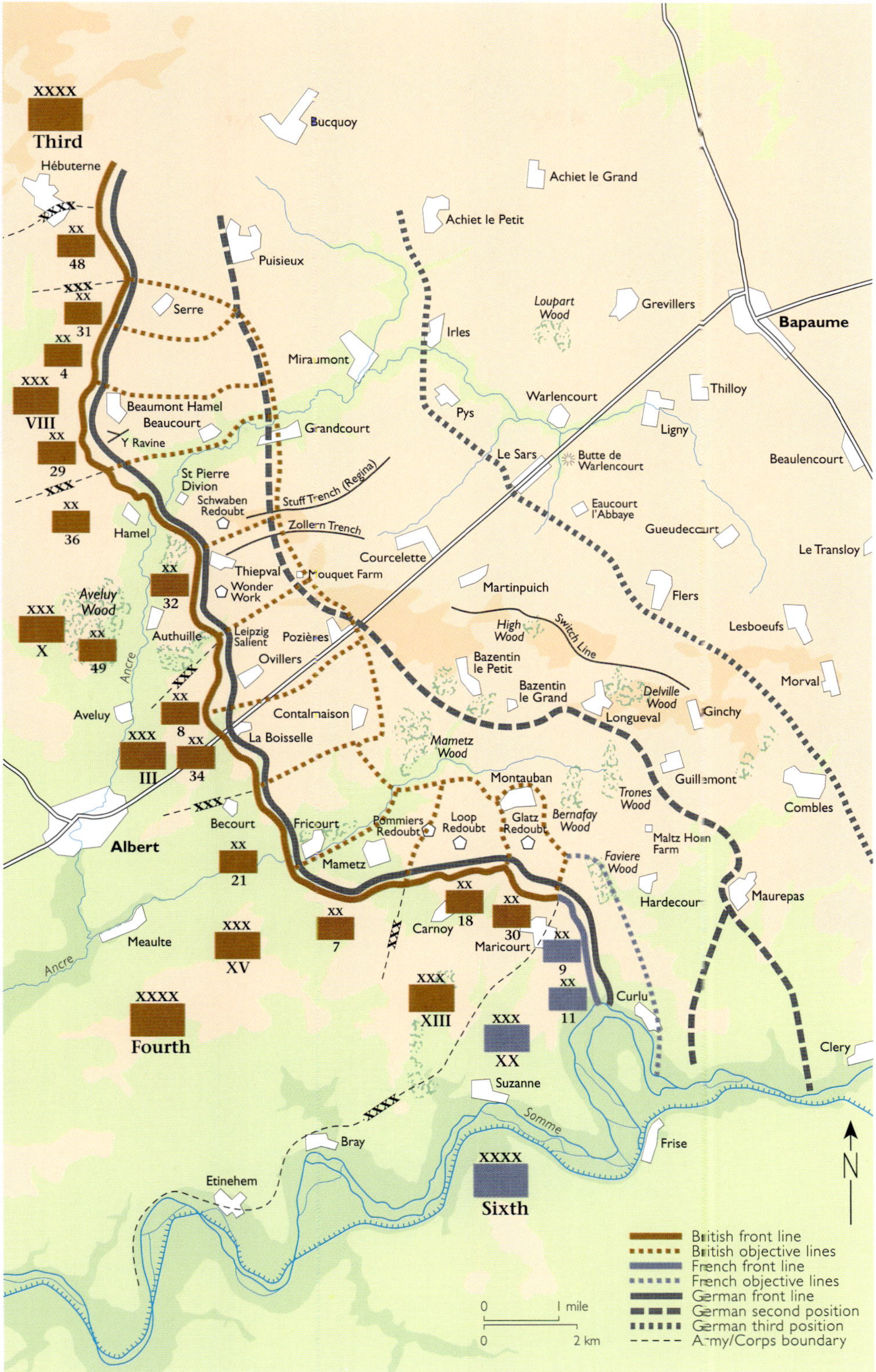
Third
Fourth
Sixth
Hébuterne
Bucquoy
Achiet le Grand
Achiet le Petit
Puisieux
Serre
Loupart Wood
Grevillers
Bapaume
Irles
Miraumont
Thilloy
Warlencourt
Pys
Ligny
Beaumont Hamel
Beaucourt
Grandcourt
Y Ravine
Le Sars
Butte de Warlencourt
Beaulencourt
St Pierre Divion
Stuff Trench (Regina)
Schwaben Redoubt
Eaucourt l'Abbaye
Gueudecourt
Hamel
Zollern Trench
Courcelette
Le Transloy
Thiepval
Mouquet Farm
Wonder Work
Martinpuich
Aveluy Wood
Flers
Switch Line
High Wood
Lesboeufs
Authuille
Leipzig Salient
Pozières
Ovillers
Bazentin le Petit
Morval
Bazentin le Grand
Delville Wood
Longueval
Ginchy
Aveluy
Contalmaison
La Boisselle
Mametz Wood
Montauban
Guillemont
Trones Wood
Combles
Becourt
Fricourt
Pommiers Redoubt
Loop Redoubt
Glatz Redoubt
Bernafay Wood
Maltz Horn Farm
Albert
Mametz
Faviere Wood
Hardecourt
Maurepas
Carnoy
Maricourt
Meaulte
Ancre
Curlu
Clery
Suzanne
Somme
Frise
Bray
Etinehem
XXXX
XX 48
XXX
XX 31
XX 4
XXX VIII
XX 29
XXX
XX 36
XX 32
XXX X
XX 49
XXX
XX 8
XXX III
XX 34
XXX
XX 21
XXX XV
XX 7
XX 18
XX 30
XX 9
XX 11
XXX XIII
XXX XX
XXXX
N
0 1 mile
0 2 km
British front line
British objective lines
French front line
French objective lines
German front line
German second position
German third position
Army/Corps boundary

dictate the pace at which troops crossed No Man's Land; nor did he insist on particular formations. The ambiguity of his instructions gave corps, divisional and brigade commanders scope to determine their own assault pace and formations with the unfortunate result that, in some sectors, over-rigid artillery timetables and infantry tactics were adopted.

This need not have mattered too much had the artillery been able to negate the distinct tactical advantages the Germans enjoyed on the Somme. Unhappily for the Fourth Army, the apparently irresistible week-long preliminary bombardment by 1,537 guns was inadequate to the task. It was widely anticipated that the artillery would destroy the German defences to such an extent that the initial assault would be a 'walk-over' and the pace of the advance therefore immaterial. In reality the number of heavy guns (467) proved too few, they relied too heavily on shrapnel rather than high explosive shells to smash trenches and cut wire, many of the rounds fired were 'duds' and the guns were spread too thinly along the front to produce the desired effect.

The bloody first day

At 7.30am on 1 July 1916 the British barrage lifted from the enemy front trenches. Along a 14-mile stretch, Rawlinson's infantry moved forward – many in long lines. In most places on that hot morning the attackers lost the 'race to the parapet', failing to get through the enemy's wire and into the front trenches before the Germans came up from their deep dug-outs

The assault of the 103rd (Tyneside Irish) Brigade on La Boisselle, 1 July 1916. (IWM Q52)

to man their machine guns. This time Rawlinson had misjudged the difficulties in seizing the German front line in a set-piece assault. Thanks to their dug-outs and the British artillery's inability to destroy the wire, many Germans survived the bombardment to mow down the attackers in rows as the latter tried to cross No Man's Land at a steady pace. To add to the Fourth Army's problems, British counter-battery work was largely ineffective and hitherto unlocated German guns now opened fire, increasing the scale of slaughter.

The explosion of huge mines under the German trenches at La Boisselle, in the British 34th Division's area, and at Hawthorn Redoubt, on the front of VIII Corps, did not materially assist the attack. In fact, the ill-conceived decision by VIII Corps to lift its barrage when the Hawthorn Redoubt mine was detonated at 7.20am merely gave the defenders an additional ten minutes to line their parapets and contribute to the British disaster between Serre and Beaumont Hamel. Elsewhere along the British front, over-optimistic and rigid fire plans – with the artillery lifting from one objective to another in accordance with an inflexible timetable – not only carried the barrage too far ahead of the infantry but also meant that it was well-nigh impossible to bring it back.

Even on that bloody morning the story was not one of unrelieved misery. On the southern flank of Fourth Army, where the attackers were much helped by the presence of French heavy guns on their right, the 30th and 18th Divisions, using more imaginative tactics, captured all their objectives in the Carnoy–Montauban sector. Next to them, the 7th Division took Mametz. The percipient Major-General Ivor Maxse, commanding the 18th (Eastern) Division, moved his assaulting infantry into No Man's Land before zero hour, giving them a head start in the 'race to the parapet'. He also employed an early form of creeping barrage, as did the 7th Division at Mametz. These limited British successes on 1 July were overshadowed by the progress of Fayolle's French Sixth Army on the right. As well as possessing a preponderance of heavy guns, the French demonstrated that they were digesting the lessons of Verdun, sending their infantry forward in small groups rather than long lines and making better use of available cover.

At other isolated spots on the British front there were tantalising early gains. The battalions of the 36th (Ulster) Division, some of which were also deployed in No Man's Land before the assault, attacked the fearsome defences at Thiepval and, displaying splendid zest and courage, took the Schwaben Redoubt. The comparative lack of movement by neighbouring divisions, however, compelled the Ulstermen to pull back by nightfall. In the north, at Gommecourt, Territorial troops of the 56th (London) Division also captured their objectives but they too were forced to withdraw when the 46th Division was repulsed.

For a shallow penetration – just a mile – on a length of front less than 4 miles wide the BEF lost 19,240 officers and men killed and 35,493 wounded. The frightful total of 57,470 casualties made 1 July 1916 the bloodiest day ever in British military history. The 34th Division alone – containing four Tyneside Scottish and four Tyneside Irish battalions – incurred 6,380 casualties, and 32 battalions suffered losses of more than 500, or over half their battle strength.

The death or maiming of such a large number of Britain's citizen-soldiers in a single day had a massive effect on the national psyche. Moreover, after the first day of the Somme offensive, the dilution of the highly localised BEF of mid-1916 was inevitable. Partly to lessen the concentrated and dramatic impact of battle losses on particular communities, it became deliberate policy – under a reorganised reserve and drafting system from the summer of 1916 onwards – to draw casualty replacements from a common pool rather than from their parent regiments. In any case, within a few months, conscripts were entering the ranks of the BEF.

Summer on the Somme

For the BEF, 1 July 1916 was undeniably the low point of the entire war. There were many more mistakes, costly setbacks and crises to come, but from that day Haig's forces on the Western Front showed clear signs of a genuine 'learning curve': the subsequent improvements in organisation, command, equipment, tactics and techniques would place the BEF at the cutting edge of the Allied armies in 1918. In the high summer of 1916, however, operations on the Somme seemed to offer the front-line troops nothing but unending sacrifice. With the slogging match at Verdun already in its fifth month, there could be no question of halting the Somme offensive after only one day. During July Haig began to drop thoughts of a swift breakthrough and to view the Somme fighting more in terms of a 'wearing-out' battle, laying the foundations for a new decisive attack, possibly in mid-September. On the other side, Falkenhayn decreed on 2 July that not one foot of ground should be surrendered, an order which helped initiate the incessant round of British attacks and German counter-attacks that characterised the Somme in 1916.

As July wore on, Gough's Reserve Army took over the northern half of the British zone on the Somme, its junction with Fourth Army running just to the south, or right, of the Albert–Bapaume road. Haig rejected Joffre's pleas for him to renew the assault in the tricky central sector of his front from Thiepval to Pozières and decided instead to try to exploit the early gains on his right, near Montauban. Accordingly, between 2 and 13 July Rawlinson's Fourth Army tried to take Contalmaison, Mametz Wood and

British gunners fire an 18-pounder in the summer heat, near Montauban, 30 July 1916. (Mary Evans Picture Library)

Trones Wood to secure the flanks of a forthcoming attack on the German second main position. Overcoming the reservations of Haig and the French, Rawlinson and the New Army units gave a glimpse of their true capabilities when, on 14 July – after a challenging night assembly in No Man's Land – a 6,000-yard section of the German second position between Bazentin le Petit and Longueval was seized in a few hours. This brilliant feat, which owed much to a more intense artillery bombardment than that before 1 July, had a disappointing sequel. At Delville Wood, near Longueval, the South African Brigade of the 9th (Scottish) Division lost over 2,300 of its 3,153 officers and men in a bitter struggle that lasted from 14 to 21 July. The wood was not completely in British hands until 27 August, while neighbouring High Wood, seemingly empty of German troops on the morning of 14 July, finally fell to Rawlinson two months later, on 15 September.

The Reserve Army, meanwhile, strove to capture the village of Pozières, which, from its dominating position on the Albert–Bapaume road, provided an alternative line of approach into the rear of the Thiepval defences.

The Australian divisions of I Anzac Corps underlined their excellent fighting reputation by capturing both the village and the fortified ruins of the windmill on the crest of the ridge beyond by 5 August, but subsequent efforts to move north-west from a constricted salient in the direction of Mouquet Farm and Thiepval were subjected to concentrated German artillery fire. Having suffered some 23,000 casualties in five weeks, the Australians were unsurprisingly critical of Gough's penchant for narrow-front attacks, while a calamitous subsidiary operation at Fromelles on 19–20 July – in which the 5th Australian Division was involved – further diminished Australian confidence in the British high command. To the south, Rawlinson did his best to assist the French Sixth Army as it crept towards Péronne, but the Fourth Army was unable to capture Guillemont and Ginchy until 3 and 9 September respectively, and Rawlinson was left in no doubt about Haig's dissatisfaction with repeated attacks by inadequate forces on narrow frontages.

Command errors, mounting losses and relentless demands on front-line troops were also to be found on the German side of the wire. Falkenhayn's order that from 11 July a strict defensive posture should be maintained at Verdun was a sure indication that British operations on the Somme were having some effect. His insistence on a tactical system of unyielding linear defence and immediate counter-attack – a policy backed by General Fritz von Below of the German Second Army – only added to the strain felt by German divisions. Given less time for rest, reorganisation and training between actions, the strength and quality of German formations began a slow but inexorable decline. The morale of German reinforcements arriving on the Somme correspondingly slumped in the face of the growing Allied superiority in matériel.

Enter the tank

The weeks between mid-July and mid-September brought a change in tactical conditions on the Somme, from siege-type operations to semi-open warfare, in which the Germans often occupied irregular lines of loosely connected shell-holes rather than continuous trenches. After Hindenburg and Ludendorff had replaced Falkenhayn in late August, there was a further shift towards elastic defence in depth, with the German forward positions even more thinly manned.

The British were now using the creeping barrage with greater frequency but it was also becoming imperative for the British and Dominion infantry to vary their tactics, placing less emphasis upon linear 'waves' and more upon the employment of small groups of men who could work their way forward with their own close-support weapons – much in the manner of the assault detachments and storm troops favoured increasingly by the Germans.

British infantry platoons and companies needed additional integrated firepower to make them more self-reliant and able to infiltrate between strongpoints instead of invariably carrying out frontal assaults. British gunners likewise continued to place too much faith in prolonged heavy bombardments and centrally controlled fire programmes which were, in fact, inappropriate in attacks on dispersed or thinly held enemy positions. These developments, and the nature of Haig's 'wearing-out' battle, were not instantly understood by all British divisional commanders and staffs as they strained to prepare more 'line-straightening' actions designed to secure improved jumping-off positions for the next big set-piece assault on a major German defensive system.

Haig faced growing criticism from politicians at home who felt that the limited progress made to date did not justify the dreadful casualties being suffered. The pressure on him to achieve more substantial results from his projected offensive in mid-September was therefore all the greater. Ready to believe the advice of his Chief of Intelligence, Brigadier-General Charteris, that the Germans were approaching exhaustion, Haig was optimistic that a breakthrough might now be forthcoming, especially as his planned large-scale set-piece attack on the German third main position would be bolstered by a new weapon, the tank. This had been conceived by Lieutenant-Colonel Ernest Swinton in 1914 as an armoured, tracked vehicle capable of crossing trenches and barbed wire and of destroying enemy machine guns. Swinton had warned against employing tanks in 'driblets' but Haig was keen to use them to deal with separate strongpoints and fortified villages that might otherwise hold up the advancing infantry. He and Rawlinson consequently deployed them along the battle line rather than sending them in to action in one concentrated body.

A British Mark I tank crosses a trench during the fighting for Thipeval, late September 1916. (Mary Evans Picture Library)

Haig hoped and anticipated that the breakthrough would be affected by fresh infantry divisions and by the artillery, the density of guns being double that of those used for the attack on 1 July though less than half the number used for 14 July. As the commander of Fourth Army, which had the principal role, Rawlinson had proposed attacking in stages on three successive nights. He was overruled by Haig, who wanted a bolder attack with no pauses, and after Fourth Army's failures in August Rawlinson was in a weak position to argue his case.

The attack, which began on 15 September, was designed to capture the German third system at Flers, followed by Morval, Lesboeufs and Gueudecourt. The Canadian Corps, part of the Reserve Army to Rawlinson's left, was ordered to seize Courcelette. Forty-nine tanks were assigned to support the infantry on the morning of the attack but only 36 arrived at their starting points. Assisted by a creeping barrage, they caused some alarm and losses among the German defenders, and in the British 41st Division's sector four tanks reached Flers. One of these advanced up the main street of the village while the others engaged machine-gun nests and strongpoints on the western and eastern outskirts. Horne's XV Corps took Flers and the Canadian Corps captured Courcelette, while Martinpuich and High Wood were also secured. Overall, however, on 15 September the gains were restricted to some 2,500 yards on a front of less than 3 miles. Lesboeufs and Morval held out for a further ten days and Combles and Gueudecourt did not fall until 26 September. Yet again the British offensive became bogged down and the oft-promised breakthrough appeared as far away as ever.

The reckoning

Haig has frequently been censured by historians and military commentators for using tanks prematurely at Flers–Courcelette on 15 September and for deploying them in 'penny packets' rather than in mass formation. Both charges are unfair. Had its debut been postponed, there was no guarantee that this untried weapon would then have proved more successful. The Mark I tanks of 1916 were slow and unreliable and it might have been an even more serious blunder to commit them on a large scale before their merits and shortcomings had been fully exposed under battle conditions. It is also often forgotten that Britain was fighting as part of a coalition: that same day Allied offensives were proceeding in Transylvania and on the Italian front as well as in the French zone of operations on the Somme to the south of the BEF. Haig might therefore be forgiven for reasoning that, should all go well, a second opportunity to employ tanks might not actually arise. Contrary to popular belief, he was certainly no reactionary so far as weapons technology was concerned. His enthusiasm for new ideas, and his

Opposite:
The battle of the Somme, July–November 1916.

Serre
Irles
Bapaume
Beaumont Hamel
Miraumont
Pys
Thilloy
Beaucourt
Grandcourt
Beaulencourt
Le Sars
Butte de Warlencourt
Eaucourt l'Abbaye
Gueudecourt
Courcelette
Le Transloy
Rocquigny
Thiepval
Mouquet Farm
Martinpuich
Flers
Ancre
High Wood
Lesboeufs
Pozières
Ovillers
Bazentin le Petit
Delville Wood
Longueval
Morval
Sailly
Saillisel
Contalmaison
Mametz Wood
Leuze Wood
La Boisselle
Ginchy
Guillemont
Frégicourt
Albert
Trones Wood
Combles
St Pierre Vaast Wood
Montauban
Rancourt
Fricourt
Mametz
Carnoy
Hardecourt
Le Forest
Bouchavesnes
Maurepas
Maricourt
Tortille
Curlu
Haut Allaines
Hem
Suzanne
Ommiécourt
Mont St Quentin
Feuillères
Frise
Bray
Péronne
Somme
Canal
Binches
Herbecourt
La Maisonette
Dompierre
Barleux
Fay
Belloy en Santerre
Foucaucourt
Brie
Villers Carbonnel
Horgny
Berny en Santerre
Soyécourt
Deniecourt
Fresnes
Vermandovillers
Ablaincourt
Marcheleport
Somme Canal
N
Lihons
Chaulnes
0 2 miles
0 2 km
Ground gained by British, 1 July–25 November 1916
Ground gained by French, 1 July–25 November 1916

personal intervention at critical moments, encouraged the development and successful tactical application of Lewis guns, Mills bombs, trench mortars, gas and aircraft as well as that of tanks.

Criticism of Haig for prolonging the British offensive on the Somme after mid-September is perhaps more justified. His persistence seems to have been motivated by the firm belief that the German Army would indeed eventually collapse provided that the BEF and its allies did not relax their constant pressure.

In the last week of September – while the Fourth Army was attacking towards Morval, Lesboeufs, Gueudecourt and Combles – Gough's Reserve Army undertook its biggest operation so far, assaulting the German positions from Courcelette to the Schwaben Redoubt. Mouquet Farm was captured by the British 11th Division on the opening day of Gough's attack, 26 September. The thorough battle training and briefing given by Ivor Maxse to his 18th Division paid off, as it cleared Thiepval village early on 27 September. However, it took until 13 October before the 39th Division was able to eject the last stubborn defenders from the Schwaben Redoubt.

On the right flank of the Reserve Army the Canadian Corps became embroiled in a furious fight for Regina Trench which dragged on until 10 November. On the Fourth Army's front, as rain turned the battlefield into a muddy swamp, Rawlinson's divisions inched painfully towards Le Transloy and secured Le Sars on 7 October.

The last phase of the Somme offensive was carried out by Gough's Fifth Army – as the Reserve Army was renamed – between 13 and 24 November. In spite of several postponements and appalling conditions, the operation was allowed to go ahead in the hope that a late success would create a favourable impression at the inter-Allied conference at Chantilly, which Haig was to attend on 15–16 November. It was hoped also that the attack would have benefits for the Russian and Romanian fronts by dissuading the Germans from switching reserves from France.

The Fifth Army's assault on 13 November was delivered astride the River Ancre, north of Thiepval, and was intended to reduce or eliminate the German-held salient between Serre and the Albert–Bapaume road. Employing a creeping barrage, and an overhead heavy machine-gun barrage by Vickers guns, the 51st (Highland) Division captured Beaumont Hamel, and the 63rd (Royal Naval) Division seized Beaucourt. However, Serre – which had been an objective on 1 July – was still occupied by the Germans when Haig brought the offensive to an end. The BEF remained some 3 miles from Bapaume; all its exertions and sacrifices during the previous 4½ months had resulted in territorial gains measuring about 20 miles wide and 6 miles deep.

The British and Dominion forces on the Somme suffered a terrifying total of 419,654 casualties. The French, though still short of Péronne, had gained over twice as much ground as the BEF for 204,253 losses – about half the cost. Estimates of German casualties vary hugely – between 237,000 and 680,000. However, statistics alone do not tell the whole story. There was increasing evidence of more progressive tactical thinking in the BEF, with outstanding division and brigade commanders like Maxse of the 18th Division and Solly-Flood of the 35th Brigade urging the adoption of flexible assault formations, meticulous battle training and greater use of Lewis guns and rifle grenades to boost the infantry's own firepower in the attack. The appointment – with Haig's active support – of a civilian expert, Sir Eric Geddes, as Director-General of Transportation at GHQ in September set in train a reorganisation of the BEF's logistics that would eventually pay rich dividends.

The German Army knew that it had been hurt by the improving BEF. On 21 September a Hindenburg memorandum stated that the Somme front was all-important and would have first claim on available divisions. Ludendorff himself admitted that the army 'had been fought to a standstill and was utterly worn out' and Crown Prince Rupprecht – who faced the BEF for most of the war – observed that what remained of the 'old first-class, peace-trained German infantry had been expended on the battlefield'.

PORTRAIT OF A SOLDIER: PRIVATE ARCHIE SURFLEET

Although, in the minds of the British public, the story of the first day of the Somme offensive has become particularly associated with the ordeal and sacrifice of the locally raised 'Pals' battalions, not all men in those units on 1 July 1916 were original 1914 recruits. Private Arthur 'Archie' Surfleet, for example, was at Serre that day with the 13th Battalion, East Yorkshire Regiment – one of four battalions raised by the city of Hull – but he had not enlisted until January 1916 and had only joined 'B' Company of his unit at the front on 8 June. From the start, however, he kept a diary, adding details in the 1920s and 1960s to form a lively and lucid account of a young soldier's service.

Archie Surfleet was born at Gainsborough, Lincolnshire, on 23 December 1896 and moved to Hull with his family in 1901. Educated at Hull Grammar School, he worked as a junior reporter for the *Hull Daily Mail* for about a year before joining a firm of manufacturing chemists, Lofthouse and Saltmer, where his father was a laboratory manager. He enlisted in the army shortly after his 19th birthday. Archie himself confessed to being 'a very ordinary

Private Archie Surfleet. (IWM)

soldier, alternately cheerful and frightened some of the time … and very frightened indeed for much of it', though he also noted how quickly he and his comrades adjusted to their new life. 'After a period of blissful ignorance', he recalled, 'many of us who saw the front line frequently often acquired a sort of fatalistic outlook, but, by some gift of Providence, we nearly always seemed to remember the happier times and forget much of the horror.'

Archie rapidly became familiar with many of the routine hardships of an infantryman's existence. He described the ubiquitous body lice as one of the most unpleasant things he had to endure – 'as soon as you warmed up they did so too, biting and irritating so that only utter exhaustion could induce sleep'. Rats were also a common nuisance, although 'strangely enough, we got partially used to them'. Some of the more primitive latrines, Surfleet remarked, 'made you feel you had plumbed the depths of indelicacy … But we even got used to that!' Food was adequate, if never over-plentiful – 'we often popped the rice pud … unsweetened anyway … into the bully-stew to give it a bit of "body"'. If one was lucky enough to obtain a quarter of a loaf, 'you felt well-fed and happy', he remembered. The constant demands for working or carrying parties always provoked widespread 'grousing' among the infantry. Even before the Somme offensive, such tasks caused Surfleet to comment that 'we all are as fed [up] as hell with this lot … The jobs we get are simply heart-breakingly … almost inhumanly impossible but they have to be done, somehow, and I marvel, daily, that we stick it.'

Entering the battle-zone for a tour of front-line duty was always a sobering moment. Approaching the Serre sector for the first time, on 11 June 1916, Surfleet noted that 'a kind of torpor peculiar to that shell-infested area came over us'. His introduction to German shelling was 'a terrible experience … The feeling was so utterly indescribable that I cannot hope to portray it; God alone knows how awfully afraid I was.' Archie estimated that 'not one in a thousand goes "up there" without some qualm or other, though most of the lads seem to be able to disguise their feelings pretty well'. There was one man, however, who suffered from shell-shock at Serre in June and succumbed again in the Laventie sector later in July. He was taken out of the line, Archie recorded, 'a really pitiable sight and most unnerving'.

Once out of the line, morale was swiftly restored. In the autumn of 1916 Archie wrote that the boys 'seem very cheerful just now; a few days of peace and sunshine makes all the difference'. The opportunity to spend some francs from their pay on egg and chips or wine and beer in local *estaminets* helped men briefly forget the terrors of the trenches. Hitherto a strict teetotaller, Surfleet warily sampled his first-ever beer on 6 July: 'I must say I did not find it unpleasant and, so far, I have not felt any of the "after-effects" usually attributed to this stuff!' He did not condemn those who over-indulged in order to blot out the realities of the war. 'There is no wonder those who have a tendency towards drink try to drown their sorrows whenever they get a chance', he commented on 21 July.

Normal grousing aside, Surfleet was clearly a dutiful soldier who respected most of his officers. Theirs was 'a thankless job', he stated in the summer of 1916, later adding, 'I wouldn't be an infantry officer for a mint of money'. He observed with approval how his officers were 'jolly decent' in carrying the rifles of exhausted men during a march in July. He was even impressed by his corps commander, Hunter-Weston, who, in Surfleet's view, 'looked such a real soldier', but he was roused to anger by the sight of a gunner, lashed to a wheel, undergoing Field Punishment No 1. To Surfleet, this seemed 'anti-British' and he wrote that 'feelings amongst our boys' were 'very near to mutiny at such inhuman punishment'.

Archie was fortunate that on 1 July the 31st Division's catastrophic assault on Serre was called off before the Hull battalions, in support, were committed to the attack. In August he was made a linesman with the signallers attached to Battalion Headquarters. Repairing damaged telephone cables under fire was a dangerous job though 'better than the rifleman's life' in Archie's opinion. When his division returned to the Somme for another attack on Serre on 13 November, he was again lucky, being among the troops left in the rear to form the nucleus of a reconstituted battalion in the event of heavy losses. He was, however, required to act as a stretcher-bearer – a harrowing job, but one allowing him to 'look the rest of the lads in the face and claim to be one of them'. Sometimes Archie understandably felt despondent, writing in September, 'our only hope is a good, serious wound to put us out of this lot', yet when in December sickness gave him the opportunity to go to hospital, he declined, not wishing to be parted from his mates. 'This may be hell', he declared, 'but I'd sooner be here, with my pals, than landed with strangers in another, maybe worse, hell'. Such comradeship was perhaps the biggest single factor in enabling soldiers to bear the horrors of the Western Front.

Surfleet continued to serve as a private until March 1918, when he went home to train for a flying commission in the Royal Flying Corps – soon to become the Royal Air Force. After the war he returned to his previous employers, Lofthouse and Saltmer, and was joint managing director of the firm before retiring in 1962. He died, aged 74, in April 1971, just after depositing a copy of his diary in the Imperial War Museum.

THE WORLD AROUND WAR: THE HOME FRONTS 1914–1916

The effects of the struggle on the Western Front were felt far beyond the battlefields and had a huge impact on domestic life. Each of the belligerents faced its own special problems. For Britain – dependent upon imports – German submarine operations represented a growing menace; Germany was increasingly affected by the Allied naval blockade; and France had to cope with the early loss of the iron and coal of its German-held northern regions. Certain problems were common to all. Each had to make mammoth efforts to mobilise both human and industrial resources and take unprecedented steps to control raw materials, food production and distribution, prices and wages, the press and transport. In many respects, the manner in which each country responded to these challenges reflected its different political, social and economic conditions.

France

French industry, still over-reliant on small workshops, lagged behind that of Britain and Germany (her steel production in 1914 being less than one-third of German output) but as a predominantly agricultural nation it was largely self-sufficient in food. The declaration of a state of siege in August 1914 allowed the French Government to assume almost unlimited powers, subjecting the press, for example, to military censorship. Such measures were vital if René Viviani's administration was to succeed in balancing France's military and industrial priorities.

Conscription in France meant that hardly a single household was left untouched from the outset. By mid-1915 the level of French sacrifice remained much greater than that of Britain, some 5,440,000 having been called up. With most rural villages denuded of young men, French women were soon bearing a bigger share of agricultural work than ever before, yet many were attracted by the higher wages on offer in the burgeoning munitions factories. Besides those replacing men in public service and commercial jobs, around 75,000 women were working in French munitions plants by October 1915, gaining a previously unknown degree of personal and financial independence.

Swelling criticism of the conduct of the war saw Viviani's government replaced in October 1915 by a broad-based coalition under the Socialist Aristide Briand. In 1916, the year of Verdun, the conflict bit really hard and deep in France, increasing the incipient war-weariness of the civilian population. Lack of price controls meant food costs had soared, and higher wages and the booming profits of war contractors had generated a 40 per cent rise in the cost of living, but despite the destruction of sugar beet factories in northern France, no critical food shortages had so far been suffered. Now, however, difficulties began to surface. To reduce the costs of importing wheat, a coarser 'national bread' was introduced in May 1916; the wheat, rye and potato harvests that year were well below normal; and, in November, a number of restrictions – including meatless days – were agreed in principle, though not all immediately implemented.

Germany

As in France, political parties in Germany concluded a *Burgfrieden* (truce), on 4 August 1914, presenting an image of solid national unity. Germany's autocratic régime could make more rapid decisions than the slower-moving democratic institutions of the Allies and so could marshal the civilian population more rigorously at an early stage than either Britain and France could. More advanced and progressive industrially – particularly in the chemical, electrical, steel and munitions fields – Germany swiftly consolidated these advantages by forming, under the able young businessman Dr Walther Rathenau, a Raw Materials Section of the War Ministry. Through a series of War Raw Materials Corporations, supplies were strictly controlled in different sectors to overcome shortages and, for a time, offset the effects of the Allied blockade.

Germany's quicker transition into top gear was also characterised by its more adroit mobilisation of women. Dr Gertrude Baumer, a leading campaigner for women's rights, was instantly recruited to organise German female labour for war work. Even so, although Germany possessed larger human resources than France, manpower problems were becoming so serious by the end of 1916, after Verdun and the Somme, that more stringent measures were required to augment the labour force. The new high command team – Hindenburg and Ludendorff – reversed earlier policies in an attempt to secure extraordinary increases in production. Under the so-called Hindenburg Programme, they first created a Supreme War Office for control of the economy and then, on 5 December, pushed through an Auxiliary Service Law providing for the compulsory employment of all German males between 17 and 60 not already in the forces.

It was in food supplies that Germany was most vulnerable. The blockade ensured that this problem would worsen steadily the longer the war continued. Whereas France by mid-1916 had only had to tighten its belt, Germany was approaching a desperate state of shortage. Bread rationing had been introduced as early as January 1915, and potato and meat supplies were also firmly regulated so that, for a while, rising prices rather than scarcities constituted the main worry. In June 1915 the Imperial Grain Office was created to oversee the purchase and distribution of grain; this was the precursor of similar bodies for other food commodities, culminating in a

War Food Office in May 1916. By then meat, potatoes, milk, sugar and butter were all rationed, but partly because of falling imports through neutral countries and also through poor harvests, these measures did not ease the situation. Many elements of diet and even articles of clothing were supplemented or replaced by *Ersatz*, or substitute, items. A sharp drop in the potato yield, for instance, compelled the German people to switch increasingly to turnips, which became a staple food in the 'turnip winter' of 1916–1917.

Britain

For the British – beset before the war by industrial unrest, the militant campaign for women's suffrage and the threat of civil strife over Irish Home Rule – the outbreak of the European conflict also brought a temporary suspension of political discord, although the attempts of Herbert Asquith's Liberal government to carry on along 'business as usual' lines soon foundered. Once the decision to create a mass army had been taken, increased State control of industry and manpower was sure to follow. Paradoxically, an otherwise instinctively anti-interventionist government quickly armed itself with considerable powers with the passage, on 8 August 1914, of the Defence of the Realm Act – DORA. As the war went on, DORA encroached into almost every aspect of daily life and led to the abrogation of personal liberties on a scale inconceivable before August 1914.

The principal need was for more efficient mobilisation and direction of military and industrial manpower. Unrestricted recruiting in the early months and the absence of a rational overall plan meant that problems were tackled in an ad hoc fashion until May 1915, when Britain faced

One of many patriotic postcards published in Britain during the voluntary recruitment period, 1914–1915. (Courtesy of Peter Simkins)

simultaneous crises in enlistment and munitions production. The formation of a coalition Cabinet and the creation of a Ministry of Munitions late that month, however, heralded the end of the government's haphazard approach to these issues, although it was not until 1916 that a more streamlined War Cabinet was created.

Between August 1914 and December 1915 a total of 2,466,719 men enlisted in the arm, but by the spring of 1915 it was already evident that voluntary recruiting would not suffice to maintain Britain's expanding New Armies in the field in a long war. From a peak of 462,901, in September 1914, enlistments had declined to 119,087 in April 1915. As calls for conscription intensified, the government began a more systematic analysis of its resources by passing the National Registration Act in July 1915, empowering the Local Government Board to compile a register of all persons between 15 and 65. When taken in August, the National Register revealed that over 5,000,000 men of military age – including 2,179,231 single men – were *not* in the forces. In the autumn a last effort to uphold the voluntary principle was undertaken through a scheme prepared by Lord Derby, then Director-General of Recruiting. All males between 18 and 45 were asked to enlist at once or attest their willingness to serve when summoned. By the close of the Derby Scheme, on 30 November, nearly half the eligible single men on the National Register had still not attested, making conscription inevitable in 1916. It was, however, applied with a velvet glove. From 1 March 1916 to 31 March 1917 only 371,000 men were compulsorily enlisted; 779,936 were granted exemption.

The Munitions of War Act of July 1915 enabled the government to adopt any measures deemed necessary to expand production and helped pave the way for Britain to become a nation in arms. Many inefficient and wasteful methods were cast aside and, with trade unions generally ready, for the time being, to forego some accepted practices and privileges, the number of strikes and disputes decreased. Here again women would play a key part in the process of industrial mobilisation, performing scores of tasks hitherto the province of men. Until mid-1915 much of this effort was channelled into charity and welfare work. In July 1914 around 212,000 women were employed in the various metal and engineering industries that would become most closely linked with war production; a year later this figure had risen only to 256,000. With the coming of Lloyd George's Ministry of Munitions, the figure climbed steeply to 520,000 by July 1916.

The fall in unemployment and higher wages which accompanied government contracts were, as elsewhere, counter-balanced by higher prices – averaging 75 per cent in essential commodities by November 1916. Britain had not yet suffered real shortages, though during 1916 the activities of German submarines caused mounting anxiety in a nation that imported most of its food supplies from overseas. In November 1916 shrinking wheat stocks led to the appearance of 'war bread' and in December the potential seriousness of the situation was signalled with the establishment of a Ministry of Food and the appointment of a Food Controller.

The realities of war had been directly felt by British citizens long before then. Raids on London by German airships had begun at the end of May 1915 and continued through that year and 1916, causing an increase in civilian casualties as well as alarm and disruption. The bombardment of Hartlepool, Scarborough and Whitby by German warships on 16 December 1914 resulted in over 700 casualties, including women and children. A serious *internal* threat also arose on Easter Monday (24 April) in 1916, when Irish nationalists seized the General Post Office in Dublin and proclaimed an Irish Republic. The Easter Rising was suppressed within five days but 64 of the insurgents, around 130 members of the Crown forces and well over 200 civilians were killed. The Rising was, in fact, initially unpopular in Ireland, but the execution in May of 14 of its leaders aroused widespread and lasting public sympathy where little previously existed.

PORTRAIT OF A CIVILIAN: WINNIFRED ADAIR ROBERTS

For many British middle-class women the war presented unexpected outlets for energies and talents that had hitherto remained wholly or partly concealed beneath a veneer of social convention. One such woman was Winnifred Adair Roberts, the seventh of nine children of Frederick Adair Roberts, an Irish-born manufacturing chemist, and his wife Janie. Winnifred, known to her family and friends as Winks, was born on 28 November 1885 in Stamford Hill, London, and in 1900 moved with her parents to Oak Hill Lodge in Hampstead. Educated initially by a governess and later at various establishments, including a Quaker school at Darlington, in the north of England, she did not pursue a career because delicate health had obliged her to become the 'daughter at home'. A Christian and a spiritualist, she taught at a local Sunday School, though her more independent qualities were revealed by her work for the Women's Social and Political Union. (Her commitment to the cause of women's suffrage was demonstrated by her smuggling of food to the WSPU's leader, Mrs Pankhurst, when the latter was in hiding from the police.)

On holiday in Switzerland at the outbreak of war, Winnifred showed something of her organisational skills by arranging sumptuous provisions for the long train journey across France. Once home, she soon joined the Women's Volunteer Reserve, founded by another eminent suffragette,

Evelina Haverfield. The Women's Volunteer Reserve adopted khaki uniforms and military ranks and Winnifred was appointed Captain in command of 'A' Company of the London Battalion.

Besides undertaking canteen duties, hospital work and fund-raising activities, the Company drilled regularly at a skating rink and in the examination hall of the School of Mines in South Kensington, even receiving instruction in rifle-shooting. By August there were 98 members but the average attendance had dropped from 61 to 31 since June. There was some unrest in the Company in June 1915, following work at the Bethnal Green Military Hospital, and Winnifred – who saw the organisation's continuing emphasis on route marches as pointless and came into conflict with her senior officer – resigned on 19 October 1915. However, a stream of sympathetic letters quickly underlined the affection and respect in which she was personally held. A week later, 37 former members of 'A' Company met at Winnifred's home and formed a new corps under her command. Within another few days Captain Roberts' Company was attached to the Women's Legion, launched by the Marchioness of Londonderry in July 1915. Convinced that the Women's Volunteer Reserve was drawn from too narrow a class, Lady Londonderry created the Women's Legion to 'provide a capable and efficient body of women whose services can be offered to the State as may be required to take the place of men needed in the firing line or in other capacities'.

Over the next 16 months Winnifred and her colleagues performed a wide range of valuable tasks. These included: eight-hour shifts day or night in canteens and YMCA huts at Euston and King's Cross stations, Woolwich Arsenal, Tottenham Court Road, Holborn and a munitions plant at Erith; bandage-making for the Red Cross; knitting woollen garments and socks; hospital work; and producing sandbags. At Christmas in 1915 Winnifred, with six helpers, catered for some 4,000 soldiers at the canteen in Horseferry Road over a ten-day period, during which the women took just two hours off each night and slept on a table in the basement. Perhaps their biggest achievement, however, was to raise over £445 for a YMCA hut – the 'Captain Roberts Company Hut' – erected near Etaples in France towards the end of 1916. To collect the necessary funds, Winnifred organised jumble sales, bazaars, whist drives, dances, snow-sweeping, carol singing, a garden party and a concert featuring the popular young composer Ivor Novello. Some evenings the women played a barrel-organ, complete with a monkey, in the London streets.

Since many in the group also held other jobs, the strain of such activities eventually began to affect their health. This prompted Winnifred to disband the company in February 1917. She declined to join the new Women's Army Auxiliary Corps (WAAC), which was to be run from the War Office, not only because of her health but also because she felt she was 'already nine-tenths pacifist' and was reluctant to belong to an organisation 'where I am only a "Yes-man". I must be conscience-free and other people's standards are not always my own.' All the same, she later recalled that she had been personally consulted about the uniform, drill and discipline of the Women's Army Auxiliary Corps, that seven of the women she had trained subsequently instructed WAAC recruits and that it was *her* 'girls' who got the responsible positions when the first WAACs went to France. She had good reason to be proud, for in two years Winnifred had made her own distinct contribution to the national war effort.

Despite her fragile health, Winnifred lived to a ripe old age. Developing her interest in spiritualism and the Church, she performed more welfare work in the Second World War, particularly on behalf of the tube shelterers in London during the Blitz. She died in June 1981, aged 95.

HOW THE PERIOD ENDED: NO END IN SIGHT

As the conflict entered its third year, the almost universal enthusiasm of 1914 had given way to a deepening sense of war-weariness and muted resignation in the belligerent countries. No one could now foresee an early end to this dour, merciless struggle. There was also a growing gulf between front-line troops and civilians. Fighting soldiers had undergone experiences that could never be fully understood by those at home. Men snatching a few precious days of leave felt like strangers in their own land and were often dismayed and disturbed by the discrepancies between their own miserly pay

A British working party, wearing trench waders and waterproof capes, near the Ancre, November 1916. (IWM)

and the high wages of war workers; by the soaring profits of war contractors; by the over-optimistic and inaccurate reports in jingoistic newspapers; and by the increasing independence and changed attitudes of wives who were suddenly more prosperous from their employment in munitions factories. For many soldiers, who were becoming closer to their comrades than their families, the trenches were the real world.

Anti-war sentiment in Britain, France and Germany was nowhere strong enough to shake each nation's overall resolve to continue the struggle until outright victory, or at least a favourable peace, had been achieved. Too much blood had been shed for either the Allies or the Central Powers to accept anything less. Tentative peace feelers from both sides in late 1916 came to nothing. Members of the ruling military, conservative and industrial élite in Germany were reluctant to relinquish their annexationist war aims – which included buffer regions to the east and west, and a dependent Belgium – yet were equally unwilling to declare them in precise terms. This presented the Allies, whose governments were also disinclined to be the first to define their intentions, with the excuse to dismiss German peace suggestions as insubstantial and insincere.

In fact, changes of political and military leadership in Britain, France and Germany in the second half of 1916 only intensified each country's pursuit of decisive victory. On 7 December Asquith was succeeded as British Prime Minister by David Lloyd George, who was determined to streamline the machinery of government and prosecute the war with greater vigour. While acknowledging the paramount need for Germany to be defeated, Lloyd George was anxious to discover a strategic alternative to the costly attrition of the Western Front and explore the possibilities offered by other theatres of operations. This policy would bring him into increasing conflict with Haig and Robertson, who wanted to concentrate resources in France.

On 12 December, the dynamic Nivelle replaced the discredited Joffre as French Commander-in-Chief. In Germany, Hindenburg and Ludendorff, who already wielded immense power and influence, similarly stood for total commitment to eventual victory. Indeed, the views of Hindenburg and Ludendorff were much less susceptible to objective military considerations than those of Falkenhayn had been. The latter had paid *some* heed to the limitations of Germany's human and economic resources. In contrast, as the American historian Gerald Feldman has remarked, the new German high command attempted to implement 'an ill-conceived total mobilisation for the attainment of irrational goals'. In so doing they 'undermined the strength of the army, promoted economic instability, created administrative chaos, and set loose an orgy of interest politics'. With such men at the helm, compromise in 1917 was, at best, unlikely.

Chapter 2

THE WESTERN FRONT 1917–1918

Previous page: Men of the Lancashire Fusiliers carry duckboards over the morass of the battlefield near Pilckem, 10 October 1917. (IWM Q6049)

BACKGROUND TO WAR: STRATEGIC CHOICES FOR 1917

On 15 and 16 October 1916, as the Somme offensive neared its end, Allied military and political leaders met at Chantilly and in Paris to discuss plans for 1917. It was confirmed at these conferences that the Western Front would again be the main theatre of Allied operations in the coming year. Joffre, still the French Commander-in-Chief, had already agreed with Haig, his British counterpart, that the next Franco-British offensive would take the form of a simultaneous assault on a broad frontage, with the French attacking between the Oise and the Somme while the BEF struck in the sector between Bapaume and Vimy Ridge. Subsidiary attacks would be made on the Aisne and in Upper Alsace. It was also decided, somewhat optimistically, that, should conditions permit, the joint offensive would be launched on or around 1 February. Backed by the War Committee at home, Haig subsequently persuaded Joffre to incorporate his long-desired Flanders offensive in the overall Allied plans for 1917. This latter operation would commence after the other attacks, probably in the summer, and would involve an advance from the Ypres Salient to clear the whole Belgian coast and capture the German-held ports at Ostend and Zeebrugge.

These plans did not long survive changes of political and military leadership in Britain and France. On 7 December 1916, David Lloyd George, the British Secretary of State for War, succeeded the discredited Asquith as Prime Minster, quickly establishing a more streamlined War Cabinet to ensure a more vigorous prosecution of Britain's war effort. Appalled by the huge casualties on the Somme and anxious to explore strategic options beyond the Western Front, Lloyd George was critical of Haig and of the Chief of the Imperial General Staff, Sir William Robertson, but, because his own political power base remained insecure, he stopped short of actually removing them. Nevertheless, events on the *other* side of the Channel presented him with an early chance to erode their individual and combined authority.

Joffre, the hero of the Marne, had come under increasing censure in the French Chamber of Deputies for Allied losses and setbacks in 1916 – especially those at Verdun. To deflect criticism away from his government, the French Prime Minister, Aristide Briand, induced Joffre to retire, sugaring the bitter pill by creating him a Marshal. On 12 December Joffre was replaced as Commander-in-Chief by General Robert Nivelle, the architect of the later successes at Verdun. An articulate and immensely self-confident gunner with an English mother, Nivelle was convinced that his recent artillery tactics, if applied on a much bigger scale, would at last bring the Allies genuine victory on the Western Front. He believed that a massive saturation bombardment, followed by a creeping barrage of great depth and by furious infantry attacks, would suffice to pierce the enemy's front defences and help his troops to reach the German gun line in a single bound. A decisive 'rupture' or breakthrough would then surely follow within two days.

General Robert Nivelle, the French Commander-in-Chief from December 1916 to May 1917. (Ann Ronan Picture library)

In Nivelle's proposed alterations to the Allied plan, it was envisaged that British and French forces would carry out preliminary attacks between Arras and the Oise to pin down German reserves. The principal blow would now be delivered by the French on the Aisne, where a 'mass of manoeuvre' comprising some 27 divisions would be kept in readiness to exploit the expected rupture of the German front. Haig, who was himself promoted to Field-Marshal on 27 December 1916, at first found Nivelle 'straightforward and soldierly' and, though he had some reservations, initially supported the new scheme in general terms. The BEF had been assigned only a subsidiary role in the modified offensive, yet, to release French formations for Nivelle's 'mass of manoeuvre', was being asked to take over an additional 20 miles of front, as far south as the Amiens–Roye area. Haig, however, was primarily concerned with his cherished Flanders plan and was prepared to co-operate in Nivelle's grand scheme as long as the projected operations in Belgium were not compromised.

Eager to seek any plausible alternative to more long months of attrition, the Allied political leaders were all too willing to be swayed by Nivelle's seductive proposals. For instance, Lloyd George – while willing to shift the emphasis of British strategy and reinforce peripheral war zones – nevertheless accepted that the German Army must be defeated on the Western Front and was therefore content to approve Nivelle's ideas. If the new French plan was successful, Lloyd George could bask in reflected glory but, if it failed, his own case for an alternative strategic approach would be greatly enhanced. Certainly Lloyd George soon glimpsed an opportunity to turn Nivelle's increasing irritation with Haig to his own account and thereby weaken the influence of his generals. When a conference was convened at Calais on 26–27 February, ostensibly to discuss the need to improve the overburdened railway communications behind the British zone of operations, it rapidly became evident that Lloyd George had conspired with the French – behind the backs of Robertson and Haig – in an attempt to make the British Commander-in-Chief permanently subordinate to Nivelle. This would deprive Haig of a role in the preparation of Allied plans and leave him with nothing much more than responsibility for the BEF's discipline and personnel. An outraged Robertson threatened to resign and Lloyd George, faced with further pressure from King George V and the War Cabinet, chose to avoid a full-blown political crisis by watering down the Calais proposals. The BEF would keep its distinct identity and Haig would be subordinate to the French Commander-in-Chief only for the duration of the coming offensive. The incident, however, did little to encourage closer co-operation between the British and French armies or boost the prospects of a unified Allied command. It also deepened the underlying antipathy between Lloyd George and his senior commanders on the Western Front.

Germany similarly witnessed growing disagreements among its military and political leaders in the opening weeks of 1917. Theobald von Bethmann-Hollweg, the German Chancellor, favoured a negotiated peace settlement, while Hindenburg, the Chief of the General Staff, and Ludendorff – his 'First Quartermaster-General' and *de facto* controller of Germany's war effort – were still totally committed to outright victory. At the insistence of the high command, the so-called 'Hindenburg Programme', designed to increase munitions production, and an Auxiliary Service Law, to mobilise the nation's human resources more systematically, had both been adopted in the last quarter of 1916. Germany was unwilling to abandon its main war aims which, at this point, included holding on to Liège and the maintenance of military, economic and political influence over Belgium – its reluctance to compromise having contributed to the failure of the recent peace feelers put out by both sides.

As in Britain and France, public opinion in Germany in early 1917 would have undoubtedly viewed anything less than a clear-cut victory as a betrayal of all who had shed their blood in the national cause. Germany's immediate future, however, looked far from bright. The Allied blockade was already causing disturbing shortages and hardship on the home front and Ludendorff recognised that Allied superiority in matériel and manpower made it unlikely that Germany could win a decisive success on land in 1917. In his mind, the surest path to victory would be to hasten Britain's collapse by ordering a resumption of unrestricted submarine warfare against Allied and neutral shipping. Such a policy carried obvious risks. The United States, angered by previous U-boat campaigns in 1915 and 1916, might this time throw in its lot with the Allies and enter the war against the Central Powers. Ludendorff, however, judged that the U-boats would achieve the necessary result before America could fully deploy its considerable military and industrial potential against Germany.

In the end Ludendorff's arguments held sway. It was decreed by the Kaiser that unrestricted submarine operations should begin on 1 February. Germany, meanwhile, would remain on the defensive on the Western Front for the foreseeable future. As Ludendorff's star approached its zenith, Bethmann-Hollweg's influence waned and he resigned, some six months later, on 13 July.

At the time of the conference at Chantilly in mid-November 1916, the Allies outnumbered the Germans in infantry divisions on the Western Front, with 169 divisions against 129. Of the Allied divisions, 107 were French, 56 were British and six were Belgian. Despite having suffered terrible losses on the Somme, the BEF continued to expand in the following months. Although the 60th Division was then preparing to move to Salonika, six more British Territorial divisions were to cross to France by the end of February 1917 while a fifth Australian division reached the Western Front in late November 1916, bringing the number of Dominion divisions in the BEF to ten – five from Australia, four from Canada and one from New Zealand. The overall strength of the BEF rose from just over 1,500,000 in November 1916 to a peak of 2,044,627 on 1 August 1917.

Crucially, the BEF also received increasing numbers of heavy guns and howitzers. In July 1916 it had possessed 761 such weapons. By November that year this total had risen to 1,157 and it was estimated that the latter figure would more than double by April 1917. The supply of heavy artillery ammunition similarly grew from 706,222 rounds in the second quarter of 1916 to over 5,000,000 in the corresponding period of 1917. Stocks of field gun ammunition rose almost to the same extent, 50 Mark II tanks were to supplement the 70 older Mark I tanks in January 1917 and the improved Mark IV model would be delivered later in the year.

During the winter of 1916–1917 the BEF made strenuous efforts to disseminate the lessons it had learned on the Somme and to make appropriate improvements in its fighting methods, particularly in its artillery and small-unit infantry tactics. These months were notable for the publication of two important manuals. December 1916 saw the issue of *Instructions for the Training of Divisions for Offensive Action,* which helped to lay the foundations of the co-ordinated all-arms tactics that would prove so effective in the final months of the war. This was followed, in February 1917, by the no less influential *Instructions for the Training of Platoons for Offensive Action,* which heralded a major change in the emphasis of infantry tactics from the company to the smaller sub-unit of the platoon. In 1915–1916 the company, composed principally of riflemen, constituted the basic tactical unit, with the specialists – such as machine-gunners, snipers and bombers (grenade-throwers) – forming *separate* sections. In 1917 the platoon

David Lloyd George, British Prime Minister from December 1916 until 1922. (IWM Q41927)

(of which there were four in each company) was itself organised into four specialist fighting sections. One contained the riflemen, including a sniper and a scout; another contained the bombers; a third was built around rifle grenades – 'the infantry's howitzer'; and the fourth was a Lewis light machine-gun section. In other words, the infantry company now comprised four flexible platoon *teams*, each capable of waging its own battle in miniature, using a variety of modern weapons. It would be some time before the full impact of these changes was felt, but there would be clear, if not yet universal, signs of improvement in the BEF's infantry tactics in 1917.

The French Army would be able to deploy 110 divisions on the Western Front by 1 April 1917 but this slight increase was more apparent than real, for there was no rise in the number of infantry battalions available. Nevertheless, the French artillery arm was still growing, with 4,970 heavy guns and howitzers expected to be available by the spring – an increase of nearly 700 pieces over the November 1916 total. In addition, the production of tanks was now in hand and the St Chamond and Schneider models would play a part in the Allied spring offensive of 1917. The French had likewise profited from the tactical lessons of 1916 but both the fighting capacity and morale of the French Army were unquestionably more brittle after the ordeal of Verdun.

The first elements of two Portuguese divisions began to arrive in France early in January 1917 and were subsequently attached to the BEF. The six large Belgian divisions were not all they seemed. Not only had Belgium deliberately adopted a defensive strategy since the end of 1914 but also, until the autumn of 1918, the standards of training and equipment and the strength of its reserves would simply not allow its forces to do more than hold quiet sectors.

The condition of the German Army at the end of 1916 was causing its commanders and senior staff officers great anxiety. For example, the German divisions which were involved in the December operations at Verdun only had a combat strength of between 3,000 and 6,000 rifles and were forced to deploy some two-thirds of their troops in the front line. About 60 per cent of the German divisions on the Western Front in 1916 had also been through the mincing-machine of the Somme, a battlefield which one staff officer described as 'the muddy grave of the German Field Army'. It did not help matters that much of the pain the Germans had suffered on the Somme had been inflicted by the relatively inexperienced citizen-soldiers and staffs of the expanding BEF. Kuhl, the distinguished Chief of Staff to Crown Prince Rupprecht of Bavaria's Army Group, warned on 17 January 1917 that 'we can no longer reckon on the old troops; there is no doubt that in the past summer and autumn our troops have been fearfully harried and wasted'. Rest and training, he advised, must come 'first and foremost' in 1917. Although the Germans decided to create more than a dozen new divisions, this could only be done by reducing existing establishments or drawing upon reserves. The increase therefore represented an organisational or administrative adjustment rather than a real reinforcement.

When 1917 began most of the German divisions in France and Belgium formed part of two Army Groups. The Army Group commanded by Crown Prince Wilhelm, the Kaiser's son and heir to the Imperial throne, held the line from the Swiss frontier to a point north of Reims and included the Third and Fifth Armies as well as the three smaller Army Detachments A, B and C. The 170-mile stretch from north of Reims to the River Lys was the responsibility of Crown Prince Rupprecht of Bavaria's Army Group, which comprised the First, Sixth and Seventh Armies. The sector from the Lys to the coast came under an independent Fourth Army, commanded by Duke Albrecht of Württemberg. In March 1917 changes were made in these arrangements. The Fourth Army, now commanded by General Sixt von Arnim, was incorporated into Crown Prince Rupprecht's Army Group; the three Army Detachments on the German left were linked together to form a third Army Group under Duke Albrecht; and the Seventh Army was transferred from Crown Prince Rupprecht's Army Group to that of Crown Prince Wilhelm so that all the formations likely to be facing the expected French offensive in the spring would be under one command.

THE FIGHTING: WAR ON THE WESTERN FRONT 1917–1918

Alberich: The Germans withdraw

Germany's decision to remain on the defensive in the west was made easier by the strides made in the construction of the fresh positions which were being established 25 miles to the rear of the existing front and which incorporated all the basic principles of the new doctrine of flexible defence in depth. The key stretch, built since September 1916, extended from Neuville Vitasse, near

Arras, through St Quentin and Laffaux to Cerny, east of Soissons. The system – named the *Siegfried Stellung* by the Germans but called the Hindenburg Line by the British – was essentially a series of defensive zones rather than a single line. Any force approaching it would first face an outpost zone, around 600 yards deep, which contained concrete dug-outs sheltering small detachments of storm troops. The latter were deployed to mount instant counter-attacks and check the momentum of an Allied advance. Behind the outpost zone was a main 'battle zone' which ran back some 2,500 yards and included the first and second trench lines as well as many concrete machine-gun posts with interlocking fields of fire. Counter-attack divisions were placed immediately to the rear of the battle zone. Subsequently two more zones were added, giving the system a depth of up to 8,000 yards. The trench lines were protected by thick belts of barbed wire, laid out in a zig-zag pattern nearest the front trench so that machine-guns could cover the angles of exit. The Germans also built the *Wotan Stellung*, a northern branch of the Hindenburg Line, between Drocourt and Quéant, near Arras.

From a military standpoint, withdrawal to the Hindenburg Line made sense for the Germans but even Ludendorff wavered, fearing that retirement might adversely affect the morale of German soldiers and civilians. The move was forced upon him by Crown Prince Rupprecht of Bavaria, the Army Group commander in whose sector the Hindenburg Line was largely located. Already under renewed pressure from the British Fifth Army on the Ancre, Rupprecht and his outstanding Chief-of-Staff, Kuhl, informed Ludendorff that the present positions were poor and that the troops were in no state to endure a repeat of the 1916 Somme battle. The order for the retirement was accordingly issued on 4 February 1917.

German barbed wire defences on the Hindenburg Line. (IWM CO3392)

A railway station and sidings are blown up by the retreating Germans, 1 April 1917. (IWM Q57515)

The scheme for the rearward movement was code-named *Alberich*, after the malicious dwarf of the *Niebelung* Saga. This was appropriate since the withdrawal was accompanied by a 'scorched earth' policy. Rupprecht was appalled by the scale and methods of the proposed destruction and was only narrowly dissuaded from resigning when it was observed that this might appear to signal a rift between Bavaria and the rest of Germany. Despite his objections, the *Alberich* programme began on 9 February. Throughout the area being abandoned, the Germans felled trees, blew up railways and roads, polluted wells, razed towns and villages to the ground and planted countless mines and booby-traps. While children, mothers and the elderly were left behind with minimal rations, over 125,000 able-bodied French civilians were transported to work elsewhere in the German-occupied zone.

The main phase of the retirement commenced on 16 March and was largely completed within four days. The evacuation of the Noyon salient, and the withdrawal from the smaller salient near Bapaume, shortened the German front by 25 miles, freed 14 divisions and seriously disrupted

Allied plans for the spring. It was not easy for the Allies to advance rapidly across a devastated region after the most severe winter of the war but it can equally be argued that the pursuit of the Germans was too cautious. The preparations for the French Northern Army Group's subsidiary part in the spring offensive were, in fact, well in hand and, on 4 March, General Franchet d'Esperey, its commander, had sought permission to attack vigorously as soon as possible in order to catch the Germans at a critical moment. Nivelle, however, would not countenance major revisions to his own operational plan and refused to sanction anything other than a limited assault to capture the German front position. Thus he missed his only real opportunity to upset the German withdrawal.

Curtain-raiser at Arras

Since Nivelle refused to modify his strategy, the BEF's contribution to the spring offensive – an attack on a 14-mile front at Arras – was still primarily intended to lure German reserves away from the main French effort on the Aisne. The British Third Army, commanded by General Sir Edmund Allenby, would strike east of Arras, attempting to penetrate the Hindenburg Line on its right and the older German defence lines opposite its centre and left. Allenby's units would then try to take the Hindenburg position from the rear and flank as well as moving on Cambrai. Vimy Ridge, to Allenby's north, would be assaulted by the Canadian Corps, part of General Sir Henry Horne's First Army. More than 2,800 guns and 48 tanks would support the initial operations.

The German withdrawal had most severely dislocated the British plan on Allenby's southern flank, in the sector of General Sir Hubert Gough's Fifth Army. One of Gough's original objectives, the Bapaume salient, had vanished and the Fifth Army experienced considerable problems in hauling its artillery across the devastated zone. Consequently, the only assistance Gough could offer Allenby was to attack the Hindenburg Line on a relatively narrow front at Bullecourt, close to its junction with the Drocourt–Quéant Line (*Wotan Stellung*). The major assault by the First and Third Armies was scheduled for 8 April while the more limited attack by the Fifth Army would be delivered a day or so later.

The French Northern Army Group's projected attack between the Somme and the Oise was similarly neutralised by the German retirement and was scaled down to a minor operation at St Quentin. This meant that, on a 60-mile length of front between Bullecourt and the Aisne, the Germans faced negligible pressure. The operations at Vimy and Arras therefore assumed even greater significance as a means of pinning down German reserve formations.

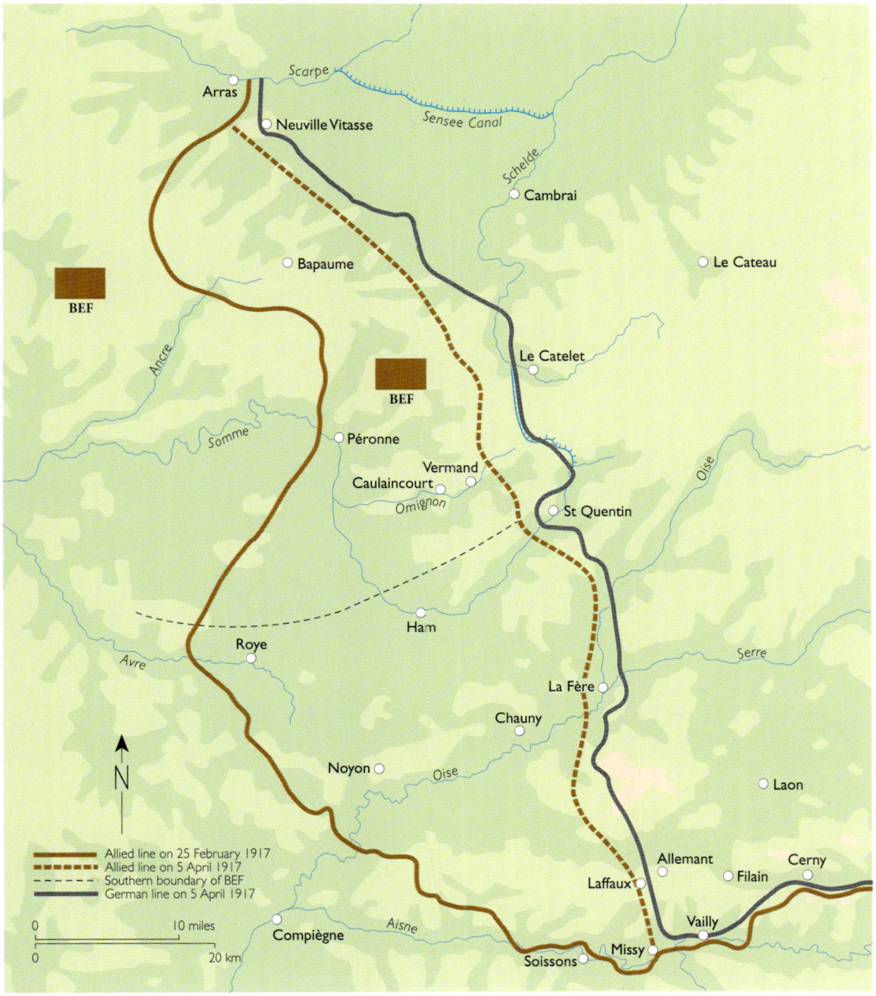

The German withdrawal, February–April 1917.

The opening stages of the battle of Arras would reveal the extent to which the BEF had acted upon the painful tactical lessons of the Somme offensive of 1916. Major-General Holland, Allenby's artillery commander, advocated a preliminary bombardment lasting only 48 hours but Haig and his own artillery adviser, Major-General Birch, opted instead for a four-day bombardment, wishing to ensure that the defenders were subjected to the maximum strain and that the German wire was properly cut. Haig and Birch also rightly judged that British artillery techniques and training were still not quite up to the tasks which Allenby and Holland proposed to set the gunners. The views of Haig and Birch prevailed and, in the event, the four-day bombardment was extended by 24 hours, partly as a result of bad weather but also at the request of the French. Forty tanks were available to support the Third Army yet were allotted to three different corps in groups of 16 or less.

British soldiers with French children in the newly liberated village of Vraignes, 20 March 1917. (IWM Q1905)

If the lengthy bombardment and the deployment of tanks in 'penny packets' were reminders of the Somme, the planning for Arras nevertheless showed evidence of considerable improvements in various areas, not least the artillery. The ratio of one gun to every 10–12 yards of front in the Arras assault compared favourably with the one gun per 20 yards of July 1916; ammunition was more reliable and supplies more abundant; the introduction of the instantaneous '106' fuze – albeit in small quantities – afforded a more efficient means of cutting enemy barbed wire without cratering the ground; much greater emphasis was placed upon precise target selection rather than indiscriminate general bombardments; and marked progress had been made in the BEF's ability to locate enemy batteries by sound-ranging and flash-spotting. Overhead machine-gun barrages to assist advancing infantry were now a standard ingredient of British offensive operations. Furthermore, through methodical and imaginative staff work, the extensive system of cellars, caves and sewers under Arras was exploited and developed to provide secure shelters for attacking troops, guaranteeing that they would be fresher for the assault. Six miles of subways – most of which were lit by electricity – were excavated for the same reason in the chalk under Vimy Ridge.

Arras: Early successes

All this planning and preparation produced impressive initial results when the BEF's assault at Arras was launched in snow and sleet on Easter Monday, 9 April 1917. On the potentially troublesome right flank of the Third Army, VII Corps captured the strongly fortified village of Neuville Vitasse and won some footholds in the Hindenburg Line's front trenches. In the centre – especially north of Telegraph Hill, where the Hindenburg Line ended – VI Corps pushed forward between 2 and 3 miles. Just south of the River Scarpe, battalions of the 15th (Scottish) and 12th (Eastern) Divisions charged down the eastern side of Observation Ridge to seize 67 German field guns which had been deployed in the open along Battery Valley. Even more dramatic gains were achieved by the troops of XVII Corps, whose thrust of 3½ miles to Fampoux represented the longest advance made in one day by any army on the Western Front since the trench deadlock imposed itself in late 1914.

The encouraging early gains made by the Third Army were more than matched by the assault on the greatly prized Vimy Ridge by the Canadian Corps under Lieutenant-General Sir Julian Byng. Although the 1st and 2nd Canadian Divisions on the right had to advance up to 4,000 yards, they soon secured their principal objectives around Thélus and Farbus. The 3rd Canadian Division, in the centre, took La Folie Farm and the western edge of La Folie Wood but ran into difficulties on its left flank, where the 4th Canadian Division was unable to secure the summit of Hill 145 – the highest point on the ridge – until the evening. On the extreme left, Hill 120 ('The Pimple') stayed in German possession for another three days, falling to an attack by the 4th Canadian Division before daybreak on 12 April. By then the Canadians had consolidated their new positions along the crest of the main ridge. The storming of Vimy Ridge, one of the truly outstanding operations of the war, had seen the four Canadian divisions attacking simultaneously for the first time. Their success, accomplished at a cost of 11,297 casualties, not only gave a huge boost to Canada's growing sense of nationhood but also provided the BEF with a physical bulwark which would prove of immense value in the defensive battles of 1918.

Meanwhile, up to 11 April, Allenby's Third Army had seized 112 guns and 7,000 prisoners, incurring only 8,238 casualties in the process. The relatively inexpensive early progress of the First and Third Armies at Arras contrasted sharply with the disasters of the opening day of the 1916 Somme offensive. However, success was more elusive on the Fifth Army's front at Bullecourt. Here Gough rashly endorsed a last-minute suggestion from a junior officer that a dozen tanks should breach the German wire for the infantry in a surprise attack, without any previous rehearsals or supporting barrage. Following a false start on 10 April, Gough again displayed poor judgement by

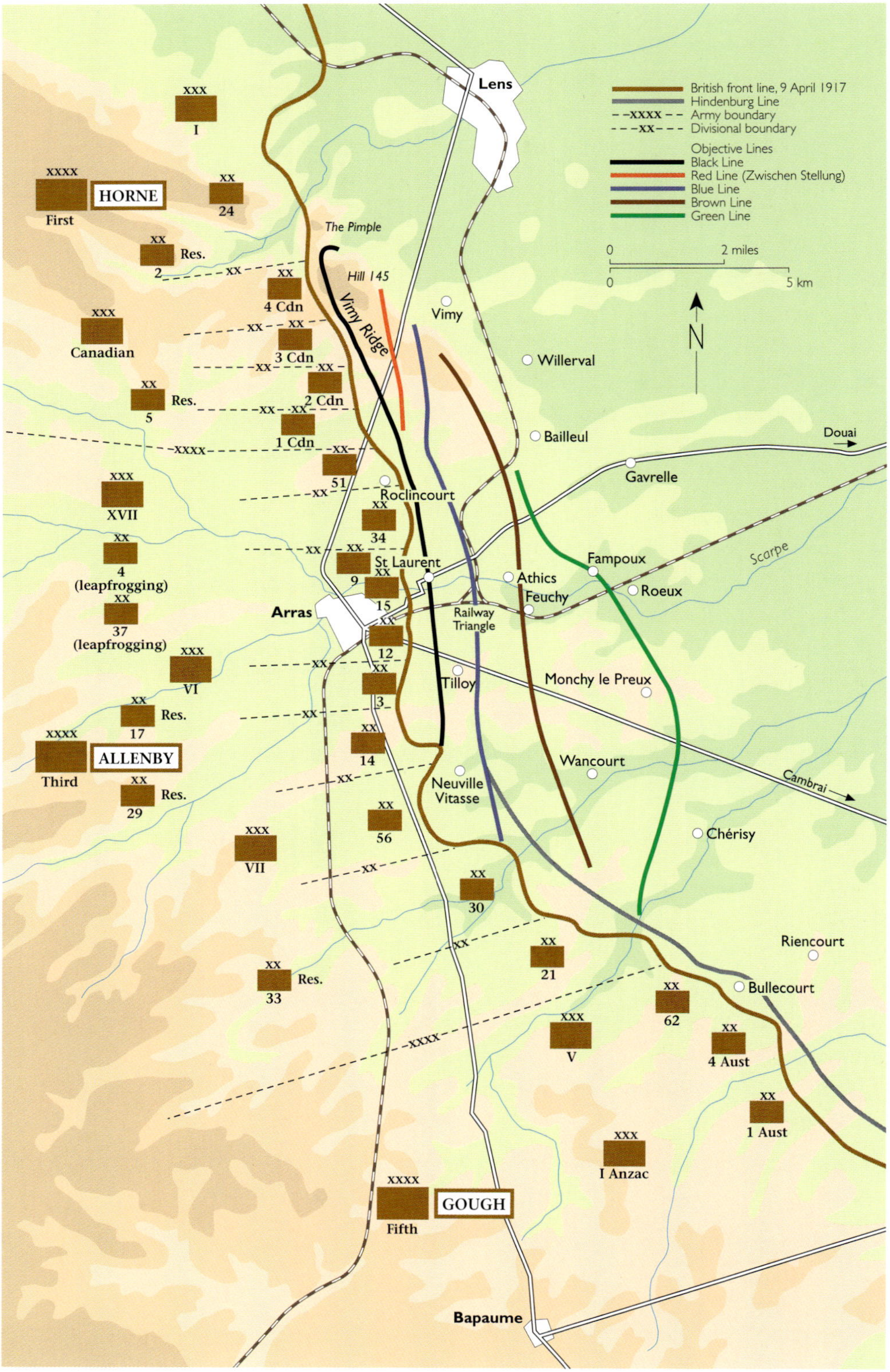
British front line, 9 April 1917
Hindenburg Line
Army boundary
Divisional boundary
Objective Lines
Black Line
Red Line (Zwischen Stellung)
Blue Line
Brown Line
Green Line
0 2 miles
0 5 km
N
Lens
Douai
Cambrai
Arras
Bapaume
The Pimple
Hill 145
Vimy Ridge
Vimy
Willerval
Bailleul
Gavrelle
Roclincourt
St Laurent
Athics
Feuchy
Fampoux
Roeux
Scarpe
Railway Triangle
Tilloy
Monchy le Preux
Wancourt
Neuville Vitasse
Chérisy
Riencourt
Bullecourt
HORNE
First
ALLENBY
Third
GOUGH
Fifth
I
24
2 Res.
4 Cdn
3 Cdn
2 Cdn
1 Cdn
Canadian
5 Res.
51
XVII
34
4 (leapfrogging)
37 (leapfrogging)
9
15
12
VI
3
17 Res.
14
29 Res.
56
VII
30
21
33 Res.
62
V
4 Aust
1 Aust
I Anzac

allowing this ill-prepared venture to proceed, essentially unchanged, the next day. All but four of the tanks failed to appear at the start line on time and most were eventually hit or broke down, leaving the attacking brigades of the 4th Australian Division to advance against the largely uncut wire of the Hindenburg Line with no accompanying barrage. Remarkably, these splendid troops reached and entered the second line of German trenches but were denied direct artillery support because of highly misleading reports about the headway made by the tanks and equally false information that men of the British 62nd Division had been spotted in Bullecourt village. The surviving Australians were forced to withdraw by early afternoon, the 4th Australian Brigade alone having suffered 2,339 casualties out of 3,000 who went into action. A total of 1,182 officers and men of I Anzac Corps were captured, the highest number of Australian prisoners in a single action during the Great War. The whole sorry episode simply served to increase Australian distrust both of tanks and of British generalship.

Opposite:
Arras: The infantry assault plan, 9 April 1917.

The Germans also committed mistakes which added to their own difficulties in the opening phases of the battle. The commander of the German Sixth Army at Arras, Colonel-General von Falkenhausen, failed to apply some key principles of the new system of defence in depth. Too many infantrymen were placed in the forward zone and his counter-attack divisions were kept so far back that they were between 12 and 24 hours' march from the battlefield. The expert tactician Colonel von Lossberg – whose nickname was 'the fireman of the Western Front' – was brought in as Chief of Staff of the Sixth Army and speedily reorganised the defence.

British infantry, 18-pounder guns and a tank near Feuchy crossroads, Arras, April 1917. (Getty Images)

The dominating village of Monchy le Preux, perched on high ground in the centre of the battlefield, was captured on 11 April by the British 37th Division and units of the 15th (Scottish) Division and 3rd Cavalry Division, although VI Corps was unable to make immediate progress eastwards, beyond Monchy, to Infantry Hill. As German reserves closed gaps in the line, the British advance lost momentum. The problems of communicating on the battlefield and of moving artillery forward across broken ground quickly enough to deal with German rear positions remained largely insoluble, and British junior officers and other ranks did not yet possess the tactical skill to adapt to semi-open warfare once the initial assault had breached the enemy line. The growing German resistance was reflected in the change in tone in Allenby's orders to the British Third Army. On 11 April he stressed that 'risks must be freely taken' in pursuing 'a defeated enemy'. The following day he merely directed that pressure on the Germans must be maintained to prevent them from consolidating their positions. However, the imminence of the Nivelle offensive made it impossible for Haig and Allenby to shut down the Arras operations at this point.

Dashed hopes: The Nivelle offensive

Haig was hardly encouraged by the fact that Nivelle's preparations had been plagued by problems. On 20 March Aristide Briand's government fell and the new French Prime Minister, Alexandre Ribot, entrusted the Ministry of War to Paul Painlevé, a Socialist with little faith in Nivelle's ideas. At the same time the German withdrawal to the Hindenburg Line largely nullified the French Northern Army Group's planned contribution to the offensive. The German retirement did have some benefits for the French since it enabled the Northern Army Group to release 13 divisions and 550 heavy artillery pieces for use elsewhere. It also gave the French the opportunity to assault the flank of the German position north of the Aisne and to direct enfilade artillery fire against the western portion of the defences on the Chemin des Dames ridge.

Pétain urged that the extra units now available should be transferred to his Central Army Group so that he could undertake a major attack astride the Suippe east of Reims – an operation that would create considerable difficulties for the Germans and more than compensate for the enforced reduction in scope of the Northern Army Group's effort. The chief drawback to Pétain's proposals was that the Central Army Group would not be ready to attack before 1 May and Nivelle felt that he could not risk postponing the principal offensive for a further two weeks. He therefore decided to restrict the Central Army Group's role to an attack by its left wing on the Moronvilliers heights, between Reims and the Suippe. Most of the reserves were allocated, in principle, to the newly created Reserve Army Group, commanded by General Micheler, but were initially kept under Nivelle's own control.

To add to Nivelle's troubles, Micheler – whose Army Group was expected to achieve and exploit the breakthrough on the Aisne – had serious misgivings about the coming offensive. In a letter to Nivelle on 22 March, Micheler pointed out that the Germans too had extra reserves available as a result of their withdrawal to the Hindenburg Line. Moreover, he observed that, since Nivelle's plan was originally conceived, the Germans had strengthened and deepened their defences in the key sector, increasing the number of successive defensive positions there from two to four. Consequently it might no longer prove possible for the Reserve Army Group to effect a breakthrough as quickly as Nivelle required.

Although Micheler's anxieties were shared by the other Army Group commanders, Nivelle would not make any fundamental amendments to his overall plan or chosen tactics. With the help of Colonel Messimy, a Deputy and former Minister of War, Micheler therefore made his views known to the Prime Minister. On 6 April, the very day that the United States declared war on Germany, a Council of War took place, in President Poincaré's presence,

The Nivelle offensive: opening phase.

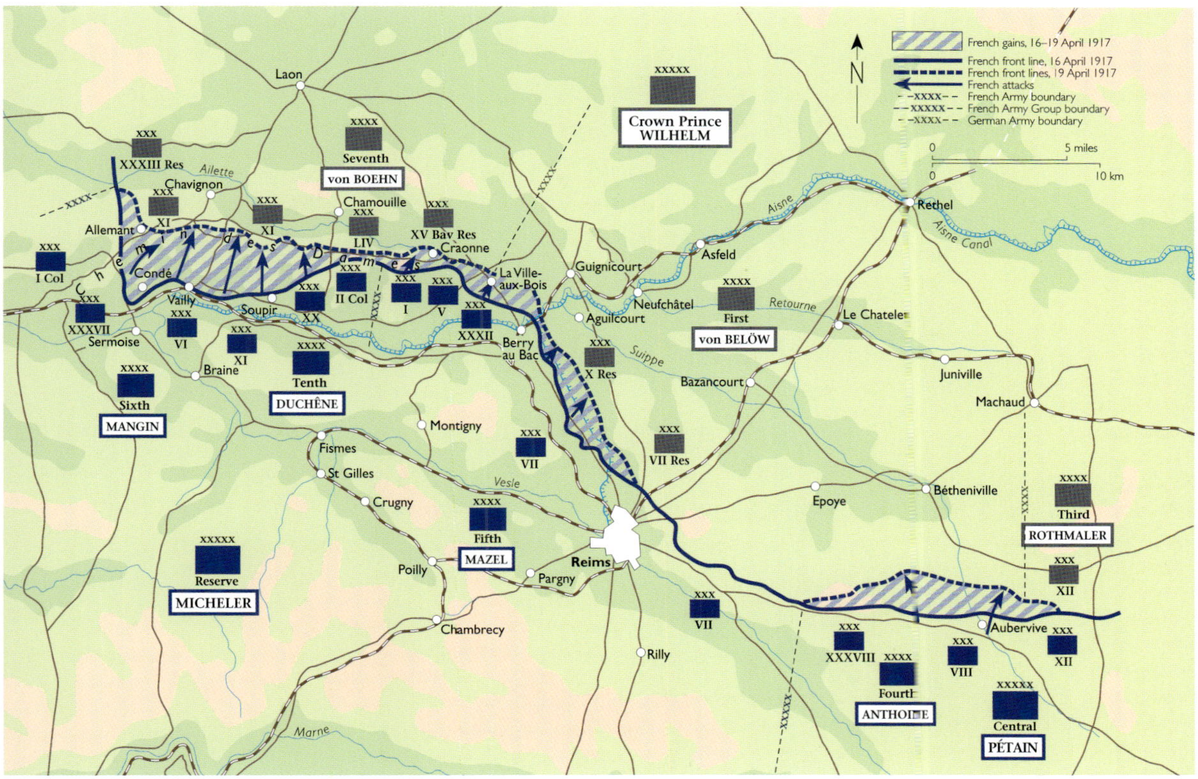

at Compiègne. Painlevé, who emphasised that the Russian Revolution in March ruled out any relief from that quarter, felt that the offensive should be postponed until the Americans could participate. Micheler and Pétain again expressed doubts that the attacking troops could penetrate the defences beyond the German second position and argued for a more limited operation. President Poincaré, summing up, proposed that the offensive should proceed but should be halted if it failed to rupture the German front. At this juncture, Nivelle decided to call the bluff of his critics by offering to resign. The assembled politicians, clearly unwilling to push matters that far, hastened to reassure Nivelle that they had complete confidence in him and the meeting ended with the main issues left unresolved. All that the protests had achieved was to impose greater pressure on the Commander-in-Chief. The following day he received more unpalatable news. During an attack south of the Aisne on 4 April, the Germans had apparently captured plans of the French assault. Even so, Nivelle obstinately refused to adapt his scheme to meet the changed circumstances.

Supported by 3,810 guns, the French Fifth and Sixth Armies began the offensive along a 25-mile front on 16 April, a week after the British assault at Arras. Their spirits lifted by Nivelle's stirring pronouncements, the French troops went into action with much of their customary *élan*. However, because the new German defensive doctrine dictated that the forward positions should be lightly held, the effects of the 14-day preliminary bombardment were greatly reduced and the French had deployed too few howitzers to reach into all the quarries, caves and ravines which dotted this sector. Hence the French captured the German first line in many places merely to find themselves facing massed machine-guns in a comparatively untouched German second position. Even the use of 128 tanks by Mazel's Fifth Army did not produce the desired breakthrough. The only gain – a 3-mile advance near Juvincourt – was, in fact, less significant than those achieved in the BEF's initial attack at Arras seven days before.

Nivelle attempted, on 17 April, to exploit the Fifth Army's progress in the right centre yet, unexpectedly, the most dramatic successes occurred on the left. Steady pressure there by Mangin's Sixth Army obliged the Germans to pull back around 4 miles, abandoning the Laffaux-Condé-Braye area as well as huge stocks of ammunition and numerous undamaged guns. In Champagne, the Central Army Group also opened its subsidiary offensive on 17 April and its Fourth Army, commanded by General Anthoine, took several important heights over the next four days. In all, by 20 April, the French Fourth, Fifth and Sixth Armies had seized over 20,000 prisoners and 147 guns. These were impressive results by the standards of previous years but there was no decisive breakthrough on the Aisne. The vast expenditure of shells by the French soon led to a worrying shell shortage and by 25 April French casualties totalled 96,125. The French medical services broke down under the strain and the growing delays in evacuating wounded from the forward zone further demoralised front-line troops.

Nivelle's personal influence on events began to diminish before the French offensive was a week old. On 21 April, Duchêne's Tenth Army was moved up into the line between the Fifth and Sixth Armies but Micheler persuaded Nivelle to scale down the offensive to a more limited operation designed to secure the whole of the Chemin des Dames ridge and drive the Germans away from Reims. Nivelle himself became increasingly depressed as every decision and order was subjected to intense scrutiny by the government and, on 29 April, his authority was further undermined when Pétain was appointed Chief of the General Staff and given powers which, in effect, made him the government's main military adviser. Mangin was another scapegoat, being removed from command of the Sixth Army on 2 May.

A fresh series of French attacks was undertaken on 4 and 5 May. The Sixth Army, now under General Maistre, thrust deep into the German-held salient opposite Laffaux and took the German positions on a 2½-mile sector along the Chemin des Dames. Meanwhile, troops of the Tenth Army captured the remainder of the Californie plateau at the eastern extremity of the ridge. These successes were not sufficient to repair Nivelle's crumbling reputation. Measured against the terrible yardstick of Verdun, the totals of 187,000 French and 163,000 German casualties for the whole offensive were not overwhelmingly high. Nevertheless, because Nivelle had promised so much, the shock of disappointment felt by the French Army and people when the breakthrough failed to materialise was all the more severe. As a wave of unrest and indiscipline engulfed the French Army, Nivelle was dismissed from the post of Commander-in-Chief on 15 May. His place was taken by Pétain, with Foch succeeding the latter as Chief of the French General Staff.

Taking the strain

The faltering start to Nivelle's offensive made it all the more vital for the BEF to continue operations at Arras, if only to deter the Germans from moving additional reserves to the Aisne. Despite his successes between 9 and 11 April, Allenby's subsequent handling of the battle caused the commanders of the 17th, 29th and 50th Divisions to register a formal protest against isolated, narrow-front operations which exposed attacking troops to concentrated flanking fire. On 15 April Allenby learned that Haig had ordered a pause to prepare another large-scale co-ordinated attack.

With all chances of surprise gone, Haig – expecting attrition rather than breakthrough – decided that this time the objectives would be less ambitious than on 9 April. After he had conferred with Allenby, Horne and Gough, it was agreed that nine British and Canadian divisions of the First and Third Armies would deliver the next set-piece blow along a 9-mile front against the line Gavrelle–Roeux–Guémappe–Fontaine lez Croisilles.

When the attack began on 23 April, the BEF realised that, under Lossberg's direction, the German Sixth Army had at last grasped the principles of flexible zonal defence. A fortnight earlier the German artillery had been overpowered but it was now present in greater strength. Furthermore, German battery positions were less precisely identified than before and many were beyond the range of British heavy guns, rendering the BEF's counter-battery fire much less effective. British and Dominion staff officers were still unaccustomed to improvising once the set-piece assault phase was over so, all too often, increasingly weary divisions were supported only by weak or patchy barrages as they advanced into the teeth of fearsome German artillery and machine-gun fire north and south of the River Scarpe. The 15th (Scottish) Division pushed the Germans out of

A French St Chamond tank at Condé-sur-Aisne, photographed on 3 May 1917. (IWM Q6963)

Guémappe and, in the First Army's sector, the 63rd (Royal Naval) Division captured Gavrelle, facilitating the seizure, within two days, of around 2 miles of tactically valuable ground near the Roeux–Gavrelle road. For the infantrymen involved, however, the fighting of 23–24 April was some of the toughest of the war, characterised by the bitter see-saw struggle for the heavily fortified village of Roeux and its chemical works.

By now Haig had cause for serious concern about the French offensive. He was prepared to press on at Arras to prevent the initiative from passing to the Germans but, as U-boats exacted a growing toll of Allied and neutral shipping, the need to reclaim the Belgian ports became even more important. Aiming to divert German attention away from both Flanders and the Aisne, to exhaust enemy reserves and secure a tenable defensive line east of Arras, Haig ordered a third big set-piece attack, which began on 3 May. However, knowing that he must save his own reserves for the forthcoming offensive in Flanders, he chose not to employ fresh divisions at Arras. Consequently, many of the formations participating in the attack of 3 May were already tired and below strength or contained a large proportion of green conscripts. The Canadian Corps, on the First Army's front, again performed well, seizing Fresnoy, and, in the Fifth Army's sector, Brigadier-General Gellibrand's 6th Australian Brigade won a precarious foothold in the Hindenburg Line close to Bullecourt but elsewhere progress was minimal. Efforts to extend the gains at Bullecourt led to a savage struggle in which seven British and Australian divisions became enmeshed before the 58th (London) Division finally cleared the village on 17 May. Further north, Roeux and the chemical works were at last taken by the British between 11 and 14 May, although the Germans had earlier recaptured Fresnoy.

In all, from 9 April to 17 May, the BEF incurred losses of 159,000 at Arras. This total represented the highest daily casualty rate – averaging 4,076 – of any major British offensive in the war. For the BEF the battle had degenerated, after the bright promise of 9 April, into yet another slogging-match that consumed not only men but also time which Haig sorely needed to ensure the success of his operations in Flanders. On the other hand, Haig had more than fulfilled his obligations to the French and was released from his subordination to Nivelle when the latter was removed from command in mid-May. Allenby was another command casualty of the offensive; his relations with Haig had never been warm and he had come under mounting criticism for his conduct of the later phases of the Arras offensive. On 6 June Allenby was transferred to Palestine to command the Egyptian Expeditionary Force and was replaced at the head of Third Army by Byng.

Mutinies

The Nivelle offensive was barely under way when, on 17 April, the French Army began to experience its worst *internal* crisis of the war. That day, 17 soldiers of the 108th Infantry Regiment left their posts in the face of the enemy. This was the first in a series of acts of collective indiscipline which, after reaching a peak in June, continued into the autumn. By 23 October some 250 such incidents had occurred, all but 12 in infantry units. Sixty-eight out of 112 French divisions were affected by the wave of mutinies.

The widespread unrest manifested itself in a variety of forms, including peace demands, the singing of revolutionary songs, stone-throwing and the breaking of windows. Far more serious were cases of incendiarism, mass demonstrations and the refusal by substantial numbers of men to return to the front line. Many indicated that while they were ready to hold defensive positions they were no longer willing to participate in apparently futile assaults. However, one should beware of exaggerating the extent of the mutinies or their revolutionary intent. Long-felt grievances about front-line conditions, envy of the relative comfort enjoyed by industrial workers on high wages and a sudden and spontaneous tide of despondency after the failure of the spring offensive all seem to have played a more fundamental role than political agitation or pacifist subversion in fomenting unrest.

Having succeeded Nivelle as Commander-in-Chief in mid-May, Pétain eventually managed to repair the morale and fighting capacity of the French Army with a combination of reform, understanding and iron discipline. A total of 3,427 French soldiers were convicted by courts-martial for offences arising from the mutinies. Of these, 554 were sentenced to death and 49 (or 8 per cent) were actually executed. At the same time, Pétain renounced the concept of the offensive at all costs, ruling out further large-scale attacks until the United States Army reached France in strength and weapons production had considerably increased. 'I am waiting for the Americans and the tanks,' Pétain frequently declared. He also took rapid action to address the most common complaints of front-line soldiers, improving medical services, welfare facilities, accommodation and food as well as granting additional leave. The French Army recovered sufficiently by late August to deliver a well-planned assault at Verdun which led to the recapture of the heights of *Le Mort Homme* and *Côte 304*. Another attack, at Malmaison in October, saw the French win possession of the crest of the Chemin des Dames ridge on the Aisne. Nevertheless these were limited affairs in the overall context of the struggle in France and Belgium. One of the most significant results of the French mutinies was that, from the summer of 1917, the British and Dominion forces under Haig had to shoulder the main burden of responsibility for Allied offensive operations on the Western Front.

Mines and method at Messines

Haig's plan for the BEF's Flanders offensive, as presented to a conference of his army commanders on 7 May, split the projected operations into two stages. The first would consist of an attack on the Wytschaete–Messines ridge, south of Ypres, around 7 June. The second, taking place some weeks later, would be a 'Northern Operation' designed to capture the Passchendaele–Staden ridge and Gheluvelt plateau to the east of Ypres before seizing the Thourout–Roulers railway link and then clearing the Belgian coast, aided by an amphibious landing. It was regarded as essential to take Messines Ridge first in order to guarantee a secure defensive flank for the subsequent advance east of Ypres and also to provide elbow-room south and south-west of Ypres for the assembly of the guns and troops needed for the attack in the centre and on the left of the Salient. Although General Sir Herbert Plumer knew the Salient better than any of his other army commanders, Haig believed that he was too careful and deliberate to lead the main operation, which was handed to the more thrustful Gough. Plumer's Second Army would instead carry out the preliminary assault against Messines Ridge.

Australian troops studying a contour model of Messines Ridge, 6 June 1917. (Great War Primary Document Archive)

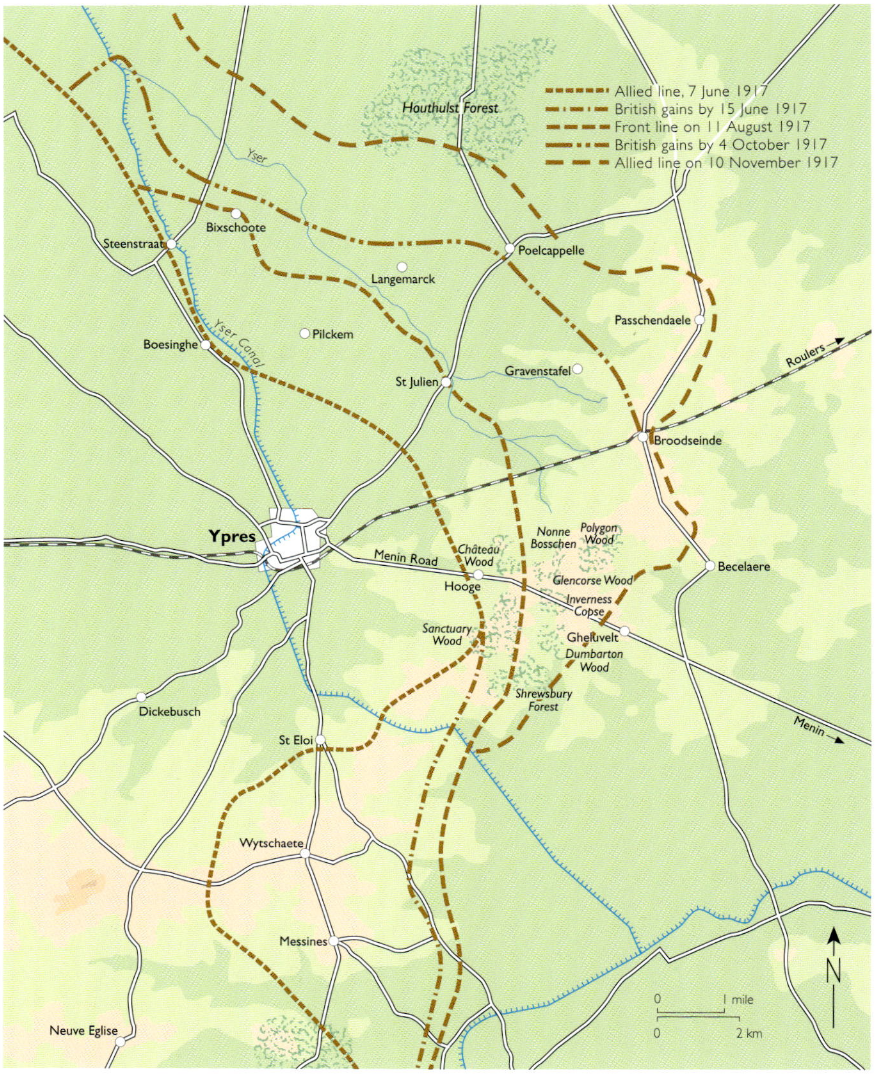

Messines Ridge and the third battle of Ypres, June–November 1917.

With his ruddy face, white moustache and corpulent figure, Plumer had the appearance of an elderly country squire rather than a successful general, but few could match his profound understanding of the principles of modern trench warfare or his concern to minimise casualties. Plumer and Major-General Charles Harington, his Chief of Staff, were a formidable team, whose watchwords were 'Trust, Training and Thoroughness'. Typically, their meticulous preparations for the Messines operation included the construction of an enormous contour model of the ridge. Seventy-two new Mark IV tanks were made available to Second Army, which could also call upon 2,266 guns. For the latter, a methodical barrage and counter-battery programme was planned, special attention being paid to the problems arising from the current

German tactics of deep defence and counter-attack. The bombardment would commence on 21 May. The feature which made the Messines attack particularly memorable, however, was the digging of 24 huge mines under the German front defences. Some of the mines had been initiated more than 12 months earlier. On the day of the attack the mines would be blown immediately before the infantry assault. The task of taking the northern sector of the ridge was assigned to X Corps; the central sector, including Wytschaete village, would be secured by IX Corps; and II Anzac Corps was ordered to seize the southern shoulder of the ridge and Messines itself.

Nineteen of the mines, containing nearly 1,000,000lbs of high explosive in all, were detonated at 3.10am on 7 June 1917. The nine assaulting divisions, advancing behind a creeping barrage, rapidly overcame those bewildered German defenders who had survived in the outpost and forward zones. Demonstrating that they had profited from painstaking battle rehearsals, from the lessons of the Somme and from the recent success at Vimy Ridge, the British and Dominion assault troops contrived to outflank or surround many German pillboxes, machine-gun posts and other strongpoints, which were subsequently cleared by trained mopping-up parties. By mid-morning, having suffered comparatively light losses, Plumer's Second Army held the crest of the ridge. During the afternoon the advance continued against the Oosttaverne Line, which ran across the eastern, or reverse, slope of the ridge. At this stage casualties began to increase as the ridge became overcrowded and, in the II Anzac Corps sector on the right, some units were even fired upon by their own artillery. However, the Oosttaverne Line was totally in Second Army's grasp after four days and all gains were consolidated within a week. The storming of Messines Ridge cost the BEF some 25,000 officers and men while German casualties were approximately 23,000, of whom 10,000 were missing.

The Messines attack, like that at Vimy Ridge, was, in most respects, a model set-piece assault, yet it also resembled the April success in the BEF's failure to follow up a brilliant initial victory. Haig and Plumer were both aware of the chance to gain ground on the western end of the Gheluvelt plateau – a possibility which the Germans themselves recognised and feared – but Plumer informed Haig on 8 June that he would require three days to bring his artillery forward. An impatient Haig thereupon transferred two of Plumer's corps to the Fifth Army and instructed Gough to prepare the operation. Ironically, Gough – possibly recalling the unfortunate outcome of his own impetuosity at Bullecourt – feared that a preliminary attack towards Gheluvelt might produce nothing more than a vulnerable minor salient on his right flank. After taking longer to study the problem than the three-day delay requested by Plumer, Gough, on 14 June, counselled against such an operation and advocated a simultaneous attack along his *entire* front, six weeks later, on the opening day of the main offensive. Since the German defences on the plateau had already been strengthened during the pause, Haig weakly agreed to the further postponement of the Gheluvelt attack – a decision that he and the BEF would shortly come to regret.

Drowned hopes: The third battle of Ypres

Haig's Flanders plan had received the War Cabinet's general approval in mid-May on the understanding that the French would similarly be taking offensive action. Now that the latter could no longer be counted upon, Lloyd George believed that it would be folly for the BEF to attack virtually on its own. Haig, however, still confidently anticipated decisive results in 1917 and there were sound strategic reasons for sticking with his scheme. The Americans were far from ready and Russian military power was nearing collapse, so there was a distinct possibility that the Germans would regain the strategic initiative and administer a fatal blow to the French Army if the BEF failed to maintain the pressure. At the very least, Haig asserted, the German Army would suffer further attrition and become easier to defeat in 1918. Haig and Robertson therefore saw considerable risks in the projected transfer of divisions to Italy, a policy which could only weaken Allied strength on the Western Front. As shipping losses to U-boats remained perilously high, Haig's scheme to clear the Flanders coast was given powerful support by the First Sea Lord, Admiral Jellicoe. These arguments notwithstanding, Lloyd George's War Cabinet did not finally authorise Haig's 'Northern Operation' until 21 July, by which time the preliminary bombardment had already been in progress five days. Haig was informed, moreover, that the

British stretcher-bearers carrying a wounded man through knee-deep mud, near Boesinghe, 1 August 1917. (IWM Q5935)

offensive might well be terminated should casualties be judged to outweigh tangible achievements.

Not all the problems Haig experienced during the third battle of Ypres were of his own making. Since the digging of deep trenches was ruled out by the boggy Ypres terrain, General von Arnim's German Fourth Army based its defence upon concrete pillboxes and fortified farms behind a thinly occupied forward zone. The pillboxes were built above ground, were sited to support each other with interlocking fire and were thick enough to withstand anything less weighty than 8-inch howitzer shells. The expert defensive tactician Lossberg was made Arnim's Chief of Staff on 13 June. Then, on 10 July, the Germans carried out a pre-emptive bombardment and attack in the Nieuport sector which badly disrupted preparations for a planned coastal advance by the British Fourth Army. The projected British amphibious landing was subsequently postponed and later dropped. Two serious mistakes can, however, be attributed to Haig. His first major error was to hand the leading role in the main offensive to Gough, thus delaying the 'Northern Operation' while the Fifth Army got into position; the second was his failure to insist on the capture of the western part of the Gheluvelt plateau before the principal attack.

Unhappily for the BEF, Haig compounded these mistakes by allowing Gough to prepare a battle plan that was far too ambitious. At the end of June Haig was envisaging a swift breakthrough but, as the opening of the offensive drew closer, he began to favour a step-by-step offensive consisting of a succession of limited advances. Because Haig tended to avoid discussing operational plans fully with his army commanders, Gough was left with the unfortunate impression that a rapid breakthrough was still the priority. Consequently he proposed that, on the first day, his Fifth Army should attempt a deep advance of 6,000 yards, penetrating beyond the main concentration of German field batteries to the German third line. If resistance proved light, the attacking troops should push on to a fourth objective. At this point there would be a pause of two to three days while artillery was moved up to support an assault against the Passchendaele ridge, scheduled for the fourth day of the offensive. As was his custom, Haig deferred to the commander on the spot, permitting Gough's unrealistic plan to stand. Haig *did* remind Gough of the vital importance of securing the Gheluvelt plateau but failed to hammer home the point when it emerged that Gough's scheme laid insufficient emphasis on its capture. In these respects, the preparations for the Ypres offensive were reminiscent of those for the Somme in 1916, for the BEF was again about to begin a major attack with ambiguous objectives and a faulty plan. The ground selected by Haig for the offensive was unsuitable and, because it was largely under German observation, necessitated a lengthy British artillery bombardment if the German batteries were to be suppressed. The preparations for the third battle of Ypres thus involved a reversion to artillery tactics that were now nearly obsolete and, to make an unpromising situation worse, the protracted bombardment ruined the already fragile drainage of the area, helping to create a swampy landscape that made rapid movement extremely unlikely, if not impossible.

Supported by 2,936 guns, including some artillery from the British Second and French First Armies, nine divisions from Gough's Fifth Army began their assault at 3.50am on 31 July. On their left two divisions of the French First Army struck between Steenstraat and Boesinghe. Units of the Second Army also attacked on their right. The initial results were heartening as much of Pilckem Ridge fell and the seizure of key observation points there and at the western extremity of the Gheluvelt plateau robbed the Germans of advantages they had enjoyed since May 1915. Plumer's troops took Hollebeke and the German outpost line west of the Lys while the French captured Steenstraat and reached the outskirts of Bixschoote. However, in the crucial Gheluvelt plateau sector the British II Corps struggled to progress beyond the German first line. Of the 48 fighting tanks allotted

'Hell Fire Corner' on the Menin Road, one of the most dangerous spots in the Ypres Salient. (IWM)

Wounded soldiers being treated at an advanced dressing station near Ypres, 20 September 1917. (Getty Images)

to II Corps only 19 went into action and a gun firing from inside a massive pillbox which commanded the Menin Road east of Hooge accounted for most of these. The setback in this sector effectively halved the Fifth Army's attack frontage. The rain which appeared during the afternoon changed from a drizzle to a persistent downpour soon after 4pm, greatly reducing visibility. In several places German counter-attacks drove the British back and, by 2 August, the continuing bad weather had forced the British to suspend operations. The initial assault had carried the Fifth Army forward about 3,000 yards but, disappointingly, Gough's divisions were still a long way short of their first-day objectives.

The persistent rain largely precluded any more major advances that month. The Ypres Salient was transformed into a gloomy expanse of mud and water-filled craters. All troops moving up to the front line had to negotiate treacherous duckboard tracks or plank roads that were targeted by enemy gunners. The Fifth Army took Langemarck on 16 August but two more attempts to seize the Gheluvelt plateau proved abortive, despite heavy fighting at Inverness Copse and Glencorse Wood close to the Menin Road. On 25 August Haig belatedly rectified his earlier mistake by transferring the leading role in the battle, as well as the frontage of II Corps, to Plumer and the Second Army.

While Haig resisted pressure from Lloyd George to halt the bogged-down offensive, Plumer was given three weeks to prepare the next step and used the opportunity to introduce more flexible assault tactics. Attacks would be led by lines of skirmishers, followed by small teams of infantry deployed loosely to outflank strongpoints and pillboxes. Each such group, with its own Mills bombers, Lewis gunners and rifle grenadiers, would fight as a self-contained unit. Other small groups, acting as mopping-up parties, would bring up the rear. Fresh reserves of infantry would be kept ready to deal with the expected German counter-attacks, which would also be subjected to intense, well-planned artillery fire and machine-gun barrages.

Plumer's methodical, step-by-step attacks with limited objectives – helped by a period of dry weather – immediately made some headway in the sub-battles of the Menin Road ridge (20–25 September) and Polygon Wood (26 September–3 October). A distinguished contribution to these operations was made by I Anzac Corps, the Australians clearly being far happier under Plumer's command than they had been under Gough. The impact of these attacks was shown by the fact that, in the Salient, the Germans were now obliged to modify their elastic defence system and again hold forward positions in greater strength, thereby making themselves more vulnerable to Plumer's artillery. On 4 October, II Anzac Corps joined in Plumer's third attack, which aimed to capture Broodseinde Ridge and the eastern end of the Gheluvelt plateau. The British X Corps drove the last German defenders from Polygon Wood and the New Zealand Division took Gravenstafel but, although the main objectives were gained, rain yet again turned the battlefield into a morass, making exploitation impossible.

Some sources maintain that Plumer and Gough advocated stopping the offensive at this point, though documentary evidence to support this

Allied soldiers, most likely Canadians from the machine gun company, 4th Division, sit in crater holes of the devastated landscape around Passchendaele Ridge following the battle in November 1917. (Corbis)

claim is difficult to find. Haig certainly wanted to reach the Passchendaele ridge to provide a firm line for the approaching winter and decided to continue operations for another month. Conditions in the Salient were now so appalling that men were drowning in liquid mud. On 6 November the Canadian Corps took the mound of pulverised rubble that had once been Passchendaele, the village that has since lent its name to the whole third battle of Ypres – which itself has come to symbolise all the worst horrors of the Great War. When the Flanders offensive finally ended on 10 November, both sides had suffered losses of approximately 250,000, though, for the British, these casualties were less than those incurred on the Somme and represented a lower daily average than at Arras in the spring of 1917. Despite an advance of some 5 miles and Plumer's impressive September operations, none of Haig's distant objectives had been attained and even the northernmost tip of Passchendaele Ridge remained in German hands.

Massed tanks at Cambrai

Although its morale and manpower were stretched almost to breaking point by the fighting at Ypres, the BEF nevertheless made one more offensive effort in 1917. On 20 November, at Cambrai, the British concentrated their tanks so that, for the first time, they were deployed for a mass attack rather than scattered in small groups along the front for local infantry support.

The assault at Cambrai evolved from a Tank Corps plan for a large-scale raid, the chief object of which was not to seize ground but to deal the Germans a bruising blow on terrain which, unlike the Ypres Salient, actually suited tanks. Byng and the Third Army staff expanded the scheme between August and November, transforming it into a major operation against the Hindenburg Line. Both Haig and Byng perceived advantages in a plan which might not only rebuild the BEF's reputation and revive morale but also simultaneously draw the enemy's gaze from the Italian front, where the Italians had suffered a near-catastrophic defeat at Caporetto on 24 October. Third Army hoped to pierce the Hindenburg system between the Canal du Nord and the Canal de l'Escaut before sending cavalry through the breach to secure crossings over the Sensée and isolate Cambrai. Infantry and tanks, after taking Bourlon Wood, were then to clear the Germans from Cambrai and the area between the principal waterways. It would be up to GHQ to decide the next step, possibly a drive towards Douai and Valenciennes. The main drawback was that the attrition at Ypres and the demands of the Italian front left the BEF with scanty reserves for any exploitation at Cambrai. In short, the plan had outgrown the resources which the BEF possessed in late 1917. Nor was it helped by Byng's desire to employ all the available tanks and infantry divisions in the breakthrough phase.

On the positive side, the plan combined some promising tactical elements. These included the decision to abandon the customary long artillery preparation and to permit the 1,003 supporting guns to deliver a surprise hurricane bombardment, capitalising on the new technique of 'predicted' shooting without prior registration of targets. Another novel aspect was the drill for tank-infantry co-operation developed by the Tank Corps and endorsed by Byng. Three hundred and seventy-eight fighting tanks, all carrying large brushwood bundles or 'fascines' to assist them in crossing trenches, would operate in groups of three. In each group, an 'advanced guard' tank would move 100 yards ahead of the two main body tanks, its task being to subdue German fire and protect the two following tanks. The latter would lead infantry sections through the German wire and over the opposing trenches. A total of 98 supporting tanks carried supplies, bridging material, telephone cables, wireless or grapnels for hauling aside barbed wire. Moreover, the British – profiting from the lessons of Third Ypres – made greater use of low-flying aircraft to strike German artillery and troops.

The opening assault, by six of Byng's 19 infantry divisions, was made along a 6-mile sector at 6.20am on 20 November 1917. The surprise achieved by the sudden bombardment and the employment of massed tanks enabled Byng's formations, in most places, to break through the Hindenburg front and support systems to a depth of 3–4 miles. However, in the left centre, the 51st (Highland) Division failed to take the key village of Flesquières on the first day. Many of its accompanying tanks either broke down short of the objective or were disabled by German gunners who had been specially

British tanks moving forward at Graincourt for the attack on Bourlon Wood, near Cambrai, 23 November 1917. (Mary Evans Picture Library)

trained in anti-tank defence. By 23 November only 92 tanks remained operational and, because the British cavalry were disappointingly unable to exploit the initial breach, the old problem of maintaining the impetus of an advance beyond the assault phase again appeared to defy solution.

Over the next few days the Third Army was involved in what was essentially a fierce infantry battle for Bourlon Ridge, west of Cambrai. For all their efforts, the British divisions never completely secured Bourlon village or the neighbouring Bourlon Wood and, after a week, were left holding a salient 9 miles wide and 4–5 miles deep. On 30 November, the German Second Army, commanded by General von der Marwitz, launched a savage counterstroke against this salient. The Germans similarly opted for a short bombardment, using smoke, gas and high-explosive shells, and also employed large numbers of aircraft for ground-attack duties. The German counter-blow was perhaps most notable for the vital part played by storm troops, employing assault and infiltration tactics developed during the past two years. The timely arrival of some British reinforcements slowed German progress but, at Haig's insistence, Byng fell back to a shorter, and more defensible, line in front of Flesquières by 5–6 December, thereby abandoning much of the ground originally gained. Casualties at Cambrai totalled more than 40,000 on each side but the most significant feature of the battle was the fact that both the British and Germans achieved a measure of success with tactical methods which at last seemed to offer a way out of the long-standing deadlock.

Taking stock

Victory had proved as elusive as ever for the Allies in 1917. Nivelle's failure, the French Army mutinies, the misery of the Passchendaele mud and the late setback after the brilliant initial success at Cambrai all combined to cast a dark cloud over Allied hopes for the immediate future. The war correspondent Philip Gibbs observed that, for the first time in the war, 'the British Army lost its spirit of optimism, and there was a sense of deadly depression among the many officers and men with whom I came in touch'. However, a brief mutiny at the infantry base depot at Etaples in September was caused by poor accommodation and a brutal training régime at that particular camp and did not signal a major collapse in morale throughout the BEF. The losses in the attrition battles at Arras and Ypres provided Lloyd George with yet more ammunition to use against Haig. Indeed, the news in December 1917 that Allenby had captured Jerusalem from the Turks appeared to buttress the position of those who argued against the primacy of the Western Front. While still unwilling to provoke a political crisis by removing Robertson and Haig, Lloyd George continued to seek ways of limiting their authority and influence.

Pétain's judicious blend of discipline and reform had brought the French Army back from the edge of the abyss into which it had stared during the spring and early summer but, in spite of its praiseworthy performance in limited operations at Verdun in August and the Chemin des Dames in October, nobody was sure how it would fare if called upon to mount large-scale attacks. Pétain himself remained reluctant to risk such offensives until the Americans arrived in force.

So far, the assembly of United States troops had proceeded at a frustratingly slow pace. By 1 December 1917 barely four American divisions had reached France. Furthermore, General John Joseph 'Black Jack' Pershing, who commanded the American Expeditionary Force (AEF), had been strictly enjoined to keep his formations together as a distinct national army and to resist any attempt to use them merely as reinforcements for weakened French and British units. On a more constructive note, the establishment of a Supreme War Council at Versailles in November 1917 promised improved co-ordination of Allied strategy in the coming year.

American soldiers marching through the streets of Liverpool, UK, following their arrival in the war. (Mary Evans Picture Library)

The German Army had some reasons for optimism, at least in the short term, at the end of 1917. The new artillery and storm-troop assault tactics tested in operations at Riga, Caporetto and Cambrai had proved highly effective. The German formations on the Western Front were therefore retrained during the winter and were simultaneously augmented by divisions released from the Eastern Front following the Bolshevik Revolution in Russia in November. A sobering factor, however, was the knowledge that the Allied blockade was causing serious shortages of oil, petrol, rubber, horses and fodder, all of which would reduce the German Army's own ability to sustain mobile operations over long periods in 1918. Ominously, troops of a previously dependable division had stopped to loot a British supply depot during the German counterstroke at Cambrai on 30 November.

1917 had certainly not been a year of total gloom for Haig and the BEF. The technical and tactical strides made by the BEF during the past 12 months were evident in the advance of XVII Corps and the success of the Canadian Corps at Arras and Vimy Ridge on 9 April; in the storming of Messines Ridge on 7 June; in Plumer's powerful blows at Ypres in late September; and in the breaking of the Hindenburg Line near Cambrai in November. Even the clinging mud of Passchendaele could not wholly obscure the achievements resulting from the BEF's collective improvement and learning process since the Somme.

Germany plans to attack

As 1917 ended, the Allies knew that they must expect a major German offensive in the west early the following year. In December 1917 both Russia and Romania suspended hostilities with the Central Powers, enabling Germany to speed up the transfer of units from the Eastern Front. Thirty-three divisions were moved to France and Belgium before 1918 dawned. The Allies, in contrast, faced severe manpower problems. Six French divisions were sent to Italy and another three were disbanded, reducing the total of French divisions on the Western Front to 100, each with an infantry strength of no more than 6,000.

The BEF was in similar difficulties. Haig requested 334,000 reinforcements but had only acquired just over 174,000 by 21 March 1918. Lloyd George, who bore the responsibility for ensuring that Britain's *industrial* manpower resources remained equal to the demands of the war, undoubtedly believed that the holding back of men in Britain might make it easier for him to limit wasteful offensives. Haig, in turn, could argue that too many men had been diverted to what *he* saw as peripheral campaigns or 'sideshows'. However, recent scholarship indicates that the general reserve was kept in Britain by Robertson and the War Office rather than by the Prime Minister and that

Haig himself may have inadvertently encouraged this policy by asserting that he could withstand a German offensive for at least 18 days with his existing forces. The manpower shortage *did* mean that, in February and March 1918, most BEF divisions were reduced from 12 battalions to nine, although the New Zealand Division, the four Canadian divisions and the five Australian divisions all retained the 12-battalion organisation. Of the British formations on the Western Front, 115 battalions were broken up, seven were converted into Pioneer battalions and 38 were amalgamated to form 19 battalions.

Little immediate assistance would be forthcoming from the Americans. Pershing had only 130,000 troops in France by 1 December 1917 and all AEF divisions would require three months' additional training on arrival. For a short period early in 1918, therefore, the Germans would enjoy the rare luxury of outnumbering the Franco-British forces, deploying 192 divisions against 156.

Acknowledging that the convoy system and air cover were now helping Britain to counter the U-boat threat, Germany's military leaders decided to seize their last real opportunity for a decisive victory on the Western Front before American strength became overwhelming. Ludendorff consequently planned to unleash a *Kaiserschlacht* ('imperial battle') of successive, inter-related attacks that would together hasten the collapse of 'the whole structure' of the Allied armies. He judged that, if the British and Dominion forces were defeated, the others would inevitably capitulate in their wake. The initial German blow would therefore be delivered mainly against the BEF. After all the possibilities had been discussed during the winter, three, in particular, appeared to meet Ludendorff's criteria. One such attack, code-named *George*, would aim to break through the front near Armentières, in Flanders, and advance against Hazebrouck, taking the British forces to the north from the flank and rear. A subsidiary operation, *George II*, would isolate and overcome the BEF's units in the Ypres Salient. The second possible attack, *Mars*, would be directed against Arras. The third, *Michael*, would involve a powerful blow against the British Third and Fifth Armies on either side of St Quentin, between Arras and La Fère. As soon as the British defences in this sector were breached, German forces could wheel north and push the BEF back towards the sea. It was obviously advisable to launch the Flanders assault in dry conditions, which might not occur until April or May, and the BEF's positions at Arras were considered too tough an obstacle for the opening attack, so, on 21 January, Ludendorff settled upon *Michael* as his first choice for the principal offensive in the spring. After another seven weeks of detailed planning, 21 March was selected as the start date.

In the final plan, Crown Prince Rupprecht's Army Group would provide the right-wing forces, namely General Otto von Below's Seventeenth Army and General von der Marwitz's Second Army. These were to attack south

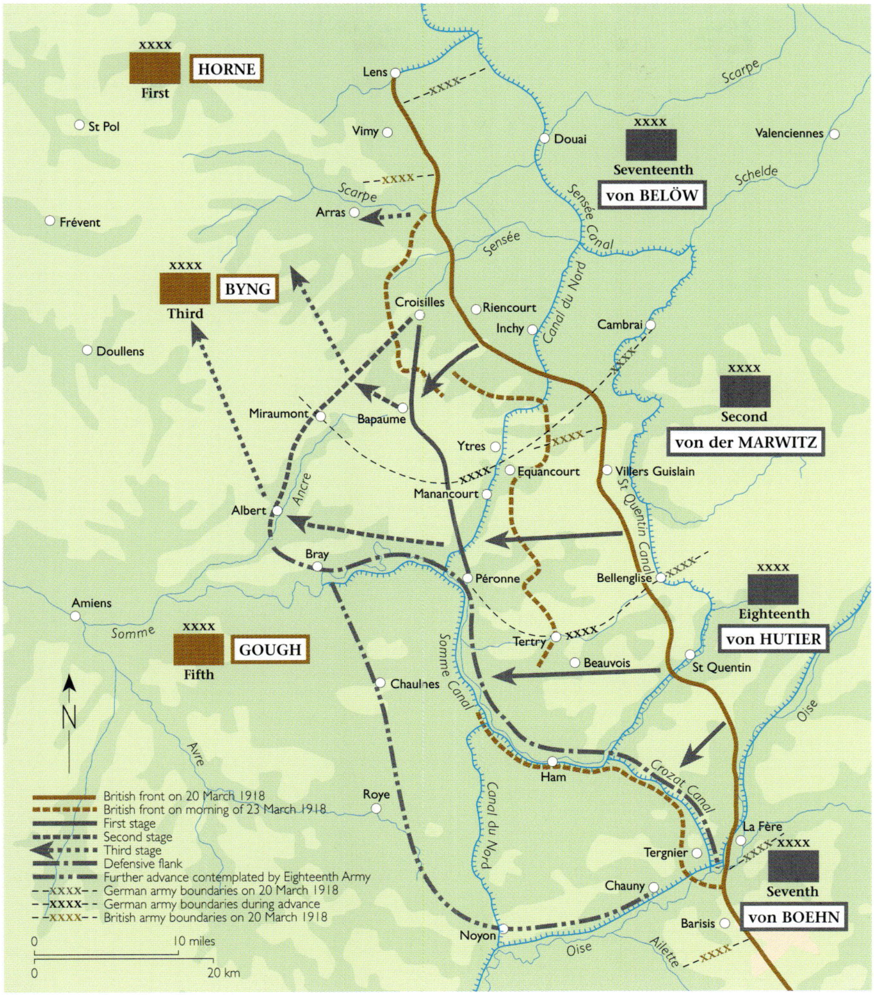

Operation *Michael*: the plan.

of Arras and pinch out the British-held Flesquières salient, near Cambrai. They would next push on towards Péronne and Bapaume, across the 1916 Somme battlefield, to a line between Arras and Albert before swinging north-west, enveloping Arras as they advanced. On their left, General von Hutier's Eighteenth Army, from the Army Group of Crown Prince Wilhelm, would attack across the River Somme and the Crozat Canal to protect the flank of the right-wing armies, deal with any French reserves moving up from the south and drive a wedge between the French and British forces. The Eighteenth Army might also help von der Marwitz around Péronne if required. *Mars* could proceed once the necessary tactical success south of Arras had been attained. Ludendorff meanwhile permitted planning for *George* to continue, just in case *Michael* failed to live up to hopes and expectations.

A major retraining programme was instituted during the winter in an attempt to acquaint more units with the tactics developed by the élite assault units, or storm troops, over the previous two years. Approximately one-quarter of German infantry divisions were designated 'attack divisions' (*Angriffsdivisionen*) and received the best new equipment and weapons, including light machine-guns. The remainder, primarily responsible for holding the line, were classified as 'trench divisions' (*Stellungsdivisionen*). Storm troops were assigned a key role in *Michael*, their task being to probe for weak spots in the opposing defences and to cause as much confusion as possible in rear areas through infiltration and envelopment. However, the artillery was arguably the most important element in the initial assault phase. The Germans would employ the gunnery methods tested and refined at Riga, Caporetto and Cambrai by such experts as Colonel Georg Bruchmüller, who was himself now attached to the Eighteenth Army and shaped the whole artillery plan for *Michael*. His scrupulously orchestrated fire plans were founded upon brief hurricane bombardments of prodigious intensity and weight, employing 'predicted' shooting techniques. Great care was taken to disrupt communications and concentration areas deep behind Allied lines, while a high proportion of gas shells was incorporated to neutralise and suppress enemy gunners.

With its formations not only weakened by recent battles and reorganisation but also containing large numbers of raw conscripts, the BEF was hardly in the ideal condition to resist the approaching German onslaught. Although Haig remained in command, several of his senior staff officers – including Kiggell, his Chief of Staff, and Charteris, his Chief of Intelligence – had been replaced. At home, Robertson resigned as Chief of the Imperial General Staff when Lloyd George tried to restrict his authority by nominating General Sir Henry Wilson as British representative on the 'Executive War Board' of the Supreme War Council. To rub salt into the wound, it was Wilson who succeeded Robertson as Chief of the Imperial General Staff on 18 February.

Both Haig and Pétain, in December, had ordered the construction of systems which would allow their armies to adopt flexible defence in depth similar to that introduced by the Germans in 1916–1917. In the BEF's area it was intended that the system would embody Forward, Battle and Rear Zones, each comprising several successive lines of continuous trenches or groups of trenches besides mutually supporting strongpoints and machine-gun posts sited for all-round defence. However, lack of time and labour shortages prevented the completion of the new positions. Not having fought a big defensive battle for well over two years, the BEF also required many more weeks than it was actually granted in order to absorb these alternative tactical ideas. The outlook was not improved by the fact that, since November, five divisions had been transferred to Italy under Plumer's command. Furthermore, in January 1918, the BEF had been called upon to take over an extra stretch of the Allied line. Its right flank now extended to Barisis, over 20 miles south of St Quentin.

Gough's Fifth Army, which held the BEF's southernmost sector, possessed only three cavalry and 12 infantry divisions to defend 42 miles, in contrast to the Third Army, on its left, which could deploy 14 divisions to defend 28 miles. The positions which Gough's troops took over from the French were rudimentary and, in any event, not all of Gough's subordinates had entirely grasped the principles of elastic defence in depth. In consequence, the Fifth Army's Forward Zone was too densely occupied when the attack came.

Albeit with the advantages of hindsight, one can fairly accuse Haig of having miscalculated the possible direction and weight of the German offensive, of being over-optimistic about the BEF's current defensive capabilities and of having underestimated the potential threat to the Fifth Army. There were admittedly few vital strategic objectives immediately behind Gough's front and east of Amiens, giving the Fifth Army more room to fall back and manoeuvre but it remains a matter of debate whether Haig was right to leave the Fifth Army quite so weak. All things considered, however, Haig was undoubtedly wise to keep most of his troops in the north, ensuring the security of Flanders and the Channel ports.

German storm troops cross a wire entanglement during training at Sedan, 1917. (Mary Evans Picture Library)

Michael

Bruchmüller's devastating prelude to Operation *Michael* began at 4.40am on 21 March 1918, when 6,473 guns and 3,532 trench mortars opened fire. The infantry assault commenced in thick fog five hours later. Nineteen divisions of the German Seventeenth Army struck the British Third Army and 43 divisions of the German Second and Eighteenth Armies attacked Gough's Fifth Army. German shelling of British rear areas severely hampered communications, while the extensive employment of gas largely subdued British batteries. Most of the defenders in the British Forward Zone were swiftly overrun. The fog that morning provided excellent cover for the infiltration tactics of the storm troops and prevented the British from bringing the full weight of their own artillery and machine-gun fire to bear on them as they approached and penetrated the main Battle Zone. In such conditions, those manning the British redoubts and strongpoints were left isolated and incapable of supporting each other.

The British front rapidly crumbled in many places, particularly on the Fifth Army's right in the sector only recently taken over from the French. Here the Germans burst through the Battle Zone, prompting Gough to pull the threatened British III Corps back to the line of the Crozat Canal. However, the Germans were not equally successful in all sectors. On their right, Below's Seventeenth Army – confronted by the more strongly held and better prepared positions of Byng's Third Army – made less satisfactory progress. Having decided against attacking the Flesquières salient frontally, the Germans failed to pinch it out as quickly as they hoped. The Second Army, under von der Marwitz, was likewise unable to achieve the planned breakthrough along its whole assault front. Even so, Haig and his senior commanders could not escape the fact that the BEF was now experiencing its biggest defensive crisis since 1914. Although the Germans had suffered close to 40,000 casualties on the first day, the British too had lost over 38,000 men and around 500 guns. Worryingly, the British casualty total included 21,000 who had been taken prisoner, a sure sign that, for many weary units and individuals, the reservoir of courage and endurance had finally run dry.

On 22 March, the second day of the offensive, the British front continued to fall apart. The normally confident and resourceful General Maxse, misunderstanding Gough's intentions, was too hasty in ordering his own XVIII Corps to withdraw to the Somme, a move which compelled XIX Corps, on his left, to retire in conformity. In a similar fashion, the right of Byng's Third Army was increasingly exposed by the disintegration of the Fifth Army's front further south. Nevertheless, Byng can perhaps be faulted for delaying the evacuation of the Flesquières salient for the best part of three days, a decision which resulted in unnecessary losses in the 2nd and 63rd (Royal Naval) Divisions and also contributed to the opening of a yawning gap at the junction of the British Third and Fifth Armies.

By the third day, the Germans had pushed some elements of the Fifth Army back more than 12 miles and Hutier's troops were thrusting westwards to secure crossings over the Crozat Canal and the Somme. As at other critical moments of the First World War, however, the Germans allowed unexpected but glittering tactical opportunities to deflect them from their original strategic aim. Thus, rather than reinforcing his stalled right wing to guarantee the success of the vital sweep to the north-west, Ludendorff strengthened the left. He also issued new orders which steered the Seventeenth Army towards Abbeville and St Pol and the Second Army westwards in the direction of Amiens. The Eighteenth Army – previously cast in the flank protection role – was to drive south-west towards Montdidier and Noyon in a much more deliberate effort to split the French and British armies. Instead of concentrating to administer a powerful left hook, the three German armies involved would, in essence, be moving in divergent directions.

Troops of the German Eighteenth Army massing in St Quentin, March 1918. (Mary Evans Picture Library)

Ludendorff's revised orders were based on the false assumption that the British Third and Fifth Armies would not recover. The BEF's immediate prospects were certainly bleak. Péronne was abandoned to the Germans on 23 March, and Bapaume was evacuated the following day. After the Fifth Army had retreated across the old Somme battlefield, Albert was lost on 26 March. The British Third Army, while largely maintaining a firm hold on its positions near Arras, was forced to draw back its right wing in order to stay in touch with the Fifth Army's left.

Whatever his intentions before 21 March, Haig was daily becoming ever more conscious of the Fifth Army's predicament and of the growing threat to Amiens, a rail centre of paramount importance to the BEF. In this situation he was therefore doubly distressed to receive what he considered to be woefully insufficient support from the French. Always the pessimist, Pétain feared that the Germans might still launch a big offensive against the French in Champagne. Above all, he was concerned with the need to shield Paris and was consequently prepared, if circumstances demanded, to withdraw south-west to Beauvais, even though this would take the French forces further away from the BEF. To be fair to Pétain, there also appeared

Men of the 20th British Division alongside troops of the 22nd French Division in hastily dug rifle pits near Nesle, 25 March 1918. (Mary Evans Picture Library)

to be a strong possibility that, if the situation deteriorated beyond repair, the BEF would retire to the north. On this occasion, however, Haig's desire for the French to cover Amiens, permitting him to retain enough reserves to protect the Channel ports, caused him to cast aside his normal objections to a unified command. Following appeals from Haig, an inter-Allied conference was hurriedly convened at Doullens on 26 March, when – again at Haig's insistence – Foch was given the necessary authority to co-ordinate the operations of the Allied armies on the Western Front. This was not an instant panacea, as the German Eighteenth Army's advance went on for a few more days, pushing the French out of Montdidier, yet Foch's appointment raised Allied morale and eased the pressure on Pétain and Haig. In addition, although French reserves did not arrive at once, there could no longer be any real doubt that the French would help to defend Amiens.

Ludendorff, whose handling of the offensive was increasingly erratic, had issued revised orders on 25 March, switching the main emphasis back to the right and centre. *Mars* – the attack against Arras – was launched on 28 April but was a costly failure. The awful truth for Ludendorff was that, when tested, the German Army was unable to sustain *prolonged* mobile operations in 1918. The German forces in France possessed a relatively small cavalry arm, no armoured cars and few tanks, while, after years of blockade, the horse-drawn and motorised transport they *did* have was not always up to the required standards. The heavy losses being suffered by the storm troops highlighted the widening gulf in quality between the élite assault formations and the 'trench divisions'. For all its skill, intellect and professionalism, the German General Staff had too often become distracted by short-term organisational and operational matters and had ultimately created an unbalanced army that could not fulfil its principal strategic purpose. The pace of the advance was dictated by the capacity of its foot soldiers and, by the end of March 1918, the German infantryman was nearing exhaustion, though cases of drunkenness and looting were not confined to the German Army alone. In a vain attempt to inject new life into the offensive, Ludendorff tinkered with his plan for the third time in a week, reducing its scope to the comparatively limited objective of taking Amiens. The blow was parried at Villers Bretonneux, approximately 10 miles east of Amiens, on 4 and 5 April by the 9th Australian Brigade and units of the British 18th Division, 58th Division and 3rd Cavalry Division. This setback convinced Ludendorff that *Michael* would not repay further sacrifice and on 5 April, its 16th day, he terminated the offensive.

Since 21 March the Germans had advanced some 40 miles, regaining much of the territory they had occupied two years before but they had not achieved the decisive result they had sought. British casualties in this period

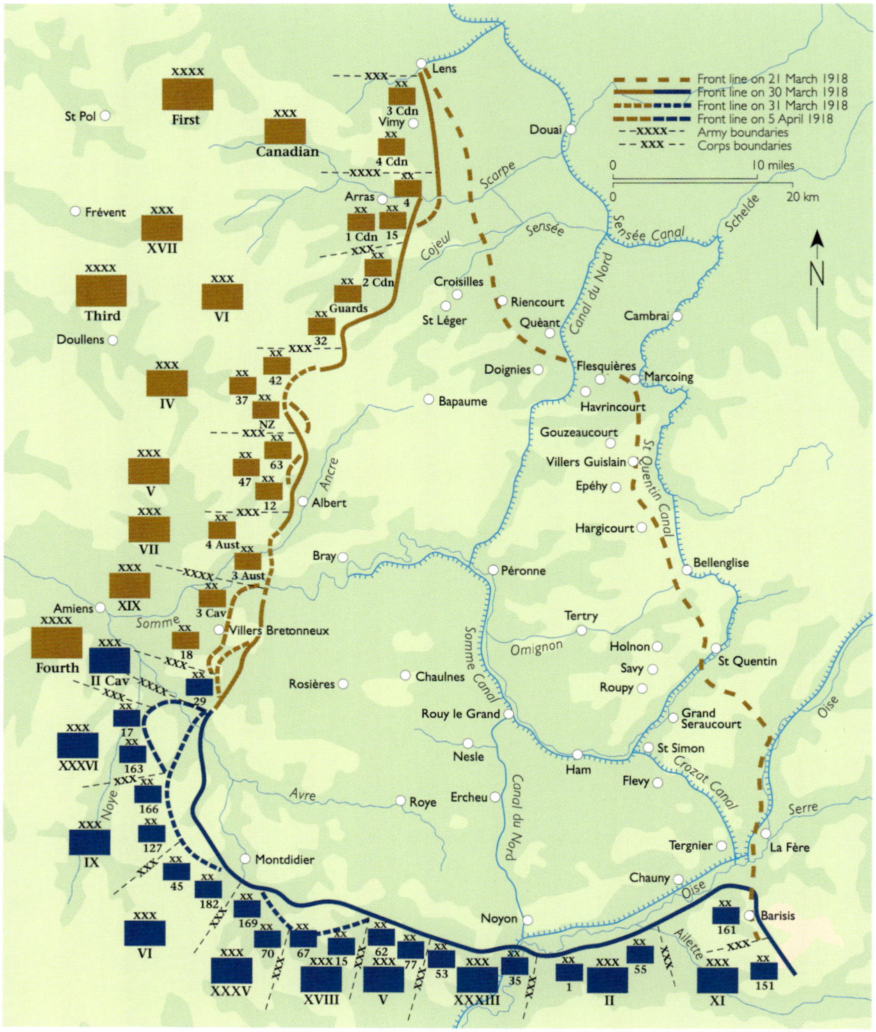

Operation *Michael*: the end of the offensive.

totalled 178,000, including 70,000 prisoners, and the French had lost approximately 77,000. German casualties numbered around 250,000, the many lost storm troops proving particularly difficult to replace. In the BEF Gough was removed from command of the Fifth Army. Though the odds had been stacked against him, he had, in fact, conducted a deft fighting retreat during which the Fifth Army's line may have been badly bent but was never fatally broken. Even so, he was singled out as the scapegoat for the Fifth Army's reverses and was succeeded on 28 March by General Sir Henry Rawlinson, who had spent the last month as British Military Representative at Versailles. In an apparent effort to wipe out the recent and unwarranted blot on its reputation, the Fifth Army was redesignated as the Fourth Army on 2 April.

'With our backs to the wall'

Ludendorff's order for the Flanders offensive to go ahead was given even before *Michael* was terminated. This second offensive, however, was scaled down from the original plan, this being symbolised by the revision of its code-name to *Georgette*. The modified plan called for the Sixth Army, under General von Quast, to strike between Givenchy and Armentières and drive north-west across the Lys valley in the direction of the important rail centre at Hazebrouck, which lay behind the junction of the British First and Second Armies. The following day, General Sixt von Arnim's Fourth Army was to attack further north towards Messines. While British defences on this front were better than those in Picardy on 21 March, the BEF's reserves were now dangerously thin. The Germans too were showing distinct signs of strain from the March fighting and the majority of their assault formations for *Georgette* were 'trench divisions' rather than 'attack divisions'.

After another classic Bruchmüller artillery bombardment, the Germans made early progress on 9 April, easily overcoming the feeble resistance of the dispirited 2nd Portuguese Division near Neuve Chapelle and advancing approximately 3½ miles at relatively small cost. On 10 April, when Arnim's Fourth Army added its weight to the offensive, Messines village fell and part of the Messines–Wytschaete ridge was yielded to the Germans. The British also withdrew from Armentières, which was situated between the converging German thrusts. Despite the Doullens agreement, Haig's pleas to Foch for assistance seemed initially to go unheeded, though even Foch was finding it difficult to force a gloomy and grudging Pétain to release the necessary reserves. As the Germans pushed on to within 5 miles of Hazebrouck, Haig knew that he again faced a crisis. On 11 April he issued a special Order of the Day, which stated:

> There is no other course open to us but to fight it out. Every position must be held to the last man: there must be no retirement. With our backs to the wall and believing in the justice of our cause each one of us must fight on to the end.

In the course of the next few days, the arrival in Flanders of the British 5th and 33rd Divisions and the 1st Australian Division eased the crisis on the Lys, and on 14 April Foch was named General-in-Chief of the Allied Armies, an additional step towards genuine unity of command. Now that he had greater control over the handling of Allied reserves, Foch rapidly introduced a rotation system permitting British divisions to move to quiet French sectors and release French formations to buttress threatened parts of the Allied line. In the British Second Army's zone of operations, the French had relieved British units along 9 miles of front by 19 April. Unfortunately for Plumer, who had returned from Italy to resume command of the Second Army, this French assistance came slightly too late. With the Germans consolidating their hold on Messines Ridge, Plumer was obliged to make the agonising but tactically necessary decision to abandon Passchendaele Ridge – won at such high cost the previous autumn – and, in an echo of May 1915, pulled his forces back to a less vulnerable perimeter closer to Ypres. The withdrawal was executed with all the Second Army's usual efficiency and thoroughness.

Ludendorff, meanwhile, was not only becoming daily more desperate but was also displaying increasing strategic inconsistency. The next significant German blow was not delivered in Flanders but took the form of a second, and belated, strike towards Amiens. This opened, on 24 April, with another attack on Villers Bretonneux. The attack was preceded by a brief artillery bombardment, which included a mixture of mustard gas and high-explosive shells, and was made in dense fog. Supported by 13 A7V tanks, the Germans quickly overwhelmed many of the inexperienced young conscripts in the British 8th Division, tore open a 3-mile gap in the defences and seized Villers Bretonneux. In front of Cachy, three British Mark IV tanks engaged three German A7Vs in the first ever tank-versus-tank combat. With negligible help from the French when it was most needed, Rawlinson and his subordinate commanders organised an audacious counter-attack, which took place that night. By dawn on 25 April – the third anniversary of the Gallipoli landings

Portuguese troops holding breastworks near Laventie early in 1918. (Mary Evans Picture Library)

A line of men, blinded by tear gas, at an advanced dressing station near Béthune, 10 April 1918. (Topfoto)

– the 13th and 15th Australian Brigades, assisted on the right by the British 18th and 58th Divisions, had driven the Germans back eastwards and, in a brilliant enveloping movement, had 'pinched out' Villers Bretonneux, which was largely cleared of the enemy by midday.

In Flanders the Allied defence had been less resilient for the same day, 25 April, the crack German Alpine Corps wrested possession of Mount Kemmel from the French. It was to be the last meaningful German success in the *Georgette* operation. On 29 April, the Germans launched a final attack against British and French positions between Ypres and Bailleul but their gains were insignificant. Like *Michael* before it, *Georgette* had run out of steam and, late in the evening of 29 April, Ludendorff suspended the Flanders offensive. Yet again Ypres, Amiens and the Channel ports had been saved by the determined resistance of the Allies.

Blücher and *Gneisenau*

Both sides desperately needed a pause in operations after *Georgette*. For the three major armies, manpower was a critical problem. The Germans had suffered around 380,000 casualties since 21 March, while the British had lost almost 240,000 men and the French some 92,000. Nevertheless, the Germans, with 206 divisions against 160, retained the strategic initiative on the Western Front. Ten of the BEF's available divisions were deemed to be exhausted, eight of them being reduced, for a short period, to cadre strength with just ten officers and 45 men per battalion. The American Expeditionary Force, of course, represented the long-term solution to the

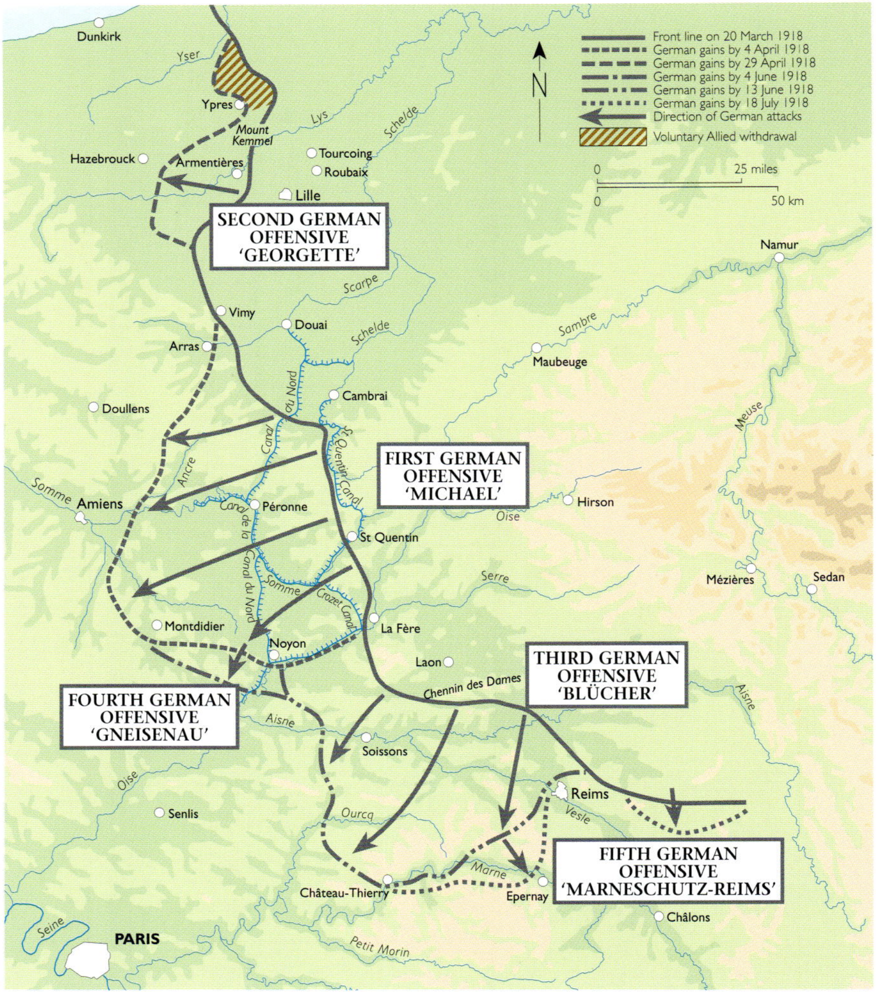

The German offensives, March–July 1918.

manpower difficulties currently being experienced by the Allies. By 1 May the AEF in France numbered 430,000 officers and men. Each American division, with 28,000 men, was two or three times the size of British or French divisions but, as yet, the US 1st Division alone had reached the front line.

The strength of the AEF increased spectacularly to more than 650,000 by the end of May. Although he relented a little during the successive crises of the spring and early summer, Pershing continued to rebuff attempts to incorporate American soldiers in British and French units and strove, as far as possible, to keep the AEF intact as a distinct component of the Allied forces, so that it could ultimately undertake offensive operations as a national army under its own commanders.

The British forces had unquestionably been badly hurt by the German March and April offensives but had survived these gigantic blows mostly without external assistance. As a result, the BEF's morale rapidly recovered from the trials of the past few months and its optimism correspondingly soared. In contrast, Ludendorff was disturbed by evidence of a sharp decline in the discipline and morale of German troops, many of whom now tended to loiter around captured Allied supply dumps. Indeed, certain divisions had shown a marked reluctance to attack during the recent operations on the Lys. Some influential figures in the German Army, including Lossberg, expressed doubts concerning the wisdom of launching more offensives. Ludendorff conceded that the German Army could no longer sustain two simultaneous offensives and that delays between big attacks were inevitable while the great German artillery 'battering train' was redeployed. However, he also knew that Germany's numerical superiority would not last and he must therefore order further offensives to achieve the elusive victory before American manpower finally and irrevocably gave the Allies the strategic advantage. For Ludendorff, the main aim was still the defeat of the BEF in Flanders but, even during the closing stages of *Georgette*, he had already concluded that it was first necessary to draw French reserves away from that sector, in order to deprive Haig of their support at the decisive moment.

German troops advancing through Pont Arcy, Aisne sector, 27 May 1918. (IWM Q55010)

With this in mind, Ludendorff chose to unleash the next major offensive – code-named Operation *Blücher* – against the French along the Chemin des Dames on the Aisne. Prospects of a German success here were enhanced by the fact that General Duchêne, the commander of the French Sixth Army, had failed to apply Pétain's instructions regarding flexible defence in depth and had placed too many troops in forward positions. In a twist of fate, five battered British divisions had been moved to the Aisne to recuperate under Foch's rotation scheme and three of them – the 8th, 21st and 50th Divisions – were in the front line.

The German artillery plan for *Blücher* was once more prepared by the brilliant Bruchmüller, who had been nicknamed *Durchbruchmüller* ('Breakthrough Müller') by German soldiers. The 160-minute bombardment by nearly 4,000 guns which opened the Aisne offensive on 27 May was the densest yet in 1918 in terms of batteries per mile and has since been described as Bruchmüller's masterpiece. By the end of the first day eight French and British divisions had been virtually destroyed and the Germans

had advanced some 12 miles – an amazing distance even in the changed conditions of 1918. On 28 May General von Boehn's Seventh Army seized Soissons and by the evening of 30 May it had reached the Marne close to Château-Thierry, less than 60 miles from Paris.

Up to this point, *Blücher* had surpassed expectations, tempting the German high command to forget that the offensive had been conceived primarily as a diversion. As Ludendorff pondered how best to capitalise upon Boehn's dazzling progress, the Allies blocked the enemy advance. Ominously for the Germans, the United States 2nd and 3rd Divisions entered the line alongside the French in the battle for Château-Thierry. On 6 June, US Marines of the 2nd Division counter-attacked German forces at Belleau Wood. The Germans now occupied a deep salient which, because of its extended flanks, was tricky to defend. Damage to railways and roads also exacerbated German supply problems. Aiming to enlarge the salient, secure better defensive positions and suck in even more French reserves, Ludendorff launched a fourth offensive, code-named *Gneisenau*, towards

The aftermath of a mustard gas attack on the Western Front in August 1918: wounded soldiers are shown being led by a medical orderly in John Singer Sargent's famous painting *Gassed.* (IWM Art 1460)

the Matz between Noyon and Montdidier. Here, like Duchêne on the Aisne, General Humbert, the commander of the French Third Army, had crowded too many troops into the forward zone. At the start of these operations on 9 June, the German Eighteenth Army, under Hutier, once more achieved dramatic first-day gains, advancing around 6 miles. On 11 June, five divisions of General Mangin's French Tenth Army, with support from ground-attack aircraft and tanks, delivered a furious counterstroke against Hutier's left flank and brought *Gneisenau* to a shuddering halt. For Hindenburg and Ludendorff both time and strategic options were rapidly diminishing.

Hitting back

Despite halting the *Blücher* and *Gneisenau* offensives, the French had little cause for self-congratulation. The loss of the Chemin des Dames so soon after Foch's appointment as General-in-Chief had been a chastening experience while some members of Foch's own staff could scarcely conceal their mounting impatience with Pétain's pessimism and sluggish reactions. After coming near to collapse on the Aisne, the French were in no position to deride the BEF's recent performance in Picardy and Flanders. Haig's stock rose accordingly over the next few months, giving him greater influence in the shaping of Allied strategy and operations. At the same time, Ludendorff's problems worsened. In at least three of the four offensives to date he had permitted dazzling initial gains to distract him from his original strategic aim or to tempt him into continuing operations longer than was sensible. He was not the first to ignore the lesson that modern railway systems almost always enabled defenders to bring reserves to a crucial sector before the attackers could push sufficient men and equipment across the battlefield to exploit any breach. German combat troops remained capable of heroic endeavours but their morale had been progressively and irreparably damaged by the failure of four successive offensives. Their sufferings were magnified when, in June, the Spanish influenza pandemic of 1918–1919 started to exact its relentless and terrible toll on units already enfeebled by food shortages, further reducing the strength of German infantry formations.

The first American attack of the war had taken place as early as 28 May, when the US 1st Division seized Cantigny, near Montdidier. By 26 June American troops had also cleared Belleau Wood. In its operations at Cantigny, Belleau Wood and Château-Thierry, the AEF had incurred more than 11,000 casualties and fought with much the same mixture of patriotism, bravery and tactical inexperience that had characterised the BEF of July 1916. Symbolically, however, the Americans had faced hardened German units and had beaten them.

At Hamel, near Amiens, on 4 July, the Australian Corps carried out a model minor attack which offered the Allies equal, if not greater, encouragement for the future. Formed in November 1917 from the five Australian divisions on the Western Front, the Australian Corps had been commanded since 31 May by Lieutenant-General Sir John Monash, who succeeded General Sir William Birdwood when the latter took over the reconstituted Fifth Army. A civil engineer before the war, Monash quickly demonstrated a capacity for painstaking and innovative operational planning that made him one of the BEF's most eminent corps commanders. Monash likened a modern battle plan to an orchestral score in which each 'instrument', or arm – artillery, tanks, aeroplanes and infantry – played a vital part in creating a harmonious whole. His insistence on teamwork and all-arms co-operation was keenly supported by the Fourth Army commander, Henry Rawlinson, who had himself learned from the brutal lessons of 1916 and was to handle his forces with distinction in the weeks and months to come.

In attacking at Hamel, Monash and Rawlinson hoped to remove a troublesome dent in the British line near Villers Bretonneux, thereby securing a straighter barrage line for future operations and depriving the Germans of a key vantage point on the spur above Hamel village. The battle plan embodied Monash's belief that infantry should no longer be expected to sacrifice themselves in bloody frontal assaults but should be given the maximum

Before the attack at Hamel, men of the US 33rd Division are photographed resting near Corbie on 3 July 1918. (IWM)

possible help by mechanised resources, including tanks, machine-guns, artillery, mortars and aircraft. A total of 60 new Mark V fighting tanks and 12 supply tanks were made available for the Hamel operation and special combined training gave the Australians a renewed trust in this weapon that had been absent since the bitter experience at Bullecourt in April 1917. Monash was therefore able to economise on infantry, deploying only eight battalions – mainly from the 4th Australian Division – along a 6,000-yard front of attack. Any sound made by the tanks during their assembly would be deliberately drowned by the noise of artillery fire and aircraft and, in the assault, the tanks would advance level with the infantry under a creeping barrage.

With the attack scheduled for America's Independence Day, it was intended to use ten companies of the US 33rd Division, then attached to the British Fourth Army for training. Almost at the last minute, Pershing refused to sanction their participation. The six rearmost companies were duly withdrawn but, to avoid further delays or disruption to the plan, Haig, Rawlinson and Monash stood firm with regard to the remaining four. In the event, the Australians and Americans captured all their objectives, together with 1,472 prisoners and 171 machine-guns, in just over 90 minutes, at a cost of fewer than 1,000 casualties. The supply of ammunition to forward troops by parachute was one of several elements of the Hamel plan which made it an invaluable blueprint for future set-piece assaults. Pershing, however, became more determined than ever to restrict or oppose French or British operational control of American formations.

Counterstroke on the Marne

A strictly defensive strategy would have been the wisest course for Ludendorff to follow by early July. However, he still hoped to persuade the Allies to seek a peace settlement on terms favourable to Germany and, with this object in view, he decided to embark upon another offensive. The defeat of the BEF in Flanders remained his overriding objective but Ludendorff was aware of Allied strength there and chose instead to make a further attempt to lure Allied reserves to a different sector. To this end, on 15 July, the Germans struck either side of Reims. The German Seventh Army, commanded by Boehn, encountered lively resistance from the US 3rd Division yet, by nightfall, had established a bridgehead 4 miles deep across the Marne. Mudra's First Army and Einem's Third Army were far less successful east of Reims. On this front, General Gouraud's French Fourth Army had fully understood and applied Pétain's strictures about elastic defence and firmly checked German progress.

Three days later, on 18 July, the French and Americans delivered a major counterstroke, which had been prepared by General Mangin, the aggressive commander of the French Tenth Army. With the French Sixth Army on

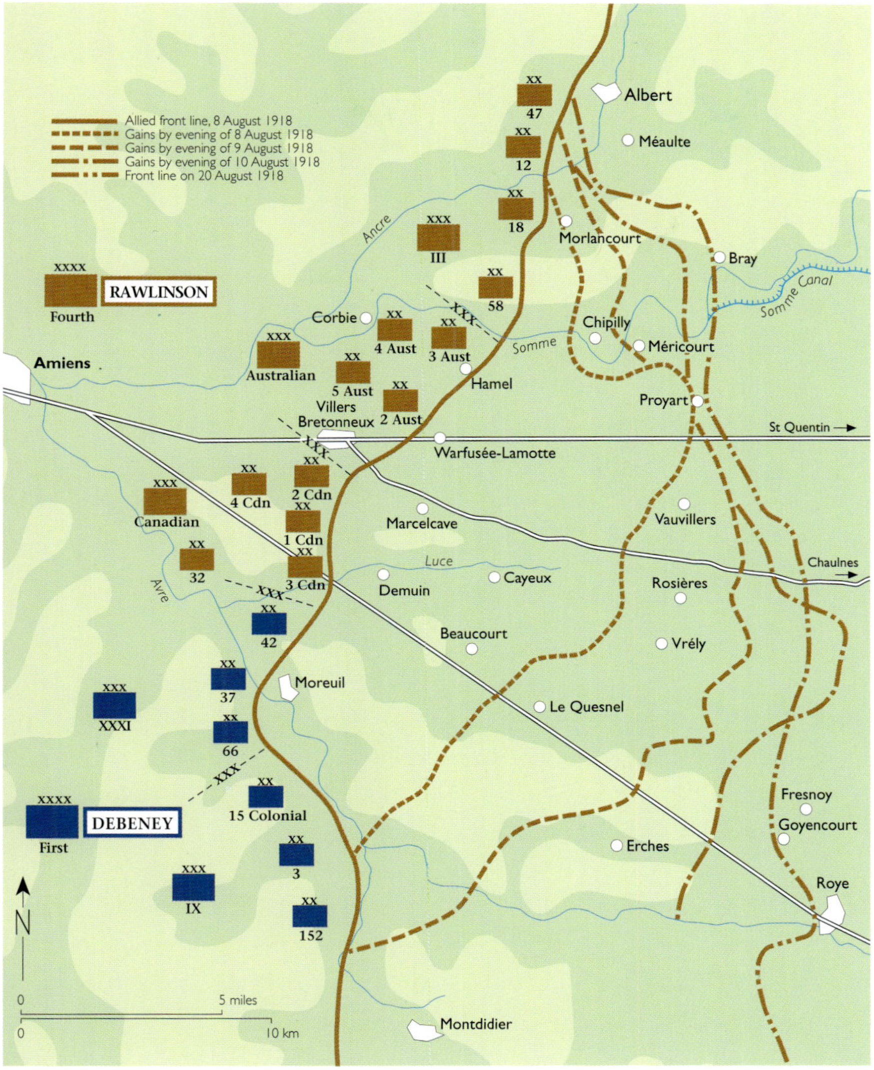

The battle of Amiens, August 1918.

their right, Mangin's units assailed the western face of the German salient between the Aisne and the Marne. The surprise counter-offensive was spearheaded by the US 1st and 2nd Divisions and supported by 225 tanks, a large proportion of which were new Renault light tanks. Within 48 hours the French Tenth Army pushed forward approximately 6 miles. By 6 August the Germans had suffered losses of 793 guns and 168,000 men, including 29,000 prisoners. Ludendorff's fifth and final gamble had ultimately proved as fruitless as its predecessors.

Like Moltke four years before, Ludendorff came close to nervous collapse in late July 1918. Increasingly erratic and uncertain, he was rapidly losing his grasp of strategic realities. Although the Germans no longer held the military initiative, Ludendorff refused to acknowledge that all hopes of offensive victories had vanished. He therefore spurned Lossberg's shrewd advice that the German Army should withdraw to the relative security of the Hindenburg Line. Early in August he regained his composure to some degree, proposing a future policy whereby the German Army would return to its former defensive posture but would continue to sap Allied morale and manpower by making sudden small-scale attacks, in specially selected sectors, from positions of considerable strength.

The black day of the German Army

The Germans were allowed no time to implement Ludendorff's revised strategy. The indefatigable Haig, whose single-mindedness contrasted sharply with Ludendorff's progressive instability, now sensed that Germany might, after all, be defeated in 1918. He had already obtained Foch's approval, in broad terms, of a plan submitted by Rawlinson for a larger-scale version of the Hamel attack, the chief aim this time being to eject the Germans from their positions between the Somme and the Avre and thus remove the lingering threat to Amiens. On 8 August, a few miles east of that city, Rawlinson's Fourth Army, with General Debeney's French First Army on its right, dealt the German Second and Eighteenth Armies a devastating blow. Ludendorff subsequently described 8 August 1918 as 'the black day of the German Army in the history of this war'.

Leading parts in the Allied attack were assigned to the Australian and Canadian Corps. Whereas British divisions were frequently switched from one corps or army to another, the Australians and Canadians kept theirs together as distinct national bodies, making it easier for them to maintain high morale and to disseminate tactical lessons learned on the battlefield. Had the movement of the Canadian Corps to the Amiens sector been detected, the Germans would have realised that an offensive was coming, and, to prevent this, two Canadian battalions remained in Flanders to generate false signals traffic. This measure – which would be echoed in the deception plans adopted before D-Day in 1944 – typified the secrecy which underpinned Rawlinson's assembly of the required men, weapons and equipment.

The Amiens attack also illustrated the progress wrought throughout the BEF in tactics and all-arms co-operation since the Somme offensive of 1916. The employment of aircraft in a ground-attack role, as well as on their normal artillery-spotting and reconnaissance duties, added extra bite to the offensive while more extensive use of wireless helped to improve battlefield communications. Three hundred and forty-two Mark V fighting tanks would lead the attack with the infantry, supported by 120 supply tanks, and, for the exploitation phase, 72 of the lighter Medium Mark A 'Whippet' models were allotted to work with the cavalry. Infantry platoons – now generally comprising two half-platoons, each with Lewis gunners, riflemen and rifle grenadiers – were better able to adapt to the more fluid conditions of 1918 and, being more self-contained and possessing greater firepower than before, were capable of sustaining the momentum of the attack for longer periods. As at Hamel, however, the bedrock of Rawlinson's planning was the emphasis placed on teamwork.

A numbing surprise bombardment from 2,070 guns, arranged by the Fourth Army's chief gunner, Major-General C. E. D. Budworth – Britain's answer to Bruchmüller – announced the opening of the Amiens attack at 4.20am on 8 August. This time the thick morning mist – so prevalent in Picardy – favoured the Allies. The preparations of the British III Corps, on the left, had been disrupted on 6 August, when the Germans reacted to an earlier Australian raid by counter-attacking near Morlancourt and were correspondingly more alert on this stretch of the front. Despite these unpropitious circumstances, III Corps managed to progress 2 miles, though its main thrust did not get beyond the first objective. The Australian Corps, in the centre, achieved a 6-mile advance while the fresher Canadians – who had not been seriously engaged in the spring fighting – pushed forward up to 8 miles. The progress of the French First Army, on the right of the Canadians, was less impressive. On 8 August the Germans lost 400 guns and 27,000 men, including 15,000 prisoners. The British Fourth Army's casualties were under 9,000.

By 12 August, as German resistance hardened in this sector, the Fourth Army's advance slowed. Only half a dozen British tanks were still in action. Nevertheless, the manner of the Allied victory at Amiens mattered more than its scale. The BEF's combat skills and confidence were growing daily at a time when the German Army as a whole was clearly in sharp decline. Their artillery and machine-gunners, and some individual German divisions, continued to fight with the old determination and professionalism but defences were no longer built or maintained with the same care and a morose and fatalistic mood had descended upon many units. As German reserves and reinforcements approached the line, they were now greeted with cries of 'You're prolonging the war!' or dubbed 'blacklegs' by troops being relieved.

Return to Albert and Bapaume

Bereft of confidence and long-term solutions following the Allied onslaught at Amiens, Ludendorff knew that the war must be ended. The Kaiser agreed and, at a conference at Spa on 14 August, instructed Admiral von Hintze, the Foreign Secretary, to open peace negotiations through the Queen of the Netherlands. Even so, as long as its forces continued to occupy large areas of Belgium and northern France, Germany might still hope to bargain from a position of some strategic strength. Ludendorff was therefore determined that, wherever possible, the existing front must be held. Influential German staff officers such as Lossberg and Kuhl believed that the most logical course was to withdraw, as in 1917, to a more defensible line behind the Somme but, for the moment, their arguments fell on deaf ears.

In stark contrast, the BEF's senior commanders were now much more flexible and receptive to sound tactical and strategic counsel from subordinates. In 1916 their response to stiffening opposition was often simply that of ordering repeated attacks in the same sector. Two years later, when German resistance increased at Amiens, Rawlinson heeded the advice of the Canadian Corps commander, Lieutenant-General Sir Arthur Currie, and recommended switching the point of the attack to the Third Army's front further north. If done soon, this would throw the Germans off balance, prevent them from concentrating reserves in one sector and deny them the time to establish new defences. Haig's support for these proposals signalled that the BEF was no longer invariably tempted to prolong offensives unnecessarily in the quest for a breakthrough and would henceforth inflict more significant damage on the Germans by unleashing a rolling series of attacks on different parts of the front. Foch initially wanted the British Fourth Army to continue battering the German positions east of Amiens but by 15 August he had allowed himself to be persuaded by Haig to accept Rawlinson's suggestions. The fact that Foch yielded relatively quickly to Haig's stand in this matter indicated that the BEF, in the latter half of 1918, was setting the pace of Allied operations. As the historians Robin Prior and Trevor Wilson have noted, this was also the last occasion on which Foch would attempt to issue orders to the British Commander-in-Chief.

The level of French performance in August was uneven though Mangin's Tenth Army was as vigorous as ever. After preparatory operations between Soissons and the Oise, Mangin's forces attacked northwards on 20 August, pushing on between 2 and 3 miles and capturing more than 8,000 prisoners from the German Ninth Army in the battle of Noyon. Ludendorff saw this as 'another black day' of 'heavy and irreplaceable losses'. On 21 August, as decided the previous week, the BEF shifted the main weight of its own offensive to Byng's sector, between Arras and the old Somme battlefield. That day, the British Third Army pushed the Germans back around 4,000 yards and, on 22 August, Rawlinson's Fourth Army retook Albert. Haig, however, sensed that greater triumphs were within reach, calling for 'all ranks to act with the utmost boldness and resolution in order to get full advantage from the present favourable situation'. Spurred on by their Commander-in-Chief, the British Third and Fourth Armies renewed their attacks along a 33-mile front on 23 August. Three days later, the right wing of General Sir Henry

Horne's First Army – to which the Canadian Corps had now returned – joined the offensive by assaulting the German defences east of Arras and south of the Scarpe.

Reeling from these successive attacks, Ludendorff was obliged to pull the Army Groups of Boehn and Crown Prince Rupprecht back to an intermediate line running from the heights north-east of Noyon to the ground east of Bapaume, the latter town being re-entered by the New Zealand Division of Byng's Third Army on 29 August. Simultaneously the Germans abandoned their salient on the Lys in Flanders, surrendering much of the territory won during the *Georgette* offensive in April. Mount Kemmel passed back into British possession and by 4 September the Second and Fifth Armies had moved forward to a line stretching from Voormezeele in the north to Givenchy, near the La Bassée Canal.

The Dominion formations under Haig's command did not rest on their laurels, carrying out yet more outstanding operations as August gave way to September. In a brilliant feat of arms on 31 August and 1 September the 2nd Australian Division, under Major-General Rosenthal, stormed and held the formidable German bastion of Mont St Quentin, facilitating the capture of Péronne, the suburbs of which were cleared of Germans by midday on 2 September. That morning the Canadian Corps broke through the Drocourt-Quéant Position, or *Wotan Stellung*, south-east of Arras. As these vital points between the Somme and the Sensée fell in turn, Ludendorff's only option was to order a retirement to the Hindenburg Line – a course of action which Kuhl and Lossberg had advocated weeks before.

Closing up to the Hindenburg Line

In the first week of September, there were increasing signs that many German soldiers were rapidly losing confidence in their military leadership. Returning to the front from sick leave, Crown Prince Rupprecht recorded on 2 September that a troop train had been seen at Nuremberg bearing the inscription 'Slaughter cattle for Wilhelm and Sons!' The German Army, nonetheless, remained a tough adversary and its front-line units still possessed sufficient collective tactical skill, patriotism and doggedness to exact a heavy toll in casualties for most local Allied successes. In the more fluid operations of August and September 1918, the Germans no longer relied principally upon linear trench systems – at least not west of the Hindenburg Line – and, during this phase of the fighting, machine-gunners provided the backbone of their resistance. All the same, as the BEF drew nearer to the outpost system of the Hindenburg Line, it faced the Alpine Corps and other formations which, because they were known to be dependable, were specially picked by the German high command to hold these vital positions.

Between 4 and 26 September the BEF battled its way forward through the strong outpost defences around Epéhy and Havrincourt to secure a suitable jumping-off line for the coming assault on the main Hindenburg Line. Since 8 August, Haig's forces had driven the Germans back some 25 miles on a 40-mile front but had again paid a high price, the First, Third and Fourth Armies having together suffered nearly 190,000 casualties in this period. However, the gathering pace of the offensive – in marked contrast to the operations of 1916 and 1917 – and the growing feeling that victory might at last be in sight made such losses somehow easier to bear.

The historian Gregory Blaxland once remarked that, in the operations of the British First, Third and Fourth Armies during August and September, the Canadian and Australian Corps 'gored the German line like the horns of a bull, while the various British divisions, and one New Zealand, gave plenty of weight to the thrust of the forehead'. The outstanding deeds of the Australians and Canadians have, perhaps, been allowed to overshadow the invaluable, if often less spectacular, contribution of British divisions to the August–September operations. The élite German storm divisions in the March, April and May offensives had undoubtedly achieved brilliant initial progress but had also invariably run out of steam after a few days.

Australian artillery in action near Hamel, 9 August 1918. (Mary Evans Picture Library)

From 8 August, on the other hand, the majority of British divisions demonstrated the ability to maintain a steady pressure on the enemy for periods of up to six weeks. This unrelenting pressure, made possible by the British soldier's traditional powers of endurance and sheer bloody-minded persistence, ultimately counted far more than dazzling breakthroughs in hastening the Imperial German Army's downfall.

It must be remembered that, by this stage of the war, most British infantry divisions contained many inexperienced young conscripts. However, co-operation between infantry and gunners had vastly improved since 1916 and the Royal Artillery was now consistently capable of shepherding even the greenest recruits towards their objectives behind creeping barrages of immense power, accuracy and depth. As officers at all levels in the BEF were given additional opportunities to display more imagination and personal initiative in the semi-open warfare of late 1918, so front-line troops gained extra faith in their leaders. But arguably the most important ingredient in the BEF's new recipe for success was the emphasis placed on teamwork and all-arms co-operation. In its organisation and infrastructure, its weapons and equipment, and its tactics, the BEF now had a much better overall balance than the German Army and thus found it easier to adapt to changing circumstances. Should one of its arms fail in any given operation, a combination of others could generally be called upon to retrieve the situation and ensure eventual success.

Foch, Haig and Pershing

Foch had sought, for some time, to widen Allied offensive efforts. The plan he placed before Pétain, Pershing and Haig on 24 July was intended to eject the Germans from the various salients created by their spring and summer attacks and also to remove the German threat to the Paris–Nancy and Paris–Amiens railway communications. Considering Foch's long-held belief in the virtues of the offensive at all costs, these aims were comparatively modest, though he accepted Pershing's proposal that the recently formed American First Army could reduce the potential menace to the Paris–Nancy railway by striking at the older German salient at St Mihiel. Early in August Foch was elevated to the rank of Marshal but, during that month, the amount of strategic and tactical co-ordination he actually attained fell far short of what was required of a Generalissimo. Of the French generals in the field, only the combative Mangin had yet inflicted significant damage on the Germans and the sluggish performance of Debeney – who commanded the French First Army on the British Fourth Army's right flank – drove Rawlinson to distraction. In truth, Foch had so far failed to exert sufficient authority over Pétain in order to infuse the French armies with the necessary urgency and dynamism.

In this light, Foch was patently unfair in making repeated demands for the BEF to intensify its pressure on some of the toughest sectors of the entire Western Front, particularly as Haig's forces were currently bearing the largest, and most effective, share of Allied offensive operations. Haig was now using a headquarters train to shuttle him between the sectors where the BEF was most heavily engaged and had a much better 'feel' for the progress of the battle than he had possessed in earlier years. Sensing, perhaps more acutely than anyone, that victory might now be possible in 1918, Haig suggested to Foch, during the last week of August, that the Americans should be playing a bigger part in the ongoing offensive. Pershing and his staff saw the eradication of the St Mihiel salient as the precursor to a thrust eastward towards Metz. Haig, on the other hand, urged that more far-reaching results would be achieved if the Americans were to drive north-west, through the Argonne and Meuse valley, towards the railway hub of Mézières. An attack in this direction would converge with the BEF's own proposed push through and beyond the Hindenburg Line in the Cambrai–St Quentin area.

Foch had been thinking along similar lines for some days when Haig incorporated his advice in a letter to the Generalissimo on 27 August. Haig's arguments appear to have helped to crystallise Foch's strategy for, from this time onwards – under the slogan *Tout le monde à la battaille!* ('Everyone into battle!') – he clearly began to envisage operations which consisted of a rolling succession of brutal and interconnected blows with broader objectives than merely freeing railway centres or eliminating salients. Certainly, after an inconclusive and sometimes fractious meeting with Pershing on 30 August, Foch left a note with the American commander which mirrored Haig's ideas and proposed that all Allied forces should join 'in one great convergent attack'. Pershing understood the advantages of an attack towards Mézières but strenuously objected to Foch's suggestion that up to 16 American divisions should participate with the French Second and Fourth Armies in operations astride the Aisne and in the Meuse–Argonne region. He hastily reminded Foch that he could not back any plan that involved employing his formations piecemeal with other Allied armies. 'I do insist that the American Army must be employed as a whole … and not four or five divisions here and six or seven there', he wrote on 31 August.

Two days later, after 'considerable sparring', Foch and Pershing reached a compromise. The attack at St Mihiel would go ahead first, but its objectives would be limited to the *Michel Stellung*, the German defence line which stretched across the base of the salient. The American Expeditionary Force would then shift its main attention to the Meuse–Argonne sector where, under Pershing's command, it would play an appropriate role in the general Allied offensive. Having successfully stood his ground on the central issue,

Pershing subsequently permitted *some* American divisions to serve with other Allied formations, such as the British Fourth Army, elsewhere on the Western Front.

St Mihiel

On 12 September, following a four-hour bombardment by 3,000 artillery pieces – mostly French, though half were fired by American gunners – seven American and two French divisions attacked the western and southern sides of the salient at St Mihiel. Other French formations assaulted the salient's 'nose'. Because of lapses in Allied security, the Germans were expecting an attack and had begun to pull back yet they could not prevent the AEF from registering a notable success in the first major American-led operation of the war. Within 30 hours, and at a cost of about 7,000 American casualties, Pershing's troops seized 460 German guns and 15,000 prisoners. No less impressive was the subsequent transfer of around 428,000 men and their equipment north-westwards to the Meuse–Argonne sector in under two weeks. The officer largely responsible for this remarkable feat of logistics was Colonel George C. Marshall of the First Army's Operations Section – a future US Chief of Staff and Secretary of State.

Australians of the 24th Battalion AIF photographed five minutes before they attacked at Mont St Quentin, 1 September 1918. (IWM)

As the detailed planning for the general Allied offensive on the Western Front was being completed, there were momentous developments in other theatres. In Palestine, Allenby's units had achieved a decisive breakthrough at Megiddo between 19 and 21 September, forcing the Turkish armies there into headlong retreat, while in Salonika the Bulgarians would shortly seek an armistice as a result of a vigorous offensive which the Allies had launched on 15 September. By the last week of the month, the Allied commanders were ready to initiate four separate but co-ordinated attacks on the Western Front over a four-day period. The first blow would be struck between Reims and the Meuse by French and American formations on 26 September. Next day, 27 September, the British First and Third Armies were to push towards Cambrai. On 28 September the rolling offensive would extend to the extreme left flank, where an attack between the Lys and the sea would be opened by a composite Flanders Army Group, commanded by Albert, King of the Belgians, and comprising the Belgian Field Army, ten divisions of Plumer's British Second Army and nine French divisions, three of which were cavalry formations. Finally, on 29 September, Rawlinson's British Fourth Army, supported on its right by the French First Army, was to assault the Hindenburg Line near St Quentin.

Hammer blows

The opening blow of the general Allied offensive – administered by the US First Army and French Fourth Army in the Meuse–Argonne region – had an immediate impact as the Americans advanced up to 3 miles on the first day. However, this rate of progress was not maintained. The Germans had sited defensive positions with their usual expertise in the thickly wooded and steeply sloping terrain between the Argonne Forest and the Meuse. Supply problems quickly multiplied in this testing countryside as Allied losses also grew. The undoubted courage of the American troops – like that of the British on the Somme in 1916 – could not always make up for their tactical naïveté or shortcomings in staff work. By the end of the month, after five days of hard fighting, the maximum penetration achieved by the Allies in the Meuse–Argonne sector was only about 8 miles.

On 27 September it was the turn of the British First and Third Armies to strike west of Cambrai. The right-hand formation of Horne's First Army was the Canadian Corps, under Lieutenant-General Sir Arthur Currie. The Canadians faced the Canal du Nord, which had been under construction in 1914 and was still dry in parts. To make the most of one of these dry stretches and thus avoid the more difficult sector directly ahead, Currie secured the approval of Haig and a more lukewarm Horne for an audacious plan involving an initial side-step to the south and a crossing on a narrow

2,600-yard front. Once over the canal, the Canadians would then spread out fanwise in a north-easterly direction on a front of over 15,000 yards. Currie's gamble paid off handsomely as the First and Third Armies thrust forward 6 miles in two days. Thereafter, stiffer German opposition was encountered and hard fighting was required but the Canadian success on the Canal du Nord opened the way for a drive against Cambrai.

The start of the offensive in Flanders on 28 September was equally promising. The first day saw the Allies under King Albert break out of the old Ypres Salient, reclaim Passchendaele Ridge and pass beyond the limits of the BEF's advance of the previous year. On 29 September Plumer's units recaptured Messines Ridge and reached Warneton on the Lys. Further north the Belgians were now only 2 miles from Roulers. The Allies progressed approximately 9 miles in this phase of operations in Flanders but then slowed down as German reserves arrived and the familiar problems of rain and mud returned. In these deteriorating conditions, the French and Belgians on the left were particularly handicapped by the inadequacy of the arrangements made by King Albert's French Chief of Staff, General Degoutte, for transporting supplies across the broken and swampy landscape of the former Ypres Salient. On 2 October another glimpse of the future was offered by an air drop of 13 tons of rations to forward Belgian and French troops. However, the overriding need to establish better lines of communication and reorganise the supply services in the French and Belgian sectors compelled the Allies to suspend major offensive operations in Flanders between 5 and 14 October.

Infantry of the 45th Battalion AIF following a creeping barrage near Le Verguier, 18 September 1918. (IWM E(AUS) 3260)

Through the Hindenburg Line

The British Fourth Army's great set-piece assault on the Hindenburg Line commenced on 29 September after a four-day preparatory bombardment by 1,637 guns and howitzers firing some 750,000 shells. The attack was launched along a 12-mile front between Vendhuille and St Quentin. Facing the IX Corps on the Fourth Army's right wing was an intimidating stretch of the St Quentin Canal, which here was about 35ft wide and passed through steep-sided, almost vertical cuttings with banks up to 60ft high. It was therefore decided to make the principal thrust further north, between Vendhuille and Bellicourt, where the canal ran underground in a tunnel. This important assault sector was entrusted to the experienced but tired Australian Corps, which had been temporarily combined with the untried US II Corps for this attack.

To the consternation of Rawlinson and Monash, the raw US 27th Division was unable to take three important German outposts in a preliminary operation on 27 September. Because it was feared that artillery fire might hit American troops who might still be holding forward positions, these strongpoints were left largely untouched for two days and, for the same reason, the 27th Division dispensed with a creeping barrage for the first 1,000 yards of its advance on 29 September itself. Thirty-four accompanying tanks were of little assistance, as 11 received direct hits and seven stuck in shell holes or trenches. Consequently, Major-General Gellibrand's 3rd Australian Division, which had been expected to take part in the exploitation rather than the assault phase, was drawn in to the ferocious struggle much sooner than planned. To the right, the American 30th Division achieved better early progress, seizing Bellicourt by noon, but did not properly mop up all the positions it had overrun. Hence, when the 5th Australian division tried to move through the Americans, it met heavy machine-gun fire from posts which the Americans had failed to clear, also becoming involved in a tough fight as it strove to push on, with the Americans, beyond Bellicourt and Nauroy. Though the Australians and Americans had advanced nearly 4,000 yards and now controlled the southern end of the canal tunnel, the day's results were less than had been hoped.

The situation was retrieved, somewhat unexpectedly, by the British IX Corps, under Lieutenant-General Sir Walter Braithwaite, on the right, and particularly by the Territorials of the unglamorous 46th (North Midland) Division under Major-General Boyd. For the canal crossing, meticulous yet ingenious preparations had been made by the corps and divisional commanders and their staffs, and included the provision of mud mats, collapsible boats, floating piers, lifelines and scaling ladders as well as 3,000 life jackets obtained from Channel steamers. On the day of the assault, screened

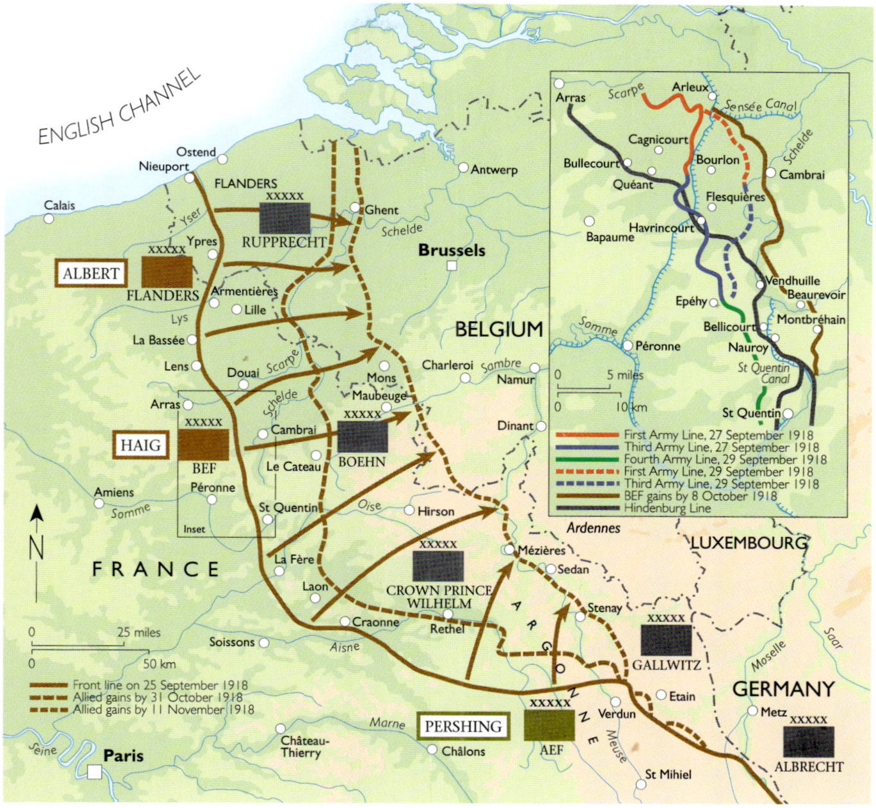

The final Allied offensive, September–November 1918.

by fog and a fast-paced creeping barrage, the 137th (Staffordshire) Brigade rushed the defences on the western bank near Bellenglise and the 1/6th North Staffords captured the bridge at Riqueval intact before the Germans could explode their demolition charges. By 3.30pm all three brigades were not only across the canal but had captured the whole of the Hindenburg Main System on the 46th Division's sector. The 32nd Division then 'leapfrogged' through to continue the advance, consolidate the bridgehead and widen the breach along the eastern bank and the high ground to the south. When night fell IX Corps had penetrated between 3 and 4 miles, capturing the Hindenburg Main Position and part of its Support Line. Fourth Army took over 5,300 prisoners, with the 46th Division alone seizing 4,200.

Despite the disappointing progress on the left flank, the 46th Division's superb assault had decisively ruptured the Hindenburg Line, enabling the French First Army – whose attacks had been frustratingly slow and half-hearted on Rawlinson's right – to enter St Quentin three days later. On 3 October another set-piece assault by five divisions of Fourth Army tore open a 6-mile gap in the Hindenburg Reserve Position or Beaurevoir Line, the rearmost trenches and fortified positions of the great *Siegfried Stellung*.

The Australians, though now exhausted, distinguished themselves yet again in their final action on the Western Front, when three battalions of the 2nd Australian Division drove elements of at least four German divisions from the strongly defended village of Montbréhain.

Pursuit

On 28 September, two days before Bulgaria became the first of Germany's allies to conclude an armistice, Ludendorff told Hindenburg that Germany itself must follow suit without further delay. The leaders parted that evening 'like men who have buried their dearest hopes', Ludendorff wrote. They were disturbed to learn the next day that Hintze had not yet acted upon the earlier proposal to make peace overtures through the Queen of the Netherlands. Even more upsetting was the Foreign Secretary's warning that revolution was inevitable if real parliamentary government was not immediately introduced. An emissary was sent to Berlin to inform the Reichstag of the current situation and, on 3 October, Prince Max von Baden, a liberal and known peace advocate, replaced Hertling as Chancellor. Both Germany and Austria at once despatched peace notes to the United States. The Fourteen Points, a set of peace conditions that had been placed before the US Congress by President Woodrow Wilson in January, constituted a basis for subsequent negotiations yet, even at this late date, Hindenburg and Ludendorff sought to avoid ceding Alsace-Lorraine or any eastern territories they regarded as rightfully German.

The strength of German infantry formations in the field was now perilously low. Over 20 divisions were disbanded in an effort to maintain battalions at a strength of 450–550 but some could only muster 150 officers and men. German artillery units and machine-gunners were still fighting obstinately, however, and slowed the pace of the Allied advance. On 8 October the British Third and Fourth Armies, with Debeney's French First Army on their right, attacked along a 17-mile front extending south from Cambrai, moving forward 4 miles. Patrols from the Canadian Corps and the British 57th Division entered Cambrai itself early on 9 October but within another 48 hours the Germans had made a stand on the River Selle, near Le Cateau. Haig's forces were again compelled to pause while a fresh set-piece attack was prepared.

In Flanders the Allies had improved their communications sufficiently to resume their most northerly offensive on 14 October. The French units in the Flanders Army Group did not perform well, the most effective blows being struck by the Belgians and the British Second Army. Uncharacteristically, Plumer deliberately disregarded orders which would have limited his contribution to that of flank protection and pressed on across the Lys.

This helped the British Fifth Army, on his right, to liberate Lille on 17 October. The same day, the Belgians freed Ostend and Horne's British First Army, to the south, entered Douai. The Belgians recaptured Zeebrugge and Bruges on 19 October while Plumer's formations occupied Courtrai. The Allies were now nearing the Dutch frontier and the British Second Army had progressed 8 miles in less than a week. Prince Max received a grave report from Crown Prince Rupprecht concerning the steep decline in the fighting spirit of German troops, who were surrendering in large numbers when faced with an Allied attack.

There was no consolation for Germany's leaders on the diplomatic front. President Wilson responded to the German peace note on 8 October, asserting that the first condition for any discussions would be for Germany to relinquish all occupied territory. The Germans signalled their willingness to comply but, on 14 October, Wilson added that submarine operations must be terminated and that the Allies would only negotiate with a democratic German government. Prince Max again declared that Germany would accept such terms but Wilson redoubled the pressure, demanding, on 23 October, what virtually amounted to Germany's *unconditional* surrender.

This was all too much for Ludendorff. On 24 October a telegram, bearing Hindenburg's signature yet probably drafted by Ludendorff, pronounced that Wilson's terms were unacceptable and that resistance should continue 'with all our strength'. Having lost touch with reality and the mood of the German people, Ludendorff could not withstand the angry reaction of the Reichstag when the text of the telegram was leaked. He resigned on 26 October and was succeeded by General Wilhelm Groener, though Hindenburg survived as Chief of the General Staff.

PORTRAIT OF A SOLDIER: PRIVATE FREDERICK 'FEN' NOAKES

Private (later Guardsman) Frederick Elias 'Fen' Noakes, a draper from Tunbridge Wells in Kent, was born on 27 January 1896 and made several attempts to join the army between 1914 and 1917, always being rejected on medical grounds. As a youth he suffered badly from asthma and was, by his own admission, thin and 'weakly' with 'little physical strength'. When turned down yet again in 1916 a mixture of patriotism and fear of being thought a 'shirker' drove him to improve his fitness by using chest-expanders and taking long walks and cycle rides. He finally passed a medical board in May 1917 and was soon called up for military service in June, being posted to Windsor for training in a reserve formation of the Household Battalion. From then until 1919 he wrote regularly to his family. He saw action during both the German March offensive and the victorious Allied advance in 1918 and was wounded twice. Even allowing for wartime censorship, his articulate letters provide an interesting commentary on the war, containing not only reports on his own daily activities but also forthright views on wider political issues. In 1934 he collated and typed these letters and then, in 1952, used them as the basis for a privately printed memoir, *The Distant Drum*, in which he added many of the previously missing military and geographical details and included some mature reflections on his opinions as a young man. Together the letters and book offer a valuable glimpse into the last 18 months of the war and can be seen as an accurate barometer of the attitudes and morale of British soldiers on the Western Front in 1918.

Noakes crossed to France in November 1917, joining the Household Battalion – a unit of the 4th Division – in the Arras area. At this stage he still retained a 'credulous idealism', counting it 'an honour to take part in the most righteous war England ever waged, the Last Crusade ... Victory is in our grasp, and we should be utterly unworthy of the trust reposed in us if we turn back now. No *peace* until Prussian militarism is in *pieces*.' After a few weeks his views began to change. On 8 January 1918 he complained about the 'spirit of savagery' in the British press. 'Could the fighting men ... of both sides come together there can be no doubt that complete unanimity would result', he remarked. Noakes now felt that 'national pride', or obstinacy, 'will prove a great obstacle in the way of a reasonable settlement'. He called for a 'much greater openness of mind and humanity' lest Britain become infected with 'the very spirit of Prussianism we set out to crush'. By 12 February he was asking when 'all this indiscriminate murder' would cease. '*Everyone*, except the people in power', he wrote, 'is heartily sick of it ... There is not a man out here who would not make peace in a moment ...' In later life, however, he declared that this was 'a temporary wave of disillusionment' which represented 'no more than the normal habit of grousing for which the British soldier is notorious'.

Private (later Guardsman) F. E. 'Fen' Noakes. (IWM)

From the end of January until early March, Noakes suffered from a poisoned finger and leg sores and was hospitalised in February at Le Tréport, near Dieppe. During this period the Household Battalion was disbanded as part of the reorganisation of the BEF and, on recovery, Noakes was sent to the 3rd Coldstream Guards, then serving in the 4th Guards Brigade attached to the 31st Division.

Between 23 and 25 March the battalion was in action near Ervillers, north of Bapaume, on the Third Army's front. Noakes recalled how tired he was following three days and nights without sleep. Eventually, as the German attacks grew heavier and more intense – and with the battalion in danger of being outflanked or surrounded – the order was given to retreat. Noakes, by then, had sunk into a mood of weary fatalism. 'I ran for some distance with the rest', he told his mother, 'and then, with a feeling of disgust for the whole job, I slowed down to a walk. I really didn't care which way things went.' He was, in fact, knocked unconscious and wounded in the forearm by a shell.

'Fen' Noakes spent over four months convalescing near Boulogne. The March crisis and the threat of defeat revived some of his former 'enthusiasm for the national cause' although 'my "patriotism" was never afterwards so unqualified and my devotion was more critical, than they had been in the past'. By 5 May he was again optimistic and commented with remarkable insight that 'I think we have got Fritz on the toasting-fork all right. He has made progress, but it has cost him far more casualties than he expected, and all the result has been is to put him in an impossible position. He is weakened out of all proportion to his gain, but he cannot stay where he is ...'

He returned to his unit in August but, towards the end of that month, was transferred to the 1st Battalion of the Coldstream Guards in the prestigious Guards Division. The Allied offensive had now been in progress for three weeks and Noakes was 'fairly certain that the war will be definitely decided, if not ended, before the winter'. In September, as the Guards Division advanced towards the Canal du Nord and Hindenburg Line, Noakes was struck, more than once, by the absence of Germans on his immediate front. On 13 September he recorded that men coming back from the forward positions were saying 'We can't find the enemy' or 'We've lost Fritz'. Noakes also noted that he had seen only three dead bodies and no wounded all day. 'I wish all battles were like that', he added. Noakes was profoundly impressed by the scale of the supporting barrage during the attack on the Canal du Nord on 27 September and, although he felt 'stark naked' when required to cross open ground under heavy fire, he also experienced 'an extraordinary sensation – curiously like relief – that I was no longer personally responsible for my own safety'. The attack was successful but Noakes and his comrades were too exhausted to care about their achievement: 'our mouths and throats were dry as lime-kilns. Nerves were on edge and tempers frayed as always after the intense strain of "going over the top".' On 9 October, in another attack at Wambaix, near Cambrai, Noakes was wounded in the left leg. 'That was the end of the war, so far as my insignificant personal part in it went', he recalled.

As the war drew to a close, Noakes was convalescing at a camp at Cayeux, near the mouth of the Somme. Attracted by the ideas of President Woodrow Wilson of the United States, Noakes was worried that Britain and France, in the elation of victory, would impose a vengeful settlement upon Germany. 'A lasting peace it must be', he told his father, 'but it must also be an absolutely *clean* peace. Otherwise, the war has been in vain.' The announcement, on 11 November, that the Armistice had been signed was, however, 'a moment of such undiluted happiness and emotion as I had never known and probably shall never know again'.

Rejoicing in his new rank of 'Guardsman', Noakes served briefly with the British occupation forces in Cologne before coming home to England in March 1919. Demobilised in October that year, he returned to work in his family's drapery business. This sensitive and perceptive former soldier died, at the relatively young age of 57, on 12 April 1953.

THE WORLD AROUND WAR: THE HOME FRONTS 1917–1918

France

1917 was the year of maximum strain for France. With the Germans still on its soil, France continued to fight for its very existence although the fierce patriotism of 1914 had largely given way to weary resignation. While most French citizens were undoubtedly willing to carry on the struggle, they were, in some respects, less regimented or amenable to discipline than their British and German counterparts and the national mood was consequently more volatile. The malaise and restlessness which followed Verdun was heightened by the Russian Revolution and the failure of the Nivelle offensive, becoming manifest in increased anti-war activities and propaganda from pacifist and defeatist elements in French society. Even if the great mass of the French people refused to be seduced by such agitation, particularly after morale had been steadied by America's declaration of war on Germany, the number of strikes in French industry and public services rose alarmingly from 98 in 1915 to 689 in 1917.

Food shortages worsened in 1917. As less than one-third of French sugar factories remained operational, supplies of this commodity were especially meagre. Bread was coarser, regulated by size and weight and barely recognisable from the pre-war product. In January 1918 bread was rationed to 10oz per head per day, a severe blow to working people who relied heavily on this item of diet. Milk, butter and eggs too were scarce and expensive and, as the nation was forced to tighten its belt yet again in 1918, cafés and restaurants closed earlier than ever while butchers shut their shops up to three days a week. In May 1918 municipal butchers' shops were introduced in Paris to reduce and control meat prices. Despite such austerity and some temporary emergencies, France's food supplies were never so precarious as those of Britain and Germany and neither were its regulations and restrictions so stringent. However, manpower shortages on the home front were sufficiently serious – even allowing for the widespread employment of women – that, between April 1917 and January 1918, some 350,000 troops were withdrawn from the firing line to work on the land, in mines, on the railways and in education.

To add to their other trials, Parisians were subjected to heavy air raids by German Gotha bombers, 120 people being killed in March 1918 alone. As the German spring offensives brought the enemy closer to the capital than at any time since 1914, Paris was once more incorporated into the Zone of the Armies and could be reached by German long-range guns. From 23 March to 9 August 1918, Paris was shelled on 44 separate days and 256 citizens were killed. The menace ended when the Allied armies began to advance.

By then, France at last had more stable and energetic political leadership. In September 1917, the government of Alexandre Ribot collapsed following the earlier resignation of Louis-Jean Malvy, the radical Minister of the Interior whose laxity in suppressing pacifist agitation and personal links with a newspaper known to have received money from Germany eventually caused him to be charged with treason. Ribot's immediate successor as Prime Minister, Paul Painlevé, in turn gave way, on 16 November, to Georges Clemenceau. Though aged 76 when he took office, 'Tiger' Clemenceau – as he was nicknamed – shared President Poincaré's determination to wage war to the finish and possessed the charisma, courage and grip needed to command the nation's support. Merciless towards pacifists and defeatists, but also prepared to respond to reasonable industrial grievances, he did much to sustain French and Allied morale during the spring of 1918 and rallied his nation for one final effort that autumn.

Britain

Like France, Britain was showing increasing signs of war-weariness by 1917. There were 688 strikes and trade disputes during the year, involving 860,000 workers. Apart from the dilution of skilled labour by unskilled men and women, reported grievances included high prices, the unequal distribution of food, poor housing and restrictions on the mobility of workers. It must be stated, however, that industrial disputes were still fewer than in the immediate pre-war period and that even the widespread strikes

For King and Country, by E. F. Skinner. (IWM Art 6513)

in 1918 mostly occurred from July onwards, when the worst of the crises on the Western Front had passed. Most people, in fact, remained prepared to 'stick it out' until victory was assured.

As the historian Gerard DeGroot has observed, many of Britain's problems stemmed from a 'sometimes obsessive adherence to outdated values' and a lingering reluctance by the government to intervene. This even applied under the supposedly more dynamic Lloyd George. A case in point was the continuing inability to ensure a rational co-ordination of military and industrial manpower demands. A scheme launched in 1917 by the newly established Department of National Service under Neville Chamberlain failed to achieve a more balanced allocation of manpower because it relied on voluntary enrolment for 'work of national importance' and lacked statutory obligation. An important step was taken in August 1917 when Auckland Geddes, formerly Director of Recruiting, succeeded Chamberlain as the head of a department that was accorded ministerial status and which, in November, took over control of recruiting from the War Office. From now on the army's demands were, in the main, given a lower priority than those of shipbuilding or aircraft and tank production. The Military Service (No. 2) Act of April 1918 conscripted men aged 41–50 and also provided for the extension of compulsory service to Ireland although, wisely, the government never sought to enforce the latter. Temporary increases in enlistment totals were achieved in the summer of 1918 but came too late to prevent the reduction in the BEF's infantry battalions.

The huge part played by Britain's women in the national war effort was a crucial factor in helping the country to surmount such manpower difficulties. Over 7,310,000 women were in paid employment by July 1918. The 947,000 who worked in munitions production represented 90 per cent of that industry's workforce, while 117,000 were employed in transport and another 228,000 in agriculture – many in the Women's Land Army which came into being in 1917. Some donned uniforms in the new women's services, performing duties as cooks, clerks, mechanics and drivers to release men to fight. The Women's Army Auxiliary Corps – later called Queen Mary's Army Auxiliary Corps – was created in July 1917, followed by the Women's Royal Naval Service in November and the Women's Royal Air Force in April 1918. This vast and vital collective contribution was duly, if cautiously, acknowledged in the Representation of the People Act of February 1918, when women aged 30 or over were finally granted the vote.

Air attacks, particularly by Gotha bombers, caused renewed anxiety in 1917, the resulting outcry hastening the creation of the Royal Air Force as an independent service in April 1918. In all, 1,413 people were killed and 3,407 injured by air raids on Britain during the war. But the biggest threat to a nation dependent upon imports for its survival came with the unrestricted submarine campaign conducted by Germany from February 1917 onwards. In April 866,000 tons of British, Allied and neutral shipping were sunk, raising the spectre of starvation in Britain. The belated introduction of the convoy system in May, and the provision of air cover for convoys, substantially cut the loss rate but could not, by themselves, alleviate all Britain's food problems. Economy schemes promoted by the Food Controller, Lord Devonport, in February 1917, had proved ineffective as they were voluntary and falsely assumed that all members of the public shared the same sense of duty. The setting up of a Food Production Department of the Board of Agriculture was more successful in boosting domestic supplies, ultimately bringing 3,000,000 additional acres under cultivation. After Lord Rhondda had replaced Devonport at the Ministry of Food in April 1917, stricter controls were introduced and 15 Divisional Food Committees were empowered to regulate prices and distribution. Nevertheless, with shipping losses still higher in December than pre-1917 levels, more stringent measures could not be indefinitely delayed. In February 1918 compulsory rationing of several basic commodities was instituted in London and the Home Counties and was extended throughout Britain in April. By July, thanks to rationing and the convoy system, the fear of starvation had largely vanished.

Germany

This could not be said of Germany, where domestic life was dominated by the ubiquitous and inescapable effects of the Allied naval blockade. For many Germans in the final 18 months of the war, the main diet consisted of adulterated bread, swedes or turnips and – when available – potatoes. Meat supplies were minimal and fats and eggs were hardly ever seen. In June 1918 citizens of Berlin were restricted to 1lb of potatoes each per week. Gnawing hunger was certainly the worst aspect of the daily ordeal on the German home front but it was not the only privation to be faced. There was little coal or other fuel for heating, lighting and transport. Closely linked with the shortages of coal and oil was the alarming deterioration of Germany's once-envied railway system, which now suffered from lack of maintenance of track and rolling-stock. Clothing too was scarce and, with shoe-leather almost unobtainable, many people took to wearing wooden-soled clogs.

One thing that was maintained was the Army high command's iron grip on the direction of the national war effort. When the Chancellor, Bethmann-Hollweg, was manoeuvred from office in July 1917, he was replaced by the little-known and ostensibly subservient Georg Michaelis, who himself held the post for under four months. Michaelis lost the confidence of the Reichstag when he blamed the Social Democratic Party for a small but ominous mutiny among German sailors at Kiel, and he was compelled to resign. His successor was the elderly Bavarian Catholic Count Georg von Hertling, under whom political stability was restored and peace agitation was muffled, if not entirely silenced.

As in Britain and France, industrial unrest was an obvious symptom of war-weariness. In April 1917 a cut in the bread ration provoked strikes in Berlin and Leipzig. In the latter city the strikers called for a peace settlement without territorial annexations. In June strikers in the Ruhr demanded political reform. January 1918 saw more major industrial disputes in Berlin and Leipzig as well as in Essen and Hamburg. Again these strikes had a strong radical, almost revolutionary, flavour. On 1 February 1918, Berlin's seven biggest industrial plants were placed under martial law and a 'state of siege' was proclaimed for the capital. The ruthless mobilisation of the German economy and society under the Auxiliary Service Law and Hindenburg Programme squeezed the last ounce of productive effort out of the increasingly regimented German people but the apparent success of the measures probably owed less to efficiency than to Germany's heightened siege mentality, which stiffened the resolve of most citizens not to yield so long as the Army remained unbeaten. Nevertheless, national morale – though briefly lifted by the transitory achievements of Ludendorff's 1918 offensives – undeniably became more brittle under the pressure of relentless physical privation. When it shattered the effects would be irreversible. It has frequently been claimed that Germany's defeat in the field followed a collapse on the home front, yet one can argue that Germany's final and sudden slide into chaos and revolution only gathered unstoppable momentum once the Hindenburg Line was threatened.

PORTRAIT OF A CIVILIAN: CAROLINE WEBB

By November 1918 some 947,000 British women were engaged in munitions production. They included Caroline Webb, a 19-year-old girl from Camberwell in South London. Born on 24 January 1899, she was employed in a shirt factory in Bermondsey early in the war before switching to munitions work at Slade Green, near Dartford in Kent, where she filled trench mortar projectiles. Her basic wage at Slade Green was around 30 shillings a week, though she received an allowance of five shillings to cover her train fares from London Bridge. She could also earn a five-shilling bonus if she filled 60 projectiles in a nine-hour working day which started at 7.30am.

The work was not without its dangers. Like many other women employed in shell-filling factories, she risked poisoning from long exposure to TNT (trinitrotoluene) and experienced the yellow skin discoloration that caused such women to be nicknamed 'canaries'. This could have unexpected advantages. As Caroline recalled in an oral history interview recorded for the Imperial War Museum in 1975, sympathetic railway employees would sometimes permit the women to travel in first class carriages. Others, however, 'used to treat us as though we was [the] scum of the earth … These old conductors used to say in the train "You'll die in two years, cock" … So we said "Well, we don't mind dying for our country."' Caroline was indeed so patriotic that she frequently spent a high proportion of her wages on parcels of chocolate, chewing gum and cigarettes for soldiers. 'I came out of the war with hardly a penny', she confirmed, 'and I thought, "Thank God my conscience is clear."'

In 1917 Caroline left Slade Green to work at Woolwich Arsenal, her new job being to fill bullets with lead. Her pay increased to £2 10s per week but her working day now lasted 12 hours, from 7.00am to 7.00pm, over a 13-day period. After one day off, she would then work for 13 nights, again on a 12-hour shift. Not surprisingly – given that her sleep was often spoiled by air raids – she rarely went out on her rest day, describing herself as a 'proper old stop-at-home'. Caroline sometimes accompanied groups of girls from Woolwich Arsenal to indulge in a little mild flirtation with soldiers in nearby Beresford Square, although, in her case, flirting was all that occurred. She was not alone, in 1917–1918, in thinking that 'it was disgusting for girls to be pregnant' but many female workers at Woolwich did succumb to temptation. 'A lot of these poor kids came from up north', Caroline asserted, '... and they were more simple Simons'. Occasional pay cuts made her more militant, prompting her to join a trade union.

When the war ended, Caroline Webb was in no mood to celebrate. Her beloved father, one of the countless victims of the Spanish influenza pandemic, died two days before the Armistice. Caroline and her 47-year-old mother – who had recently had another baby – had to register the death on 11 November and were barely aware of outside events. When they heard maroons signalling the Armistice, 'we thought it was another air raid', Caroline admitted.

After the war, Caroline married, becoming Mrs Rennles. She and her husband – himself a former soldier – possessed little money at first and soon had a child. Caroline had even bought the boots which her husband wore on their wedding day. Bitter about being thrown 'on the slag heap', she took part in a protest march to Westminster that was dispersed by mounted police. Nevertheless, she was still working at the age of 76, running a shop in Coldharbour Lane, Brixton. She died in 1985. Her recorded reminiscences remain as testimony to the part which she, and nearly a million other British 'munitionettes' played in ensuring an Allied victory.

HOW THE WAR ON THE WESTERN FRONT ENDED: THE FINAL MONTH

In presenting his peace conditions to Germany, President Wilson did not always fully consult his allies and some leading players felt that the terms might be too harsh. Haig, for one, prophetically remarked to his wife that Allied statesmen should 'not attempt to so humiliate Germany as to produce a desire for revenge in years to come'. Haig was particularly anxious to seek victory in 1918. He knew that the BEF was battle-weary and short of reinforcements, that the French Army probably lacked the capacity to mount a decisive offensive by itself and that the Americans were still not totally combat-hardened. Even so, he wished to deny the Germans any opportunity of establishing a new defensive line during the winter and, while hoping that moderate armistice terms might induce the Germans to capitulate, he simultaneously strove to keep the enemy off balance and moving backwards.

To this end, Rawlinson's Fourth Army struck the German positions on the Selle on 17 October. The main objective was a line from the Sambre and Oise Canal to Valenciennes, which would bring the Allies within artillery range of Aulnoye – a communications centre where the Mézières–Hirson railway joined that which stretched back to Germany through Maubeuge and Charleroi. Rawlinson's units, attacking on a 10-mile front south of Le Cateau, forced the passage of the Selle despite strong German opposition and, although the advance subsequently slowed, the Fourth Army's right wing managed to push forward around 5 miles to the Sambre Canal by the evening of 19 October. Horne's First Army also gained some 6 miles, bringing it level with the Third Army so that a joint night attack could be made across the Selle, north of Le Cateau, early on 20 October. As on other sectors, dogged resistance from their rearguards won the Germans

Brigadier-General J. V. Campbell VC addresses the 137th Brigade, 46th Division, from Riqueval Bridge, 2 October 1918. (IWM)

enough breathing-space to bolster their defences east of the river with wire entanglements and the British First and Third Armies needed all day to move 2 miles and reach their immediate objectives. Determined not to let the enemy off the hook, Haig launched yet another combined night attack – by the First, Third and Fourth Armies – on 23 October, driving on 6 miles in two days. Further north, the Second and Fifth Armies were approaching the line of the Schelde. However, a pause was now required so that the next round of Allied attacks could be properly co-ordinated. Strategically, October had been a productive month for the BEF but, since breaking the Hindenburg Line, Haig's formations had, perhaps, met stiffer opposition than anticipated, suffering 120,000 casualties for an overall gain of approximately 20 miles.

Unknown to the front-line troops of both sides, the war now had less than two weeks to run. Following more than a month of fierce fighting in the Meuse–Argonne region, the US First Army breached the last significant German defence line on 1 November and, two days later, cut the crucial Lille–Metz railway. In the BEF's zone of operations, the Canadians took Valenciennes on 2 November preparatory to the larger set-piece assault on 4 November by the First, Third and Fourth Armies. This attack, supported by just 37 tanks, was delivered on a 30-mile front from Valenciennes to the River Sambre, on both sides of the Mormal Forest. In an almost symbolic minor operation that day, men of the New Zealand Division bravely scaled the ramparts of the walled town of Le Quesnoy to avoid a protracted siege and hasten the surrender of the garrison.

For the Central Powers the situation was beyond recovery. Turkey had already signed an armistice with the Allies on 30 October and Austria-Hungary followed on 3 November. Sailors of the German High Seas Fleet, when ordered to put to sea for a pointless last sortie, mutinied on 29–30 October. By the evening of 4 November, Kiel was controlled by the mutineers and revolution was spreading inexorably throughout Germany. On Thursday 7 November a Bavarian Republic was declared in Munich, a few hours before a German delegation crossed the front lines to negotiate an armistice with Foch.

Even at this point the Allies did not relax the pressure. By 9 November, a Saturday, French forces were closing in on Mézières and two American corps gained the heights overlooking Sedan. On the opposite, or northern, flank the Allies were across the Schelde as the Germans pulled back to the Antwerp–Meuse line. The British Second Army was now nearly 50 miles from its fields of sacrifice in the Ypres Salient. That day, Prince Max prematurely announced that the Kaiser had abdicated and, after a German Republic had been proclaimed from the Reichstag, the only course left for Wilhelm II was to relinquish the throne and escape to exile in Holland. Around 5.00am on 11 November, the Armistice was signed in a railway coach of Foch's special train at Rethondes in the Forest of Compiègne. During the morning Canadian troops appropriately entered Mons, the scene of the BEF's first battle of the war. Then, at 11.00am, after 1,568 days of conflict, the guns at last fell silent and the long agony of the Western Front was ended.

Chapter 3

THE EASTERN FRONT 1914–1918

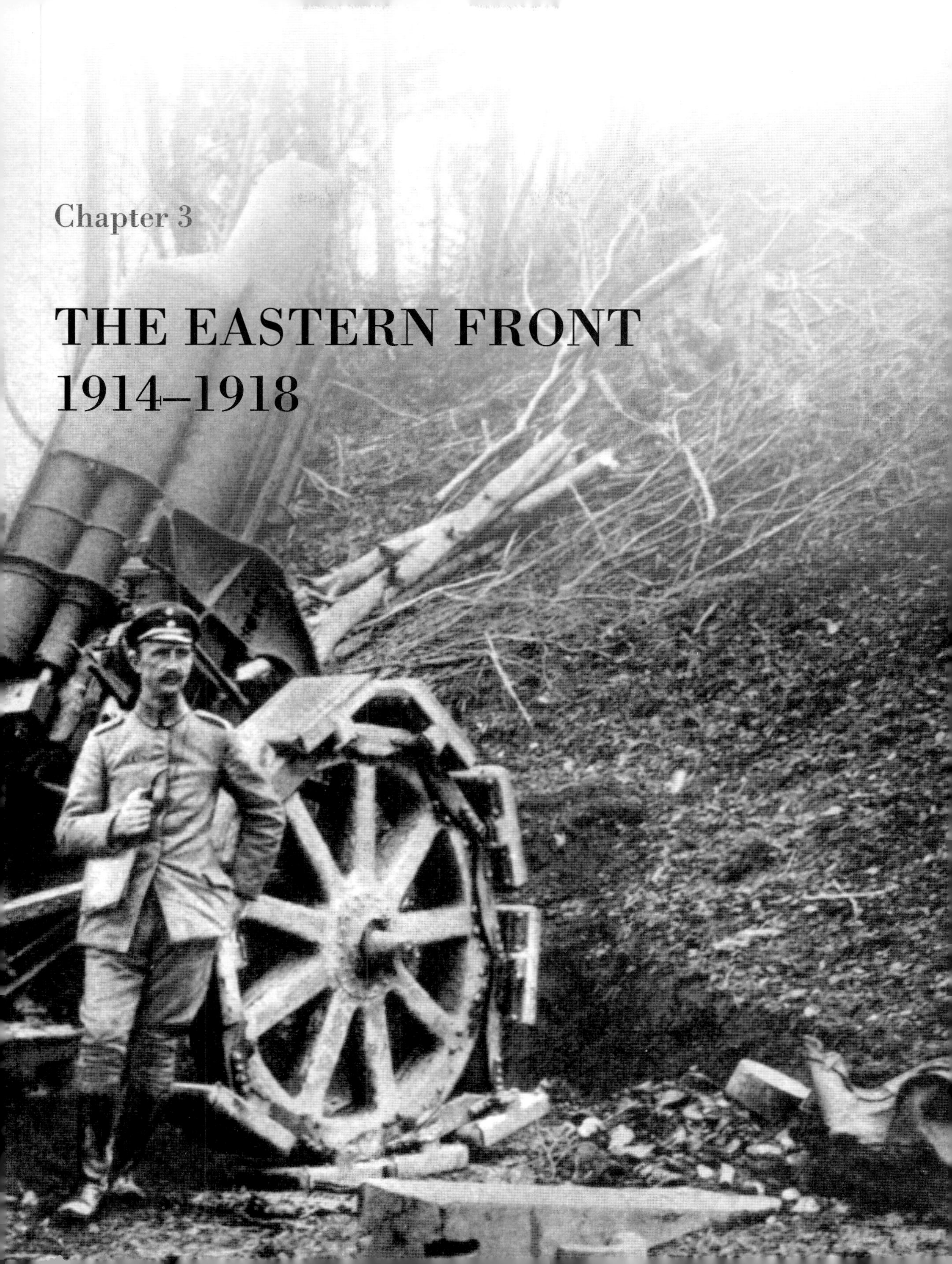

Previous page: German mortar in a position near Predeal, Transylvania, Romania, 1916. (Getty Images)

BACKGROUND TO WAR: RUSSIAN AMBITIONS

That Russia, the most autocratically ruled of all the empires involved in the First World War, should in 1914 find itself aligned with the relatively democratic British and French Empires against the other autocracies of Germany, Austria-Hungary and Ottoman Turkey was neither inevitable nor accidental. Russia joined Britain and France to secure Greek independence from Ottoman rule in 1829, but for most of the next 80 years Britain and Russia were arch rivals, coming close to war several times, and actually going to war once, in the Crimea in 1853–1856. The British and French supported Turkey then, mainly to thwart Russia's designs on the Turkish Straits, control over which would have placed it across the main route to their possessions in the Asia-Pacific region.

Temporarily frustrated there, Russia sought expansion on land to the south and east. It annexed the independent Khanates of central Asia, and combined them with land taken from China into the Governorates of the Steppe (now Kazakhstan) and Turkestan (now Turkmenistan, Uzbekistan, Kyrgyzstan and Tajikistan). Its southward expansion brought it close to the borders of British India, and increased their rivalry, the British fearing Russian invasion of India, the Russians anxious of British expansion into central Asia, and both contending for control over Iran, Afghanistan and Tibet.

In the east, Russia gained vast territories in the Amur valley and on the Pacific coast at China's expense, then sought hegemony over Manchuria and Korea. However, its ambitions collided there with those of Japan, which emerged in 1868 from over two centuries of isolation to adopt a European modernisation model complete with imperialism. Russia's defeats on land and sea in the Russo-Japanese War of 1904–1905 led to nation-wide anti-regime disturbances in 1905. The Tsar sent in the police and Cossacks, established a Parliament, the Duma, but gave it no executive powers, and turned his attention back to Europe.

Expansion in Asia had never precluded continued Russian interest in the fellow-Slavs (Serbs, Croats, Slovenes, Bulgars, Czechs, Slovaks, Ruthenians, Poles) and Orthodox co-religionists (Serbs, Romanians, Bulgars) under Muslim Turkish or Catholic Austro-Hungarian control, where Russia could present itself as 'big brother'. In 1877–1878 its victory over Ottoman Turkey ensured the independence of Romania, Serbia and Bulgaria; but British diplomacy again frustrated Russia's aim of controlling the Turkish Straits. That this remained an objective would be shown in 1915, when Russia secured British and French consent to include annexation of the Straits and the land on both shores, including the Ottoman capital, Constantinople (Istanbul), among its war aims.

The Triple Alliance Treaty between Germany, Austria-Hungary and Italy went through five versions, in 1882, 1887, 1891, 1902 and 1912. All five obliged the signatories to go to war if France attacked Germany or Italy, or if two or more Great Powers attacked any of them. The last four were also implicitly anti-Russian in their references to maintaining 'as far as possible' the status quo in 'the Orient', specified as 'the Ottoman coasts and islands in the Adriatic and Aegean' and, in an accompanying Austro-Italian Treaty of 1887, also 'the Balkans'. The third renewal, in May 1891, additionally mentioned the possibility of seeking British accession to the articles dealing with the Orient.

This prompted the French and Russian governments in August 1891 to reach a secret 'understanding on the measures whose immediate and simultaneous adoption would be imposed on the two governments' by a threat of aggression against either. In August 1892 their General Staffs composed a secret Draft Military Convention. If Germany attacked either France or Russia, if Italy supported by Germany attacked France, or if Austria-Hungary supported by Germany attacked Russia, each would employ 'all her available forces to the full, with all speed, so that Germany may have to fight at the same time on the East and on the West', and neither would make peace separately. Russia was slow to accept the convention, but did so in December 1893. In 1912 this was supplemented by a Naval Convention, to cover 'every eventuality where the alliance contemplates and stipulates combined action of the land armies'. The Triple Alliance riposted in 1913 with a Naval Convention that even listed the ships each would deploy in the Mediterranean.

The Franco-Russian Conventions stipulated regular discussions between the General Staffs. These became especially frequent from 1911, and the French insistently advocated that the simultaneous offensives begin on the 15th day of mobilisation. This was feasible for France, but Russia needed 40 days to mobilise, and at most only one-third of those mobilised could be on the Russo-German border in 15 days. Russia nevertheless accepted the French proposal, but undertook only to invade East Prussia, not to strike directly towards Berlin, as the French urged. In a war that made a bonfire of treaties and conventions, Russia's attempts to fulfil its obligations to France would be noteworthy, but would bring it military disaster in each year of the war.

In 1907, recognising Germany as a greater threat to both than either was to the other, Russia and Britain settled their differences in Iran, Afghanistan and Tibet. In Iran each defined a sphere of influence adjacent to its imperial borders in Transcaucasus and India, with an Iranian-controlled buffer zone between them. Russia acknowledged Afghanistan as 'outside the Russian sphere of influence', and Britain undertook not to occupy or annex any part of it. Both agreed to stay out of Tibet, and to respect China's suzerainty. Neither undertook any obligation to support the other in war; so the alliance with France remained central to Russia's military planning, and disrupting it central to Germany's.

WARRING SIDES: RUSSIA, GERMANY AND AUSTRIA-HUNGARY

Ambitions

Conflict between Slav and Teuton had a long history, but Russia and Germany had not fought each other in modern times. Kaiser Wilhelm II and Tsar Nicholas II were cousins (both were grandsons of Queen Victoria), and Wilhelm's expansionist ambitions were directed not against Russia, but towards acquiring an overseas empire and challenging British hegemony at sea. He cultivated Nicholas as a potential ally or at least benevolent neutral, and to that end played on Nicholas' anti-British feelings, which were considerable, notwithstanding that King Edward VII was their uncle, and his successor, George V, their cousin.

Tsar Nicholas II, Tsaritsa Alexandra and their son, Alexey. (Edimedia, Paris)

Nicholas was convinced that without the Anglo-Japanese alliance of 1902 Japan would not have dared challenge Russia. In the war of 1904–1905 Russia was soundly beaten on land by the German-trained and largely German-equipped Japanese Army, but most humiliating of all was the navy's virtual annihilation by Admiral Togo's British-built and British-trained fleet. Wilhelm encouraged Nicholas' ambition to gain control of the Turkish Straits, assuming that the British would automatically oppose this. He was apparently unaware that in 1895 the British Government had decided that its communications with its Asian dependencies were sufficiently secure that it was no longer vital to keep Russia out of the Mediterranean.

In 1905 Wilhelm even induced Nicholas to sign a treaty of alliance. This would have destroyed the more important alliance with France and prospects for French investment, so Nicholas' foreign minister, Lamsdorf, persuaded him to renounce it. Wilhelm continued cultivating Nicholas, but so did the British, ultimately with more success. The Anglo-Russian Convention of 1907 – apparently, like the Anglo-French Entente of 1904, only a settlement of potential colonial squabbles – did not mention Germany, but was a sign that both empires saw Germany as a threat. However, neither undertook to go to war in support of the other.

Russia's size and population (in 1914 about 167 million, versus Germany's 65 million and Austria-Hungary's 51 million) rooted the idea that it was an inexhaustible manpower reservoir ('the Russian steamroller') among allies and enemies alike. But the true position was different. Profligate and inefficient use of manpower was endemic in industry and agriculture. Mass illiteracy increased armed forces' training problems, and the low level of mechanisation engendered not only low labour productivity but also low military 'teeth to tail' ratios. To maintain one Russian front-line soldier required two in rear services, compared to one in the rear for two at the front in the German and French armies. And large sections of the population were exempt from conscription.

All four empires on the Eastern Front were autocracies, but the Tsar had more absolute power than his counterparts in Berlin, Vienna and Constantinople. He appointed all government ministers, and they were answerable only to him. Moreover, Nicholas II had come to the throne in 1894 eager but untrained to rule – his father, Alexander III, planned to begin preparing him at the age of 30, but died four years too soon. Nicholas' German wife, Alexandra, was equally eager for power, but equally untrained, and her political views were reactionary by any standards. Had either been an outstanding individual, or Russia a constitutional monarchy, their shortcomings might have mattered less, but they were rather unexceptional people given exceptional powers; and as devoted parents, their main concern was to keep the autocratic powers intact for their son, Alexey, to inherit. Unfortunately his inheritance included, through his mother, another of Queen Victoria's grandchildren, haemophilia. From 1912 at the latest, the dissolute monk Rasputin had more influence over Alexey's parents than the Duma or any Cabinet minister because of his reputation as a faith healer and his uncanny ability to relieve the pain Alexey suffered from knocks or bruises.

Geography increased the gulf between rulers and ruled in Russia. The capital, Peter the Great's 'window on Europe', was a West-oriented enclave, mostly the work of Italian architects, closer geographically and intellectually to the other European capitals than to its own provinces. Even its name, 'Petersburg' (the 'Saint' was a later affectation), was German, Russianised to 'Petrograd' only after the outbreak of war; its aristocrats often spoke better French than Russian, Baltic Germans held high governmental and military posts, and Nicholas and Alexandra communicated with each other mostly in English. About 75 per cent of their subjects were illiterate peasant tenant farmers.

Russia in 1914.

Industry, though growing fast, had come late to Russia, and an industrial working class existed in only a few cities. Peasant discontent over land tenure was matched by industrial unrest over low wages and poor working conditions, which in the summer of 1914 had workers overturning tramcars and building barricades in the capital's main streets. But as war approached, patriotic fervour erupted, and when the Tsar appeared in Palace Square, the crowd fell to its knees. Mobilisation was accompanied by considerable disorder, looting and riots, but they were caused by reservists *en route* to their units – that is, by men who did not question their duty to serve. They were the consequences of inadequate provision for feeding them, or of delays in paying allowances to wives and families, not signs of opposition to the war.

There were, nevertheless, numerous potential time bombs in the multinational Russian Empire, additional to political discontent. First, like its rulers, the empire was not especially Russian. In 1897 its first census showed that only 44.3 per cent of the population was 'Great Russian'. Only by adding Belorussia ('White Russia' – a reference to soil colour, not politics) and Ukraine ('Little Russia') could the 'Tsar of all the Russias' claim two-thirds of his subjects as Russian. Turkestan and Steppe Governorates were overwhelmingly Muslim, and there were also large Muslim populations in Transcaucasus and Tatarstan. Doubt about the wisdom of giving Muslims weapons and military training was the main reason for exempting them from conscription. The Ottoman Emperor was *ex officio* Caliph of Islam, empowered in principle to proclaim any war a *Jihad* (Holy War), and he might do just that in a war with Russia.

Nationalism elsewhere in the empire, compounded by cultural and religious differences, was a growing problem. The Russian Orthodox Church was widely (and rightly) seen as an arm of the Russian state by the predominantly Lutheran Finns, Estonians and Latvians, Catholic Lithuanians and Poles and Ukrainian Uniate Catholics, and all these retained strong religious and cultural links with Scandinavia, central or Western Europe. The Georgians and Armenians had their own Orthodox churches, much older than Russia's, and not accountable to the Russian Synod. Finnish nationalism became enough of a problem in the pre-war decade for the Russian Army's Finnish regiments to be temporarily disbanded and the conscription of Finns suspended. Poland, divided between Prussia, Austria-Hungary and Russia, would become the focus of a triangular contest of promises for post-war independence and reunification. Nor could Russia take Ukraine for granted; nationalism was resurgent there, among Orthodox as well as Uniates.

The uneasy Austro-Hungarian Dual Monarchy contained similar time bombs, because about 60 per cent of its subjects – Czechs, Slovaks, Poles, Ruthenians, Slovenes, Croats and Bosnian Serbs – were Slavs. The Chief of Staff, Conrad von Hötzendorff, had long been advocating preventive war on Serbia for encouraging unrest among the Habsburgs' South Slav subjects, and saw Franz Ferdinand's assassination as his opportunity. Russia inevitably lined up to support Slav Orthodox Serbia, and Germany to support Austria-Hungary against the Russian threat.

Germany had come late to empire building, and had a contiguous empire, like Russia, Austria-Hungary and Turkey, only in the sense that from 1871 the King of Prussia was also Emperor (Kaiser) of Germany. Its overseas dependencies were too small to contribute much to its war effort, and Entente, mainly British, sea power soon had them

Grigoriy Rasputin, the dissolute monk whose influence over the Russian royal family helped bring down the regime. He is shown here seated between Colonel Loma and Prince Putianin. (Ann Ronan Picture Library)

cut off or occupied. On the positive side, the Kingdoms of Prussia, Bavaria, Württemberg and Saxony, the several Grand Duchies, German Poland and Alsace-Lorraine contained no serious threat to unity; Alsace-Lorraine was not big enough to pose one, and most Poles saw Russia, not Germany, as the main obstacle to restoration of independence. Resentment of Prussian overlordship was widespread in the other German states, but did not affect their contribution to the Eastern Front.

Ottoman Turkey's Army had performed poorly in 1912 against Greece, Serbia and Bulgaria, but was being reorganised and partly re-equipped by Germany. Its main roles in Germany's plans were to prevent the British and French using the Turkish Straits as a supply route to Russia, and to tie up some Russian forces in Transcaucasus. Turkey was effectively dragged into the war when German Admiral Souchon, commanding its navy, bombarded Odessa on the night of 29–30 October 1914. Russia declared war on Turkey on 2 November.

Field Marshal Conrad von Hötzendorff, Austrian Chief of Staff. (Ann Ronan Picture Library)

Turkey's biggest potential time bomb was in its Arab dependencies, and affected the Eastern Front only in that Turkish troops fighting Arabs and their British or French patrons could not be used elsewhere. However, its Third Army confronted Russia's Army of the Caucasus in Eastern Anatolia, formerly part of Armenia. It had one specific war aim, the recovery of territory – Kars, Ardahan and Batum – annexed by Russia in 1878, and one much more grandiose objective, the ambition of Enver Pasha, Minister of War, to destroy the Army of the Caucasus, hoping thereby to kindle a revolt among Russia's overwhelmingly Turkic Muslim subjects in Transcaucasus and central Asia that would spread to Afghanistan and India.

Bulgaria and Romania joined the war on opposite sides in 1915 and 1916 respectively. Both did so in pursuit of territorial claims – Bulgaria against Serbia, Romania and Greece; Romania against Austro-Hungarian-ruled Transylvania.

Soldiers and equipment

The German Army on the Eastern Front would always be outnumbered, but would always be superior in training, leadership, supply and weaponry, built on a concept of the 'Nation in Arms' that was not yet fully accepted in 1914 by the other belligerents. Its core was the belief that conscripts, if well trained, equipped and led, would provide adequate front-line troops in larger numbers than those of other belligerents that used conscript reservists only for secondary or garrison duties. As in the West, Germany's Eastern Front infantry was backed by lavish artillery support, especially superior to Russia's in heavy guns and howitzers. Expecting only a short and mobile war, the German high command had not yet fully grasped the importance of machine guns, but was much closer to doing so than the Russians, and equipped its troops with them on about eight times the Russian scale. With railways dominating land transport, the density and excellence of Germany's network gave it a great advantage in the speed with which it could supply its front-line troops, or transfer them between the Western and Eastern fronts, or between north and south when the Austro-Hungarians needed support. Faced with an unexpected protracted war, Germany's industrial strength and communications enabled it to adapt better and faster than Russia or Austria-Hungary.

Enver Pasha, War Minister of the Ottoman Turkish Empire. (Ann Ronan Picture Library)

Prussia had once been described as an army possessing a state, rather than a state possessing an army. However, while Prussia undoubtedly provided the leadership and most formidable forces, those of the Kingdoms of Württemberg, Bavaria and Saxony, or Archduchies such as Baden, proved far more reliable than Slavs in Austria-Hungary's armies or non-Slavs in Russia's. Doubts about the reliability of French-speaking conscripts from Alsace-Lorraine generally precluded their use against France, but they fought well enough on the Eastern Front.

Austria-Hungary's annual intake of conscripts in the last pre-war years averaged 159,500, about 20 per cent lower proportional to its population than Germany, but nearly 50 per cent higher than Russia. However, only units from the empire's twin cores, the Ostmark (Austria) and Hungary, were completely reliable. Almost two-thirds of the empire's population shared ethnicity with countries across the borders, Italians in the west, Czechs, Slovaks, Ruthenians, Poles and Romanians in the east and Slovenes, Croats and Serbs in the south. Some attempt was made to keep ethnic kin apart, but there were not enough Austrians or Hungarians to man the Eastern Front without Slav troops, and they would prove unreliable against Russians, especially after mid-1916.

Part of the Russian women's battalion in training. They were rounded up without fighting at the Winter Palace and told to go home. (Ann Ronan Picture Library)

Parsimony was the rule in Austria-Hungary's defence spending. As late as 1911 it was less than a quarter of Germany's, and just over a quarter of Russia's. It rose with the adoption in that year of plans to increase the wartime army from 900,000 to 1,500,000, but remained comparatively low. In consequence, Austria-Hungary's armies were little better equipped than Russia's. Despite this, the Chief of Staff, Conrad, saw the assassination of Franz Ferdinand in June 1914 as an opportunity to flex military muscle that, unaided, proved insufficient even to beat Serbia.

Because it envisaged a short war, Germany saw no need to co-ordinate its Eastern Front operations with Austria-Hungary's, and contacts between the two General Staffs were almost completely in abeyance from 1896 to 1909. They resumed then at Conrad's insistence, but in 1914 the two countries still had no plans for joint action against Russia. At once differences in outlook emerged. With 70 of its initial 80 divisions engaged in the West, Germany envisaged only defence by the ten divisions in the East for the 36–40 days that the conquest of France was expected to take. Russia would then, it was expected, sue for peace, either at once or after briefly experiencing what 80 German divisions could do. Conrad, on the other hand, urged priority to attacking the southern flank (the 'Warsaw bulge') of Russian Poland. The Central Powers never fully resolved the problem of priorities between East and West.

Russia's peacetime army, of 1,423,000, was intended to rise within six weeks to 4,538,000, and a subsequent wartime peak of 6.5 million. However, its conscription system, based on a law of 1874, amended only slightly in 1912, did not foresee the colossal casualties of industrialised warfare and granted widespread exemptions. Many non-Slavs, including all Muslims, were altogether exempt for perceived backwardness, remoteness or fear of the dangers of arming them. Sole breadwinners or only sons were exempt in peacetime, and liable only for garrison or auxiliary service in war. No records were kept of them, or of men with elder brothers already serving, or of second breadwinners, also seldom conscripted in peacetime. Their availability for war depended on their willingness to serve and police diligence in finding the unwilling. The German equivalent, the Ersatz or 'substitute' reserve, was as fully documented as the primary reserve, and mobilised on the outbreak of war.

Equally misconceived was Russia's policy in regard to the 1.1 per cent of men with higher education. Teachers, doctors or chemists were mostly not conscripted in peacetime, and graduates in other disciplines served only one to three years instead of four; the system thus forfeited most possibilities for turning suitable graduates into reserve officers. These privileges, accorded only to the highly educated, overwhelmingly the sons of the wealthy, not surprisingly helped condition the masses to see conscription as a burden, not a civic duty, and to try to avoid it.

In Germany only about 2 per cent of men of military age could claim exemption for family or educational reasons, whereas in Russia 48 per cent could, and about half of those remained exempt even in wartime. The required numbers were achieved only by accepting the lowest physical standards in Europe. In Germany 37 per cent of conscripts were rejected on medical grounds, in Russia only 17 per cent. This meant not only higher sickness rates in the field, but also a more rapid decline in available reservists. On average 3 per cent of German reservists, but over 4 per cent of Russians, were de-listed annually on medical grounds. This meant that after ten years 75 per cent of German, but only 66 per cent of Russian reservists were still available; and when the call-up extended to men aged over 37, Germany had more available than Russia.

In the last pre-war years Germany trained on average 280,000 conscripts annually, while Russia, with over two and a half times Germany's population, trained 335,000, only 20 per cent more than Germany. And the average Russian conscript was of lower physical and educational standards than his German counterpart, as well as less well trained and equipped. In most armies, non-commissioned and warrant officers provide much of a unit's professional backbone. They averaged 12 per company in the German Army, but only two in the Russian.

When it came to equipment, Russia did not lack inventive minds, but application of their ideas lagged far behind the other principal belligerents. Only one plant, the Petrograd Arsenal, could make field guns, and only five others could repair them. When the armed forces expanded to wartime levels, artillery shortages at once became, and remained, endemic.

Machine guns were in equally short supply. In 1914 Russia had just over 4,100 (less than one per infantry battalion), and only the Tula Arsenal manufactured them. Contracts were placed with private firms, and attempts made to place orders abroad; but the other belligerents had already filled the foreign producers' order books, and as late as 1916 Russia's armies had only one-eighth of the machine guns they needed.

But the most acute shortage was in rifles and rifle ammunition, where requirements were underestimated by over one-third. There was a deficiency of 350,000 rifles at the outbreak of war, and by the end of 1914 recruits were commonly arriving unarmed at the front, some to be sent back, others sent into battle unarmed and told to take rifles from dead comrades. With a monthly need for 200,000 rifles, production averaged 71,000 in 1915, and rose in 1916 only to 111,000.

In 1914 only three factories in Russia produced rifle ammunition. Monthly production, though trebled, remained only half of requirements throughout 1915, and not till April 1916 was it decided to build an additional manufacturing plant. By then the ammunition shortage was less acute, but only because the armies had only two-thirds of the rifles they needed. Meanwhile they had suffered a series of defeats, had enormous numbers of men captured and lost large tracts of territory.

All First World War armies depended heavily on horses. Apart from cavalry (of which they all had more than they could use on battlefields dominated by machine guns, trenches and barbed wire), artillery and field kitchens were horse-drawn, as were the carts that carried supplies from railheads to the front line. Horse fodder was usually the largest single item of supply, and the need to transport so much of it was an important factor in overloading the Russian railways.

The Turkish Army was directly engaged against Russia only in Eastern Anatolia. The head of the German military mission, General Otto Liman von Sanders, had great power over the army through its German Chief of Staff, General Bronsart von Schellendorf; a German Admiral, Souchon, commanded the Turkish Navy and German staff officers occupied many senior positions. Their influence was, however, limited by War Minister Enver Pasha, who, as mentioned above, envisaged a much more ambitious role for Turkey's 36 divisions than Germany required of them.

THE FIGHTING: WAR ON THE EASTERN FRONT 1914–1918

On 31 July 1914, Russia began mobilisation. Only five days later the French ambassador 'entreated' the Tsar to attack immediately to relieve the pressure on the French Army. Invasion of East Prussia by General Rennenkampf's First and General Samsonov's Second Army was hastily arranged. They outnumbered the ten divisions of the German Eighth Army (commanded by General von Prittwitz und Gaffron) by about two to one, so the Germans planned holding actions in Masuria, followed, if need be, by withdrawal to the strongly fortified lower Vistula river line, there to await reinforcement by the conquerors of France. Russia's prospects were not enhanced when the Commander-in-Chief, Grand Duke Nikolay, responded on 8 August to more French pleas for help by taking two infantry corps from Rennenkampf for the attack towards Berlin that the French wanted.

Russia invades East Prussia

The Russians entered East Prussia on 12–13 August. At Stallupönen (17 August) and Gumbinnen (20 August) the First Army pushed the Germans back, placing East Prussia's capital, Königsberg (now Kaliningrad), in danger. Prittwitz, a court favourite rather than a good professional, panicked, so on 22 August Moltke replaced him and his Chief of Staff with generals Hindenburg and Ludendorff. They arrived the next day, to begin the war's most formidable strategic partnership.

They inherited a critical but not hopeless situation. Rennenkampf's supplies were running short, and he could not use East Prussia's railways to resupply because the Germans had removed the rolling stock, and Russia's was of different gauge. When the Germans retreated after Gumbinnen he did not pursue them, but waited for two days for supplies to catch up. And when he did move, on 23 August, he gave avoiding a German flank attack priority over supporting the Second Army, continuing west towards Königsberg instead of turning south to meet Samsonov.

The Second Army had communication and supply problems, and was being imprudently urged on by the Front (Army Group) Commander, General Zhilinsky, over sandy soil that made progress difficult for infantry and even harder for draft horses. The Russians made much use of radio, sending messages in plain text or a simple cipher that was easily broken. On 25 August the Germans intercepted two plain text messages, one by

Some of the Russians captured at Tannenberg. The Germans claimed 92,000, while the Russians admitted only 60,000 taken prisoner. (Ann Ronan Picture Library)

Rennenkampf, giving the distances his troops were to march on the next day, the other from Samsonov, with orders for pursuing an enemy he believed to be in full retreat. They showed that the First Army would not be coming to meet the Second, and these messages were such a gift that some wondered if they were a trap. However, the Eighth Army's Chief of Operations, Colonel Hoffman, had been an observer in the Russo-Japanese War and knew that Samsonov had suffered a defeat there because Rennenkampf had failed to support him, and that they had publicly come to blows over it. Hoffman claimed thereafter that this knowledge convinced him mutual dislike would prevent them co-operating, and that the messages were genuine. However that may be, he acted on them, and was proved right. Leaving two divisions facing Rennenkampf, the Eighth Army hurled the other eight against Samsonov. Between 27 and 31 August Samsonov's army was trapped; 18,000 were killed and 92,000 captured, and on 29 August Samsonov shot himself.

The Germans named the battle after nearby Tannenberg, then turned on Rennenkampf, and in the battle of the Masurian Lakes (7–17 September 1914) drove him out of East Prussia. His army did not disintegrate, but 45,000 were captured, and General Pflug's Tenth Army, on his left, also had to withdraw. By the end of September the Russians were back along the River Niemen, minus over 250,000 dead, wounded or captured. Their sacrifice did, however, help France to survive. Five German divisions, rushed from the west in response to Prittwitz's panicky reports, arrived only after Tannenberg had shown they were not needed. They were immediately returned west, but arrived too late for the battle of the Marne. Colonel Dupont, Head of French Intelligence, later said of the Russians that 'their débâcle was one of the elements of our victory'.

Russian offensive in Galicia

While Samsonov and Rennenkampf were heading into disaster, other Russian armies were trundling into Galicia (Austrian Poland). The 'Warsaw bulge' laid Galicia open to invasion from the northern as well as from the eastern, Ukrainian, side; Austria-Hungary's heterogeneous armies were believed less formidable than the Kaiser's, and some Russian generals favoured knocking out Austria-Hungary before seriously tackling Germany.

Stavka (Russian GHQ) planned to take the Austrians in flank and rear by attacking south from the 'bulge' with the Fourth Army commanded by General Evert, while the Third and Eighth, commanded by generals Ruzhsky and Brusilov respectively, advanced into Eastern Galicia. However, Conrad expected Russia's slow mobilisation to give him numerical superiority until late August, and was preparing to attack the 'bulge'.

The battle of Tannenberg and the battle of the Masurian Lakes.

Strategically each side stood to lose, as both proposed to attack forces that greatly outnumbered them. But misfortune for once came to Russia's aid. General Lechitsky's Ninth Army, assigned to the intended drive on Berlin, was deployed along the Vistula between Warsaw and Krasnik, and when the East Prussian disasters temporarily foreclosed the Berlin option, it was already deployed where it could be best used against the Austrians.

In Eastern Galicia, the Austrian general Brudermann's Third Army, along the Grula Lipa River, was intended only as flank guard for the First and Fourth Armies, and was assisted only by the lightly armed Kövess Group, deployed south and west of it. Conrad intended also to use the Second Army, under the command of General Böhm-Ermolli, here, but it was *en route* to Serbia when he belatedly realised that its departure left Galicia weak. He recalled it on 30 July, but railway congestion slowed its return; not until 25 August was it in position, east of Sambor.

The Austrians attacked General Plehve's Fifth Army on 26 August, and the ensuing battle of Komarów proved disastrous for Brudermann. When Ruzhsky's and Brusilov's advance guards fell upon the Third Army, he did not realise that their main bodies were close behind. On the 26th he counter-attacked without co-ordinating the two infantry corps involved, or arranging artillery support for either, and was routed. Russian ponderousness saved the Austrians' front from collapse, but they lost 350,000 killed, wounded or captured (almost half their total force) and most of Austrian Poland, and had 150,000 troops isolated in the fortress of Przemysl. By 16 September they had withdrawn behind the Dunajec River.

The Russian victory illustrated a dilemma that would plague Stavka throughout the war. German forces were closer than Austro-Hungarian to Russia's vital centres, and Germany was the main enemy, while Austria-Hungary's weaker forces could be contained or beaten with a relatively small proportion of Russia's, and the rest used against Germany. But it was also arguable that Germany could not survive alone, so there were two schools of thought among Russian generals, one giving priority to Germany, the other to the 'soft underbelly', Austria-Hungary.

On the German side, there was a tussle between 'Eastern' and 'Western' strategies. Moltke's plan staked everything on overrunning France before Russia completed mobilisation, and when it miscarried the Kaiser replaced him with the Prussian War Minister, General von Falkenhayn, on 14 September. He had to work out how to fight a completely unforeseen protracted war, and his most immediate problem was settling priorities.

The fighting in Galicia had highlighted Austria-Hungary's shortcomings, while the battles in East Prussia demonstrated Russia's. To dig in on a defensible line in France and send most troops east to knock out Russia was an option. Falkenhayn, however, believed the Russians could avoid decisive battles by retreating, and victory must be sought in France, where the defenders had less room to trade space for time, and where the British, Germany's main enemy in his view, were involved.

Falkenhayn endorsed Moltke's belief that Germany must bolster the Austrian front, but

Grand Duke Nikolay, Russian Commander-in-Chief, 1914–1915. (Ann Ronan Picture Library)

without transferring forces from the west. On 16 September he approved Ludendorff's proposal to move most of the Eighth Army south to Silesia, to form a 'new' Ninth Army, commanded by Hindenburg. Ludendorff, its Chief of Staff, met Conrad on 18 September to discuss further action. Conrad resisted putting Austro-Hungarian troops under German command, and Ludendorff did not press him. He realised the Austrians needed a breathing space that only the Ninth Army could provide, and had already issued appropriate orders before going to meet Conrad. The Ninth Army began advancing north-east on 29 September, aiming to push the Russians back to the upper Vistula between Warsaw and Ivangorod (now Deblin) and draw Russian forces off from the Austrians, who would then, he hoped, resume their offensive.

Battles of Warsaw

Stavka knew by 23 September that German forces were in Galicia, and the Grand Duke laid a trap, switching all bar the Eighth and Third Armies to the German front. The Second and Fifth were sent north to the Vistula between Sandomierz and Warsaw, the First moved south from the Niemen to Warsaw, and the Tenth prepared a diversion on the Niemen. The Germans would be allowed to advance to the Vistula, then the First Army, plus most of the Second and Fifth, would attack their left flank south of Warsaw. The Germans did not discover the moves, assumed the Russians would attack the Austrians, and diverted three corps to meet the expected threat. In East Prussia, the Tenth Army advanced on 29 September, but had been halted by 5 October, and played no part in the main battle.

The Austrians realised by 4 October that they faced only a screening force, so they advanced to the River San, and relieved Przemysl on the 9th. Russian resistance then stiffened, and the Austrians were stopped. Belated realisation that the main Russian force was at least 30 miles further north than expected forced Ludendorff to regroup. On 9 October an intercepted Russian radio message disclosed that seven Russian corps would be in the Warsaw area by 11 October, the day on which Mackensen, commanding the Ninth Army's left flank, was supposed to capture Warsaw with only two corps.

On 10 October a copy of the Russian plan found on a dead officer showed Ludendorff that not only was the Ninth Army's left flank threatened from the Warsaw area, its right was also imperilled by the Russian Fourth and Ninth Armies, from bridgeheads on the west bank of the Vistula. On 11 October he ordered Mackensen to prepare for retreat. Falkenhayn spared only one corps from the west, where the first battle of Ypres was imminent, and sent it to protect East Prussia; so relieving the pressure on the Ninth Army depended on the Austrians resuming the offensive on the San. Conrad, however, refused to do so, and rejected Ludendorff's alternative request to rush troops north to help Mackensen. The Kaiser appealed to Emperor Franz Josef; he upheld Conrad's refusal, but the Austrians took over the German Guard Reserve Corps' front at Ivangorod, freeing its two divisions to go north.

The Russians were now very strongly placed, with the Second Army west of Warsaw, and the Fifth in the city, preparing to pounce on Mackensen. On the 19th he began withdrawing, and a week later Ludendorff ordered a full-speed retreat of about 60 miles to a line between Kielce and Radom, to avoid being encircled. Preserving German forces now took precedence over helping allies, so the Austrians were left to their own devices, and their First Army also had to withdraw hastily, to prevent encirclement by the Russian Fourth and Ninth Armies. By the end of October the Russians had outrun their supplies, and the first battle of Warsaw ended. The Germans had lost all their initial gains, the Austrians rather more, and Przemysl was again isolated. Mackensen had evaded the Grand Duke's trap, but on the whole the Russians had had the better of it.

Inspired by this, the Grand Duke resumed planning a direct advance to Berlin. By early November nine armies stood in Russian Poland, a 'spearhead' of the Second, Fifth, Fourth and Ninth in the Vistula bend, with the Tenth and First protecting their right flank and the Third, Eleventh and Eighth their left. With seven-eighths of Germany's forces still on the Western Front, this concentration of more than 60 divisions, barely 300 miles from Berlin, clearly had great potential.

However, the South-West Front's commander, Ivanov, advocated acting first against the Austro-Hungarians in Galicia, to remove their threat to the south flank of the 'spearhead'. His Chief of Staff, Alexeyev, proposed sending the Third, Fourth and Ninth Armies south against Kraków and the battered Austrian First Army. This would halve the 'spearhead', so the Grand Duke rejected it, but he compromised by leaving the Third Army on the River San, and removing the Ninth from 'spearhead' to flank guard, covering the Kraków direction.

The 'spearhead' nevertheless remained large, and the northern flank guard's two armies were also to attack – General Sievers' Tenth to re-invade East Prussia with 20 divisions, Rennenkampf's First to advance along the Vistula west of Warsaw with six. The three 'spearhead' armies – the Second, the Fifth and the Fourth, commanded by Scheidemann, Plehve and Evert respectively – totalling 26 divisions, were to advance west, the Fourth into Silesia, the others on to the flank of the German Ninth Army, now commanded by Mackensen and deployed between Kalisz and Czestochowa.

Battle of Lódz

The retreating Germans had systematically destroyed roads and railways, and consequent supply problems meant that the Russians' offensive could not start before 14 November. Eavesdropping on their radio traffic gave Hindenburg, now *Oberost* (Commander-in-Chief East), detailed information on their intentions. On 3 November he took the bold decision to move the entire Ninth Army to Thorn (now Torun) to attack south-eastwards into the flanks of the Russian First and Second Armies. His railways moved over 250,000 men in five days, and by 10 November the Ninth Army, plus a corps from East Prussia, was in position. Only four German divisions remained to defend Silesia, but Conrad reinforced them with the five of Böhm-Ermolli's Second Army.

The Ninth Army attacked on 11 November. At Wloclawek on the 11th and 12th, it pushed V Siberian Corps aside, but failed to destroy it. The battle of Kutno (13–16 November) was more decisive; V Siberian and II Corps were badly mauled, a 40-mile gap opened between the First and Second Armies, and three German infantry and one cavalry corps poured south, ending the second battle of Warsaw and beginning the battle of Lódz. By the 18th Lódz was surrounded on all bar the south side.

The battle of Lódz to the second battle of Warsaw.

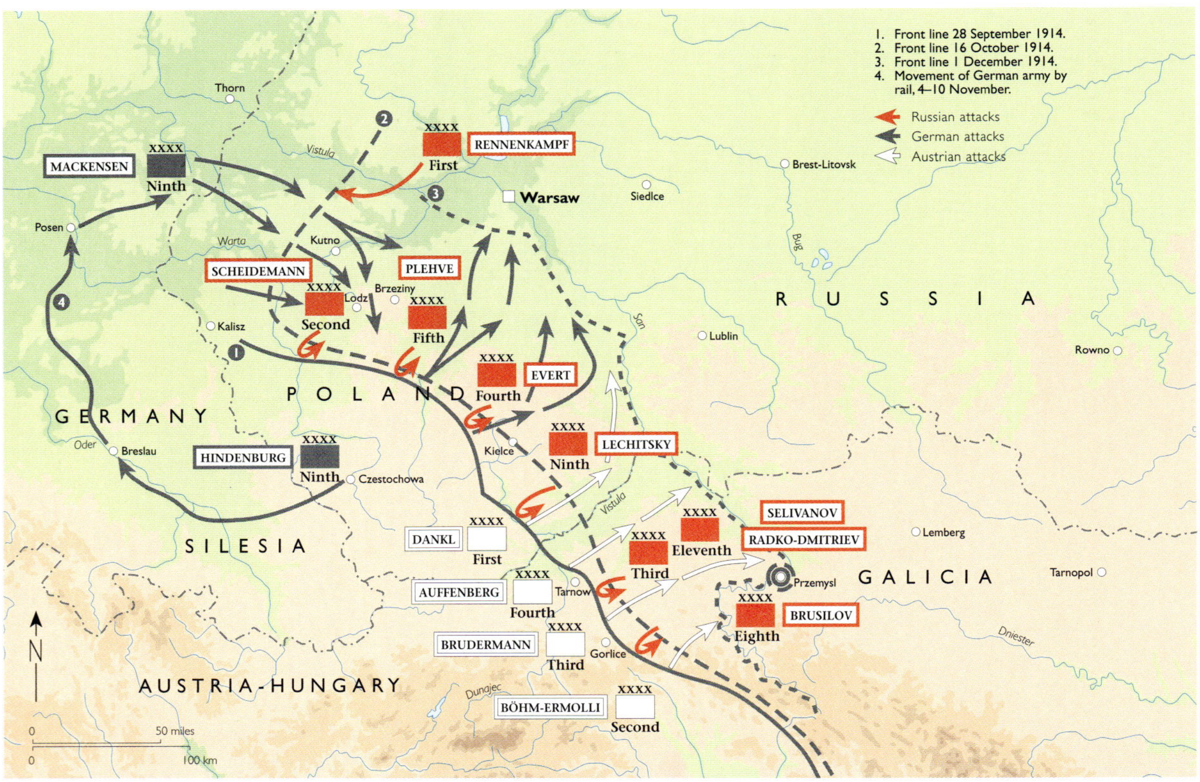

By forced marches the Russian Second Army had brought up 500,000 troops in three days, outnumbering the Germans by about two to one, but arriving exhausted. For the moment Lódz was saved, but it desperately needed support. The nearest supporter was the First Army, north of the city; but Rennenkampf helped the Second Army there as little as he had at Tannenberg.

That Russia narrowly avoided another Tannenberg owed most to a broken promise by Falkenhayn. A few days before Hindenburg attacked, Falkenhayn, expecting to win the first battle of Ypres quickly, promised to reinforce him by 24 November, and Hindenburg planned his offensive accordingly. But by the 18th First Ypres was lost, Falkenhayn had no troops to spare and Mackensen's Kutno victory had improved Germany's position in the east as much as Falkenhayn's defeat had worsened it in the west. On the 18th Falkenhayn told Hindenburg he would get no reinforcements; he was so convinced of the Western Front's primacy that he was pressuring Prime Minister Bethmann-Hollweg to seek peace with Russia.

The battle of Lódz was hard fought, and fraught with miscalculations on both sides. The Germans attacked on 19 November, expecting an easy win, but the weather suddenly turned cold with snow, favouring the far more numerous defenders. Nevertheless, General Scheffer's group (XXV Corps, a cavalry force and the Guard Division) advanced eastwards south of the city, threatening to encircle it and the Russian Second Army, and on the 21st one of its brigades got within a mile of the city centre. However, the defenders forced it out, and by nightfall on the 21st Scheffer had been halted. On the 22nd fresh Russian divisions encircled his force at Brzeziny, and ordered up trains to take away the expected prisoners. However, Scheffer's boldness, Russian lack of co-ordination and Rennenkampf's inactivity combined to save Scheffer's group. In three days it pushed over 20 miles through superior Russian forces, taking with it not only 2,000 wounded, but 16,000 captured Russians and 64 Russian guns. Russian reconnaissance mistook the march-column of prisoners for Germans, and judged the enemy too strong for their nearby forces to attack. Scheffer lost half his force, but evaded the trap. Thus, on 25 November, ended the battle of Lódz, again aborting Russia's plan to drive to Berlin.

For the moment this gave the ascendancy to the 'soft underbelly' school. To support Mackensen, Conrad had attacked northwards from Kraków on 18 November. However, the Russians' unexpectedly strong resistance at Lódz and on the Kraków front nullified hopes of encircling them or sweeping them back over the Vistula. Worse still, Conrad had denuded his front from Kraków eastwards, leaving its defence to the 11 divisions of General Boroevic's Third Army and a few divisions hastily assembled just south of

Kraków. When Stavka realised this, it at once launched Radko-Dmitriev's Third and Brusilov's Eighth Armies, each with ten divisions, against the entire front from Kraków east to the Bukovina.

Brusilov was very successful, advancing through the Carpathians almost on to the Hungarian Plain. But the Russians had co-ordination problems, because the North-West and South-West Fronts were diverging, their communications with each other and with Stavka at Siedlce were unreliable, and their experiences were different. When their commanders met the Grand Duke on 29–30 November, Ruzhsky urged withdrawal almost all the way to the Vistula, to regroup, resupply and restore units battered at Lódz and await the German attack he believed imminent.

To do so would expose the South-West Front's northern flank, obliging it also to withdraw, and Ivanov rejected that. His forces had stopped the Austrians north of Kraków, made considerable gains south and east of it, and taken many prisoners, so he advocated another offensive. The Grand Duke vetoed Ruzhsky's proposal and accepted Ivanov's, for the Ninth Army to attack Kraków from the north and the Third from the south, each with four corps, while two corps of the Eighth Army maintained pressure in the Carpathians to prevent the Austrians reinforcing Kraków.

Conrad's four understrength armies between the Vistula and Carpathians were outnumbered by about two to one, and with Brusilov almost into Hungary the Dual Monarchy's heartland was directly threatened. So Conrad sent part of the Fourth Army under Archduke Josef Ferdinand and one full-strength German division south from Kraków on to the Third Army's left flank, beginning the battle of Limanowa-Lapanów. General Roth's four infantry and three cavalry divisions pushed forward on 3–6 December, forcing Radko-Dmitriev to halt and seek Brusilov's help. Brusilov sent General Orlov's VIII and Tsurikov's XXIV Corps into Roth's right flank, and the battle entered its second phase on 8 December, the Russians now trying to outflank Roth from the east.

They did not succeed, and the removal of two of Brusilov's corps to this battle left only one facing the entire Austrian Third Army. It also attacked on 8 December, and took the vital Dukla, Lupka and Uzhok passes, again thwarting Brusilov's advance on Hungary. The single corps retreated to north of the mountains, and this relieved the pressure on Roth, because Brusilov's two corps facing him had to withdraw in conformity. By 15 December the Russians had retreated to a shorter line along the Dunajec River. Some divisions had suffered 70 per cent losses, and the Austro-Hungarians had proved more hard nut than soft underbelly. That school therefore lost favour; though in fact Austria-Hungary never again did as well.

Turkish front, winter 1914–1915

Since Turkey and Russia were at war only from 2 November, with the severe Anatolian Highland winter beginning, Russia's Army of the Caucasus neither expected nor planned a major offensive, especially as Stavka had told its commander, Myslayevsky, to expect no reinforcements. However, I Corps, under General Bergmann, tried a limited offensive on 2 November. The Turkish Third Army's commander, Hasan Izzet Pasha, enticed him forward for several days, then launched a counter-offensive threatening the Russians with encirclement. Bergmann pulled back hastily, but lost about 40 per cent of his force before fighting died down on 16 November. Russia suffered other defeats on the northern sector, where irregulars ejected several garrisons, and for a time the port of Batum appeared vulnerable. The Grand Duke

Russian trenches at Galicia. (Ann Ronan Picture Library)

was sufficiently perturbed to ask for an Anglo-French 'demonstration' at the Straits to draw Turkish forces away. However, by 19 February 1915, when the Allies responded with the first attempt by warships to force a passage, the crisis in Transcaucasus was long past.

The main reason for this was that the November victories went to Enver Pasha's head. On 6 December he arrived in Erzerum, intent on destroying Russia's Caucasian Army and sparking revolts among Russia's Turkic subjects. His German advisers were privately sceptical, but failure would not affect the Eastern Front, while success would draw Russians away from it, so they did not try to dissuade him. Izzet Pasha and two of his corps commanders expressed doubts, so Enver dismissed them. The third corps commander said success was possible, given careful planning, winter clothing and extra rations, establishment of advance bases and one additional corps. Enver kept him, but ignored his advice.

The offensive began on 22 December. It included an outflanking manoeuvre that required two divisions to spend two days traversing a barren high plateau with no warm clothing, no hot food and minimal rations. In a blizzard on the 24th one division lost 40 per cent of its men. Another spent a night in the open in a temperature of -36°F. Several hundred froze to death, thousands suffered frostbite and thousands more fled to the nearest villages for shelter; 50 per cent of the division was lost that night. Another lost one-third in a 19-hour march at nearly 10,000ft altitude.

The decisive battle of Sarikamis began on 29 December, and the Russians finished mopping up on 17 January 1915. Of the 95,000 Turks engaged, 75,000 met death, wounding, frostbite or captivity. Of 65,000 Russians, 16,000 were dead and 12,000 wounded or frost bitten.

The battle of Limanowa-Lapanów.

Winter campaigns, 1915

On 1 January Falkenhayn met Conrad and Ludendorff in Berlin. A week later, under pressure from the Kaiser and Bethmann-Hollweg, he reluctantly agreed to send a few Eastern Front divisions to support Austria-Hungary in the Carpathians, and on 12 January he went to Hindenburg's headquarters at Posen (Poznan) to discuss his plans. On 23 January he agreed to give Hindenburg three newly raised corps that he would rather have sent west, and one transferred from the west because it was raised mostly in Lorraine, and not thought reliable for fighting the French. Three of these corps would form a new Tenth Army, which was to be commanded by Colonel-General von Eichhorn. This new army was to take over the northern part of the front, from Gumbinnen to the Niemen River, and form the northern jaw of a pincer aimed at encircling the Russian Tenth Army, then under the command of General Sievers. General Otto von Below's Eighth Army, reinforced by the fourth new corps, would form the southern jaw of what was hoped would be a second Tannenberg.

The two armies totalled 15 infantry and two cavalry divisions, versus the 11 infantry and two and a half cavalry divisions of Russian Tenth, but Russian divisions had 16 battalions and German only 12, so they slightly outnumbered the Germans. However, the Germans had much more artillery, 924 light and 291 heavy guns, versus Sievers' 308 and 88, and a better supply network.

The Russians were again arguing about priorities. Ivanov cited the failures against the Germans as reasons for concentrating on Austria-Hungary, arguing that a convincing defeat would prompt Italy and Romania to invade it; it would then collapse, leaving Germany isolated. Ruzhsky argued that Germany was the main enemy, and force used against Austria-Hungary was wasted. The Grand Duke saw a flank attack from East Prussia as the greatest threat to his planned drive on Berlin, and came down on Ruzhsky's side, giving Ivanov only one extra corps – the Finnish XXII – and telling him not to attack. The bulk of reinforcements went to form a new Twelfth Army, under General Plehve, deployed south of the Tenth, to invade East Prussia from the south, by-passing the Masurian Lakes, while the Tenth invaded from the east.

Which side would be ready first depended on the railways. Here the Germans won hands down. On 5 February documents found on a dead German officer told the Russians that East Prussia had been reinforced, but they had no time to act on the information. Their offensive could not begin until 23 February, but the German Eighth Army attacked on the 7th, and the Tenth on the 8th. The weather was atrocious, varying from blizzards to daytime thaws, freezing again at night, so that even though both sides' troops had winter clothing, casualties from frostbite far outnumbered those of battle. The conditions favoured the defence because closing the trap required the Germans to move faster than the Russians. Movement of any kind was difficult through snowdrifts and mud, fast movement impossible, and bringing supplies from railheads took up to 12 horses per cartload. But here, too, superior German organisation told; by 9 February most of the Russian artillery was out of ammunition, and under constant bombardment the Russian Tenth's north flank crumpled. By 17 February the Germans had taken over 60,000 prisoners, and had another 70,000 trapped in the Augustów forests. The east side cordon was too thin to stop some escaping, but about half were captured by the 22nd, and two days later another 10,000 surrendered at Przasnysz.

The Germans were now nearing exhaustion, and Russian counter-attacks in the last days of February prompted Hindenburg to end the offensive and pull back from the most exposed positions. By the end of March another 40,000 Russians had been captured, and the front was stable just east of the frontier. The Russians had lost 150,000 in prisoners alone, and three-quarters of the Tenth Army's 396 guns. But the grander aim of forcing Russia to abandon the Vistula line had not been achieved, and the accompanying Austro-Hungarian offensive failed. However, the Russian public did not know Hindenburg's aim, or that he fell short of achieving it. They knew only that another army had been wiped out, and that soldiers' letters spoke of overwhelming German artillery bombardments, Russian guns silent for lack of shells and infantry mown down or captured by the tens of thousands.

The Austro-Hungarian front offered Russia more cheer. Since mid-September it had the fortress of Przemysl, with over 100,000 defenders, under siege – though the length of siege reflected Russia's lack of heavy artillery. Ivanov stuck to his plan to invade Hungary through the Carpathians, while Conrad saw an attack from them as Austria-Hungary's contribution to forcing the Russians off the Vistula line.

So both planned winter offensives in the Eastern Carpathians. Terrain less suited to a winter campaign is hard to imagine. The mountains, though not very high, are steep sided, intersected by few passes and even fewer passable roads, and blocked by snow on most days, and by mud during the occasional thaws. Thousands of troops on both sides died of exposure that winter.

The Austrians moved first. On 23 January 1915, 20 divisions attacked at the Dukla, Lupka and Uzhok passes. Simultaneously the new 'German South Army' (mostly Austrian, but under a German general, Linsingen) attacked the eastern Verecke and Wyszkow passes. The Eighth Army, with approximately equal strength, held the attacks, and they were called off on the 26th. Brusilov then attacked at the Dukla and Lupka passes, sowing havoc among Boroevic's Third Army, which in three weeks lost over 65,000 of its 100,000-plus manpower to battle or frostbite.

By mid-February the Russians had captured the important railway junction of Mezölaborcz, and were prevented from exploiting their success only by having to divert resources to counter General Pflanzer-Baltin's advance towards the Dniestr River at the eastern end of the front. A second Austrian offensive from 27 February achieved only limited success in the Carpathians, but Linsingen and Pflanzer-Baltin succeeded by mid-March in forcing the Russians back across the Dniestr.

On 22 March the Russians captured Przemysl, taking 100,000 prisoners and freeing the Russian Eleventh Army for use elsewhere. Another Russian assault through the Carpathians began the same day, and by mid-April the Austrians were fortifying the Danube line between Vienna and Budapest, anticipating a Russian exodus on to the plain. But by then the Eighth Army had again run out of artillery ammunition, and German reinforcements helped stabilise the line. Most of Austria's regular officer cadre had by now been lost, and though the Russians were in a no better state, their 'soft underbelly' advocates seemed triumphant.

Winter 1914–1915 in the Carpathians. (Edimedia, Paris)

Breakthrough at Gorlice-Tarnów

However, Falkenhayn now had to look more to the east, because Austria-Hungary's reverses prompted Italian and Romanian hints that only territorial concessions could prevent their declaring war. Conrad and Falkenhayn opted to overawe them by crippling Russia's offensive power. They planned a surprise attack on the Russian Third Army over a 78-mile front between Tarnów in the north and the Lupka pass in the south. Its focal point was the city of Gorlice, and it went into history as Gorlice-Tarnów.

Falkenhayn took his decision on 9 April, and after discussion with Conrad eight German divisions received orders on the 15th to move secretly from the Western to the Eastern Front, to form a new Eleventh Army under Mackensen, deployed west of Gorlice. Conrad gave Mackensen control over the Austrian Fourth Army, on the Tarnów sector to his north, and the Third to his south, covering the Dukla and Lupka passes. 'Army Group Mackensen', with one cavalry and 22 infantry divisions, faced 19 Russian divisions, all understrength and short of artillery. The Eleventh Army was to break through at Gorlice and force the Russian Third back to the River San, the Austrians providing flank support and attacking to roll back the Carpathian front.

The attack on 2 May achieved almost complete surprise. By 3 May Gorlice had been taken, and a 12-mile hole ripped in Radko-Dmitriev's line. Three of his divisions broke and fled, the rest were down to an average of only 1,000 men by evening on 4 May, and his only option was withdrawal behind the Vistula. Destruction of his centre uncovered the northern flanks of two of his corps in the Carpathians, but if they withdrew Brusilov would also

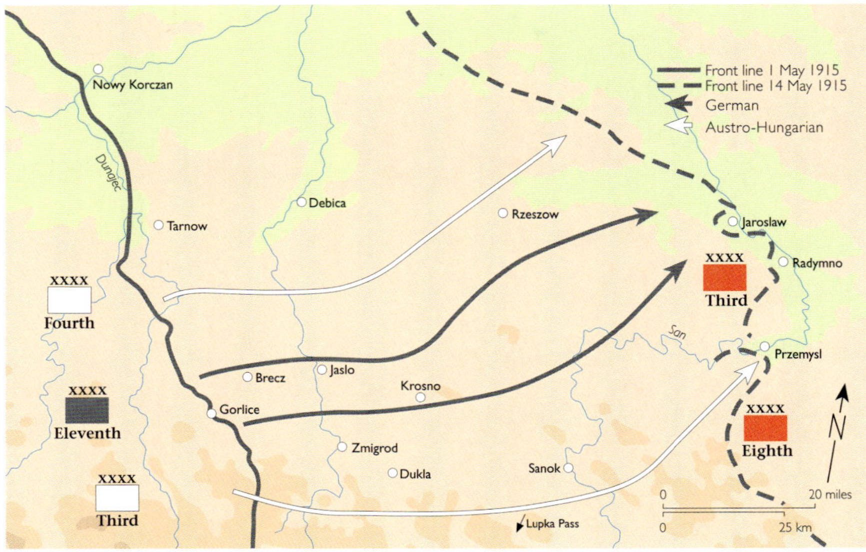

The battle of Gorlice-Tarnów.

have to pull back, aborting the invasion of Hungary yet again. On 5 May the Grand Duke vetoed withdrawal, but that same day further thrusts by the Austrian Third Army towards Lupka and the German Eleventh towards Sanok forced the Third Army into an unstoppable retreat. By 10 May, Radko-Dmitriev reported that it had 'bled to death', and Ivanov ordered withdrawal from the Carpathians. The Grand Duke asked the British and French to attack urgently to draw off German forces, and to nudge Italy into the war, drawing off the Austrians.

Falkenhayn saw the victory of Gorlice-Tarnów as important enough to transfer the Supreme Command from the west to Silesia, and plan a joint Austro-German effort to cripple Russia permanently. A local success by the Russian Ninth Army, pushing Pflanzer-Baltin back from the Dniestr to the Prut, was the only bright spot for Russia, and too remote to affect matters in Galicia, where both the Third and Eighth Armies lost heavily in the battle of Sanok (9–10 May). On the 13th, the German Eleventh Army reached the San, and forced a crossing in the five-day battle of Jaroslaw. An attempted Russian counter-offensive was unsuccessful.

Nor did Italy's declaration of war on Austria-Hungary on 23 May provide any immediate relief. Austrians began leaving for the Italian front only on 3 June, and Germans arrived to replace them. The Austrian Third Army was disbanded, its divisions shared between the Second and Fourth, and regrouped with the German Eleventh for a new venture – recapture of Lemberg (now Lviv), capital of Galicia.

Russian retreat

By now Russian losses were soaring. In May alone, the South-West Front lost 412,000 killed, wounded or captured. Mackensen resumed his offensive on 12 June, and by the 17th had advanced to the line Rava Russkaya–Zolkiew, while the Austrian Second Army was closing on Lemberg.

The Vistula line, already threatened with outflanking from the north, was now also vulnerable from the south. There were insufficient guns, small arms and ammunition for a counter-offensive. Galicia would have to be abandoned, to shorten the line and free troops for a strategic reserve, so on 17 June the Grand Duke ordered a fighting retreat. It was 'to be deferred as long as possible', but events were moving fast. On 20 June the loss of the Rava Russkaya–Zolkiew line bared Brusilov's right flank, so he ordered war stores evacuated from Lemberg and all forces in Galicia prepared to withdraw. The battle of Lemberg began that day, with two of Brusilov's corps – VIII and XVIII – facing the numerically superior and fresher German XLI Reserve and Austro-Hungarian VI Corps. On the 22nd, the Austrians broke into the outskirts, and Brusilov avoided entrapment only by abandoning the city.

Gorlice-Tarnów and Lemberg, immediately followed by the third battle of Warsaw, were cumulatively even more disastrous for Russia than Tannenberg. Fifteen divisions were wiped out, and about 20 more reduced to skeletons. The retreat from Galicia left the Vistula line untenable, and it, too, was abandoned.

Warsaw fell on 5 August. The Grand Duke, like Kutuzov in 1812, had traded space for time. But the armies of 1812 were tiny compared to those of 1914–1915, there was neither a continuous front line nor streams of refugees, and the country, apart from the narrow belt traversed by the armies, was little affected. In 1915 the consequences of retreat were far greater.

The front-line troops' retreat from Poland was orderly. But ahead of them were over two and a half million refugees, forced to leave by having their towns and villages burned under the Grand Duke's 'scorched earth' policy. The refugees were being dumped from trains in towns, some as far away as central Asia or Siberia, that were too gripped by shortages of food, fuel and accommodation to provide adequately for them. The impression this left on rear-service troops and the population was far worse than the purely military situation warranted. Apparently believing the army had cracked, Nicholas decreed draconian punishments for surrender, including cessation of allowances to families, and post-war exile to Siberia. These decrees merely reinforced the public's impression of disaster. The new War Minister, General Polivanov, told the Council of Ministers on 30 July, 'demoralisation, surrender and desertion are assuming huge proportions', and the Minister of Agriculture, Krivoshein, warned that 'the second great migration of peoples, staged by Stavka, will bring Russia to the abyss, revolution and ruin'.

The immediate consequence was the dismissal of the Grand Duke, for which Alexandra and Rasputin had long been lobbying. Alexandra suspected him of plotting to become Tsar, and saw his support for representative government as intended to undermine the autocracy. The retreat gave them the opportunity to pressure Nicholas. On 7 August, two days after Warsaw fell, Nicholas dismissed him and appointed himself Commander-in-Chief. The soldiers grieved, Ludendorff (later to say 'The Grand Duke was a great soldier and strategist') rejoiced. The Council of Ministers was aghast, believing Nicholas' action would now focus the nation's anger on himself. The generals were less upset, seeing him as a figurehead, with a professional Chief of Staff taking the important decisions. Nicholas' appointee, General Mikhail Vasilyevich Alexeyev, was highly respected by his colleagues, and with Polivanov in office they believed that supply would never again be as bad. The British and French governments heaved sighs of relief, taking Nicholas' action as evidence that Russia meant to stay in the war.

The retreats continued and public anger mounted. The Falkenhayn–Conrad plan to cripple Russia permanently seemed to have succeeded, and as the autumn rains began, Falkenhayn started returning troops to the west. Yet Austria-Hungary was in little better state than Russia. It, too, had suffered supply shortages and immense casualties – over 800,000 in the Carpathian winter campaign alone, increased to 1,250,000 by the summer campaign of 1915. Only massive German reinforcement had saved the Austrian front from collapse, and the Habsburgs had become satellites of the Hohenzollerns, with German generals such as Linsingen, Bothmer and Mackensen commanding Austrian forces, and German priorities determinant. The home front faced a food crisis nearly as bad as Russia's, for the same reason – the blockade added to unmechanised agriculture's difficulty in maintaining production when most of the able-bodied peasants had been conscripted. Conrad's last attempt at independent military action was an offensive in the Rovno area in September 1915, and it failed. So an energetic assault might break Austria-Hungary.

Russian offensive in Turkey

After Sarikamis the Russo-Turkish front was quiet for almost a year, except for localised campaigns in Persian Azerbaijan in April and around Lake Van in May–June. The Turks were preoccupied with reorganisation, the Gallipoli campaign and 'ethnic cleansing' in Turkish Armenia, and the Russians could not contemplate an offensive because the Caucasus Army's needs had low priority compared to those of the Eastern Front proper. The situation began to change following the arrival of the Grand Duke Nikolay, whom the Tsar appointed Viceroy and Commander in the Caucasus in September. On the night of 19–20 December the Allies evacuated Gallipoli, and the Caucasus Army's Chief of Staff, General Yudenich, realised that this would free Turkish forces for use elsewhere, principally against his front. Secondly, Serbia's collapse in October and Bulgaria's entry into the war on Germany's side had reopened the land route from Germany to Turkey. German weapons, especially artillery pieces, could now flow unimpeded to the Turks. Thirdly, Turkish supply routes and services were so inadequate that neither of these could happen quickly.

There was a 'window of opportunity' of several weeks for destroying the Turkish Third Army, and there was another appeal for help from an ally. This time it came from the British in Mesopotamia (now Iraq), whose attempt to advance to Baghdad had been stopped at Ctesiphon. They had had to retreat, and since 7 December had been besieged in Kut al-Amara by Turkish forces in daily increasing numbers. The British therefore asked for a Russian attack in Anatolia, to draw some Turks away, and this gave the Grand Duke an additional reason to act quickly. He approved Yudenich's plan on 31 December, and the offensive began on 10 January 1916.

The fall of Trabzon.

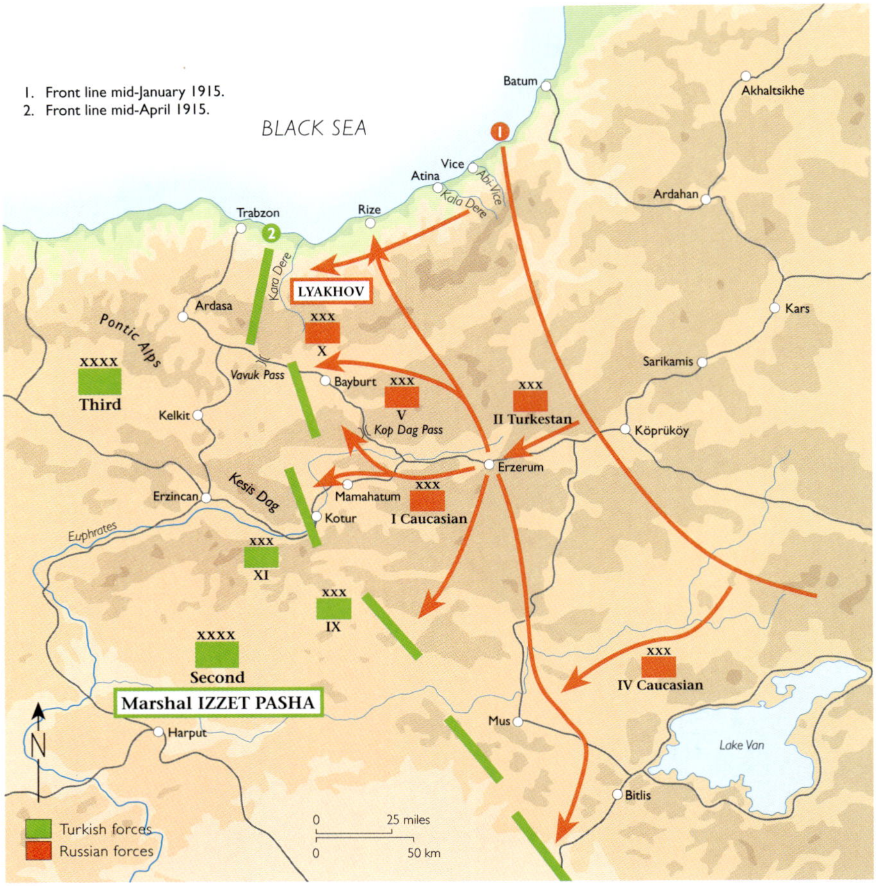

Yudenich assumed, correctly, that the Turks would not expect a Russian offensive in the depths of winter – the Third Army's commander, Kamil Pasha, and Chief of Staff, a German, Major Guse, were both away. The Russians had 325,000 troops available, the Turks 78,000, and Russian supply services, which included 150 lorries, were superior to their Turkish equivalents. These were entirely dependent on beasts of burden, had few good roads and had been disrupted by deportation or worse of the Armenian conscripts who provided clerical and labour services in the Third Army, and of the Armenian farmers who provided much of its food. The Russians also controlled the sea, and had air superiority – the 20 aircraft of the Siberian Air Squadron.

Like Enver's 1914 plan, Yudenich's required the troops to march over high mountain plateaux and ridges in blizzards and deep snow. But unlike Enver's troops, the Russians were adequately clad and fed, and carefully trained beforehand. The Turks chose to stand at Köprüköy, 40 miles east of Erzerum, and concentrated five divisions there, leaving only one to guard the south–north road from Bitlis, at the west end of Lake Van, to Erzerum, along which most of Erzerum's supplies came. The Russian 4th Caucasian Rifle Division marched over the high Cakirbaba ridge to split the Turkish defences on 14 January. Some 25,000 Turks were killed or captured, and the rest fled to Erzerum.

The fortifications of Erzerum comprised 15 forts with about 300 mostly obsolete guns. A ridge, over 9,600ft high, between the northern and central forts was presumed impassable, so was neither fortified nor occupied. The Russians moved on to it, but after an entire battalion froze to death they rotated troops so that most spent only a few hours there at a time. As the fort system could be adequately manned only by about twice the 40,000 defenders, it was to be attacked at several points, and simultaneously the town of Mus on the north–south road was to be captured, to block any Turkish reinforcements or supplies that might be on their way.

Victorious Russian cavalry entering Trabzon. (Ann Ronan Picture Library)

The assault began on 11 February, and four days later the Third Army abandoned Erzerum. The Russians entered the city the next morning, and captured Mus on the same day. Only about 25,000 Turks escaped; the Russians captured over 12,000, and 327 guns, at a cost of about 3,000 killed in battle or by exposure, 7,000 wounded and about 4,000 non-fatal frostbite cases.

The next phase of Yudenich's plan involved an advance along the Black Sea coast, and was noteworthy for skilfully conducted combined operations using shallow-draft barges to land troops, and the big guns of warships to provide the heavy artillery support that the army elsewhere lacked. The Russian Black Sea Fleet, under the command of Admiral Eberhardt, had maritime supremacy, challenged only sporadically by two modern German warships (*Goeben* and *Breslau*) and one submarine (U33), and its main operating difficulty was the 450-mile distance from its main base, Sevastopol, and nearest subsidiary base, Novorossiisk.

Between 5 February and 6 March the Turkish Third Army was turned out of several defensive positions along the coast by a combination of naval bombardment and landings of troops behind them. The Russians halted about 30 miles east of Trabzon because of faulty intelligence reports that a large Turkish force was in the vicinity, but resumed the offensive on 14 April, and entered Trabzon on the 18th. The Turkish Second Army had been brought into the area in February as part of a German-devised plan for a south–north drive across the Russian lines of communication; but it managed no more than a temporary blockage of the Russian drive towards Erzincan.

Brusilov's offensive

On the Eastern Front proper, neither Allies nor enemies thought Russia capable of a major offensive in 1916, so Falkenhayn continued transferring troops to the west for his battle of attrition at Verdun. The Allies, too, resolved on a major Western Front offensive, on the Somme, to begin on 1 July, and sought limited Russian support, to inhibit German westward transfers. Stavka therefore ordered North and West Fronts – commanded by generals Kuropatkin and Ever – to plan an offensive towards the important rail centre of Vilnius for some time in May. However, the Verdun battle, which began on 21 February, spurred more frantic French appeals for help, so the offensive was advanced to 1 March.

The North Front, along the Dvina River, comprised two armies (Fifth and Twelfth), the West Front five (First, Second, Third, Fourth and Tenth). One from each front was to attack, the Fifth to advance its right wing out of its Yakobshtadt (Jekabpils) bridgehead, the Second to advance north and south of Lake Narozh, to meet the Fifth, closing a pincer on the German XXI Corps, then advance to Vilnius. The Twelfth, Fifth and First Armies were to pin down German reserves. The West Front's assault force totalled 30 divisions, with about 400,000 men, on a 43-mile front.

The artillery support was modest by German standards, but Russia's heaviest yet. However, the prolonged concentration process was, as usual, detected, and the Germans reinforced beforehand. The 1 March deadline could not be met, for lack of rifles; so Stavka ordered the West Front to move on 18 March, and the North on the 21st.

On 17 March the spring thaw began unexpectedly early, turning the ground ahead of the Russians into an almost impassable quagmire. Nevertheless, the offensive proceeded. Despite unprecedented expenditure of shells, and disregard for casualties, the West Front failed utterly. In three weeks it took an area slightly more than 1 mile deep by 2 miles wide, at the price of 70,000 killed, wounded or captured, and in one day, 14 April, the Germans retook it all.

On the North Front, General Gurko fared somewhat better, by attacking later (21 March), and desisting sooner (26 March). He committed only four of his eight divisions; they had over 28,000 casualties, more than one-third of their strength. Diversionary attacks south of Riga and west of Dvinsk neither prospered nor drew off Germans. The two fronts' casualties totalled 110,000, but the main casualty was morale. This time immense efforts had been made to provide enough weapons and ammunition, but failure was again complete.

Stavka blamed the commanders for bad organisation, the artillery for not supporting the infantry, and the infantry for lacking dash. But the real culprit was Stavka's blithe insouciance in going ahead despite the thaw. Nor did the offensive draw off any Germans from Verdun. However, when Alexeyev began to plan 1916's main operation – the offensive to support the Somme – he produced only an expanded version of it.

For supporting the Somme it did not matter whether German troops stayed in the east defending themselves or helping Austria-Hungary. But Alexeyev had no doubt that the major effort should be against Germany, and proposed a renewed attempt to recapture Vilnius using the West Front, supported by the North. The South-West Front would join in only after the West's advance had exposed the Austrians' left flank, and would receive no extra resources. Most of Stavka's artillery and infantry reserves would go to Evert, the rest to Kuropatkin.

The South-West Front's commander, Ivanov, had become chronically depressed, and was replaced by Brusilov at the end of March. On 14 April Nicholas summoned a Council of War at Mogilev, to consider Alexeyev's

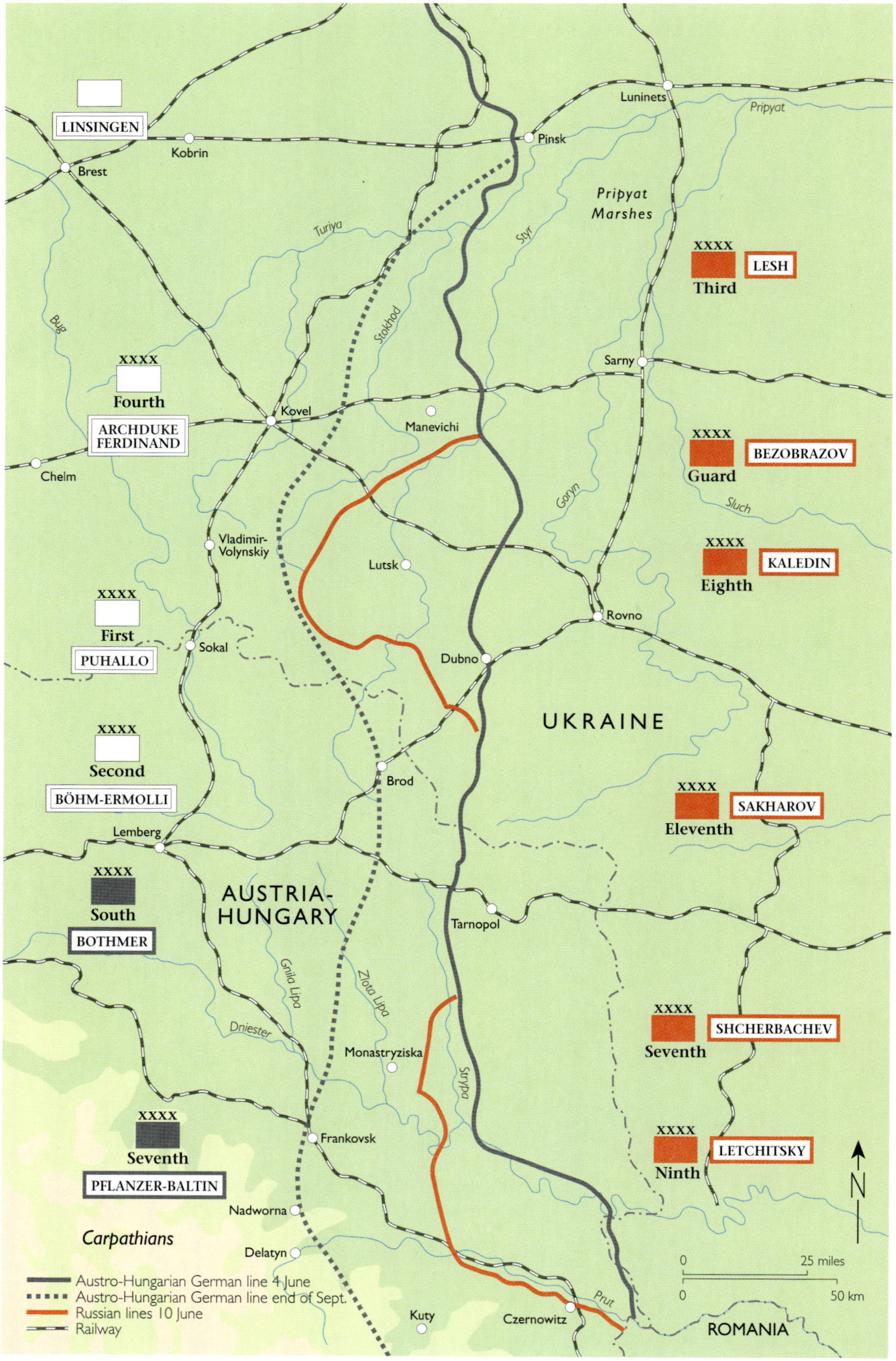
LINSINGEN
Kobrin
Brest
Luninets
Pinsk
Pripyat
Pripyat Marshes
Turiya
Styr
Stokhod
Bug
XXXX
Third
LESH
XXXX
Fourth
ARCHDUKE FERDINAND
Kovel
Manevichi
Sarny
Chelm
XXXX
Guard
BEZOBRAZOV
Goryn
Sluch
Vladimir-Volynskiy
Lutsk
XXXX
Eighth
KALEDIN
Rovno
XXXX
First
PUHALLO
Sokal
Dubno
UKRAINE
XXXX
Second
BÖHM-ERMOLLI
Brod
XXXX
Eleventh
SAKHAROV
Lemberg
XXXX
South
BOTHMER
AUSTRIA-HUNGARY
Tarnopol
Gnila Lipa
Zlota Lipa
Dniester
Monastryziska
Strypa
XXXX
Seventh
SHCHERBACHEV
XXXX
Seventh
PFLANZER-BALTIN
Frankovsk
XXXX
Ninth
LETCHITSKY
N
Nadworna
Carpathians
Delatyn
0 25 miles
0 50 km
Austro-Hungarian German line 4 June
Austro-Hungarian German line end of Sept.
Russian lines 10 June
Railway
Kuty
Czernowitz
Prut
ROMANIA

Opposite:
The Brusilov offensive.

proposal. At the Council Kuropatkin predicted immense casualties, for lack of heavy artillery ammunition. War Minister Shuvayev and Head of Artillery Grand Duke Sergey confirmed that heavy shells would remain scarce, whereupon Evert endorsed Kuropatkin's objections, opposing any offensive until artillery supply improved.

At this point Brusilov sought permission to attack simultaneously with Evert and Kuropatkin, arguing that at worst he would improve their chances by pinning down enemy forces. Alexeyev agreed in principle, and Evert and Kuropatkin then grudgingly accepted his plan, with a provisional deadline in May.

The North and West Fronts' preparations followed the conventional pattern. A sector about 28 miles wide was chosen west of Molodechno, and 47 divisions assembled in it. The main force was General Ragoza's Fourth Army consisting of 22 infantry divisions, while south of it were Radkevich's Tenth Army with 15 infantry and three cavalry divisions, and the new Guard Army under Bezobrazov, composing four infantry and three cavalry divisions. Ammunition dumps were established, roads improved and artillery and supplies brought in; and, as usual, German air reconnaissance and spies saw them come.

Since the front north from the Pripyat River to the Baltic was the nearer to Russia's and Germany's vital centres, all bar four German Eastern Front divisions were north of the Pripyat Marshes, and the preparations caused them no anxiety. The planned operation was orthodox and therefore predictable; they would have ample advance notice of its starting, and could withstand it.

Brusilov rejected the orthodox approach. Troop and supply concentrations and trench-digging could not be concealed, so he decided to confuse the Austrians by having all four armies dig trenches along their entire front, and each have all its corps attack somewhere. The main assault would be by General Kaledin's Eighth Army towards Kovel, where the north–south railway behind the enemy front crossed two west–east lines; but the Austrians could not extract this from a picture of frenzied activity everywhere. He deliberately violated the principle of 'concentration of force' to increase his chances of surprise.

His four armies (from north to south, the Eighth, Eleventh, Seventh and Ninth) occupied a front about 300 miles long, between the Pripyat Marshes and the Romanian frontier, with 36 infantry and 12½ cavalry divisions, comparable to the 37 infantry and 9 cavalry (42 Austro-Hungarian, 4 German) divisions facing them. Brusilov's efficient combination of aerial reconnaissance and spies kept him better informed than the enemy about the forces facing him.

From north to south they were an 'Army-sized Group' under Linsingen, the Austrian Fourth and Second Armies, led by Archduke Josef Ferdinand and Böhm-Ermolli, the German Southern Army, which despite its name and its Bavarian commander, Bothmer, was mostly Austro-Hungarian, and the Austrian Seventh Army, under the command of Pflanzer-Baltin. More than half the Austro-Hungarian troops were Slavs, mostly better disposed towards Russians than towards their Austrian or Hungarian overlords. Since March 1916 Ludendorff had advocated a unified eastern command under Hindenburg, but the Austrians opposed publicising their subservience, so no such command yet existed; the front facing Brusilov was under the Austrian Archduke Friedrich.

Brusilov could not set an attack date until he knew that of the main offensive. On 20 April he ordered his armies to be ready any time after 11 May, but Evert's preparations proceeded so slowly that a co-ordinated offensive clearly could not begin until June. Then, as before, events elsewhere forced a change of plan.

On 15 May the Austrians attacked on the Italian front, and their initial successes prompted urgent Italian appeals for Russian help. Evert was still dragging his feet, but Brusilov's preparations were so advanced that on 24 May Alexeyev asked him if he could attack alone. Alexeyev can only have done this on the Tsar's orders, and like the responses to appeals by the French in 1914 and February 1916, and the British in 1915, it put fidelity to allies above Russia's own interest. Sending the South-West Front alone into action destroyed the entire concept of a co-ordinated offensive. Brusilov, attempting to retain it, offered to attack on 1 June, provided Evert attacked simultaneously, to prevent the Germans moving troops to his front. Alexeyev told him Evert could not attack before 14 June, and asked him to postpone his own offensive to 4 June. On being assured that there would be no further postponement, he agreed. However, late on 3 June Alexeyev telephoned, expressed grave doubts about Brusilov's plan and suggested postponement to regroup for an orthodox single blow. Brusilov refused and offered his resignation; Alexeyev, having covered himself and Stavka against possible failure, withdrew his suggestion.

When the offensive opened on 4 June, two questions were crucial. Did the Austrians know what to expect? How would the troops perform? The answer to the first soon became clear: they did not. The second had less simple answers. Most performed well, but there was a worrying desertion rate. Between 15 May and 1 July, 10,432 men deserted from the Seventh Army, 24,621 from the Eighth, 9,855 from the Ninth and 13,108 from the Eleventh. Thus, during three weeks of quiescence and four weeks of a successful offensive, enough men for three full-strength divisions deserted.

The Eighth Army, at the north of Brusilov's line, attacked on a 16-mile front with two corps. After a long artillery bombardment on 4 June, Kaledin unleashed his infantry on the 5th and captured Lutsk by nightfall on the 9th. The Austrian Fourth Army was forced back, and its southern neighbour, the Second Army, also had to withdraw, as the Fourth's retreat exposed its northern flank.

Kaledin's southern neighbour, General Sakharov's Eleventh Army, attacking towards Vorobyevka, was somewhat less successful. The German Southern Army's right, almost all Slav troops, soon folded, but its centre and left held firm.

The guns of General Shcherbachev's Seventh Army opened up at 4.00am on 4 June and continued, with occasional breaks, for 46 hours, shelling wire, trenches and observation posts by day, and firing sporadically during darkness to hinder repairs. At 2.00am on 6 June, II Corps attacked with two infantry divisions and one regiment on a 4½-mile front; within two hours it took the first two lines of Austrian trenches and most of the third. That evening II Cavalry Corps arrived, and on the 7th the two corps drove the enemy back across the Strypa River. On the 8th the adjacent XVI and XXII Corps joined in on the north, and by the 10th the breach in the Austrian front was 30 miles wide, with over 16,000 prisoners.

Russian infantry charge. Five casualties are already shown in the attack. (Ann Ronan Picture Library)

Previous page:
Russian gunners in 1914, pictured with light field guns laid out in direct line-of-sight formation on the Eastern Front.
(Getty Images)

At the front's southern end, Lechitsky's Ninth Army faced Pflanzer-Baltin's Seventh. Lechitsky had only slightly more infantry (ten divisions against eight and a half) and no more cavalry (each had four divisions), but he prepared his attack carefully. He assembled his force in narrow ravines along the Dniestr River that the Austrian artillery could not penetrate, and chose two narrow sectors for the main assault, about 3,000 and 4,000yds respectively. All 16 battalions of the 3rd Trans-Amur Division assembled in the shorter northern sector, and 20 from the 11th and 32nd Divisions gathered in the southern. His bombardment began at 4.30am on 4 June, and lasted until noon in the southern sector, 12.30am in the northern. As the barrage lifted, the infantry rushed the Austrian trenches, and took them all by evening.

Pflanzer-Baltin, under cover of counter-attacks, prepared to evacuate his east-bank bridgeheads, and on 10 June pulled back to the River Prut. Several days of torrential rain hampered pursuit, so the Austrians averted total disaster; but they were forced back across the Prut, retaining only one bridgehead on its east bank, just north of Czernowitz (now Chernivtsi), capital of Austrian Bukovina. Here they held for five days, but on the 19th XII Corps took Czernowitz, and two days later Pflanzer-Baltin withdrew to the Seret River.

Thus in the first two weeks Brusilov's two flank armies, the Eighth and Ninth, achieved considerable penetrations, but success in the centre was more limited. Casualties in all three armies were heavy, and most of the artillery ammunition had been fired. The inner flanks of the Eighth and Ninth Armies were vulnerable to counter-attacks, so the line needed to be straightened by advancing the centre. This raised the issue of pinning-down attacks and the West Front's passivity. Successful though Brusilov's offensive was proving, it was officially only a curtain-raiser for Evert's. That was due to start on 14 June, but Evert requested four days' postponement for bad weather, then claimed that the German concentration of troops and guns at Molodechno was too strong to beat, and proposed attacking at Baranovichi instead. The Tsar consented, but the need to regroup imposed further delay.

Brusilov protested hotly at being left unsupported, scorned Evert's Baranovichi plan as needing at least six weeks to prepare, and asked Alexeyev to persuade the Tsar to order Evert to attack as planned. Alexeyev replied that Evert had orders to attack by 3 July, and offered Brusilov two additional corps. Brusilov grumbled that Evert's attack would fail because it could not be properly prepared so quickly, that two corps were no compensation for Evert's foot-dragging and that moving them would take a long time, during which they would obstruct transport of his supplies; but he did not refuse them.

Events justified Brusilov's scepticism, and his fears of German counter-action. When Evert finally moved, at Lake Narozh and Baranovichi, he did not even succeed in pinning any German forces down. The Germans realised that Brusilov's successes threatened a death-blow to Austria-Hungary, and began moving troops south even before Evert's offensive petered out, on 9 July.

The Somme offensive it was meant to support was a disaster, and the only bright spot was the South-West Front. By 23 June it had taken 204,000 prisoners, so on 24 June Stavka decided to reinforce success and temporarily subordinated the Third Army under General Lesh to Brusilov. He ordered his two wings to maintain their offensives, while the Eleventh Army stood its ground.

The Germans' principal concern was to hold Kovel because its loss would cut the north–south railway, hampering movement between the Austrian and German fronts. A mixed German–Austrian force was assembling in the Kovel–Manevichi area to attack the Eighth Army's north flank, but Lesh and Kaledin disrupted its preparations by attacking first, on 4 July.

The Germans then planned a counter-offensive in the centre, to push back the Eleventh Army, which had been weakened by dispatching its reserves to its neighbours. However, the South-West Front's spies notified Brusilov that the counter-offensive was scheduled for 18 July, and he ordered the Eleventh Army to pre-empt it. At night on 15 July, Sakharov's troops attacked north of Brody, taking 13,000 prisoners and, more importantly, destroying the three dumps of ammunition stockpiled for the counter-offensive. The Germans had to call it off.

Elsewhere, however, the Central Powers' situation looked better. Kaledin was halted on 8 July, 25 miles short of Kovel. His advance to the River Stokhod eliminated a threat to his right flank, but brought him no nearer Kovel, now heavily protected by German forces.

Both sides now raced to reinforce. The Germans moved troops from the Western Front, the Austrians from the Italian and Serbian fronts. Stavka sent Brusilov units from the West Front and the rear. Thanks to superior railways, the Central Powers were reinforcing slightly the faster, but not yet fast enough to replace their losses. Brusilov's strengthened north and south flank armies pressed forward, and the Eleventh Army straightened the line in the centre by advancing to the Koshev–Lishnev area, taking another 34,000 prisoners.

The Third and Eighth Armies halted on the Stokhod on 14 July, and began regrouping to advance on Kovel and Vladimir-Volynski. The elite Guard Army now arrived. Commanded by General Bezobrazov, it had four infantry corps (I and II Guard, I and XXX Infantry), each of two divisions.

and the Guard Cavalry Corps, of three divisions, under General the Khan of Nakhichevan. It was deployed between the Third and Eighth Armies, where its 134,000 men greatly outnumbered the two German and two Austrian divisions facing it.

Brusilov planned to resume his offensive in two stages. The Seventh and Ninth Armies in the south were to start advancing north-west along the Dniestr on 23 July, the Third, the Guard and the Eighth were to follow on 28 July over the Stokhod, the first two towards Kovel, the third towards Vladimir-Volynski, also on the north–south railway. Torrential rain forced postponement in the south, and all attacked on 28 July.

The Stokhod's east bank was marshy and wooded, and the Guards were confined to three narrow causeways. They advanced with all the expected *élan*, driving the mixed Austro-German force across the river and taking some 11,000 prisoners. However, machine guns and marshy terrain exacted an enormous price, as did enemy use of air superiority to deny reconnaissance and impede artillery support by shooting down observation balloons. In its first two weeks at the front (21 July–2 August) the Guard Army lost about 30,000 men, and Brusilov's belief that Kovel could be taken in a week proved unrealistic. The Eighth Army took 9,000 prisoners, but Vladimir-Volynski also proved beyond reach, and all three northern armies had to dig in against fierce counter-attacks. The Eleventh Army stormed Brody on 28 July, advanced to the Graberka and Seret rivers and took another 8,000 prisoners.

On 3 August Brusilov conferred with Kaledin and Bezobrazov at Lutsk, and decided to continue towards Kovel. The Guard Army's sector was too marshy for cavalry, so its Cavalry Corps was dismounted and used to man quiet sectors, releasing three infantry divisions for the main blow. This would be delivered by I Guards and I Corps north-westward from Velitsk, supported by a westward thrust by I Siberian and XVI Corps of the Third Army north of them, and an assault on the fortified village of Vitoney by the Guard Rifle Division south of them.

It was hoped that concentrating 64 battalions against nine German and 16 Hungarian would overcome the enemy's advantage of prepared positions and the lack of maps or photographs of the defences – these were mostly in woodland, and German aircraft thwarted attempts to photograph those visible from the air. But the attack, launched on 8 August, failed completely. By next morning the Guard was back on its start line, minus almost 9,000 men. The Third Army fared no better, and the Guard Rifle Division occupied Vitoney, but heavy artillery fire drove it out. Nicholas dismissed Bezobrazov, renamed the Guard the 'Special Army' and removed it. At the same time, mid-August, the Third Army was returned to the West Front, leaving Brusilov only his original four armies.

On 2 August Hindenburg was at last given charge of the entire Eastern Front. However, no sooner had the Austrian General Staff agreed than it partly reneged, stipulating that the two armies south of the Tarnopol–Lemberg railway, the 'German Southern' and the Seventh, should remain under Archduke Charles and Austrian GHQ.

On the southern sector, the Russian Seventh and Ninth Armies pushed together along the River Korobtsa towards the regional centre of Monastryziska, and on 9 August the Ninth Army broke the Austrian line near Stanislav. The Eleventh pushed southwards west of the River Strypa, threatening to outflank Bothmer. The Kaiser had visited Bothmer's positions during the previous winter, and pronounced them impregnable; but now they were untenable. Bothmer withdrew some 10 miles, to the Zlota Lipa River. On 12 August the Ninth Army took Nadworna, and the Seventh Monastryziska. The front in the south then stabilised temporarily.

In the ten weeks to 12 August Brusilov's offensive had captured 8,255 officers and 370,153 men. Including killed and wounded, it had deprived the Central Powers of over 700,000, and taken over 15,000 square miles of territory, by far the Entente's biggest success so far. Brusilov's unorthodoxy had been brilliantly vindicated.

But the price had been high. Russian casualties were over 550,000, and three-quarters of the front's 400,000-man reserve had been expended. Success also brought increased commitments in the south, where the Ninth Army's advance into the Carpathian foothills more than doubled its front line. But a much greater additional burden was about to materialise.

Campaign in Romanian

The Entente had long been wooing Romania, which had an interest in joining the war. This interest was Transylvania, Hungarian ruled, but mostly Romanian populated. However, Romania could only hope to get it if the Entente won, and up to mid-1916 that did not look very likely. Besides, should a Central Powers' victory put Transylvania out of reach, Russian Bessarabia (now Moldova), also mostly Romanian populated, could be a consolation prize.

Strategic vulnerability also dictated caution. Romania had very long frontiers relative to its area. Bulgaria had joined the Central Powers in September 1915, had a territorial claim against Romanian Dobrudja and could well pursue it militarily if Romania joined the Entente. Bucharest would then be particularly endangered, as it was only 30 miles from the Bulgarian border. The Romanian Army numbered 23 divisions, but all were poorly equipped and trained, and deficient in wheeled transport; the road system was inadequate, the railways not much better. Prudence probably dictated staying neutral, but Brusilov's successes created a chance for Romania to seize Transylvania while Austria-Hungary was fully stretched, so on 27 August Romania declared war.

One division was left to guard Dobrudja, and almost all the rest were sent into Transylvania. Hungary had few troops there, a few days would suffice to take it, and then Dobrudja could be reinforced. However, as insurance, the Romanian high command asked Russia for troops, and Alexeyev agreed to send the minimum three divisions specified by the Russo-Romanian military convention to Dobrudja.

Unfortunately, this proved only the first, and smallest, burden that Romania's entry into the war imposed on Russia. Bulgaria was not at war with Russia, and diplomatic manoeuvre and a token military presence might deter it from invading Dobrudja. But Austria-Hungary and Germany were already at war, so diplomacy could not neutralise the threat from Galicia.

To counter it, Alexeyev dispatched one cavalry and seven infantry divisions to the Ninth Army between 23 July and 31 August, one from the rear, the rest by taking one each from the First, Fourth, Fifth and Sixth Armies, two from the Seventh and the cavalry division from the Third. Thus Lechitsky had 17 infantry and five cavalry divisions, although 14 of them, having been in action since 4 June, were understrength.

Romanian infantry in their trenches, November 1915. (Ann Ronan Picture Library)

The Central Powers had grasped the danger that Lechitsky's advance posed, and reinforced the Austrian Seventh Army with five German divisions, plus two divisions and two mountain brigades from Austria's Italian front. The Austrian Seventh grew to 16½ infantry and four cavalry divisions. Half its infantry and all its cavalry were in no better shape than Lechitsky's, but the five German divisions were formidable, and so were the Austrian mountain brigades. They had fought in the Dolomites, whereas most Russian soldiers had never seen mountains before, let alone fought in them.

For Dobrudja, Alexeyev could spare only two Russian divisions, while the convention stipulated at least three. A '1st Serbian Volunteer Division' was being formed from prisoners of war, and Alexeyev decided to include it in the 'Dobrudja Detachment'. He was presumably unaware that to find Russia allied with Romanians and Serbs, whom they had fought as recently as 1913, would extend Bulgarian hostility from them to their Russian mentors.

The South-West Front was partially reorganised. The Special (ex-Guard) Army, now commanded by Gurko, returned, and took over the Eighth Army's northern sector. Reconnaissance reported the enemy positions in the Lutsk salient east of Kovel (held by Linsigen's German 'Army of Manoeuvre' and Archduke Josef Ferdinand's Austrian Fourth) too strong to take, so Brusilov decided to substitute a westward thrust towards Vladimir-Volynski by the Special Army and the right wing of the Eighth. His two centre armies, the Eleventh and Seventh, in line from Brody to Stanislav, were given no major task, as both were much understrength. Two divisions and a corps staff of the Seventh were transferred to its southern neighbour, the Ninth, which received the major assignment for September, and the lion's share of reinforcements. To help secure Romania, it was to seize the north–south passes through the Carpathians.

While Romania was invading Transylvania, and the Russo-Serbian force was moving into Dobrudja, the Ninth Army advanced into the Carpathian foothills on a front of about 75 miles between Nadworna and Dorna Watra (now Vatra Dorne). Lechitsky had superiority of about two to one in infantry and five to one in cavalry, but his advance was necessarily channelled along three main roads, from Delatyn, Kuty and Cimpulung, which converged at Marmarössziget. His cavalry was almost useless in the hills, and enemy howitzers, deployed on reverse slopes out of sight of his artillery spotters, poured fire down on his troops. For lack of aircraft the Russians could seldom locate them, and could not deal effectively with those they did locate because they had few howitzers and little howitzer ammunition. Morale was high, but shortages, enemy artillery and unfamiliarity with mountain warfare made the going hard.

The Romanians had completely occupied Transylvania by 6 September, but the Central Powers riposted quickly. Falkenhayn's failure at Verdun had led to his replacement by Hindenburg on 28 August and he was appointed to command the German Ninth Army, assembling in Galicia. Bulgaria declared war on Romania on 1 September, and a mixed force under Mackensen immediately invaded Dobrudja, sweeping the Romanian division aside, reducing the 1st Serbian and 61st Russian divisions to 3,000 men each, and forcing them out. On 19 September Falkenhayn entered Transylvania and was as little hindered as Mackensen. On 3 October both won major victories, Mackensen forcing withdrawal north of the Danube, and Falkenhayn driving a retreat from Transylvania by his win at Kronstadt.

For ten days Falkenhayn rolled the Romanians back towards Lechitsky's troops. Near Dorna Watra, on the night of 13 October, six Romanian battalions decamped. Lechitsky plugged the gap temporarily with two cavalry divisions, but the Ninth Army had to take over the empty sector or its flank would be turned.

Germans man-handling their field weaponry. (Ann Ronan Picture Library)

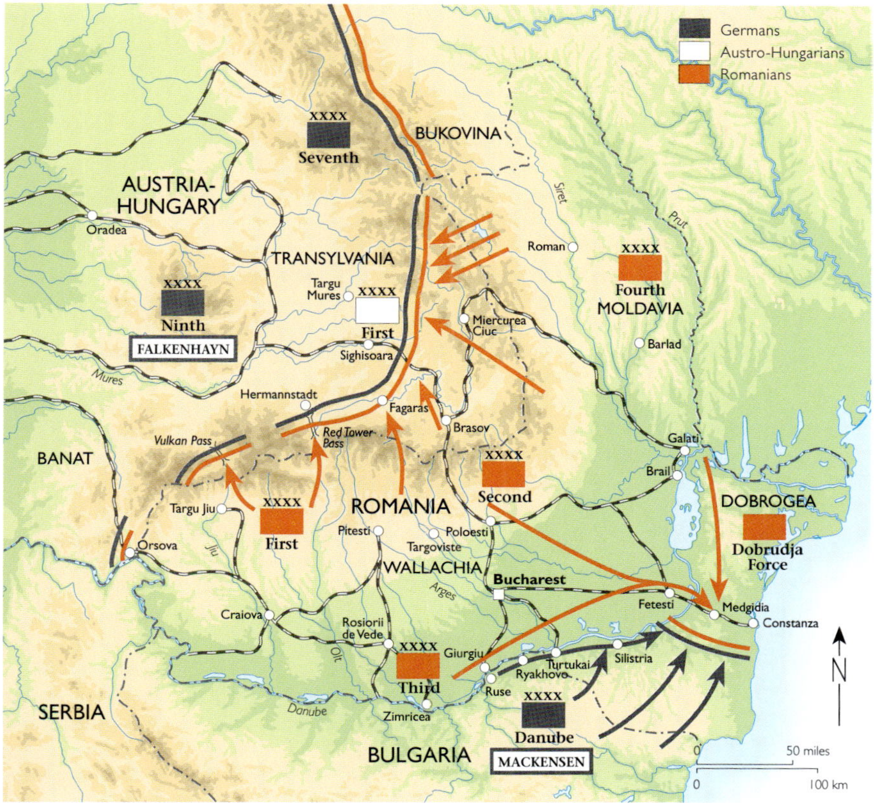

The invasion of Romania.

The South-West Front's mission was no longer to eliminate Austro-Hungary, but to prevent Romania's collapse. This necessitated abandoning Brusilov's offensive, and Nicholas ordered its end on 10 October. The extension of the Ninth Army's front meant an additional army was needed. The Eighth Army's Staff was transferred in mid-October from Lutsk to Czernowitz, the Ninth's front was divided in two, and most of its troops were allocated to the new Eighth Army. The Dobrudja Detachment grew to ten divisions and became the 'Danube Army', under Sakharov, who was replaced at the Eleventh by General Klembovsky.

Eighth Army forces remaining on the Vladimir-Volynski axis were subordinated to the Special Army, inflating Gurko's command to 25 infantry and five cavalry divisions. It fell to him to throw the last dice, when on 16–17 October he committed 15 divisions to a final thrust at Vladimir-Volynski. The German artillery drove out his infantry wherever they penetrated German lines, and punished them further as they withdrew to their own. After two days of this Gurko called a halt, and the front settled into the mud and mists of autumn. Since 4 June the South-West Front had incurred 1.2 million casualties, including 212,000 taken prisoner.

The onset of winter brought little relief. Defence of the Romanian front became Stavka's main preoccupation because failure could open the way into Ukraine and the Russian rear. All offensive plans were scrapped. The North and West Fronts would undertake only minor operations, and many of their units would be sent to the new Romanian Front, formed from the Danube Army and the remnants of four Romanian armies. This was nominally commanded by the Romanian King Ferdinand, but really by General Sakharov. Bucharest fell on 6 December. Romanian and Russian pleas to the French to activate the expeditionary force at Salonika against Bulgaria produced no significant result. The Western Allies pronounced Romania solely Russia's responsibility; and extension of the front line by about 250 miles to the Black Sea coast forced Russia to provide 55 infantry and 15 cavalry divisions to man it.

Suffering on the Russian home front, 1917

Though Ludendorff later admitted that the German Army 'had been fought to a standstill, and was utterly worn out', the Germans considered that they had done well enough in the east to transfer eight divisions to the west. They were somewhat surprised when in January–February 1917 the Russian Eighth, Seventh and Ninth Armies attacked, gaining some ground in Bukovina, but at the end of February joint German–Austrian counter-attacks recovered it all.

Meanwhile popular discontent with Nicholas' leadership was increasing and the home front was starting to collapse under the weight of food and fuel shortages, high prices and continued military failure. On 12 January 1917, British ambassador Buchanan told the Tsar that he must regain the people's confidence. Nicholas' response was: 'Do you mean I am to regain the confidence of my people, or they are to regain my confidence?' Buchanan diplomatically replied 'both', but warned that 'in the event of revolution, only a small part of the army can be counted on to defend the dynasty'. Eight days later Rodzyanko, President of the Duma, delivered a similar warning. But Nicholas took no notice.

February 1917 was a month of extreme cold and heavy snow. The railways were brought almost to a standstill, and Petrograd began to run out of flour, coal and firewood. On 8 March food riots erupted, the next day crowds began looting bakeries and the Cossacks sent to disperse them fraternised instead, and on the 10th the workers went on strike. On the 11th, Garrison Commander General Khabalov, on Nicholas' orders, forbade all public assembly, but a company of the Pavlovsky Life Guard Regiment, ordered to fire on a crowd, shot its officer instead. One after another regimental commanders notified Khabalov that only some of their troops were still obeying orders; and they could not undertake street duties because if they left barracks the rest would mutiny. By evening on the 12th almost the whole 170,000-man garrison had mutinied, and Khabalov controlled only the Winter Palace, with a mere 1,500 troops.

Revolutionary propagandists had long been at work among the troops, but they did not cause the rising, and no faction stood ready to take over. The Duma hastily set up a 'Provisional Committee' only when it heard on 12 March that a crowd of 80,000 was approaching. By that time an alternative source of power, the Petrograd Soviet, had come into existence.

In 1905 a short-lived 'Soviet (Council) of Workers' Deputies' had been formed to direct a general strike. Now a similar Soviet was set up, mostly by show of hands at open-air meetings. On 13 March both it and the Provisional Committee were at work in the Duma building. That evening Nicholas' ministers resigned, and arrived at the Duma asking to be taken into protective custody.

Nicholas had left on 7 March for Stavka at Mogilev, 500 miles away. During the next few days Rodzyanko and others advised him that only his abdication could save the monarchy. He attempted to return to Petrograd on 13 March. At 2.00am on the 14th, when his train arrived at Malaya Vishera, 100 miles from the capital, he was told that the line to Petrograd was blocked by troops with artillery and machine guns, but he could go east to Moscow or west to Pskov. The North Front's headquarters were at Pskov, so he went there, to be met by the Front commander, General Ruzhsky, with the news that the entire Petrograd Garrison had mutinied, and four regiments sent to restore order had been stopped on the outskirts, then had deserted *en masse.*

While Nicholas was travelling to Pskov, Rodzyanko spoke to Alexeyev, who agreed that Nicholas must abdicate, and sent telegrams seeking all the Front commanders' opinions. Their replies, received on 15 March, all recommended abdication. That day Nicholas abdicated.

Russia now had no head of state, but it still had a war. A Provisional Government was hastily formed, but the Soviet at once claimed authority over the garrison. On 14 March it issued 'Army Order Number One', proclaiming itself the 'Soviet of Workers' and Soldiers' Deputies' and decreeing that in all political actions military units must obey only its orders. Discipline must be observed on duty, but off-duty standing to attention and saluting were abolished and titles were replaced by 'Mr General', 'Mr Colonel', etc. Company Committees must control all weapons, and in no circumstances issue any to officers.

The preamble made it clear that the order applied only to the Petrograd Garrison, but copies reached the front, and discipline crumbled in their

Opposite:
Soviet myth making. The Winter Palace was not stormed – the Red Guards got in through an unguarded side entrance. (Ann Ronan Picture Library)

wake. In April two Duma members visited the front and concluded that the morale of the artillery and Cossacks appeared intact, but the cavalry's was unknown, and much of the infantry 'shaken'.

The German Great General Staff now decided to stir the pot by providing the so-called 'Sealed Train' (actually a carriage) to convey Lenin across Germany to Sweden, whence he arrived in Petrograd on 16 April. There he advocated fraternisation, immediate peace and conversion of the war into a class struggle – that is, civil wars between the peoples and their governments. This was an open challenge to the Provisional Government, whose members saw an Entente victory as essential, since a victorious Germany would restore autocracy. They strove to keep the Eastern Front in being, and prevent enemy transfers to the west, by mounting a summer offensive.

Tension between the Provisional Government and troops increased as Bolshevik and Left Socialist Revolutionary (SR) peace propaganda spread alongside rumours of the impending offensive. However, senior officers remained optimistic, and the West Front told Stavka in mid-April that an offensive would be possible in one or two months, after revolutionary excitement had abated. The Fronts' reports probably erred on the optimistic side because pessimistic officers were deemed counter-revolutionary; War Minister Guchkov and his successor, Kerensky, dismissed large numbers of them.

Before the insurrection, Russia had undertaken to co-ordinate its operations with those of Britain and France, and in particular to attack within three weeks of the start of the Anglo-French offensive. Alexeyev, now Commander-in-Chief, notified the Allies that Russia could not meet this commitment until May, and by 12 March he was convinced it could not do so before the end of July. In any case, the Russian Army's condition made it impossible to co-ordinate action with Nivelle's offensive in France, scheduled for mid-April.

The Sealed Train.

News of the USA's entry into the war on 6 April offered some encouragement, but was followed only ten days later by the collapse of Nivelle's offensive, and mutinies in the French Army. There was now doubt whether the Western Front could last out the several months that would elapse before the Americans arrived in force, and this increased Allied anxiety to keep the Eastern Front in being. They stepped up deliveries, and soon the material situation was better than ever.

Vladimir Ilyich Ulyanov, better known as Lenin. (Ann Ronan Picture Library)

But psychologically things could hardly be worse. Guchkov resigned on 1 May, and on the 2nd Alexeyev and the Front commanders addressed a joint meeting of Provisional Government and Soviet. Alexeyev told them bluntly that 'the army is on the brink of ruin', and others gave instances of the troops' interpretation of Bolshevik calls for 'peace without annexations' as meaning they need not attack even to recover occupied Russian territory. The Soviet would not act to restore discipline; the Provisional Government could not. All that resulted was that on 22 May the new War Minister, Kerensky, replaced Alexeyev with Brusilov, who began planning a scaled-down version of his 1916 offensive, an attempt by the Seventh and Eleventh Armies to take Lemberg, with pinning-down attacks by other Fronts and the Eighth Army (under General Kornilov).

The Central Powers advance

The front had been static since October 1916, the Germans preferring not to risk restoring Russian unity by attacking, so artillery and ammunition were plentiful. A new factor was volunteer shock battalions, which Alexeyev, doubting the ordinary soldier's reliability, had formed from men who specifically asked to continue fighting.

On 18 June the South-West Front's assault began. The shock battalions led the way, but the infantry followed only reluctantly, and after two days refused to go on. On their left, Kornilov attacked on 23 June, against low-quality Austro-Hungarian forces, and took 7,000 prisoners; but as his shock battalions became casualties, the Eighth Army's infantry proved as recalcitrant as the Seventh and Eleventh's. By 2 July the offensive was over. Total losses, 38,700 officers and men, were infinitesimal compared with those tolerated in previous years, but were now unendurable. The Germans and Austrians counter-attacked the Eleventh Army on 6 July, and with nine divisions routed 20, driving the Russians back to the Seret. So complete was the Eleventh's collapse that even its Soldiers' Committees approved shooting of deserters, but apparently no one was prepared to do any shooting.

The North Front's offensive began on 8 July and ended on the 10th. Of six divisions allocated, only two took part, and one of them had to be forced into the line at gunpoint. The other took two lines of German trenches, but then refused to continue and returned to its own lines. When the West Front attempted to attack, with 138 battalions against 17 German, the same happened.

On the Romanian Front the position was slightly better. The Romanian Army had greatly improved, and was unaffected by the Russian Revolution, so it was planned to use Romanian forces alongside Russian. Here the shock battalions were not used to lead, but deployed behind the troops, to shoot any who ran away. The assault began on 10 July, and was attended with some success. However, the failures elsewhere had eroded Kerensky's confidence in Brusilov, and he replaced him with the Cossack Kornilov. His first act was to stop the offensive, and the Romanian Front did so on 13 July. From then on, only the Germans would attack.

Nor did the Russians have long to wait. The next German move was near the Baltic coast, where the front, almost unchanged since December 1915, ran along the lower course of the River Dvina, except for a large Russian bridgehead from 12 miles above Riga to a point on the coast 25 miles west of the city. It was held by the Russian Twelfth Army commanded by General Klembovsky, with two corps – II and VI Siberian – in the bridgehead, and another two – XXI and XLIII – behind the Dvina. By August 1917 it was in

Germans crossing the Dvina River during the Riga operation, September 1917, with no apparent opposition. (Ann Ronan Picture Library)

an advanced state of disintegration. Many soldiers had deserted; those who had not were mostly beyond control by their officers, and had killed many of them. General von Hutier's German Eighth Army, facing the bridgehead, had seven and a half divisions, but was reinforced by eight infantry and two cavalry divisions, and by as much heavy artillery as could be brought up in time from elsewhere on the front.

Hutier had two options, a frontal assault on the bridgehead, or crossing the Dvina upstream of it and attacking it from behind. The first would involve crossing the estuarine Tirul marshes, the second an opposed river crossing, then taking several fortified positions in succession. He chose the second option, the starting date of 1 September and the place a point about half way between Jakobshtadt (Jekabpils) and Riga, near two islands, Borkowitz and Elster. After crossing, the main force of three infantry and both cavalry divisions was to head north to the coast, to cut the Twelfth Army's line of retreat towards Petrograd. A second force of two divisions was to follow, to reinforce the main body and guard its flank against any counter-attack from the landward side.

The Russians knew of Hutier's preparations, but misread them as presaging an assault on the bridgehead. So Klembovsky removed his least reliable divisions from there to the east bank of the Dvina, and, fortuitously, deployed them precisely where Hutier intended to cross.

From 4.00am on 1 September the Germans fired gas shells for two hours, then changed to high explosive. The two islands were taken by 9.00am, and ten minutes later the river crossing began. The Russian positions were mostly found abandoned; by 5.00pm the bridgehead was 7½ miles wide, and two lines had been taken. But for once the Russians moved faster than the Germans. Hutier learned early on 2 September that Klembovsky had evacuated the bridgehead, and with his few reliable units as rearguard, was retreating along the Riga–Pskov road and railway, which the Germans had not yet reached. By the time they did, on the afternoon of the 4th, most of the Twelfth Army had gone. The Germans gained much territory and took 24,000 prisoners, but failed to destroy the Twelfth Army. That proved not to matter; apart from brief German actions to seize three islands at the mouth of the Gulf of Riga (12–20 October), the front remained quiescent until on 7 November the Bolsheviks seized power and began taking Russia out of the war.

The fiasco of the 1917 offensive had shown the depths to which the army's morale had sunk, and on 12 July the Provisional Government had voted to restore both capital punishment and courts-martial. Kerensky was now Prime Minister, but the government was still competing with the Soviet for the loyalty of the armed forces, and had just survived a premature attempt to seize power by a Bolshevik faction. He could not therefore implement the draconian measures that Kornilov wanted, so Kornilov began plotting to take power himself. The Cossacks looked to him for leadership, and, importantly, he had the support of the Don Cossack Ataman (Headman), General Kaledin. The Allies backed Kornilov, seeing his efforts to restore discipline as the only guarantee of Russia's staying in the war, while conservative Russian politicians and financiers backed him as defender against a Bolshevik takeover.

Kornilov concentrated III Cavalry Corps (mostly Cossacks) near Petrograd, and arranged to have about 2,000 'Kornilovist' officers posted to the capital. The putsch was to begin by provoking riots, then marching troops into the city on the pretext of protecting the government, while the 2,000 officers would arrest the leaders of all left-wing parties and seize the government buildings. It was planned to take place no later than 1 September.

However, Kornilov's intentions became known, so Kerensky ordered Kornilov to Petrograd, and when he began to move troops Kerensky proclaimed him a traitor. But Kerensky had no real force at his disposal, and it was the Soviet that stopped Kornilov; it armed the workers (including Bolshevik Red Guards, who thus obtained thousands of weapons to use later), ordered railway workers to block movement of troops by train and fetched in sailors from the Baltic Fleet's Kronstadt base. On 27 August, representatives who went to meet Kornilov's troops persuaded them to refuse to go further. The Soviet also told the front-line troops what was happening; many Kornilovist senior officers, including the South-West Front's commander, Denikin, and all his army commanders, were arrested by their men. The Soviet gained most from Kornilov's attempt to establish a military dictatorship, and its failure showed that the army and population had lost interest in the war. The German capture of Riga a few days later passed almost unnoticed.

Kornilov's failure further fragmented the army. The men now saw their officers as the chief obstacles to peace, and many moderate military committees were replaced by radical ones. Bolshevik and German propaganda exploited war-weariness to increasing effect, and by the time the Bolsheviks seized power on 7 November (25 October by the old

The Kaiser in Riga, September 1917. (Ann Ronan Picture Library)

calendar), the army's attitude, as described in Stavka's report for the second half of October, was

> one of highly nervous expectancy. Now, as before, irresistible thirst for peace [and] universal desire to leave the front ... constitute the main motives on which the attitude of most of our troops is based. The army is simply a huge, weary, shabby and ill-fed mob of angry men, united by their common thirst for peace and common disappointment.

On 25 November the newly appointed Communist Commander-in-Chief, Krylenko, sent a peace delegation to the German lines. General Hoffman replied on the 27th, indicating willingness to grant an armistice. It took effect on 17 December, and both sides prepared to negotiate peace.

PORTRAIT OF A SOLDIER: A TROOPER, AN ENSIGN AND A SERGEANT

German Eastern Front soldiers were regularly required to beat numerically superior Russian forces, and almost invariably did. Their leaders seldom exposed them to pointless risk, and normally fed, equipped and rested them adequately. The infantryman could see that his artillery, machine-gun and air support was vastly superior to the Russian, and his feeling of having the edge seldom left him. There was no breakdown of morale in 1918 comparable to that on the Western Front; it was historical irony that, after the failure of a strategy explicitly devised to avoid a two-front war, Germany fought one for three and a half years successfully enough to eliminate one of the fronts, only to concede defeat on the single front in only eight more months.

The heterogeneous Austro-Hungarian forces were not much better equipped than the Russians, and about 60 per cent of them were Slavs – Czechs, Slovaks, Poles, Slovenes, Croats, Bosnian Serbs and Ruthenians. Most of these initially fought reliably, but in time became less reliable, especially the Czechs, who were encouraged to surrender or defect by a reconnaissance unit of Czechs living in the Russian Empire. Attempts to form units from them were initially frustrated by the Tsar's reluctance to arm them while his own troops lacked weapons, then by the Czechs' unwillingness to fight for a Russia that refused public support for Czech independence (the Tsar feared 'infection' spreading to his non-Russian subjects), and by other ministries' desire to use them as industrial or agricultural labour. Some units were formed, but too late to affect the Eastern Front war, though one, the Czechoslovak Legion, played a prominent part in the ensuing Civil War.

The Russian view of military service was expressed in a four-line verse: 'clever to the artillery, drinker to the navy, rich to the cavalry, stupid to the infantry.' It was meant for newly commissioned officers, but the 20–25 per cent of literate conscripts tended to be sent to the artillery or cavalry, and the rest to the infantry. The average soldier could keep no diary or journal, and in the turmoil that followed the 1917 collapse, almost nothing was published about the ordinary soldier's experiences. However, enough military censorship reports survived to give a general picture, and significant accounts were written later by a cavalry trooper and sergeant, and an infantry junior officer (ensign).

The three soldiers served on the same front (South-West), in different units; their accounts are generally consistent with each other, and with the censors' reports. All three were villagers, the trooper and sergeant born into peasant families, the ensign son of a village priest. They were typical in that their families subsisted only by their fathers taking on extra work, and their mothers and sisters making gloves and mittens for sale during winter. They were untypical in receiving education – the ensign (intended for the priesthood) was schooled to the age of 19, the others to the age of ten – and in 'escaping' their rural background early, the ensign to a theological seminary, the others apprenticed to a shoemaker and a furrier. The trooper was conscripted in 1912, the others in 1915 – the ensign in January, the sergeant in August.

The ensign underwent officer training from February to May 1915. The programme paid much attention to drill, but taught nothing about surviving on battlefields dominated by 'field obstacles' (trenches, barbed wire, machine guns), or about the possible roles of motor vehicles and aircraft, and next to nothing about co-operation between the different arms of service. He joined an infantry regiment as an ensign in autumn 1915, and noted that the Russian trenches were primitive, uncomfortable and badly laid out compared to those of the opposing Austrian Seventh Army (the trooper made the same point after inspecting abandoned Russian and German trenches in 1916). The soldiers had no blankets; and slept in their greatcoats.

The regiment was entirely equipped with captured Austrian rifles, and had only two machine guns per battalion; the artillery was short of howitzers, heavy guns and ammunition of all calibres. After rest and training during the winter, the regiment returned to the line for Brusilov's offensive. The men, and most of the officers, welcomed facing Austrians, not Germans, and heaved collective sighs of relief when shell-bursts showed the pink smoke of Austrian high-explosive, an indication of the moral ascendancy that the Germans had established over the Russian soldier by mid-1916.

The trooper was at war from the outset. Like the sergeant he noted the lack of contact between officers and men, and that soldiers were frequently beaten for minor infractions. The ensign was told to impose discipline by the 'Prussian rule', that 'the soldier must fear the Corporal's stick more than the enemy's bullet'. The sergeant noted 'One aim was pursued, the soldier was to be an obedient automaton … The regulations did not provide for corporal punishment, but it was rather widely employed.'

Career officers came from the richer families, and few attempted to adapt to wartime circumstances, in which officer casualties could only be replaced by commissioning the less privileged, such as the ensign, or promoting warrant officers and sergeants. For example, two sergeants in the trooper's regiment, decorated for bravery and promoted to ensign, 'were suddenly posted to another regiment; our regiment's officers and gentlemen were unwilling to shake hands with ex-rankers'. He went on to say:

> when the general withdrawal [from Galicia in 1915] began … depression became more and more marked, and derogatory comments about the High Command became frequent … Reinforcements reaching us from the rear depressed us even more with their talk of imminent famine and our rulers' incompetence. The troops also found it hard to tolerate our officers' disregard for their most basic needs.

The sergeant said that during training he saw his company commander only twice, and that both times the officer was drunk. He described lack of rapport and unity between officers and men as the most characteristic feature of the Tsarist Army, though, contradictorily, he also gave instances of considerate and understanding officer behaviour. He also noted that the influx of officers from less privileged backgrounds improved relations up

A priest visits a primitive military hospital. (Ann Ronan Picture Library)

to battalion level, but that the higher commands remained dominated by officers 'alien' to the soldiers.

The typical Russian soldier with whom these three men served was a peasant who, unlike them, had not 'escaped' his background. He lived in a village with no electricity, gas, piped water or sewers, served by unsurfaced roads that were impassable for several weeks at a time during the autumn rains and spring thaw. He was used to hardship and a monotonous diet, described in another popular epigram as 'cabbage soup and buckwheat porridge', and to ill-treatment by 'gentry', whether landlords, factory owners or his military superiors. He was also, however, unused to handling and maintaining even the simplest machinery. Only the literate minority could do the paperwork of administration, and if they became battle casualties, a unit could soon find itself short of food, fodder or ammunition, or unable to operate the primitive radios used for communicating with higher formations.

Another junior officer, serving on the West Front in February 1916, summed up his men optimistically in a letter home:

> Whomever you ask 'well, brother, fed up with sitting around?' replies, '… we'd like to go forward now. We've got shells, we can push on …' And in our brigade they've all been under fire, they're experienced soldiers … they survived the painful time when we had no shells … people here don't weep or grieve, they're just full of energy and faith in the future, they can even joke happily in their own circle, here you don't meet mournful, sad faces, calm and confidence are written on them … about the war, in the sense of assessing results, betrayals or horrors, they don't talk; rest is devoted to laughter and gossip.

His assessment was made before the Allies' unsuccessful offensives on the Russian West Front of March and July 1916, and his subsequent letters made no reference to his men's morale. The trooper, sergeant and ensign, and the military censors' reports, point to its deterioration during 1916, particularly in its last few months. The sergeant, en route to the front in August 1916, mentioned conversations with wounded, from which he learned that 'our armies were very poorly armed, the senior commanders had a bad reputation, it was widely held among the soldiers that traitors, bought by the Germans, sat in the High Command, and the troops were poorly fed'. He went on to say that in September 1916 disaffection among the troops mounted, 'especially after letters from home told them of hunger and dreadful disorganisation'. In October he was seriously wounded, and he returned to the front only in December, where 'talking with the men I realised they were not burning with a desire to "sniff gunpowder", and didn't want the war. They already had different thoughts, about land and peace.'

Estimates of Russia's losses differ considerably, but on the latest available assessment 1.45 million were killed, 3.41 million captured, 3.22 million wounded and over 1 million missing. The ratio of 251 captured or missing to every 100 dead was by far the highest for any of the belligerents. In the first two years, the captures resulted mostly from inept generalship, but in 1916–1917 they were accompanied by high rates of desertion, indicating erosion of the will to fight. The signs of decay began to accumulate in the last months of 1916.

Russia contributed troops to the Anglo-French forces in Greece. They went by ship to a French Channel port, then by train to Marseilles. On 2 August 1916 soldiers travelling by train from Marseilles to embark for the Salonika front, beat their commanding officer to death. Their comrades refused to identify the killers until threatened with the shooting of every tenth man. Twenty-six were court-martialled, and eight of them shot. The men were officially said to have been exposed to revolutionary propaganda while in a transit camp in Marseilles, but there had already been disorders aboard ship between Archangel and France.

Unrest was not exceptional, as military censors' reports showed, and the commanders knew it was fragile. However, optimists, such as Brusilov's General Quartermaster, Dukhonin, expected the winter lull to provide relief, and morale to be much improved by the spring of 1917.

That this view was unrealistic soon became apparent. On 1 and 2 October 1916, in the Eastern Carpathians, two Siberian regiments of the Seventh Army refused orders to attack. On 9 October a regiment of the Special (ex-Guard) Army was forced at gunpoint by the two adjacent regiments to cease working on defences. Another threatened to fire on its neighbours if they obeyed orders to attack. Two more regiments were found to have been distributing peace propaganda for several months, including an anti-war manifesto written by the commanding officer of one of them; this in an 'elite' army raised in 1915, with specially selected officers and men.

In April 1916 the head of the Petrograd Okhrana (Security) could write: 'The Petrograd Garrison does not believe Russian arms can succeed, and finds prolongation of the war useless, but soldiers in fighting units express confidence that victory is possible.' By the end of 1916, this distinction was disappearing. Military censors' reports referred both to the depressive effect of letters from home ('Almost every letter … expresses a wish for the war to end as soon as possible'), and to the disgruntled tone of many soldiers' letters.

Food and fuel shortages and escalating prices affected morale. The Petrograd Military Censorship Commission on 27 November quoted soldiers' complaints of shortages of food, warm clothing and equipment, and added, 'in letters from the army, just as mostly in letters to the army, dissatisfaction begins showing itself more and more acutely about the country's internal political situation ... Rumours reach the army about disorders, strikes in factories, and mutinies in rear units, and cause morale to decline.'

To free Russian troops for the front line, on 25 June 1916 the Tsar had ordered conscription for non-combatant duties from populations hitherto exempt, including the Muslims of Turkestan (to provide 250,000), and Steppe (243,000) Governorates. This sparked risings throughout central Asia, which continued until December; barely had they been put down, and about half the desired numbers conscripted, when the regime collapsed.

Even had the full number been available, they would have made little difference. A report to Alexeyev on 15 October 1916 estimated that reserves available after 1 November would total only 1.4 million, almost all of low quality: 350,000 aged 37–40, 700,000 youths not due for conscription until 1919, and 200,000 previously rejected as physically unfit. Even with replacements cut to 300,000 a month, numbers would begin to fall from March 1917. This decline was accelerated, but not caused, by the events of 1917.

In 1914 nationalism had prevailed over class solidarity among most European socialists. A small minority, led by Vladimir Ilich Ulyanov (Lenin), argued for turning the 'imperialist' war into a class war, in which the conscripts, instead of fighting other countries' conscripts, would turn their guns on their rulers. The revolutionaries' linking of anti-war sentiment, social reforms, especially land reform, and opposition to the autocracy had some early effect. In January 1915, the Interior Ministry noted that many soldiers' letters home instructed the recipients to stop paying rent for their land; the Grand Duke ordered them destroyed. The revolutionaries then intensified their propaganda among training units in the rear, worrying the Grand Duke enough for him to have the Orthodox Church Synod ask bishops to appoint experienced priests as chaplains, capable of 'countering corruption by revolutionary propaganda'.

However, the success of anti-war propaganda among troops in the rear was not yet matched in the front line. There the shared purpose of self-preservation, unit pride, comradeship among men who had been under fire together and measures taken to keep out anti-war propaganda, defeated Bolshevik efforts. The party then infiltrated members into the military zone, but on 26 May 1915, the Grand Duke prohibited front-line visits by persons of 'dubious political reliability', and had some leaflet distributors exiled to Siberia.

Foiled yet again, the Bolsheviks ordered party members without police records to volunteer for military service. This was much harder to counter, as fellow-soldiers would hardly betray an agitator, even if they rejected his views. From then until the regime's collapse, subversives in uniform were a source of anxiety to the military leadership.

The socialist parties organised a conference in September 1915 in Switzerland, aimed at trying to end the war by international working-class action. Most participants supported a vague appeal to workers to 'struggle for peace', but Lenin headed a minority who advocated civil wars of peoples against their rulers there and at a second conference in April 1916. Lenin did not speculate on what would happen if Russians answered the call while Germans did not, because he believed that revolutions were imminent, and would render frontiers and nationalism obsolete.

As the 1916 campaigning season approached, revolutionary propaganda intensified, including spreading false rumours that soldiers on both sides were already refusing orders to attack. Henceforth claims that German troops were mutinous and Germany ripe for revolution became increasingly prominent in Bolshevik propaganda. The front-line soldiers knew they were false, but troops in the rear and civilians were more credulous. On 14 April 1916, the head of the Petrograd Okhrana reported: '[Petrograd Garrison] soldiers say openly that … revolution has already begun in Germany, and as soon as success has been achieved there, we shall follow Germany's example.'

In fact the Germans had other reasons to keep the Eastern Front quiescent. They were withdrawing troops from there for the Verdun offensive, they had also had to help Bulgaria and Austria-Hungary conquer Serbia and they saw no point in attacking in the winter snow or the spring mud. No offensive could be decisive, given Germany's commitments elsewhere, and to mount one might make the Russians sink their differences.

One reason for the impact of anti-war propaganda was military reliance solely on repression to maintain discipline. Stavka never attempted persuasion, or even telling the troops why Russia was at war – the trooper said that only by talking to officers' orderlies did the men learn that Russia was about to go to war. To explain the autocrat's decisions implicitly undermined the principle that they must be obeyed unquestioningly; but eschewing counter-indoctrination meant taking the troops' docility for granted, an ever less realistic attitude as time passed.

In the circumstances, it was surprising not that Russian troops sometimes performed badly, but that they often performed well. Defeatist revolutionary activities constantly worried the high command, but the examples cited above suggest that reliability was the norm, not the exception, among front-line units until the last quarter of 1916. And in March 1917 it was not the front-line troops but the Petrograd Garrison that mutinied and brought down the regime.

Three of the four sources cited above were chosen because of their subsequent careers. The sergeant was Georgiy Zhukov, of the 10th Novgorod Dragoons. The ensign, later Staff-Captain, was Alexander Vasilevsky of the 409th Infantry Regiment, and the trooper Alexander Gorbatov of the

Chernigov Hussars. All three rose high in the Red Army. In the Second World War, Zhukov and Vasilevsky, both Marshals, held its two top posts, respectively Deputy Supreme Commander and Chief of General Staff, and masterminded the victories that eluded their Tsarist predecessors. Gorbatov became a full General and commanded an army. Their views 'from below' can therefore be taken as fairly authoritative. The fourth source, Alexander Zhiglinsky, who assessed his men so optimistically in February 1916, was less fortunate. He was invalided out of the army in December 1916, went to the Crimea and took no part in the Civil War. In December 1920 the newly installed Soviet authorities there shot all ex-Tsarist officers.

THE WORLD AROUND WAR: THE LAST DAYS OF TSARIST RUSSIA

Throughout the war Russia's main problem was supplying its troops with the necessities of war, and its cities with food and fuel. Russia's size, an asset in some other respects, was a drawback when it came to meeting these objectives. Its thinly spread railway system could cope with peacetime loads, but the war soon overloaded it. First came the transport of reservists to their units, and of units (men, guns, horses, carts) to the front. Then came the burden of maintaining a regular supply to the army of food, ammunition, weapons and (the largest single item) fodder for horses. Added to that was the increase in industrial demand, particularly for coal.

Most of the heavy industry was in the north-west of European Russia, particularly in the Petrograd and Moscow areas, and was fuelled in peacetime, as also were most households, by Welsh coal delivered by ship to the Baltic ports. When Germany closed off access to or from the Baltic, coal had instead to come by rail from mines in Ukraine, over 1,000 miles away, and a crisis in coal supply began a mere six months into the war. Similarly, Turkey's entry into the war closed off access to the Black Sea ports, and the Allies' failure at Gallipoli to reopen the Turkish Straits cut off Russia's possibilities for importing machine tools, weapons and ammunition via the Mediterranean.

External links could be maintained only through Vladivostok in the Far East and Archangel on the north coast. Vladivostok had good port facilities, and icebreakers could keep them working in winter. But it was 6,000 miles from the front line, and necessitated immensely long transits, first across the Pacific and then via the mostly single-track Trans-Siberian Railway. And until July 1916, when a major bridge over the Amur west of Khabarovsk was completed, everything had to be ferried across the river. Ships delivered supplies faster than the Trans-Siberian could remove them, so they piled up on the wharves.

The sea and rail routes via Archangel were much shorter, but the port froze for almost half the year; a subsidiary port, Ekonomiya, was constructed downriver, and was ice free for most months, but its capacity was limited, and it had not been open long before the regime collapsed. Ships could deliver in six months more than the railway, also single-track, could remove in a year, and here, too, cargoes piled up. The Gulf Stream kept the north-coast fishing village of Alexandrovsk (now Murmansk) ice free, and a railway was being built to it, but it was completed only at the end of 1916, less than three months before the collapse.

Attempts to improve domestic supply began in March 1915, when the Ministry of Transport was empowered to control fuel producers. In May, after the supply crisis spread to food and fodder, the Ministry of Commerce and Industry was given powers to control agricultural supplies, food prices and the supply of food and fodder to the army. But attempts by the ministry and municipalities to control supplies and prices foundered on inefficiency, corruption, lack of funds and the declining capacity of the railways. In 1914 Russia had just over 20,000 locomotives and about 540,000 rail wagons. Those were modest enough totals (Britain, one-hundredth the area of Russia, had more locomotives), but by 1917, through labour and materials shortages and plain bad management, they had shrunk to 9,000 and 150,000 respectively. Inevitably, supplies of fuel and food to the cities suffered, and when the bad weather of February 1917 put 1,200 locomotives out of action with boilers or piping burst by freezing of the water inside them, food and fuel vanished from Petrograd. The food riots that began on 8 March escalated into revolution, and the Tsar abdicated a week later.

Soviet poster. 'Comrade Lenin is cleansing the world of dirt', by sweeping away kings, priests and capitalists. (Edimedia, Paris)

Considering that it was originally meant only as a diversion, the Brusilov offensive was a remarkable feat. It brought Austria-Hungary close to collapse, and forced both it and Germany to transfer troops from elsewhere. Forty-three divisions (15 from the Western Front, 19 from elsewhere on the Eastern Front, seven from Italy and two from Turkey) were so transferred. Their removal both weakened the

German effort at Verdun and forced Falkenhayn to abandon plans to disrupt the expected Somme offensive by attacking first. The Austrians could not exploit their success against the Italians in the Trentino because they had to transfer seven divisions to the East.

But the need to sustain Romania saw no fewer than 27 Russian divisions sent there in the ten weeks following its declaration of war. The Allied failure on the Somme enabled the Germans to send troops east to bolster their faltering Austro-Hungarian allies, and Falkenhayn's dismissal was another negative consequence for the Entente, as the far more formidable Hindenburg–Ludendorff team replaced him. Even so, the success was remarkable for an army that had suffered so many serious defeats in the previous two years. Brusilov's novel tactic of eschewing concentration and instead 'nibbling' simultaneously at a large number of points, initially proved itself; but the Russian regime and armed forces collapsed before any Russian generals could emulate it. And despite the improvements in supply wrought by General Polivanov, Russian armies remained technically inferior to their opponents, particularly the Germans. Casualties were inevitably high and the biggest casualty of all was the Russian soldiers' morale, which collapsed dramatically in 1917.

Throughout the war Nicholas, urged on by Alexandra and Rasputin, refused to dilute his autocratic powers, which he sincerely believed were God given, by forming a government based on majority support in the Duma. But public discontent was such that some spreading, if not of responsibility for decisions, at least of the odium they incurred, would have been advisable. The summer 1915 Duma session (19 June–3 September) offered an opportunity, when a new group, the 'Progressive Bloc', was formed. It was supported by all except the extreme left- and right-wing parties, comprised over two-thirds of the Duma and demanded representative government. Nicholas' only response was to prorogue the Duma, and he recalled it only after nation-wide demonstrations.

Alexandra constantly attacked Cabinet ministers who incurred Rasputin's or her displeasure. With the Tsar away at Stavka, his normal receptiveness to her suggestions increased, and from mid-1915 capable ministers were replaced by nonentities. First of these was the replacement of Goremykin as Prime Minister by Stürmer, a notorious pro-German. Next was the War Minister, General Polivanov. In the few months since he replaced the incompetent Sukhomlinov, he had effected immense improvements in army supply and training. However, like Grand Duke Nikolay, he hated Rasputin and favoured seeking Duma support, a combination that doomed him in Alexandra's eyes. On 25 March 1916, Nicholas replaced him with General Shuvayev, whom coming events would show to be a poor substitute.

Foreign Minister Sazonov's liberalism also made him suspect to Alexandra. In particular, she saw his advocacy of a post-war united autonomous Poland, linked to Russia only by acknowledging the Tsar as head of state, as threatening her husband's present and son's future autocratic rule, because other provinces would be likely to demand the same status. Nicholas dismissed him in July 1916, despite British and French protests. Sturmer added Sazonov's duties to his own, to the further detriment of relations with Britain and France, which deemed him totally untrustworthy.

But the most disastrous appointment Alexandra and Rasputin engineered was that of Alexander Protopopov in October 1916 as Minister of the Interior. To his control of the police Alexandra then added responsibility for food distribution. Given the poor state of the railways, a much more effective minister would have had difficulty maintaining food supplies to the cities in the 1916–1917 winter. Protopopov found it impossible, and his fifth and last month in office ended with food riots that escalated into revolution, and brought the regime down within a week. Rasputin had been assassinated on 31 December 1916 by ultra-monarchists who wanted to save the regime by purging it of his malign influence, but it was too late.

The Provisional Government's attempt to keep Russia in the war was only to a very minor extent governed by the undertaking Russia had given in the Treaty of London not to make a separate peace. The main reason for it was that if the Central Powers won the war, autocracy would be restored in the rump Russian state that they would permit to exist. The mutinies in the French Army in April 1917 marked the low point of the Entente's fortunes, raising at least to outsiders the question of whether the Western Front could last out until the Americans arrived.

The Allies were painfully aware of the effect an additional 40 or more enemy divisions could have if transferred from the east. But apart from their natural distaste for Lenin's calls on their workers to overthrow them, the Allies' governments cherished two illusions. The first, that the Bolsheviks were German agents, had some basis in fact, and the Germans shared it for a while. They had eased Lenin's return to Russia so that he could erode its will to fight, and he had done just that. They had not, however, expected him to come to power, and he kept calling on German and Austrian workers, peasants and soldiers to follow Russia's example and overthrow their rulers.

The Allied governments' second illusion was not shared by the Germans, and had no factual basis. It was the belief that there were large numbers in Russia who wanted to continue the war. In that belief the Allies stepped up deliveries of military equipment to unprecedented levels. However, the railways' capacity to move them had declined almost to nothing, and the army for which they were intended was melting away. Huge stocks accumulated at

Archangel and Vladivostok, and some at the ice-free port of Alexandrovsk (Murmansk). Among the reasons for the Allied intervention in formally non-belligerent Russia was the fear that the Bolshevik government would hand these stocks over to the Germans.

The Brest-Litovsk Treaty was signed on 3 March 1918. British troops landed at Murmansk in May; British, French and American troops at Archangel in July; Japanese, American, British and French at Vladivostok in July and August; and also in August British troops were fighting the Turks at Baku, attempting to prevent a Central Powers takeover of the oilfields. Meanwhile the Germans were in the Baltic provinces and Finland and, together with the Austro-Hungarians, in Ukraine.

These interventions had a mixture of motives. Germany and Austria-Hungary wanted Ukrainian food, coal and iron ore, and Caspian oil. Japan had imperialist designs on part of the Russian Far East. Turkey wanted to recover Kars, Ardahan and Batum, which Russia had annexed in 1878, and add Georgia and Azerbaijan to them. All the European governments on both sides, and the US administration, took the Bolshevik calls for revolutions seriously, perhaps more seriously than the masses to whom they were directed. They saw the new Russian Government as dangerous enough to justify crusading against it, the Entente powers having the additional motive of keeping the stockpiled supplies out of German hands.

However, to the Bolsheviks the fact that countries that elsewhere were fighting each other were, as they saw it, all making common cause against Communism, appeared to justify their view of capitalism as a worldwide conspiracy of the rulers against the peoples. The siege mentality that characterised the Soviet Union for most of its existence originated in the months following the signing of the Treaty of Brest-Litovsk.

The signing of the Russo-German peace treaty at Brest-Litovsk, 2 March 1918. (Ann Ronan Picture Library)

PORTRAIT OF A CIVILIAN: 'LIVING ON CEREALS AND PORRIDGE'

Before the war Germany imported about one-third of its food, including 12 per cent of fats and 28 per cent of proteins, so the civilian population suffered increasing shortages of flour, butter, cooking fat and meat as the war progressed. By mid-1916, weekly meat consumption had fallen from the pre-war 2½lb to 1lb, flour from 5lb to 2½lb, and fats from 14oz to 4oz. Not only was the quantity more than halved, but the quality fell; the wartime flour contained much bran, the meat much bone and gristle. The reduced rations were partly a consequence of cessation of imports, especially grain, from Russia, but resulted mainly from the blockade. German civilians were not actually starving, but malnutrition was becoming widespread enough to arouse popular discontent.

The wave of strikes that began in April 1917 owed something to the Petrograd Soviet's call for 'peace without annexations or indemnities', but more to the hardships of the just-ended 'turnip winter' (so called because turnips often had to substitute for unavailable potatoes), and a cut in the bread ration from 4lb to 3lb a week. The Social Democrats and others in the Reichstag could argue about the need for peace, but the military-dominated leadership wanted a victor's peace, and with America just entering the war, there was no way the Entente powers would give it to them. The civilian population simply had to continue suffering, with only such sporadic relief as foodstuffs delivered from conquered Romania under the armistice it signed in December 1917, or those that Ukraine undertook to deliver in return for Germany's recognition of its independence in February 1918.

Austria-Hungary's civilian population suffered similar hardships, again mostly caused by the blockade, but exacerbated by difficulties in maintaining food production when most able-bodied peasants were in the army and rail distribution was disrupted by military traffic. As in Germany, there were widespread strikes in Austria-Hungary in early 1917; here, too, they owed more to hunger than to the Russian revolutionary example.

As with all the other belligerents, how the war affected Russia's civilians depended on where they lived and how a family's breadwinners earned their livings. However, the effects were more acute here than elsewhere for several reasons. The standard of living was very low to begin with, and sank more as the war progressed. Agriculture was almost totally dependent on muscle power, and rural families suffered when the army conscripted most of the able-bodied peasants. In the winter it was common for male peasants to seek work in towns, often 100 miles away or more, and their wages, though small, were more than the allowances paid to their families when they were conscripted – moreover, after mid-1915 the allowance was terminated if the soldier was captured.

The most detailed descriptions of peasant life come from the relatively small number who 'escaped' from it. One fairly typical example was as follows.

The family had ten children. Large families were common because there were no social services, so the parents needed the children's labour and later their support in old age, and some of the children were likely to die in infancy. Clothes were bought new only for the eldest boy and girl, and handed down, increasingly patched, to the younger ones. The family had one cow, which the mother tended, but its milk went to market, and so did its annual calf, because the grain and potatoes they grew were never enough to last the year, and the money was needed to buy bread. There was also a horse, always an old one, bought cheaply, and carefully skinned when it died, as the money obtained for the skin went towards purchase of its replacement. The nearby woods and marshes provided mushrooms and berries, the best sold, the worst eaten, hay and fodder for the cow and horse, and wood for fires. In the winter all males over 12 years of age went to the nearby town and worked cleaning sheepskins. The wages were meagre, but they were allowed to keep the wool scraped off the skins, and this was taken home for their womenfolk to spin and make into mittens for sale. Many girls aged 12 or over worked in textile factories in the nearby town. The author of this account had three years' schooling, from age seven to ten, then went to join his father cleaning sheepskins.

The effects of the war on a family already barely subsisting were serious. The three eldest brothers were called up, and two of them were killed; the money they contributed from their work, and their labour at harvest time, ceased on call-up, and were replaced only by a small allowance paid in respect of one of them. When the surviving son arrived home in March 1918 he found his father ill, the house and outbuildings in a ruinous state, and no seed grain or potatoes left for sowing. Survival was possible only because the men of his regiment, before decamping, had shared out the regimental stores among themselves, and he was able to sell his portion to buy seed.

Most peasants saw the February–March revolution as a signal to drive out the landlords and divide their estates among themselves. Mass desertions from the army took place during the summer and autumn of 1917 when the soldiers, overwhelmingly peasants, headed for home to ensure they got their fair share of redistributed land. A governess on one estate described the consequences:

> the garden very much spoilt by the peasants and miners, who already considered it theirs by right, and we had to stay near our home or run the risk of being insulted … we left with the sad feeling that we looked for the last time upon the dear old place. And so it was, for a few months later it lay in a heap of ruins.

The war's effects on town dwellers were equally drastic. Food supplies dwindled because only women, children, the old, unfit or disabled were left to grow them. The 1915 harvest was so poor that even in the grain-growing Volga provinces flour-mills were periodically idle, while elsewhere they stopped for months for lack of grain. Even in the bread-basket of Ukraine and North Caucasus, the cities and towns reported flour and bread shortages, while meat and sugar also became scarce. Not one of the main cities abounded in all four; many lacked them all. Some residents had 'dachas' (smallholdings outside town) and planted vegetables there in their free time, but increasingly often they arrived to find the produce had been stolen.

Food prices rose in all the warring countries, but more so in Russia than elsewhere. Compared to 1913–1914, by early 1916 they were up 50–70 per cent in Britain, and 20–50 per cent in France. But in Russia the increases averaged 114 per cent, and in some cities were much larger. For example, in Moscow in June 1916 butter was 220 per cent, beef 371 per cent, mutton 381 per cent and rye bread 150 per cent above July 1914 levels. Fuel and clothing prices increased comparably, while wages, very low in 1914, had less than doubled. Municipalities' attempts to cap price increases merely drove more goods on to the black market, and their efforts to improve supply by bulk purchase were frustrated by lack of funds.

The Union of Towns, representing town councils, several times approached the Special Council for Supply seeking an overall plan to overcome the shortages by improving distribution. However, the Council, though specifically charged with 'co-ordinating all measures relating to problems of supplying the army and civilian population, and all institutions concerned with the same', proved reluctant to follow that line, mainly because the information needed for control was not available. Only in February 1916 did it introduce a draft scheme combining price control with regulation of rail transport, providing for rationing if necessary, and taking an agricultural census to provide the information needed for controlling prices and regulating supply.

This attempt to control the crisis was belated and inadequate. In particular, the local machinery for the supply scheme proved unworkable, mainly because it had separate commissioners to control supply to the army and the civilian population, and these acted independently, often competing with one another. Some imposed prices fixed arbitrarily or under pressure from interested parties. Others published permissible profit margins, thereby tempting merchants to inflate costs so as to increase profits. Yet others banned all price increases, and introduced severe penalties for offenders. Since some increases were inevitable, this drove commodities on to the black market.

Nor was it possible to co-ordinate and systematise freight transport, because of the overstrained railways and the priority accorded military traffic. In the Moscow Regional Committee's six provinces, for example, shipments in June 1916 were only 34.9 per cent of those planned. In most areas the 1916 grain harvest was excellent, but supply barely improved because landlords hoarded the grain to secure higher winter prices. Inevitably, bread shortages in towns, alongside known abundance of grain, strained urban–rural relations. The municipalities justly accused landlords and peasants of profiteering, while rural spokesmen pointed out equally justly that controlling prices of food but not of industrial products was discriminatory.

Amidst mutual recriminations, supply continued to deteriorate. The moneyed classes could eat well on food bought on the black market or brought from their estates, but for the ordinary citizen late 1916 was a time of 'queuing for thirteen hours for black bread, and living on cereals and porridge'. This continued until the run-down railways finally buckled under the cold in February 1917, and the food riots in March swiftly escalated into demands for the 'Nemka' ('German woman' – the Tsaritsa) to be removed and the Tsar to abdicate.

By then Petrograd had shed its urbanity. Streets lay uncleared of snow. Improvised stove-pipes poked out of windows because heating systems had broken down for lack of coal and the residents were making do with wood-burning stoves. There were no trams, almost no street lighting, and queues for bread outside bakers' shops formed before dawn.

Under the Provisional Government urban living conditions got even worse. By July 1917 the price of bread had trebled and that of potatoes, shoes and clothing more than trebled, while wages had risen by only one-third. Fuel and raw materials shortages, and cancelled orders, saw 568 firms in Petrograd close by July, throwing over 100,000 out of work. The workers' response was to establish factory committees to oversee owners, managers and accountants, and by August these were Bolshevik dominated. The Bolshevik seizure of power and consequent peace treaty brought some easing, but the Civil War soon broke out, and nothing resembling normal conditions returned to Russia's towns for at least another two years.

HOW THE WAR ON THE EASTERN FRONT ENDED: THE BOLSHEVIKS SEIZE POWER

The Russian Empire began to break up after the Bolsheviks seized power. The Ukrainian Rada declared independence on 22 January 1918, and on 9 February Germany signed a peace treaty with it, together with an economic deal for delivery of a million tons of grain to Germany and Austria-Hungary.

A German armoured train in Finland, 1918. (Ann Ronan Picture Library)

When Soviet government forces drove the Rada from Kiev, the Germans invaded Ukraine because they needed its grain, iron ore and coal to mitigate the effects of the blockade. Ukrainian co-operation was not sought; instead German firms were brought in to run Ukraine's mines and railways, and a puppet regime under the aptly named Skoropadsky ('quick-fall') was installed. The Germans' demands for food supplies alienated the peasants; their arrogance and profiteering alienated the industrial and mine workers. Saboteurs proliferated, as did Bolshevik propaganda. The German commander, Field-Marshal von Eichhorn, was assassinated in July 1918, and when the Germans withdrew following the November Armistice, their puppet regime quickly fell.

Finland declared independence soon after the Bolsheviks seized power. Although this action had Lenin's approval, a civil war broke out in January 1918. The 'Reds' seized Helsinki and a 'White' government was formed in the north, with small forces under Mannerheim, a former Russian Army general. He appealed to Germany for help, and a German division arrived in April. With its help the Reds were beaten before the year's end, but Germany's defeat aborted plans to install a German prince as king. Mannerheim became regent, and a republic was proclaimed in July 1919 and formally recognised by Soviet Russia in the 1920 Treaty of Tartu.

Opposite:
The front line at peace and after.

NORWAY
ARCTIC OCEAN
SWEDEN
FINLAND
Petrograd
ESTONIA
BALTIC SEA
LATVIA
RUSSIA
Moscow
LITHUANIA
GERMANY
Berlin
POLAND
Brest-Litovsk
UKRAINE
AUSTRIA-HUNGARY
Budapest
ROMANIA
Bucharest
CRIMEAN REPUBLIC
SERBIA
MONTENEGRO
BULGARIA
BLACK SEA
ALBANIA
GREECE
Athens
TURKEY
N
0 250 miles
0 500 km
Russia
Entente Powers
Central Powers
Neutrals
15 December 1917 front line at the time of the armistice
Line set by the Brest-Litovsk Treaty
Limit of area occupied by central powers
LATVIA States recognised as independent by the treaty

The Kaiser wanted to annex the former Russian Baltic provinces (Estonia, Courland, Livonia and Lithuania) to Prussia. The Reichstag wanted to annex them to the Reich. A group within the Foreign Office advocated their independence as non-Communist states, which, being small and economically dominated by ethnic German 'Baltic barons', would naturally gravitate towards Germany rather than Russia. Bolshevik sympathies were widespread among the locals, and German behaviour during the occupation tended to alienate them.

The 'barons' set up pseudo-parliaments, lobbied influential relatives in Germany, especially in the army, and appealed to the Kaiser to intervene. In February 1918, German troops went in as 'peacekeepers', and made secret deals with the biggest barons to have the pseudo-parliaments declare independence, then immediately vote for annexation by Germany. These moves were frustrated by Germany's defeat, and after its surrender the provinces became the independent states of Estonia, Latvia and Lithuania.

Harsh as the Treaty of Brest-Litovsk was, German behaviour was even harsher. Lenin had agreed to the treaty because Russia had no choice, with an army whose will to fight had been destroyed largely by his own propaganda; in any case, he believed the other belligerents would soon follow Russia's example, and the treaty would then lapse. He was right on the last point, though wrong about the reason for it.

Germany's behaviour in the east in 1918 did nothing to help it win the war, and may have helped Germany to lose it. The 100-plus German and Austro-Hungarian Eastern Front divisions used to further plans for annexations there would not have been needed if the Russian Empire had simply been left to disintegrate. They could have been shipped to the Western Front and almost doubled the force available for the 1918 spring offensive, the Central Powers' last chance of winning before the Americans arrived.

Paradoxically, it was the military's dominance in German decision-making that brought about this militarily counter-productive situation. Initially Hindenburg and Ludendorff sought a quick conclusion to the Brest-Litovsk negotiations precisely so that they could transfer troops to the West as soon as possible. But they kept the troops at hand to pressure the Russian negotiators because they wanted a peace that reflected the completeness of their victory. In seeking it they behaved as if they had already won the whole war, rather than just what they agreed was the less important half of it. The stick used to beat the Bolshevik negotiators was the threat that if Germany's demands were not met, the advance would resume, and the treaty not negotiated at Brest-Litovsk would be dictated in Petrograd.

PUNCH, OR THE LONDON CHARIVARI.—March 27, 1918.

A WALK-OVER?

The Kaiser. "THIS IS THE DOORMAT OF OUR NEW PREMISES."
Emperor Karl. "ARE YOU QUITE SURE IT'S DEAD?"

Cartoon, originally from *Punch*. (Ann Ronan Picture Library)

The German Government was less ambitious than the military. Foreign Minister von Kühlmann did not share the generals' belief that complete victory was possible. Even if the German Army were victorious on the Western Front, Germany did not have the sea power to confront the world's two strongest navies and invade the United Kingdom, its Dominions or the United States. Peace could be imposed on Russia and France by victory on land, but peace with the 'Anglo-Saxons' would at best have to be negotiated.

Kühlmann was as keen as the generals to take territory in the east, but only to use as bargaining counters in peace negotiations, by offering to yield territory there in order to avoid having to do so in the west. He also wanted a settlement with the Russians that would not be held against Germany by its future negotiating partners.

So when the new Soviet Government invited all the belligerents to negotiate peace on the basis of 'no annexations, no indemnities, and the principle of self-determination', Kühlmann and his Austrian counterpart, Czernin, agreed. But when the other Entente powers rejected the formula, leaving Russia to negotiate alone, the German military insisted not only on a speedy settlement, but on a victor's peace that extracted as much as possible from the vanquished.

The Soviet delegation, headed by Trotsky, was motivated to prolong the negotiations as much as possible, to give time for the proletariat and peasantry in the other belligerent countries to absorb and, they hoped, copy the example of Russia's Bolshevik revolution. Trotsky succeeded in dragging negotiations out for six weeks. But on 9 February 1918, the Central Powers forced his hand, by recognising Ukraine as independent, and signing the peace treaty. On the 10th Trotsky declared the war ended but the Central Powers' terms rejected, proclaimed 'neither war nor peace' and left for Petrograd, apparently believing that the Central Powers needed peace as much as Russia did, and would soon come to heel.

All his flamboyant gesture achieved was to hand the initiative back from the diplomats to the soldiers. Despite strong protests by Kühlmann and Czernin, Hindenburg and Ludendorff secured the Kaiser's reluctant consent to resuming hostilities. What remained of Russia's Army melted away before the German troops, who advanced to within 80 miles of Petrograd in a few days, virtually unopposed. The Bolsheviks then gave in and asked for peace terms. The Germans set them out as an ultimatum to be accepted within three days, and a treaty to be ratified within two weeks of signing. The Bolshevik leadership was split, and Lenin had some trouble in getting his own way. But in reality they had no choice but to comply, and the Treaty of Brest-Litovsk was signed on 3 March 1918.

It was a very punitive treaty. Russia had to recognise the independence of Finland, Ukraine and Georgia, yield sovereignty over its four Baltic provinces and adjacent islands to Germany, over Russian Poland to Germany and Austria-Hungary, over Kars, Ardahan and Batum to Turkey, and pay six billion Marks in reparations. Since Marx had predicted that the socialist revolution was most likely to happen first in highly industrialised countries, Lenin signed in the belief that it would soon be rendered inoperative by revolutions throughout Europe. In fact, it and the supplementary treaty of August became inoperative before the year was out, as a result not of revolution, but of Germany's defeat by the capitalist Entente powers. Both treaties were annulled on 13 November, two days after the Armistice.

But even that Armistice did not bring peace to Russia. The Allied forces which in the first instance had come primarily to prevent the handover of military supplies to the Germans, and to keep the Caspian oilfields out of German hands, did not leave when the war's end removed the threat. The prospect of strangling the Communist state at birth would lead to increasing foreign interventions on the side of the 'Whites' in the ensuing Civil War. To win that war the Bolsheviks, who had subverted the old army during 1917, and dissolved it in 1918, would now have to build the new 'Workers' and Peasants' Red Army' from its remnants.

Chapter 4

THE MEDITERRANEAN FRONT 1914–1923

Previous page:
A 60-pounder gun of the Royal Garrison Artillery in action at Cape Helles, Gallipoli. A chronic shortage of field artillery and ammunition severely inhibited the performance of British troops throughout this ill-starred campaign. By August 1915 most of the 60-pounders had broken down and a lack of spares had reduced their number to a single gun. (Topfoto)

BACKGROUND TO WAR: THE DECLINE OF THE OTTOMAN EMPIRE

To understand the complex factors affecting the Mediterranean war it is necessary to look into the histories of the numerous nations involved. Many of the conflicts can be traced back to the middle ages and beyond. The Ottoman Empire arose from the fall of the eastern Christian Empire in 1453 and the vigour of militant Islam. Successive sultans' armies fought their way westward, by 1529 to the gates of Vienna, bringing whole provinces of the Balkans, Arabia, North Africa and much of the Iberian peninsula under Ottoman rule. Vienna, however, saw the first serious reverse; a Turkish Army of some 120,000 men under Suleiman the Magnificent was repulsed by the city's 16,000 defenders and with the raising of that siege the Ottoman military machine began slowly to decline. In 1683 it reached Vienna again, to be defeated with enormous loss by 70,000 Christians. Ottoman sea power in the Mediterranean was broken in 1571 at Lepanto when the Venetian and Spanish battle fleets shattered the Turks in the last great battle fought by oar-propelled ships.

The Ottoman decline was irreversible. The empire had overrun many Christian states and these territories were in continual turmoil, their struggles for independence aided, when it suited them, by the western powers. The Orthodox Christian Slav population of Serbia gained autonomy in 1817 and 12 years later Russian pressure and the participation of idealistic individuals – notably Lord Byron – enabled Greece to break away from Constantinople. There was growing concern in London over increasing Russian influence in the Balkans, where Pan-Slavism, the awareness of the brotherhood of Slavs, fuelled rebellion against Ottomans and Austrians alike. Russia backed this movement, and was seen throughout the 19th century as a threat to British interests in India. In Vienna there was alarm at the rise of Pan-Slavism on the doorstep, especially as Austria had enough problems of its own among its non-Germanic populations. France favoured the Christian populations of the Levant, supported them in their struggles to escape from the Turks, and sought to colonise sub-Saharan and North Africa. French advisers helped the remarkable Pasha Mehmet Ali to become ruler of Egypt in 1806. In 1823 his French-trained army pushed south into the Sudan to found Khartoum. Mehmet's son Ibrahim, defying orders from Constantinople (as had his father), moved north and took Damascus in 1832, defeated the Turkish Army sent to bring him to book, and headed for Constantinople. Hurried discussions between Austrian and Russian diplomats led to the Treaty of Umkiar Skelessi, which appointed Russia as military protector of Turkey, with the right to close the Dardanelles to warships of any other power. But Britain and France regarded the treaty with dismay and resolved to get it abolished or at least revised as soon as possible.

Quinine parade for British troops in the field. The revolting taste of the medicine made it difficult to enforce health discipline and the only answer was to hold compulsory parades such as this. Malaria caused more casualties to British troops than combat in this theatre. (IWM Q32159)

In 1839 the Turkish sultan Mahmoud II died, having failed to recover Syria from Ibrahim. The great powers hurried to take advantage of the Ottoman decline but disagreed as to how they should act, all having their own selfish objectives. France was keen to install the ageing Mehmet as hereditary ruler of Syria and Egypt but the Foreign Office in London saw a dangerous opening for Russian expansion in the direction of India. Palmerston, the British Foreign Secretary, produced a formula acceptable to Russia, Prussia and Austria whereby Mehmet was granted the hereditary right to rule over Egypt and (if he agreed immediately) the administration of Syria for life. The French, his patrons, were excluded from the deal and objected vehemently; Mehmet declined the offer but was nonetheless granted government of Egypt. France was re-admitted to the club and a new treaty was drafted to replace that of Umkiar Skelessi: the Treaty of London, signed in 1840, under which the Dardanelles and Bosphorus remained closed to all foreign warships *as long as the Ottoman Empire stayed peaceful.* Palmerston's crafty diplomacy had successfully scrapped the older treaty and displaced Russian influence in Turkey, which now enjoyed 12 years of relative peace.

The sultan, gaining confidence, supported reforms of the civil service and military systems and declared the equality of all citizens of the empire. But corruption remained endemic and religious fanaticism continued to deny the large Christian population their rights. In 1852 the new French Emperor, Napoleon III, decided to assert himself by insisting that France should have guardianship of the holy places in Palestine, hitherto in the custody of the Orthodox churches. In response Tsar Nicholas, who detested the upstart Napoleon, told the Turks to acknowledge Russian protection of the Orthodox Church throughout the empire, including the Balkans.

Nicholas (who coined the expression that the Turkish Empire was 'the sick man of Europe') then suggested an Anglo-Russian partition of the tottering empire. Rebuffed by Palmerston, Nicholas ordered his troops into the provinces of Wallachia and Moldavia. As war loomed, the French and British fleets entered the Dardanelles. Turkey declared war on Russia in October 1853 and immediately lost a disastrous naval encounter with the Russians at Sinope. The Anglo-French fleet entered the Black Sea in January 1854, and the two nations went to war with Russia two months later in support of Turkey in what became known later as the Crimean War. The war ended with a treaty signed at Paris in 1856. The Ottoman decline continued. Wallachia and Moldavia achieved autonomy and became Romania under a German prince, Charles of Hohenzollern, who reigned wisely as Carol I until 1914.

Ottoman rule eventually broke down in Syria with civil war following a massacre of Maronite Christians by Druse Muslims, which gave the opportunistic Napoleon III another chance to assert himself. The French Army savagely put down the Druse in Lebanon, and a Christian governor was appointed. In Greece, independent since 1833, there was a rebellion against King Otto, a Bavarian, and he was replaced by King George I of the Hellenes, a Dane, who reigned from 1863 to 1913 when he was assassinated in Salonika. George was succeeded by his son Constantine, whose wife Sophia was the sister of Kaiser Wilhelm II of Germany. Constantine was educated in Germany and attended the Prussian Military Academy. As a professional soldier he served with distinction in the Balkan Wars but his pro-German sympathies lay uneasily with his professed neutrality on the outbreak of war in 1914.

Rebellion against Ottoman rule continued to spread in the latter half of the 19th century. Limited self-rule was granted to the Cretans following an uprising in 1863, and in 1867 the Turks abandoned seven great fortresses in Serbia. In 1875 a revolt in Herzegovina spread like wildfire through Bosnia, Serbia, Montenegro and Bulgaria. Austria, Russia and Germany now put pressure on the Sublime Porte, the seat of Ottoman Government

Serbia and Salonika, 1914–1916.

in Constantinople (in what was termed the 'Berlin Memorandum') to implement long-overdue reforms under threat of armed intervention by the signatory powers. Britain firmly declined to join in, and the 'Concert of Europe' failed. The results were calamitous. Serbia and Montenegro declared war on Turkey, a revolution in Constantinople deposed the Sultan and Turkish troops massacred thousands of Bulgars. In London, Gladstone called for the expulsion of the Turks 'bag and baggage' from Europe. A new sultan, Murad V, was swiftly deposed in turn and replaced by Abdul Hamid ('the Damned') who was to reign until 1909. His refusal to grant autonomy to his Christian provinces and implement reform led to a declaration of war by Russia in April 1877. Romania, Montenegro and Serbia gladly joined in and by December that year Russian troops were within sight of Constantinople. Under the terms of the Treaty of San Stefano, signed in March 1878, independence was granted to Serbia, Montenegro, Romania and Bulgaria, including Macedonia.

The victorious partners immediately fell out over the division of the spoils. Once more there was alarm in Western Europe and Britain's prime minister Disraeli ordered the Mediterranean Fleet through the Dardanelles.

Russia was persuaded to modify the San Stefano Treaty at the Congress of Berlin in the summer of 1878 (the Berlin Treaty) but Turkey still had to grant Serbia, Montenegro and Romania their independence. Russia acquired Bessarabia, Kars in eastern Anatolia, and Batum. Bosnia and Herzegovina passed under Austrian protection and Bulgaria was partitioned in two. Macedonia remained Turkish. Under a separate convention Britain garrisoned and administered Cyprus and guaranteed the sultan's remaining Asian territories. The Berlin Congress was a way-point in the disintegration of the Ottoman Empire. Eleven million Christians were freed from Ottoman rule at a stroke and 30 years of peace in the Middle East ensued. Turkey's outstations were there for the picking by opportunists and France took over in Tunis in 1881. Britain, having defeated the Egyptian Army at Tel-el-Kebir in 1882, established a *de facto* government over Egypt to protect the Suez Canal. A string of inter-Balkan agreements brought about a series of border re-alignments that Turkey was now too feeble to prevent. None of the treaties prevented the bellicose Serbs from taking up arms against Bulgaria, to be soundly beaten in a two-week campaign. The Bulgars were in turn threatened by the Austrians and their ruler, Prince Alexander, was forced to resign in 1886, to be replaced by yet another spare German prince, Ferdinand of Saxe-Coburg. Closely related to Queen Victoria, he ruled with moderation, restyling himself as Tsar in 1908. Serbia fell prey to blood feuds, the Obrenovitch family coming to a grisly end in 1903 when the king and his morganatic queen Draga were slaughtered in their palace by dissident army officers. The rival Karageorgevitch family took over the throne.

Greece went to war again with Turkey in 1897 over Muslim persecution of Cretan Christians, but the fighting was stopped by the great powers when it seemed the Turks were about to win.

Turkey's situation in 1900 was unhappy. Of the Sultan's remaining subjects no fewer than four million were Christians of one sort or other. Although Austria now occupied Bosnia and Herzegovina the Sultanate still regarded them and Bulgaria as Turkish lands. Balkan history was still affected by resonances of the battle of Kosovo in 1398, when the Turks under Murad I had destroyed the combined forces of Serbia, Bosnia and Albania. Kosovo, with its predominantly Muslim population, remained an almost holy place for Serbs and the mythology surrounding the disaster of 1398 sustains their national identity to this day. The result of that battle ensured Turkish political, cultural and religious domination of Kosovo for the next six centuries.

Another side effect of the Berlin Treaty was a resurgence of Pan-Slavism as Croats, Slovenes and Montenegrins who had shed Turkish rule sought to join hands with their Serb brethren and the ethnic South Slavs of

Opposite:
General Count Luigi Cadorna. He was appointed Chief of Staff in 1914 to face the problems of reinvigorating an army depleted in strength by its recent North African campaign. He was forced to lead it in war from 1915 despite its manifest inadequacies of equipment and training. Believing that offensive action alone held the key to victory he persisted in launching a succession of bloody assaults on the Austrians in the Isonzo sector. Widely considered to be arrogant, ruthless and unapproachable, he was removed from command following the catastrophic defeat of the Italians at Caporetto in 1917. (Topfoto)

Bosnia-Herzegovina. The concept of a greater Serbia struck dread into Austrians, Hungarians and Turks alike and threatened to antagonise Bulgaria, which nurtured designs on the assorted population of Macedonia and (more alarmingly) on Greece.

In Turkey a new political force was at work, threatening the old regime. The new constitution of 1878 drafted by the Grand Vizier Midhat Pasha had promised widespread civil liberties and parliamentary government, but the Sultan saw to it that the western-style parliament (the first of its kind in an Islamic country) only convened once. A new, educated middle-class began to feel its strength, breeding the Young Turk movement, which was instrumental in firing the revolution of 1908 that forced the revival of the Midhat constitution that followed. The leader of the Young Turks was an army officer, Enver Bey, ably assisted by a small group who all became ministers in the government he led in 1914 when it brought Turkey into the war on the side of the Central Powers. All of them came to violent ends in the years immediately following the war.

The *putsch* instigated by the Young Turks triggered several reactions. Bulgaria declared independence, Austria annexed Bosnia-Herzegovina and neither sought representation in the Ottoman Parliament promised under the Midhat constitution. Ripples spread out from Constantinople: the Serbs mobilised, and early in 1909 Berlin warned the Russians – Bulgaria's sponsors – to recognise the Austrian annexation, implying that failure to comply would involve war with both Germany and Austria-Hungary. Russia and Serbia took the hint; but it was clear for all to see that Germany was prepared to invade Belgium and France, using Balkan instability as an excuse. Britain's answer was to lay the keels of eight dreadnoughts instead of the four or six originally budgeted for in the 1909 Naval Estimates. War was in the air, and Russia, France and Britain nervously closed ranks. Italy, formerly bound to Germany and Austria by the Triple Alliance Treaty of 1882, began to shuffle aside, its leaders knowing full well that she was utterly unprepared for a major war. In Austria the 'War Party', in which Count Berchthold the Foreign Minister was a moving spirit, urged the emperor to attack the Serbs at once before the Russians could mobilise for their protection.

Italy's position at this time was nominally governed by its membership of the Triple Alliance, which it had entered into primarily out of concern about France. Progressively revised over the years the terms of the alliance came to embrace North Africa, but in 1902 the Italians and French had come secretly to an agreement by which, in return for a free hand in Tripolitania, Italy declared that its share in the Triple Alliance was *not* directed at France. Austria's annexation of Bosnia-Herzegovina in 1908 complicated things. It implied that Italy would join the Central Powers in war against France. Neither the Germans nor the Austrians believed that the Italians could be relied on. When in 1895 Count von Schlieffen drafted his celebrated plan for the subjugation of France he based it on the assumption that the Italians would do no more than face the French from their home ground on the heights of Piedmont. At the German Imperial manoeuvres of 1913 the Kaiser tried in vain to extract a promise from General Pollo, the Italian Chief of Staff, that in the event of general war Italy would commit no fewer than five army corps to the upper Rhine. As late as February 1914 Pollo confirmed the deployment of three army corps and two cavalry divisions against France. But nothing came of this and in 1914 General Pollo died. His successor, General Count Luigi Cadorna, found that the army was in no state to fight any sort of war, having used up most of its equipment in the North African campaign of 1911–1912. Cadorna faced a gigantic task of modernisation and reorganisation before the army could meet the role he had in mind – no less than the invasion and defeat of Austria. Italy lacked the raw materials required for a war industry. Short of all types of ammunition and without the medium and heavy artillery required to tackle the formidable Austrian border defences, it opted for neutrality in August 1914. There were two valid excuses for this apparent breach of faith: a secret clause in the Triple Alliance treaty absolved the Italians from fighting the British, and under Article 7 Austria undertook to consult the Italian Government before taking any military action in the Balkans. The invasion of Serbia in 1914 by the Austro-Hungarian Army justified Italy's neutrality and this neutrality was the signal for which the French and British governments had been waiting. Italy's entry into the war on their side in 1915 was the result of energetic work by politicians and diplomats to produce a deal politically and financially acceptable in Rome.

The decay of the Ottoman Empire was carefully monitored in Berlin where finely judged diplomacy ensured that the Sultan, however unpopular, retained his throne as long as his friendship with Germany lasted. Turkey's tottering economy was sustained by hard-headed loans like that granted to construct the Turkish section of the Berlin–Baghdad railway, a key element in German strategic planning. Help was given from the 1880s in training and equipping the Turkish Army but it was not until 1913 that a full training mission was sent from Germany, under the formidable General Otto Liman von Sanders. Kaiser Wilhelm II paid two state visits to Constantinople in the 1880s and 1890s and the diplomats selected as German ambassadors to the Sublime Porte were men of the highest calibre.

WARRING SIDES: THE OPPOSING ARMIES

The British fleet

Having successfully avoided involvement in European wars since 1815, British defence policy in 1914 relied on a strong navy to secure the sea-lanes and deny them to Germany. The fleet, recently assembled for the royal review at Spithead, was ready for war. Its reservists were in post and the fleet fully armed and bunkered. The Grand (or main battle) Fleet was held in home waters to deal with any attempt by the German High Seas Fleet to break out from its home bases, to provide defence against invasion and to support other naval forces in home waters. Of the nine naval commands for overseas waters, tasked with keeping the sea-lanes open, foremost was the prestigious Mediterranean Fleet based at Malta.

The Royal Navy enjoyed the status earned by its stupendous performance during the Napoleonic wars, but was professionally conservative. When Britain went to war with Russia in 1853 the battle line still consisted of wooden battleships scarcely distinguishable from Nelson's *Victory*, carrying up to 120 muzzle-loading cannon and a full set of sails. Although the newer ones were fitted with steam propulsion, the very idea of this innovation was anathema to many older admirals. When Fisher, destined to be the most innovative First Sea Lord of all time, joined the service as a midshipman in 1854 he was signed in by the last of Nelson's captains. As he rose steadily through the ranks his ambition and ability secured accelerated promotion. A gunnery officer in the fleet as it passed through the Dardanelles in 1878, he had carefully noted the fixed batteries guarding the Chanak Narrows. As he successively occupied the key posts in the navy's hierarchy his vision turned the service on its head, forcing the adoption of the torpedo, steam turbines, oil fuel, mines, submarines, wireless and, most importantly, the all-big-gun dreadnought battleship. On his way he made many enemies, for he waged ferocious vendettas. When he retired in 1910, Britain had achieved superiority in capital ships over all other European nations, with a 60 per cent lead over Germany. In August 1914 Britain possessed 24 dreadnoughts with another 13 under construction, to Germany's 13 and ten on the stocks. Counting pre-dreadnoughts, some of which dated back to the early 1890s and were unfit for the line of battle, the Royal Navy could boast a total of 65 battleships.

The other category of capital ship was the battle cruiser (a concept developed by Fisher), designed for high speed and heavy armament, albeit at the cost of armoured protection, for hunting German commerce raiders and acting as scouts for the main battle fleet. Britain had ten of these, armed with 12-inch or 13.5-inch guns.

Discounting a mass of ancient armoured and light cruisers designed for colonial protection duties, there were 16 modern cruisers. The Royal Navy had 225 destroyers, half of which were of modern design and the rest serviceable for escort duties. British submarine design had lagged behind that of France, Germany and Italy and although the navy could deploy 75, many were only suitable for harbour protection and coastal operations.

Manning this huge fleet was no problem, for in addition to the normal reserve system, Churchill (First Lord of the Admiralty since 1911) had created an 'Immediate Reserve' of men available prior to general mobilisation. In his years as First Sea Lord, Fisher had scrapped over 150 obsolete warships. As a result, on mobilisation, several thousand reserve officers and ratings were without seagoing berths. Formed into the Royal Naval Division and re-trained as infantry, they served initially in the futile defence of Antwerp in the autumn of 1914, then at Gallipoli, and finally on the Western Front.

Despite the Royal Navy's numerical superiority, there were some shortcomings. In the design of armour-piercing shells, moored mines and torpedoes Britain had lagged behind other naval powers. But in naval aviation, Britain was ahead. The world's first purpose-built aircraft carrier, *Ark Royal*, had joined the fleet and was to serve in the Mediterranean in support of the Dardanelles operations, and several capital ships had been modified to carry seaplanes.

The super-dreadnought, HMS *Queen Elizabeth*, under fire from the Turkish shore batteries at the entrance to the Dardanelles, 18 March 1915, during the ill-fated attempt of the Anglo-French fleet to force the Narrows at Chanak and fight its way into the Sea of Marmara and on to Constantinople. (Liddle Centre for World War I)

Italy

Prior to Italian unification in the second half of the 19th century, armies had been raised by various states up and down the peninsula. None of these was strong enough to stand by itself against more powerful neighbours and as a result Italy was ruled for centuries by Austria under the Habsburgs in the north and by Bourbon Spain in the south. The Papal states managed to retain a degree of autonomy, as did the Piedmontese, who had a strong military tradition. By 1866 guerrilla warfare led by Garibaldi culminated in the proclamation of the United Kingdom of Italy which, allied with Prussia against Austria, extended its territory by acquisition of the Venetian provinces. Austria's desire to recover these would be a primary excuse for its bellicose attitudes in the period leading to war in 1914. The Army of Savoy saw service in the Crimea and some of its regiments, like the *Bersaglieri* and *Alpini*, were famed throughout Europe. The emergence of a truly national army was slow, for the northerners looked down on Garibaldi's irregulars and Neapolitans. There was little public enthusiasm for conscription, introduced after 1861 and it became a folk tradition for young men in the south to evade military service by taking to the hills at call-up time.

By 1910 conscription had become acceptable although about 20 per cent of the population successfully dodged their military service. The army liked to think of itself as the school of the nation in the old Prussian manner, but its Ethiopian campaign of 1896 was disastrous; hundreds of Italian soldiers taken prisoner were murdered or castrated. The army redeemed its name by beating the Turks in Libya in 1911–1912, deploying nearly 100,000 troops to Tripolitania and Cyrenaica. As a result, the army was short of virtually every sort of munition and armament in 1914. There were still four classes of conscript serving with the colours (as opposed to the normal two) but from a peacetime strength of 14,000 officers and 852,000 soldiers the army, on mobilisation in May 1915, could raise and equip only 35 divisions – even with the recall of older classes of reservists – and was short of artillery and ammunition reserves. For this reason Italy's entry into the war was delayed until General Cadorna, the Chief of Staff, was satisfied that the army was fully ready. By 1917 he was commanding 67 divisions in the field, despite appalling casualties as the result of his bovine assaults against the near-impregnable Austrian defences on the Isonzo front.

Serbia

The Serbian military system demanded universal service for all able-bodied males aged 18–45. The army conspicuously lacked motorised transport, due in part to the appalling standard of Serbian roads, generally impassable to motors after rain. Instead, the army's transportation relied on animals;

baggage trains, bridging equipment and artillery were all drawn by oxen. Country wagons hauled by two or four animals were the usual method of carrying supplies. The strength of the Serbian Army lay in the endurance and courage of its officers and soldiers, who displayed amazing powers of survival in their campaigns. In peacetime the army comprised five active divisions, each of which had its own reserve division, thus the mobilised strength was ten self-contained divisions; a 'bayonet strength' of some 180,000.

Austria-Hungary

The Austrian Army was strong on tradition, many of its regiments claiming descent from those that had fought the Turks in the 17th century (the Hoch-und-Deutschmeister regiment, founded by the Teutonic knights in 1696, claimed an even more venerable ancestry as the military wing of an order founded in the 12th century). With the steady expansion of the empire, however, it had been necessary to recruit increasingly from non-German elements. Problems of loyalty and language arose as German-speaking units became outnumbered by the other ethnic groups. By 1914 less than 30 per cent of the army was Germanic. Germans, Hungarians and Czechs, being

Serbian artillery on the move – the guns were normally drawn by oxen, as the roads were of poor quality and usually impassable to motor vehicles. (Corbis)

the better educated, went into the artillery, engineers and cavalry. Almost 70 per cent of men in the so-called Common Infantry regiments were Slavs. Magyars hated Slavs, and care had to be taken in mixing their formations. Language was a major problem, tackled by using a universal *patois* known as 'Army Slav' in addition to which recruits were required to learn up to 80 German words of command.

Manning was a huge problem in peacetime. In 1910, out of the empire's total population of some 50 million, only 125,000 were available for conscription. The army's peace establishment was under 500,000, expanding on full mobilisation to 3,350,000. This included various second-line categories such as Landwehr, Landsturm, Ersatz reserve and, in Hungary, the Honved. In theory every fit man from the age of 19 was liable for conscription, serving an initial two years with the colours before entering the reserve system.

Turkey

The Turkish Army had been defeated by four small Balkan states in the three years prior to the outbreak of war in 1914. Despite this it was to fight doggedly until its final defeats in 1918. Much of the credit for its performance was due to the training teams of Germans under General Otto Liman von Sanders (active in Turkey from 1913) and the drastic reforms carried through by Enver Pasha, the War Minister, on their advice. Elderly time-serving officers were replaced by young, well-educated men from the Turkish middle classes. The German instructors had faced serious problems, apart from the conservatism and national pride of Turkish officers who resented their presence. There was a shortage of manpower, and communications in Asia Minor were appallingly bad. The Turkish population in 1914 was about 19 million in the core provinces, and perhaps another six million in outlying ones where non-Muslim populations paid higher tax in lieu of military service. Muslims could also evade service and the prosperous, better-educated urban classes tended to escape the draft in this way. In wartime, units of poor Christian Greeks and Armenians, regarded as untrustworthy in the line, were assigned to fatigue duties; the fighting cadre of the army was the Anatolian peasant soldier: patriotic, generally ill-educated, brave, devout and enduring. About 100,000 young men were liable for call-up each year but administrative incompetence meant that only 75 per cent of these actually reached the training depots. The peacetime strength of the army was some 250,000, comprising two years' call-up classes. On mobilisation, numbers rose to 800,000 but this took up to six months to achieve. In France and Germany some 10 per cent of the population could be conscripted; the figure for Turkey was less than half this.

Turkish conscripts were liable to a total of 17 years active and reserve service with the navy, 25 years in the infantry, or 20 in the technical arms like the engineers and artillery. Of these, naval conscripts served five years full time (*nizam*) in the navy, two in the infantry and three in the technical troops, before passing into successive grades of reserve or *redif*. At the end of the reserve obligation there was still the territorial force, a militia known as the *Musathfiz*, an obligation so tenuous that there was not even a peacetime cadre. The *Jandarma*, a paramilitary internal security force, was recruited from reliable ex-regular and conscript soldiers.

The reformed Ottoman Army of 1915 was grouped in four regional armies, based in Constantinople, Baghdad, Erzerum and Erzinjan. A further five armies were created during the war, and the pre-mobilisation strength of 36 divisions increased to 70 by 1917. Army corps were formed by pairing a *redif* division with a *nizam*; even so, few divisions or army corps ever reached their full war establishment. A division consisted of three regiments, each of three battalions. The artillery branch was historically independent, enjoying an elite status stemming back to the days of Mehmet II, conqueror of Constantinople in 1453 and the world's first great artillery commander. The standard field gun was the Krupp 75mm, but a wide assortment of elderly pieces were in service; the large-calibre fortress guns, like those installed in the defences of the Dardanelles, were mostly obsolete and short of suitable ammunition. But some of the batteries closer to the Chanak Narrows were equipped with relatively modern Krupp and Schneider-Creusot 150mm howitzers dating from the 1890s.

On the basis of scanty intelligence assessments of the Turkish Army's equipment and the perceived incompetence of much of its officer class the British and French seriously underestimated their opponent; the true strength of the Turks lay in their ordinary soldiers and the patriotism that inspired them to defend their native soil.

Greece

The ambivalent position of Greece in the First World War stemmed from the polarity between Prime Minister Eleftherios Venizelos and King Constantine, exacerbated by chronic political turbulence. In 1833, independence had been secured by a raggle-taggle army of idealistic irregulars, foreign Hellenists and unashamed bandit gangs. The first King of the Hellenes, Otto, brought with him 3,500 fellow Bavarians as the unpopular cadre of a 'national' army. Only a few Greeks were allowed to serve, primarily as garrison troops in Athens, and these mutinied in 1843 to secure the Hellenisation of the entire army. When Otto was deposed in 1863 the army had been developed on Germanic lines. In the next reign, that of a Danish prince, the bond between throne and army was strengthened and Crown Prince Constantine, who ably commanded in the field in the Balkan Wars of 1912–1913, was a graduate of the Prussian Staff College. By 1914 he was king, favouring the cause of the Central Powers and hoping devoutly for their victory.

Prime Minister Venizelos was a rabid Greek nationalist, infused by what became known in 19th-century Greece as the 'Great Idea'. Recalling the glories of ancient Greece, it visualised the annexation of all areas of south-west Europe with Greek-speaking populations plus Crete and Cyprus, Constantinople and parts of western Anatolia. The idea was enthusiastically taken up by the Greek intelligentsia and the army became steadily more and more politicised. When international pressure in 1909 compelled the Greek Government temporarily to shelve the idea of annexing Crete, the army revolted and Venizelos, himself a Cretan, became prime minister. In 1915, as Constantine and many of the senior generals backed a German victory, he openly declared for the Anglo-French alliance, seeing this as a chance to be rewarded in due course with a large slice of Turkish Anatolia. Deposed by the King, Venizelos set up a government in exile on Crete until the Allies acted to disarm the royalist army and forced Constantine to resign in 1916. The Greek Army, purged of most of its senior officers, then took the field on the Allied side.

THE FIGHTING: WAR ON THE MEDITERRANEAN FRONT 1914–1923

The strategies adopted in the Mediterranean campaigns were governed by geographical as well as by political factors. The Central Powers enjoyed few outlets to the open seas. Germany's were effectively closed from the start by the presence of the British Grand Fleet at Scapa Flow and the North Sea and Channel ports. The Austrian Navy, though not insignificant, was based on the Adriatic, which could be closed across the Straits of Otranto by a hostile fleet. In 1914 it was unprepared for major operations and was kept at Pola, its main base. The Turkish Navy, comprising mostly ancient ships until the acquisition of the powerful former German warships *Goeben* and *Breslau*, could readily be confined within the Dardanelles by an Allied blockading fleet based on adjacent Greek islands. Italy had an extensive coastline on the Adriatic and Mediterranean and following its entry into the war in 1915 its fleet's main preoccupation was the neutralisation of the Austrian Adriatic fleet. The French Mediterranean fleet's planned war role had been to confront the Austrian and Italian fleets, but as the Austrians were shut in the Adriatic and the Italians failed to join the Central Powers in the Triple Alliance it found itself contributing to the Allied blockade of the Dardanelles.

British strategic interests centred on the Suez Canal, the route to India. Turkey's entry into the war on the side of the Central Powers was not unexpected, though it might have been avoided had the British Government matched the Germans in their diplomatic handling of the Sublime Porte in the years before the war. Turkey's closure of the Dardanelles cut Russia off from its Western Allies, preventing the export of Ukrainian grain and oil that would have financed its war effort. It also denied the Allies the ability to supply Russia with munitions and weapons. Strategically, Turkey's entry into the war threatened the Suez Canal and Russian territory in the Caucasus. The proclamation of *jihad* by the Sultan/Caliph on the outbreak of war seemed to pose a threat to the structure of the Indian Army and its Muslim soldiers. Although this danger did not materialise it inhibited the use of these valuable regiments against soldiers of their own faith. The threat posed to India by Russia had largely evaporated since 1904, but a significant garrison still had to be maintained in India on the north-west frontier and for internal security. The Persian Gulf assumed a new strategic significance with the development of oil fields, largely under Anglo-French control, on the fringe of the Ottoman Empire. This oil was essential to the fuelling of the battle fleets, which were then changing over from coal to oil fuel. The threat of German influence in this area via the Berlin–Baghdad railway, even though this was still incomplete, necessitated an expeditionary force from

Minesweeping operations in the Dardanelles. The destroyer HMS *Racoon*, hit by fire from shore batteries, blows off steam as another destroyer closes with her to take her on tow; a battleship – either *Agamemnon* or *Lord Nelson* – provides cover. In the far distance, aground at Sedd-el-Bahr, can be seen the collier *River Clyde*, used as the 'Trojan Horse' for the landings on 25 April. (IWM SP1117)

India to secure the oilfields and advance up the Tigris and Euphrates rivers. As if these problems were not enough, the British Commander-in-Chief Egypt had to face the threat of insurrection in his rear. Enver Pasha, encouraged by the Germans, was stirring up the dissident tribes of Libya, where the Italians had supplanted the Turks in 1912, but now found the subjects of the Grand Senussi of Sollum agitated by the proclamation of Holy War against the infidel.

The Mediterranean war can be said to have started on the day the French declared war, when the two German warships on the loose in the western Mediterranean materialised off the North African coast and bombarded two ports. But it was on the Serbian border that the serious fighting began.

Invasion of Serbia

Serbia's geographical position made it the strategic keystone of the Balkan peninsula. The terrain was wild and mountainous but two historic Balkan trade routes passed through it along the Morava–Maritza Trench, known as the 'Diagonal Furrow' (the line selected for the Berlin–Baghdad railway), and the Morava–Vardar Trench, connecting Central Europe with the Aegean. Serbia's northern frontier was shielded by natural barriers, the rivers Drina and Danube. Neither was fordable and in 1914 the only bridge over the Danube in Serbia was at Belgrade. A third barrier, the River Sava, was lined with near-impassable marshes. Road communication throughout the country was extremely poor. The population consisted mostly of hardy peasant farmers.

The Serbs began to mobilise on 26 July 1914. The Austrian Chief of Staff, Conrad, was discovering that despite his haste to go to war, the army was ill-prepared for active service. He also had to deploy eight army corps to the Russian border. Despite this Austria declared war on Serbia on 28 July. A day later, Austrian warships on the Danube bombarded Belgrade as their Second, Fourth and Sixth Armies under General Oskar Potiorek prepared to cross the rivers Sava and Drina. The Serbs, with 450,000 men supported by partly trained Montenegrins, all under command of Marshal Radomir Putnik, resolved to sell their lives dearly. Putnik, with some 450 miles of frontier with Austria and Bulgaria to defend, deployed his three armies centrally to meet threats from either direction. He aimed to hold the key river lines with small formations then, having located the main crossings, to attack them in strength on ground of his own choice. He correctly forecast the Austrians' main thrust lines and was ready when they came. Potiorek's approach was hesitant and many of his ill-trained troops were unwilling to fight fellow Slavs. There was much indiscipline in the ranks and horrific atrocities were committed by Austrian units against Serbian civilians.

Battle was joined in earnest on 12 August when, in nine days of ferocious fighting, the Serbs threw the Austrians back across their start lines in the battle of Jadar and advanced into Bosnia in hot pursuit. The Austrians fled in disorder. On 7 September Potiorek tried again, forcing the over-extended Serbs back out of Bosnia. By early November it seemed that all was up, but at that point the frail and elderly King Peter, carrying a private soldier's rifle, entered the trenches with his sons, inspiring his troops with the words:

> Heroes – you have taken two oaths: one to me, your King, and the other to your country. I am an old broken man on the edge of the grave and I release you from your oath to me. From your other oath no one can release you. If you feel you cannot go on, go to your homes, and I pledge my word that after the war, if we come out of it, nothing shall happen to you. But I and my sons stay here.

Not a man left the line. Sheer weight of numbers forced the Serbs to evacuate Belgrade on 29 November but on 3 December Putnik, having completed a withdrawal in good order to the south-west, turned and counter-attacked on the line of the Kolubara River, King Peter still in the front line with his rifle and 50 rounds of ammunition. The Austrians again fled in confusion. By 15 December Serbian patrols were back in Belgrade where the King attended a solemn *Te Deum* in the cathedral. The third Austrian invasion had collapsed ignominiously with the loss of 41,000 prisoners and 133 guns. Potiorek was replaced by the Archduke Eugene.

The Serbian front now went quiet as the Austrians endeavoured to cope with the alarming situation on their Russian front. In response to Serbian appeals, Admiral Troubridge of the British Mediterranean fleet, eccentrically clad in the uniform of a Serbian general to confound German intelligence, arrived in Belgrade in February 1915 with a naval detachment including eight 4.7-inch guns for the city's defence. Meanwhile typhus was decimating the Serb Army; by April 48,000 soldiers were in hospital. The summer of 1915 saw little more than skirmishing as the Serbs built up their strength for what they realised would be a hard winter. Germany was desperate to reopen the Berlin–Baghdad rail link and could not do so until Serbia was conquered. The Austrians, appalled by their losses to date and unwilling to tackle the Serbs on their own, looked to Bulgaria, whose government was sitting on the fence. There was a hint that they would consider joining Britain and France if given large tracts of land including Serbian and Greek Macedonia. Eventually German patience ran out; on 6 September 1915 a convention was signed between Germany, Austria and Bulgaria, aimed at crushing Serbian resistance. The Allies, alarmed, made a final unconditional offer to Bulgaria of part of Macedonia. It was turned down, and Serbia's fate was sealed. German forces joined the Austrians on the northern border and the Allies belatedly realised that they had lost a major diplomatic battle by not insisting that the Greeks fulfilled the treaty terms binding them to help Serbia. On 22 September a French mission arrived at Salonika to assess its suitability as a base for the support of the Serbs. In an effort to involve the Greeks, Serbia offered them territory on the border. Constantine reluctantly gave permission for Allied troops to land at Salonika as his prime minister made a vain last-ditch appeal for the Bulgars to suspend mobilisation if the Greeks did likewise. It was too late; the die had been cast.

The Austro-German forces massing on the northern frontier were commanded by Field Marshal August Mackensen, fresh from his crushing defeat of the Russians at Gorlice-Tarnów. Charged with the total defeat of the Serbs he headed a joint force including the newly mobilised Bulgarians.

On 5 October a huge artillery bombardment began the offensive. The next day Belgrade came under attack and the British naval gunners fought to the end as the capital fell on the 9th after savage street fighting costing the Austrians 7,000 casualties. The Serb retirement continued. Morale was still high, men were flocking to enlist, and the fighting qualities of the Serb Army remained as strong as ever; but they were steadily forced to give ground and the great arsenal of Kragujevac was abandoned and blown up on 1 November. The army retreated onto the Kosovo Plain as the new seat of government was set up at Mitrovica.

On 16 November, as winter closed in, the city of Monastir fell; the army was now in dire straits, its last links with Greece cut, typhus raging, all troops on half rations and only 200 field guns left. The balance had tipped in favour of the Central Powers, and the great fortress of Mitrovica eventually fell to the Austrians on 23 November as the Serbs withdrew south and west. On the same day the Bulgars linked hands with General von Gallwitz's German troops. The Bulgarian advance had cut the Serbs off from the Anglo-French force now established in its bridgehead around Salonika, from which it had earlier been possible to supply Putnik's army. As Mitrovica and Pristina fell on 23 November the surviving 200,000 Serbian troops faced a nightmare march over mountains in the grip of winter, to safety on the Adriatic coast. The Serbian rearguard was overwhelmed on the White Drin River, losing masses of precious supplies in the process as the retreat went on in dreadful weather. A new seat of government and General Headquarters were established at Scutari on the Albanian coast as the Allies rushed shipping into the Adriatic to embark the battered survivors.

A French force that had belatedly set out from Salonika up the Vardar valley to help the Serbs was met by overwhelming Bulgarian forces and compelled to fall back in some disorder with a British division, the 10th (Irish), shielding its left flank. The Allies withdrew to a defended line, the so-called 'Entrenched Camp', some 14 miles inland from Salonika itself, where they remained for the rest of the winter. It had not been an auspicious start. The Greek king was informed that the surviving Serbs were going to the island of Corfu, already occupied by French marines without the Greeks' permission; the transfer began on 12 January 1916 as the Salonika garrison blew the bridge over the River Struma in the presence of indignant Greek troops. The Salonika campaign had got under way.

The Mesopotamian sideshow

The British Government had already appreciated the vulnerability of strategic oil supplies from the Persian Gulf. It was decided that military operations in that area should be directed from India, under political control of the India and Colonial Offices in London. Initially there was no input from the War Office as the troops involved were from the Indian Army. This split command system led to confusion and near-disaster. A small force was dispatched from India in September 1914 to secure the Anglo-Persian Oil Company's installations at Abadan and the pipe-head from the up-country oilfields, and to ensure the continuing loyalty of the various sheikhdoms along the Gulf in view of the *jihad* proclaimed in Constantinople. With the initial objectives secured, more troops were sent from India to implement the second phase of the operation, an advance up the Shatt-el-Arab to Basra, which was entered on 22 November.

The Mesopotamian theatre, 1914–1917.

After further reinforcements had arrived from India the force pushed up the Tigris and Euphrates rivers, supplied by a small armada of steamers and towed barges. Two infantry divisions and a cavalry brigade made up an improvised army corps under General Sir John Nixon of the Indian Army. As the Turks resisted vigorously along the Euphrates a second force under Major-General Townshend advanced up the less heavily defended Tigris. Townshend drove his men hard through the blazing summer of 1915. In September he reached Ctesiphon, only 22 miles from Baghdad. Short of rations, weary and low-spirited, his Indian troops failed in a mishandled attack on 22 November. The Tigris was running low and the river steamers were unable to support the force, so Townshend fell back on Kut and dug a strong defensive position in a loop of the river, confident that he could sit it out until reinforcements of men and material reached him when the river returned to its winter flow. The Turks, now under the command of the former adviser to the Sultan, General (Field Marshal in the Ottoman Army) Colmar von der Goltz, closely invested the garrison. A number of attempts to rescue Townshend failed ignominiously. By January 1916 supplies were running low and the garrison slaughtered their horses for food, an idea repulsive to most of the Indian troops. A final overland relief attempt on 16 April, by which time the defenders were on starvation rations, also failed and Townshend was given authority to negotiate a surrender. Some supplies were now reaching him, dropped from machines of the Royal Flying Corps, but the quantities were insufficient. Meanwhile von der Goltz died in Baghdad, probably of cholera (though some thought he was poisoned by a cabal of Young Turks). Khalil Pasha, the Turkish commander at Kut, assured Townshend that were he to capitulate, 'your gallant troops will be our most sincere and precious guests'. The subsequent treatment of Townshend's rank and file was appalling; he was escorted to Constantinople and regally treated but his men were subjected to a brutal 1,200-mile forced march to Anatolia on short rations, in the course of which over 4,000 died.

An ambulance wagon makes its way up Gully Ravine, Helles, at the height of the Gallipoli Campaign. Earlier in the summer of 1915 this had been the scene of savage fighting. Sudden downpours of rain turned the normally dry watercourse into a raging torrent, and afterwards all traffic had to contend with deep mud. (IWM)

In August 1916 the arrival of General Sir Frederick Maude as Commander-in-Chief transformed the campaign. Control passed to the War Office in London. Maude insisted on massive reinforcements and the establishment of an efficient logistics system before resuming the offensive, which he did in December 1916. The Turks, though still fighting stubbornly, were racked by disease; their supply system was inefficient and they failed to stem Maude's relentless advance. He re-took Kut in February 1917 and entered Baghdad in triumph on 11 March, only to die there of cholera in October, in the same house in which von der Goltz had died.

Although Maude had a four-to-one numerical superiority over the Turks (who had barely 42,000 men) his army had overcome severe physical and psychological difficulties following Townshend's humiliation, and although the Dardanelles and Palestine campaigns were to create far more news and still retain an aura of glamour, he had successfully destroyed a main Turkish Army. After the capture of Baghdad the urgency went out of the campaign; in any case the Russians were all but finished by the end of 1917 and Turkey was now so weakened that its armies no longer posed a serious threat to the Allies outside Palestine.

Gallipoli and the Dardanelles

The campaign in the Dardanelles and on the Gallipoli peninsula was one of the most intriguing and tragic of the war. On 2 January 1915 the Russians appealed for some sort of demonstration by the Allies that would divert attention from the Caucasus, where the Tsar's troops were facing an ill-conceived Turkish offensive mounted, against the advice of his German Allies, by Enver Pasha the War Minister.

For some time Winston Churchill had tried to persuade his colleagues in Prime Minister Asquith's Cabinet to adopt a strategy of indirect approach to resolve the deadlock on the Western Front. Churchill's idea was to force the Dardanelles, seize Constantinople and, by knocking Turkey out of the war, undermine the entire strategy of the Central Powers. Kitchener was reluctant to divert any effort from the west, and was supported by the General Staff and Field Marshal Sir John French, commander of the British Expeditionary Force, who believed that it was only in France that the German main army could be beaten and the war won. Faced with Kitchener's refusal to allocate ground forces for an expedition, Churchill sought and obtained sanction to mount a purely naval attack. His First Sea Lord, 'Jacky' Fisher, immediately raised objections; he had seen the Dardanelles defences for himself in 1878 and was convinced that their guns could still inflict catastrophic damage to any battle fleet trying to negotiate the Chanak Narrows. Once in the Sea of Marmara, the fleet would still require servicing by its oilers, colliers, victualling and ammunition ships and these, being unarmoured, would not stand a chance of survival at the close ranges involved. As it was, Fisher had declined to allot any modern battleships to the Anglo-French fleet blockading the Straits. A desultory bombardment was opened on the outer forts on 19 February 1915, surrendering any advantage of surprise.

As early as 13 December 1914 the British submarine B-11 had torpedoed the ancient Turkish battleship *Messudieh* off the town of Chanak; before long, British and French submarines were braving mines and submarine nets to enter the Sea of Marmara, there to cause chaos to Turkish maritime trade. In February and March 1915 landing parties went ashore to complete the destruction of the outer forts on the European and Asiatic shores of the entry to the Straits. On German advice the Turks improved their defences against the expected Allied attack, deploying mobile howitzers on both sides of the Straits. Early in March Vice-Admiral Carden, the fleet commander, announced he was ready to launch the naval attack on the Narrows, timed for the 18th. Meanwhile in London, Churchill's persistence had secured the use of ground troops, who would land after a successful naval operation to secure the forts and

Turkish Marines on the march to the Dardenelles

Opposite:
Gallipoli, 1915.

The 42nd (East Lancashire) Division of the British Army dug in at Gully Beach, Helles, in the summer 1915. Concealed from the view of Turkish observers and to some extent shielded from enemy artillery fire, this was an almost idyllic spot on an otherwise unpleasant part of the front. Staff officers' memoirs recall their delight at sitting on their terraced hillside, drinking whisky as the sun went down behind the island of Samothrace. (Corbis)

batteries. The Australian Imperial Force (AIF) and several thousand New Zealanders had reached Alexandria *en route* to Britain and the Western Front. Formed into the Australian and New Zealand Army Corps (Anzac) under Lieutenant-General Sir William Birdwood of the Indian Army, they were retained in Egypt, ostensibly for further training and the defence of the Suez Canal. Another force available to Churchill was the Royal Naval Division (RND). Its battalions were made up of naval reservists and the Royal Marine Light Infantry, mainly enthusiastic men who had responded to Kitchener's call for volunteers on the outbreak of war.

Early in March 1916 Kitchener appointed General Sir Ian Hamilton to command the Mediterranean Expeditionary Force (MEF). He received only the sketchiest of briefings from Kitchener before leaving London on 13 March, accompanied by a few staff officers, and with only meagre intelligence on the defences of the Dardanelles and Gallipoli Peninsula. He arrived with the fleet off the Dardanelles in time to observe the Anglo-French fleet's attempt to force the Narrows, and found that Vice-Admiral Carden, after a complete nervous breakdown, had been replaced by his deputy, Vice-Admiral de Robeck.

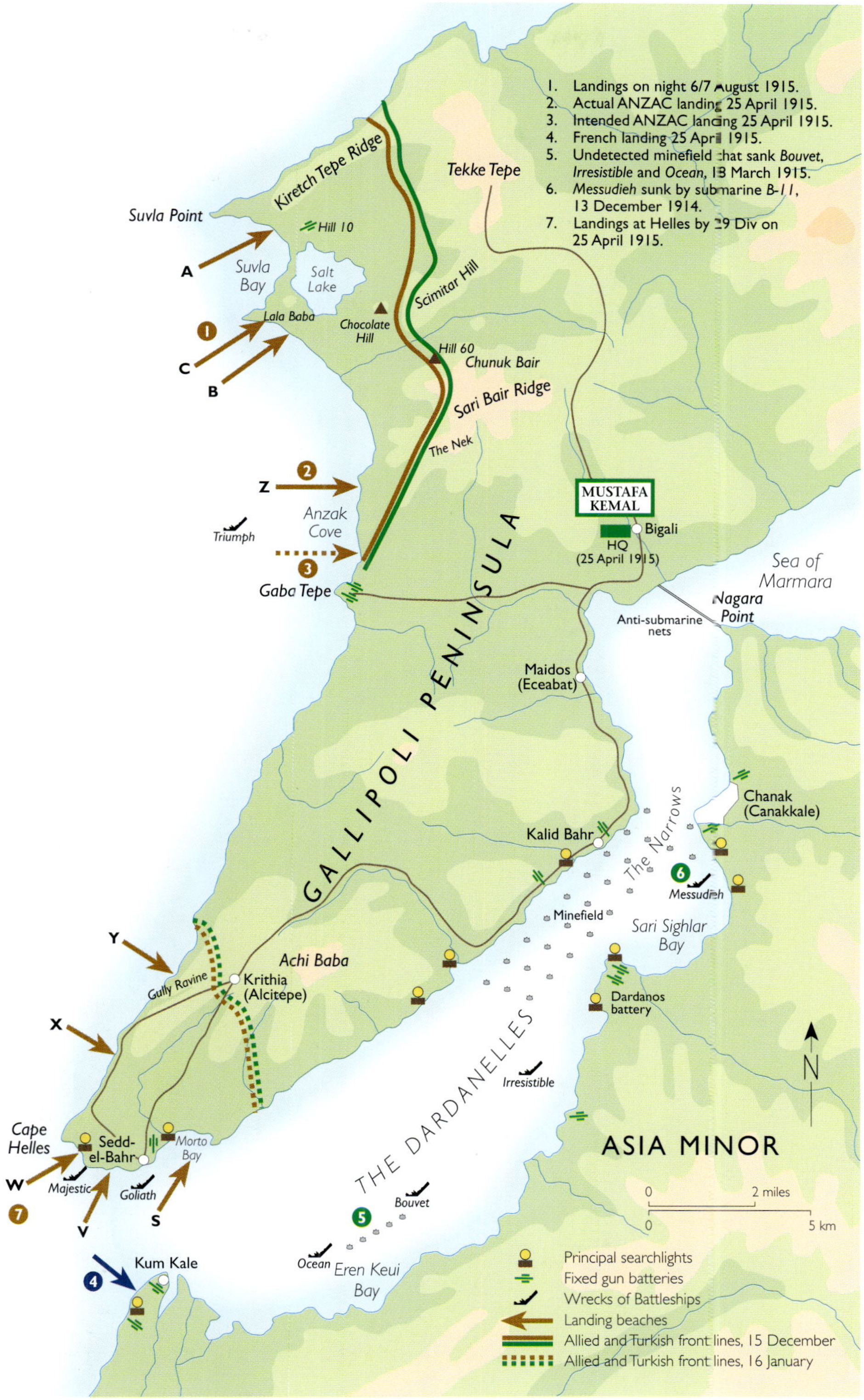
1. Landings on night 6/7 August 1915.
2. Actual ANZAC landing 25 April 1915.
3. Intended ANZAC landing 25 April 1915.
4. French landing 25 April 1915.
5. Undetected minefield that sank Bouvet, Irresistible and Ocean, 18 March 1915.
6. Messudieh sunk by submarine B-11, 13 December 1914.
7. Landings at Helles by 29 Div on 25 April 1915.
Suvla Point
Kiretch Tepe Ridge
Hill 10
Tekke Tepe
Suvla Bay
Salt Lake
A
Lala Baba
Chocolate Hill
Scimitar Hill
C
B
Hill 60
Chunuk Bair
Sari Bair Ridge
The Nek
Z
Anzak Cove
Triumph
Gaba Tepe
MUSTAFA KEMAL
HQ (25 April 1915)
Bigali
Sea of Marmara
Nagara Point
Anti-submarine nets
GALLIPOLI PENINSULA
Maidos (Eceabat)
Chanak (Canakkale)
Kalid Bahr
The Narrows
Messudieh
Minefield
Sari Sighlar Bay
Achi Baba
Y
Gully Ravine
Krithia (Alcitepe)
Dardanos battery
X
THE DARDANELLES
Irresistible
Cape Helles
Sedd-el-Bahr
Morto Bay
W
Majestic
Goliath
V
S
ASIA MINOR
N
0 2 miles
0 5 km
Bouvet
Kum Kale
Ocean
Eren Keui Bay
Principal searchlights
Fixed gun batteries
Wrecks of Battleships
Landing beaches
Allied and Turkish front lines, 15 December
Allied and Turkish front lines, 16 January

The naval attack of the 18th had been defeated, with the loss of three battleships and severe damage to several more. The Germans and Turks had secretly laid an undetected minefield well down the Straits in an area where the bombarding fleet had been manoeuvring, resulting in the spectacular loss of the French pre-dreadnought *Bouvet* with almost her entire crew, together with the elderly British battleships *Ocean* and *Irresistible.* The battlecruiser *Inflexible* and the French battleships *Gaulois* and *Suffren* were severely damaged. The new British super-dreadnought *Queen Elizabeth,* diverted from gunnery trials prior to joining the Grand Fleet, escaped damage, and her eight 15-inch guns wrought considerable destruction on the defences before a furious Fisher ordered her return to home waters, where she joined the Grand Fleet.

It was clear that the fleet would never get through to Marmara unless a large ground force was landed to secure the shores of the Dardanelles and Narrows, where the defenders, although on the verge of collapse at the end of the day on 18 March, had been heartened by success. German advisers supervised the repair of damaged fortifications and the construction of beach defences on the most likely landing places. In command of the Turkish 19th Division based at Maidos was the unknown Lieutenant-Colonel Mustafa Kemal, promoted over the heads of hundreds of others by Liman von Sanders, who had a gift for spotting talent. Kemal trained his command rigorously. Instead of dispersing the defence thinly all around the coast of the peninsula, Liman held the bulk of it well back from the beaches, poised to move rapidly in strength to deal with landings when they came, and holding the main reserve of two divisions back at the Isthmus of Bulair.

The ships bringing equipment out to the Greek islands from England had been loaded without thought of what would be needed first after a beach assault. In the absence of wharfage at the harbour of Mudros the ships had to be sent for reloading to Alexandria, where Hamilton established his temporary headquarters. After much haggling in London Kitchener agreed to release the 29th Infantry Division for the eastern Mediterranean. This formation consisted of regular units brought home in the autumn of 1914 from all corners of the empire to join the BEF in France. Over the protests of Field Marshal French and his generals it was shipped to the Mediterranean to join the Anzacs, Royal Naval Division and the French Expeditionary Force commanded by Hamilton's old friend General d'Amade.

Hamilton was told by Admiral de Robeck that the fleet could no longer penetrate deeply into the Dardanelles because of the improved batteries ashore. De Robeck also believed that the Turks had laid further undetected minefields. The plan of attack therefore hinged on landings by the

29th Division under the guns of the fleet at the tip of the peninsula and by the Anzacs some 15 miles up the coast. The Anzac landings were planned to keep Liman's reserve divisions from rushing down to attack the Allied beach-heads. The French were to land at Kum Kale on the Asiatic shore as a further diversion, but would re-embark and join the 29th Division at Helles after two days, Kitchener having specifically forbidden sustained operations on the Asiatic side of the Straits. Given the resources available, Hamilton's plan was imaginative and sound. Its execution was anything but.

The landings took place on the morning of 25 April. The Anzacs went ashore at first light, but were landed a mile north of the intended beach due to a strong off-shore current. Instead of a gently sloping hinterland and open country all the way to the Narrows (only 5 miles away across the peninsula) they were confronted with steep slopes – up which they rushed. Their impetus carried them to the heights of the Sari Bair ridge, brushing aside the resistance of Turkish detachments covering the beach; but as they arrived on the summits, blown and disorganised, they met a furious counter-attack led by Mustafa Kemal, which swept them back to the edge of the ridge. There they grimly held on to positions that became their front line for the rest of the campaign. That night, a despondent Birdwood signalled Hamilton, afloat in the battleship *Queen Elizabeth*, that the situation was so confused that re-embarkation was the only solution. Hamilton ordered him to stick it out and 'Dig, dig, dig', unwittingly creating a legend.

At Helles on the tip of the peninsula the commander of the 29th Division, Major-General Hunter-Weston, had chosen to land in broad daylight, a decision for which his troops paid dearly. Coming ashore under tow in ship's boats, rowed for the last hundred yards by bluejackets, they came under devastating fire at 'V' beach from the defenders. A naval aviator flying overhead was appalled to see that the water for 50 yards out from the beach was red with blood. At 'V' beach the landing was augmented by a 'Trojan Horse'; the collier *River Clyde* had been modified, with extra ports in its sides, to beach itself and disgorge two battalions down ramps and across a bridge of boats to the shore. These troops also met withering fire as they emerged

A seaplane of the Royal Naval Air Service (RNAS) at Mudros harbour, Lemnos, during the Dardanelles operations. Lord Kitchener had specifically ruled out the use of the Royal Flying Corps at Gallipoli but the RNAS, using a miscellany of primitive aircraft, carried out reconnaissance, spotting for the guns of the fleet, photographic sorties and before long, torpedo bombing of any Turkish ships that could be found in the Sea of Marmara. (IWM)

from the ship and were pinned down with the others on the shore. At 'W' beach on the other side of Cape Helles, only a mile away, the first battalion ashore, the Lancashire Fusiliers, fought their way off the beach through dense barbed wire, winning six Victoria Crosses in the process. Elsewhere around the Helles area the landings met little resistance, but Hunter-Weston ignored this, concentrating on reinforcing the slaughter at 'W' and 'V'. By last light the 29th Division was shattered and incapable of exploiting inland. The day's final objective, the dominating high ground of Achi Baba, 5 miles from the landing beaches, was never taken during the campaign.

The French landings at Kum Kale stirred up a hornet's nest and fierce fighting took place before the troops were ferried across the Straits to join their British comrades at Helles.

Through the furnace heat of summer a series of futile attacks at Helles failed to take Achi Baba or the village of Krithia at its foot. Disease took its toll, brought on by insanitary conditions and the vast number of flies feeding on thousands of unburied corpses. The Turkish soldier, previously regarded as no more than an unlettered brute, earned the respect of his opponents. At Anzac, as the precarious beach-head became known, the attackers had

Australian infantry going ashore at Anzac Cove on the morning of 25 April 1915. At this stage most of the troops of the Australian Imperial Force still wore uniforms similar to those of the British Army. (IWM)

to cling to a ridgeline subjected to incessant sniper and artillery fire. A great Turkish assault in May, aimed at sweeping the Anzacs into the sea, was fought off, leaving thousands of putrefying dead in the open. So appalling was the smell and health hazard that a truce was agreed in which both sides buried their dead, fraternising briefly as they did so.

Hamilton's force was now effectively stranded and Kitchener belatedly sent reinforcements: a territorial division from Egypt, and another from Scotland. Both were committed to ill-planned and costly attacks producing little or no gain. More troops were called for: territorial divisions stripped of their best officers and men to feed the Western Front, and partly trained 'Kitchener' divisions shipped out to the eastern Mediterranean as the IX Army Corps, for what Hamilton hoped would be the decisive battle. His August offensive aimed to take the summits of the Sari Bair ridge; a diversionary attack at Helles was to pin down Turkish reinforcements, and IX Corps made a new landing some miles north of Anzac, in Suvla Bay. In theory a sound plan, it was disastrously bungled by the commanders on the ground, while Hamilton fumed impotently at his headquarters on the island of Imbros. Lieutenant-General Sir Frederick Stopford, commanding IX Corps, had been picked out of retirement, as had many of his subordinates. The citizen soldiers landed at Suvla were virtually all volunteers: patriotic, brave, bewildered and worthy of far better leadership than they got.

The assault on the Sari Bair Heights was pressed home with utmost courage by New Zealanders who drove the Turks off Chunuk Bair. A diversionary attack by the Australian Light Horse serving as infantry along a ridgeline known as The Nek (graphically portrayed in the film *Gallipoli*) failed despite the Australians' sublime gallantry. Elsewhere on Sari Bair a battalion of Gurkhas reached the summit, only to be destroyed by 'friendly fire'. At Helles the diversionary assault also failed. Mustafa Kemal, in command of the defence at Sari Bair, ordered a massive counter-attack on 10 August that swept all before it as the close-packed Turkish infantry surged over the crest. The objective of the last great British attack, on 21 August, included a spur known as Scimitar Hill. The attack failed amidst scenes of horror as the scrub ignited, cremating hundreds of wounded in the blazing undergrowth.

No further offensive action was possible at Gallipoli; priority for reinforcements went to the Western Front, and the need to send troops to Salonika progressively weakened the force's ability to do any more than hold on. Hamilton was recalled in October and replaced by General Monro, who took stock of the dismal situation and immediately recommended evacuation, prompting an embittered Churchill (shifted from the Admiralty to the anodyne appointment of Chancellor of the Duchy of Lancaster) to comment, 'He came, he saw, he capitulated.'

The naval campaign in the Dardanelles had started with the exploit of submarine B-11, followed by the leisurely bombardment of the forts and the disastrous attempt to force the Narrows on 18 March. It took a turn for the worse in mid-May with the loss of the battleship *Goliath*, and the arrival in the eastern Mediterranean of a number of U-boats. Two more pre-dreadnoughts, *Triumph* and *Majestic*, were torpedoed in full view of the horrified troops ashore, and most of the fleet abruptly departed to safer anchorages in the Greek islands, a move that further lowered the morale of the army ashore. As the U-boats ran riot, sinking numerous troopships with great loss of life, the situation at sea got worse. In one aspect, however, the navy earned undying fame. Ever since the initial landings, boldly handled British, Australian and French submarines had braved the Dardanelles defences to force their way into the Sea of Marmara to eliminate the Turkish merchant marine. They sank numerous warships and on several occasions penetrated into the harbour at Constantinople, causing widespread panic. Naval aviation also played a prominent part. Kitchener had expressly prohibited the use of the Royal Flying Corps in the expeditionary force but the Royal Naval Air Service, initially equipped with underpowered primitive machines, grew in strength and confidence to the extent that it scored the first success with torpedo-carrying floatplanes against Turkish ships in the Sea of Marmara.

An extraordinary picture, taken by a machine gunner in the bows of the *River Clyde* during the landing at 'V' Beach, Helles, on the morning of 25 April 1915. Men of the Royal Munster Fusiliers ashore can be seen taking cover under the walls of Sedd-el-Bahr castle; many others lie dead, piled on the decks of the lighters. So great was the slaughter to the Munsters that the disembarkation of the Hampshires was cancelled until after dark. (IWM)

The approach of winter brought torrential rain, followed by hard frost and snow, creating appalling conditions for the hapless infantry in their open trenches. Thousands were evacuated with frostbite, hypothermia and trench foot; hundreds froze to death. Kitchener briefly came to see things for himself and, aghast at what he had required of Hamilton and his troops, confirmed the order for evacuation. On the nights of 19 December 1915 and 8 January 1916 the troops at Anzac-Suvla, then Helles, were taken off from under the noses of the unsuspecting Turks in a brilliantly planned and executed operation in which not a single man was lost.

Of some 410,000 British and Empire troops and 70,000 French who went ashore, 252,000 were killed, wounded, missing, prisoners or evacuated sick. Estimates of Turkish casualties vary between 218,000 and 400,000 with at least 66,000 killed in action. Great heroism was displayed on both sides but to pit inexperienced troops against the best of the Turkish Army, fighting for its own soil and fired by patriotism, was asking too much. Amphibious operations are the hardest of all to bring off, requiring careful training and rehearsal, neither of which was given to the soldiers that fought at Gallipoli.

Defence of the Suez Canal

Egypt, technically still part of the Ottoman Empire in 1914, had been under effective control of a British 'Agent' since 1882. The army was in the hands of a British Commander-in-Chief or *Sirdar*. British officials headed most government departments in Egypt including the police. The nominal Egyptian head of government and viceroy of the Ottoman Sultan was the *Khedive*, Abbas El Hilmi: an anglophobe mostly resident in Constantinople, he was summarily deposed by the British in December 1914. The British closure of the Canal in August 1914 to ships of hostile nations was illegal under international law but reasonable in the circumstances. The small British peacetime garrison of regular troops was replaced by territorial infantry and mounted Yeomanry, joined before Christmas by the vanguard of the Australians and New Zealanders destined for the Western Front.

The declaration of *jihad* by the Sultan in his capacity as Caliph in November was ignored where it should most have taken fire – the holy places of Islam in Arabia. Sherif Hussein of Mecca and his extended Hashemite family saw that the grip of the Sultan had slipped to the extent that they could make a bid for power on their own account. But there were places where the idea of holy war did appeal to Muslim leaders. The Libyan provinces of Tripolitania and Cyrenaica, under Italian control since 1912, were inhabited by tribes owing religious and some political loyalty to Ahmad al-Sharif, Grand Senussi of Sollum. Known collectively as the Senussi these people had fought against the Italians with the help of Turkish advisers.

In 1914 the Turks sought Senussi aid in distracting British attention from the Suez Canal, and in the hope of spreading *jihad* westwards to afflict the French in their North African territories.

West of the Nile Delta rises a low plateau; to the south extends the great Libyan desert, its boundary marked by a string of great oases whose inhabitants acknowledged the authority of Senussi Ahmad. Nominally a dependant of the Egyptian Government, he was required to keep the tribes in reasonable order. The Turks saw an opportunity to re-assert their authority in this area early in 1915 when Enver sent his half-brother Nuri Bey to the Senussi, accompanied by one Jafar Pasha, a German officer who had embraced Islam. If Ahmad proclaimed his own holy war against the British in Egypt, he was promised German money and arms. Intelligence of Nuri's and Jafar's activities reached GHQ in Cairo and measures were taken to forestall insurrection spreading into Egypt, where many of the Delta peasantry owed allegiance to Senussi Ahmad as their religious leader. An improvised Western Desert Force assembled at Alexandria including British, Australians, New Zealanders, South Africans, Sikhs of the Indian Army and Egyptians. Apart from skirmishes along the frontier, little happened until the end of 1915, by which time the Senussi had received several shipments of German arms. Some sharp encounters took place on ground destined to become familiar in the Second World War.

In January 1916 the Grand Senussi, emerging from his base in the great Siwa oasis, personally led an advance eastward along the coast from Mersah Matruh with a force commanded by Jafar. In what turned out to be the decisive engagement of this miniature campaign, at Aqqaquia on 26 February, the Western Desert Force defeated and captured Jafar, who, having recovered from his wounds, changed sides to become a successful commander of one of Sherif Hussein's irregular armies in the Arab Revolt.

Turkish and German eyes turned toward the Canal as the vital focus of a strategy threatening Egypt, the coaling and signal station at Aden, British interests in the Persian Gulf and India. The Turks needed little persuasion to mount a major operation against the Canal, assigning it to their Eighth Army under Djemal Pasha, whose Chief of Staff, Colonel (later General) Baron Friedrich Kress von Kressenstein boldly decided early in 1915 to approach the canal by a direct march across the Sinai desert. Water was the great problem. The force had to cover about 120 miles from Gaza in Palestine to Kantara on the Canal; at least 12 days' supply was needed for men, horses and camels. A diversionary force advanced down the Mediterranean coast, while the main body advanced across Sinai to halt in an area close to the canal where a tract of sand dunes offered cover as pontoons and collapsible boats carried across the desert were assembled.

War in the desert, 1915–1918.

To manhandle these and field artillery across Sinai was a remarkable feat. The defenders, alerted by aerial reconnaissance, deployed to meet the threat. During the night of 1 February several attempts were made to get across the Canal but few Turks made it. At dawn the next day the battle spread as further Turkish units reached the Canal. Gunboats hastened to the scene and shot the Turkish boats out of the water. The Turks withdrew, taking their guns with them back over the Sinai. There was no further action on the canal in 1915, and General Maxwell strengthened the defences. At one time that year he commanded no fewer than 13 divisions but these were progressively withdrawn to meet crises elsewhere in the theatre.

Advance into Sinai and Palestine

Early in 1916 Lieutenant-General Sir Archibald Murray succeeded Maxwell; his command was re-designated the Egyptian Expeditionary Force, including all troops in the Eastern Mediterranean theatre. Murray was ordered to begin a deliberate advance up the coast towards Palestine. The cavalry patrolled deep into the desert on his landward flank. A railway and a water pipeline accompanied the laborious advance as the rough track was improved to take heavy motor transport. Kress harassed the advance effectively, but by the end of May 1916 Murray had set up a railhead at El Rumana, deploying a division to defend it. Realising that Kress would try to turn his right flank, Murray threw out a force of cavalry; the Turks attacked this vigorously on 4 August and were beaten off, suffering heavily in the process. The Turkish soldier was already recognised as a formidable opponent, brave and enduring; respect for him mounted accordingly.

By the end of 1916 the British had edged forward against stubborn resistance to El Arish, less than 30 miles from the border of Palestine. The vigour of the Turks defending the frontier posts at Maghdaba and Rafah warned Murray to advance cautiously, the first major objective being the town of Gaza. Murray placed Major-General Sir Charles Dobell in charge of the operation. Dobell had masses of mounted troops, including General Chetwode's 'Desert Column' but they brought with them the problem of watering 10,000 horses. The wells at Gaza were therefore essential to success. The town, protected by a natural barrier of dense cactus hedges, was held by 4,000 determined Turks. Dobell decided to shield his right flank with cavalry and attack frontally from the south. On 26 March 1917 the infantry advanced in a dense fog and all went well until the cavalry, short of water, had to be recalled. Due to a staff error the infantry also retired from positions they had gained, which had to be retaken next day. Kress counter-attacked and drove in Dobell's right flank. At this point the battle was broken off.

The second battle of Gaza took place on 17 April. By now the Turks had improved their positions and were strongly dug in along the line of the Gaza–Beersheba road. Dobell decided to attack on a 2-mile frontage with a single division. Although he had given Dobell *carte blanche* in the execution of the attack, Murray entirely neglected to check the staff-work, resulting in hopeless muddle and failure. The attackers sustained 6,500 casualties to 2,000 Turkish losses. Murray was held to blame by London and removed from command in June. His relief, from the Third Army in France, was General Sir Edmund Allenby, who insisted on getting all the reinforcements he asked for and visited every unit in his command to restore morale. A large man (known as 'the Bull') with a terrible temper, his evident professionalism quickly motivated the troops and gained their unqualified support.

Allenby's force was substantially reinforced. Two mounted divisions were formed in Egypt and two more came from Mesopotamia and Macedonia. He now had seven infantry divisions, and formed them into two army corps, under generals Chetwode and Bulfin. After careful personal reconnaissance he planned two hammer blows, at Gaza and Beersheba. The Turks would be pinned down at the former as the Anzacs took Beersheba and its essential water supplies. Some tanks (the only ones to leave the Western Front in the entire war) had been sent to Palestine and made their debut at Beersheba, which was taken on 31 October. The Turks failed to destroy the vital wells and their whole line was rolled up from east to west; Gaza was bombarded by the Anglo-French fleet and occupied on 16 November. This battle, known as the third battle of Gaza, was the start of a victorious progress for Allenby and his rejuvenated army.

The Germans, alarmed by the turn of events, sent one of their star performers, General Erich von Falkenhayn, to sort things out. Having rejected a hare-brained scheme of Enver's to retake Baghdad, he launched an attack on Allenby's vulnerable right flank but lacked resources for a decisive result. After much bitter fighting, Jerusalem fell and Allenby entered the city on foot on 11 December. The symbolic humility of the gesture was not lost on the world at large.

Review of Turkish, Austrian and German troops in Palestine by Djemal Pasha. Although a reasonably competent commander his German allies lost confidence in him and he was side-tracked after the battles of Gaza and replaced by German generals. (IWM)

Adana
Alexandretta
Aleppo
CYPRUS
(British)
Homs
Beirut
Damascus
MEDITERRANEAN
SEA
Lake
Galilee
Haifa
Nazareth
Deraa
Megiddo
Wadi
Fara
Nablus
Jaffa
Jericho
Amman
British military railway,
extended progressively,
May 1916 to April 1917
Jerusalem
Gaza
Dead
Sea
Port
Said
Rafa
Beersheba
Hedjaz Railway
Alexandria
El Arish
Kantara
Romani
Ismailia
Bitter
Lake
Ma'an
Cairo
Suez
Western
Desert
EGYPT
Sinai
Aqaba
N
Gulf of Suez
Nile
0
100 miles
0
100 km
Front Line March to October 1917
Front Line December 1917 to September 1918
Railway
Railway under construction in 1915
Area taken by Turks in February 1915
Turkish attack, February 1915
RED SEA

Opposite:
Campaigns in Sinai and Palestine.

Torrential rains now halted the campaign. In March 1918 Allenby pushed east to Amman in Transjordan to cut the Hedjaz railway that supplied all the Turkish garrisons to the south. The foray was unsuccessful; although Amman was besieged, the primary target, a great railway viaduct, remained intact. The German March offensive in France deprived Allenby of many of his best units – a total of 90,000 men in two infantry divisions, nine Yeomanry regiments and some of the heavy artillery went to France. Allenby's force now included untried Indian Army troops but also a splendid Indian cavalry division that had been wasted in France. He still enjoyed a two-to-one numerical superiority over the Turks, whose strength had never exceeded 30,000, but there was still one German division in Palestine, well trained and heavily armed.

In Arabia, stirrings of nationalism were already evident and Sherif Hussein, to whom Kitchener had already offered conditional independence, began negotiations with the British in 1915. Hussein's terms were explicit; he would fight the Turks in return for recognition of independence for Arab countries south of the 37th parallel of latitude; this was rejected by the British as it

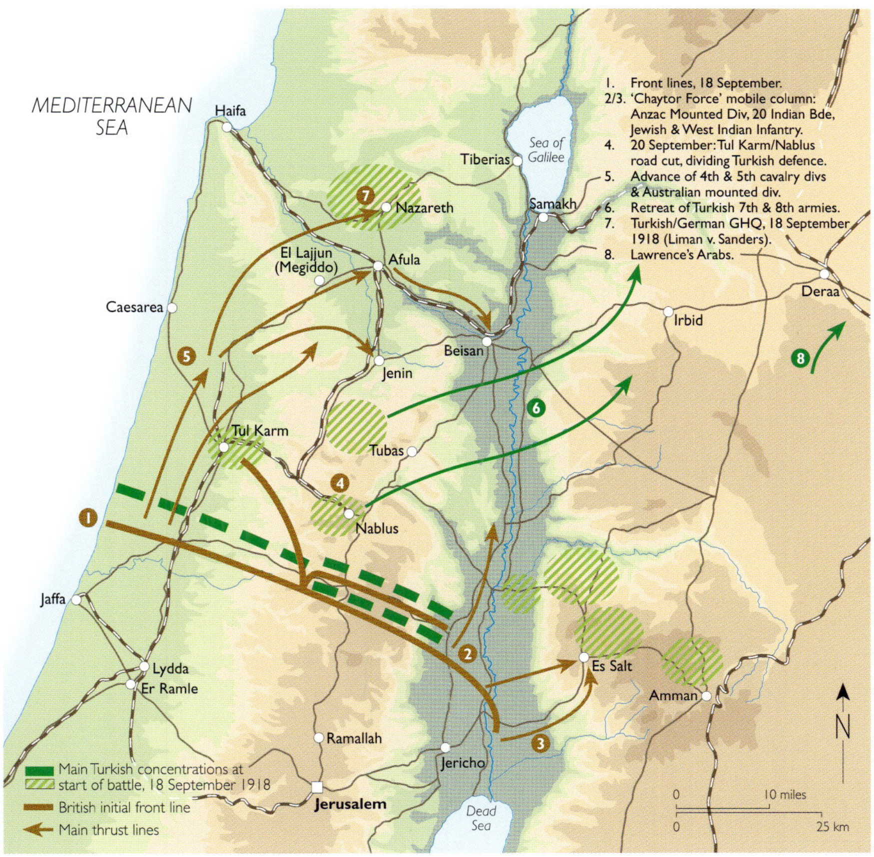

Megiddo, Allenby's master stroke, 19–21 September 1918.

would have included large tracts of Asia Minor and Syria. A compromise was reached, although the future of Baghdad and Basra was left vague.

As Hussein had to be armed and financed it was not until mid-1916 that the Arab revolt got under way in the Hedjaz with an attack on the Turkish garrison of Medina. Hussein proclaimed the independence of the Hedjaz and the garrison of Mecca surrendered in June. Hussein then, to the consternation of the British Government, proclaimed himself King of all the Arabs and appealed to Arabs everywhere to take up arms against the Turks. His claim of kingship of the Hedjaz was recognised by London at the end of the year.

The course of the Arab revolt was punctuated by quarrels between various factions and tribes involved, and the duplicity of British and French politicians preparing their respective post-war spheres of influence in the Near East. The key British personality on the ground was the gifted Captain (later Colonel) T. E. Lawrence, a young Oxford archaeologist with profound knowledge of, and sympathy for, the Arab cause. Working for the Arab Bureau, he gained the confidence of Hussein and his sons and quickly revealed a genius for guerrilla warfare, leading highly mobile columns of camel-mounted irregulars to attack the vulnerable Hedjaz railway, cutting the tracks, blowing bridges along its length and overwhelming isolated garrisons. By mid-1917 Lawrence and his men were ranging widely and on 3 June, while sounding out the Syrian Arab tribes, they blew up a length of the Aleppo-Damascus railway. A month later Lawrence took the surrender of the Turkish garrison at Aqaba, then went to Cairo to meet Allenby and discuss future operations. Allenby recognised Lawrence's talents and agreed to co-operate. By the end of the year the two men were co-ordinating operations with the Arab irregulars to inflict maximum disruption on the Turks and their German allies. Having disposed of the Hedjaz railway, for which the stocks of replacement rails had long run out, Lawrence protected Allenby's right flank in the offensive that both hoped would end the campaign. The Turks were now commanded by the talented Otto Liman von Sanders who had a small German contingent and three shaky Turkish armies at his disposal. On 19 September 1918 Allenby struck. His plan for the attack at Megiddo relied on secrecy, deception and surprise. The Turkish right flank collapsed, and Liman only narrowly avoided capture when his command post was overrun. On 20 September the British crossed the Jordan as Nazareth fell and Allenby's cavalry were loosed in pursuit. The Turkish armies collapsed and the Seventh, caught as it jammed the Wadi Fara, was virtually destroyed in a lethal bombing attack by aircraft of the RAF. Allenby and Lawrence entered Damascus simultaneously on 1 October, Beirut fell to the French on 7 October and by the end of the month they had occupied Homs and Aleppo.

This was the end for the Ottoman armies. The new Turkish Sultan, Mehmet VI, sacked the Young Turk ministry and appealed to President Wilson of the United States to seek an armistice on Turkey's behalf. In the absence of a reply the Turks took the bizarre step of releasing General Townshend from his comfortable detention, sending him as their emissary to Admiral Calthorpe, Flag Officer Royal Navy in the Aegean. The armistice was signed at Mudros on the island of Lemnos on 30 October. Under its terms Turkey opened the Dardanelles, released all prisoners of war, formally ended her alliance with the Central Powers, and placed Turkish territory at the Allies' disposal for further operations of war. On 12 November the Allied fleet passed through the Chanak Narrows and sailed to Constantinople, where the great city lay under its guns.

The Italian campaign

At the end of 1914 Italy was being courted by both the Central Powers and the Allies. The Italian Government had prudently declared neutrality on 3 August, despite the implications of the Triple Alliance that should have taken Italy into the war on the side of Germany and Austria. Her army and navy were the most powerful of the neutrals in Europe and her geographical position was strategically important, lying on the flanks of both the Central Powers and the Allies. Italy had the naval power to control the Mediterranean sea-lanes, notably in the Sicilian Narrows, where a combined Austro-Italian navy could have denied access to the Suez Canal. But intensive diplomatic and political activity secured Italy's signature to the Treaty of London in April 1915, bringing her into alliance with Great Britain, France, Belgium and Russia for prosecution of war against Austria, against whom Italy declared war on 23 May.

The Austro-Italian frontier had been created artificially by a Treaty in 1866 engineered by Bismarck, providing Austria with a barrier of mountains from which her army could sweep down at will onto the north Italian Plain. Any Italian offensive would have to be conducted uphill. Italy's difficulties were increased by the shape of the frontier, a giant 'S' on its side, with a huge salient projecting into Italy in the Trentino district, and the Udine salient extending into Austrian territory. Of these the Trentino was potentially the more dangerous, but its poor road and rail communications also presented problems to Austria's military planners. From the Swiss border to the Adriatic the battle line extended for nearly 400 miles, divided into three segments: Trentino, Alpine and Isonzo. Except for about 30 moderately hilly miles on the Isonzo, the entire line lay in mountain terrain. Anticipating war with Austria, whose intentions towards her former Venetian provinces were all too clear, Italy had fortified all three fronts, covering the northern Plain with a network of strategic roads and railways to permit rapid movement of troops to any threatened sector. On their side of the frontier the Austrian General Staff had constructed permanent defensive positions and had improved the transportation infrastructure in the rear areas. The existence of fixed defences on both sides dictated that from the outset the campaign would be mainly static.

The Italian Chief of Staff General Cadorna planned to attack on the Isonzo front, where the objectives of Trieste and the route to Vienna lay within reach, along with the tempting opportunity to link with the armies of Serbia and Russia. The Italians' Achilles heel was the Trentino front, where a successful Austrian breakthrough would isolate Cadorna's armies on the Isonzo. The lay-out of the Italian railway system in the region acknowledged this; a double-track route ran parallel to the frontier, with spurs branching off up the valleys. The Austrian rail system provided a main line following their side of the frontier but was deficient in branch lines, and this was eventually to lose them the momentum of their offensive in Trentino.

On the outbreak of hostilities the Italians deployed 35 divisions, facing some 20 Austrian divisions in strong, near-impregnable positions along the front. Soldiers of both sides faced arduous conditions in the mountains. Cadorna planned a sustained offensive on the Isonzo and aggressive defence on the Trentino, whilst securing advantageous positions for his *Alpini* fighting in the high Carnic Alps. The Italian Army was ill-prepared, having exhausted most of its material reserves in the Libyan war, and left-wing political pressure had prevented their replacement. Artillery, machine guns and the materials for constructing field defences were all deficient. The air wing, eventually to become outstandingly effective, was still at an early stage of development.

Field Marshal Lord Kitchener reviews troops of the 10th (Irish) Division prior to their embarkation for the eastern Mediterranean in June 1915. Eyewitnesses of this parade, held near Basingstoke, long remembered the sight of 'K' mounted on a huge black charger, 'immobile as a graven image' as the battalions trooped past him. If he entertained doubts as to the prudence of dispatching such raw units to fight the Turks, his impassive features revealed nothing. (IWM Q27688)

Despite these problems the Italians advanced on all fronts on 23 May 1915, surprising the Austrians. Initial results were gratifying and the Italians secured a number of positions inside Austrian territory on the Isonzo front, where the line stabilised, setting the scene for successive attritional battles. The first of these got under way on 23 June – 11 more would almost bleed the Italian Army white. At the same time, however, these bloody slogging matches, resembling the Allied offensives in France, were also to drain the Austrian war effort and pin down whole armies badly needed on the Eastern Front.

General Count Luigi Cadorna came from an old Piedmontese military family. His father had commanded the army that entered Rome in 1870, sealing Italian unity. On the death of General Pollo in 1914 Cadorna saw that the army was operationally unfit, and did much in the next few months to prepare it for war. From the outbreak of war he persisted with repeated head-on assaults, incurring enormous casualties. An austere and aloof man, ruthless to under-performing subordinates, he lacked the humanity that endears successful generals to their men. By the end of 1915 he had fought four battles on the Isonzo, struggling to take the important town of Gorizia, protected by an Austrian bridgehead and covered by fire from surrounding hills. The Austrian positions were enormously strong and both sides suffered terrible casualties. These were titanic battles; in the second battle of the Isonzo the Italians pitched 260 battalions against 129 Austrian, but despite this superiority the defences proved too strong. Cadorna, never noted for

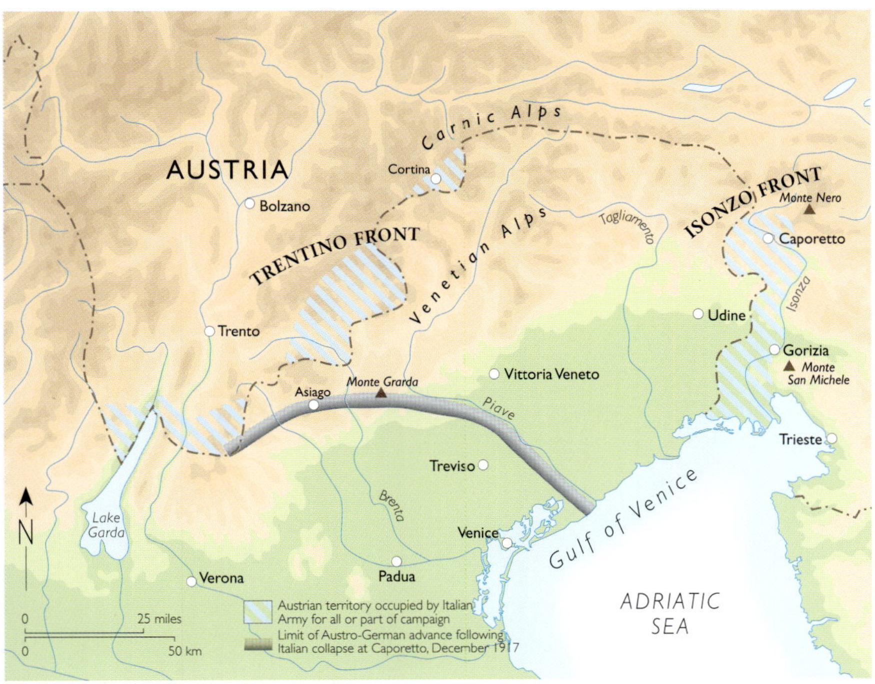

The Italian front, 1915–1918.

his tolerance, had already sacked 27 generals and he removed many more in the months ahead. In their first four Isonzo attacks alone the Italians lost 161,000 men and the Austrians nearly 147,000 killed, wounded, captured and missing. More Italians were called from the reserve to the colours. One 32-year-old reservist rejoining the *Bersaglieri* in August 1915 was destined to make his mark on Italian history – Benito Mussolini, the editor of a socialist newspaper, was invalided out of the army following injuries sustained in a trench mortar accident, but not before he had been decorated for gallantry.

As winter descended the tempo of operations slowed, and cholera, supposedly contracted from the Austrians, spread through the Italian Army. The Italians were still short of artillery, especially the heavy guns needed to break up the Austrian defences. At an Allied summit conference at Chantilly it was agreed that Britain and France would provide additional guns and equipment to buttress the Italian war effort.

The Austrian Chief of Staff, Conrad, was expected by his German Allies to concentrate his main efforts against the Russians, freeing German formations for use on the Western Front. But he had ideas of his own. One was to mount a decisive attack in the Trentino, advancing rapidly across the Italian Plain to seize the great cities of the north. He selected the area around the Asiago plateau for the attack. The prospect appalled the Chief of the German General Staff, General Erich von Falkenhayn. Conrad held on to a mass of heavy artillery that Falkenhayn badly needed to reduce the French forts at Verdun, and his Trentino plan diverted a number of divisions from the Eastern Front. Falkenhayn also believed that the 18 divisions assembled by Conrad would prove inadequate, even though the Austrians enjoyed a marked superiority in artillery – 2,000 guns including nearly 500 pieces of heavy artillery against the Italians' 588 field and 36 heavy guns.

The Trentino attack began at dawn on 15 May 1916, using the novelty of a short but concentrated artillery bombardment that virtually destroyed the Italian trench systems. The Austrian heavy artillery was devastating in the confined valleys, causing avalanches and rock falls; but the rugged terrain saved the Italians from overwhelming defeat, as it slowed the Austrian advance to a crawl. The skill of the *Alpini*, fighting on their home ground, bought time for the defence to stabilise. Even so, by 4 June the Austrians, who had captured the Italian code books and were intercepting their wireless traffic, were within 20 miles of Vicenza and the vital lateral railway supplying the Isonzo front. Here they ran out of momentum, and Cadorna's counter-attack on 16 June steadily drove the Austrians back to their start lines. Falkenhayn was furious, for by diverting troops and guns from the east, Conrad had enabled the Russian General Brusilov to launch a successful offensive.

Five further battles of the Isonzo took place in 1916 as casualties mounted. The Italians were rewarded in August by the capture of Gorizia and briefly it seemed that a breakthrough had been achieved; but the momentum went out of the attack. Cadorna had done better than he had hoped, with gains of up to 4 miles on a 15-mile front. With the return of winter, offensive action once more came to a virtual halt apart from raids and patrols.

At an Allied conference in Rome in January 1917, Cadorna called for eight British and French divisions and 300 heavy guns to capture Trieste and knock Austria out of the war. He was promised artillery, but only on loan for two or three months. The situation in Macedonia, where pressure on Salonika was increasing, made equally urgent demands on the Allies, and the Russian Revolution, beginning in March, enabled the Austrians to transfer formations from the East to augment their forces on the Isonzo and Trentino fronts. Undeterred, Cadorna ordered two further attacks, the tenth and eleventh, on the Isonzo. At the end of August the Italians seemed on the point of final victory; Austrian morale was crumbling as non-Germanic regiments lost their stomach for the war. The Allies had responded to Cadorna's pleas for heavy artillery and British 6-inch batteries were serving under his command. General Ludendorff, Falkenhayn's successor as Chief of Staff, recognised that Austrian political and military collapse could follow a twelfth battle of the Isonzo and sent massive reinforcements for Conrad's army. These included elite German units trained in new tactics whereby assault troops ('storm troops'), advancing rapidly, by-passed centres of resistance and struck at the enemy's headquarters and gun lines. In one such unit served an officer with a future. Major Erwin Rommel commanded a company in a Württemberg mountain battalion that was to play a key role in the forthcoming twelfth battle of the Isonzo.

In this battle the newly formed Fourteenth Austro-German Army came close to winning the campaign outright. Its commander was General Otto von Below, who had an outstanding record of victories already to his credit. Italian military intelligence had correctly predicted the date and place of the offensive. The Italian line was held at the point of attack by the Second Army, whose commander, General Capello, a sick man, relinquished command on 20 October. His dispositions were better suited to the offensive than a sound defence (an Italian offensive had been planned, but postponed), as became clear when Below attacked near Caporetto early on the 24th. A storm of artillery overwhelmed the Second Army, destroying its fieldworks and throwing its communications into chaos. Gas was widely used and the Italian respirators proved ineffective. Fog and rain helped the storm troops to infiltrate the Italian rear areas. The Fourteenth Army crossed the Isonzo and by nightfall on the first day

Previous page:
Italian soldiers in a trench on the Carso Plateau during World War I, c.1916. (Getty Images)

Below had penetrated the Italian reserve lines and taken the high ground on the defenders' side of the river. The Second Army disintegrated, although some units stood firm as the German storm troops swept round them. So great was the impetus of the attack that a withdrawal to an intermediate line ordered by Capello, who rose from his sick bed only to collapse again, was overtaken by the onrushing Germans. On the left of the Second Army, the Third Army commanded by the Duke of Aosta held firm, but as its flank was about to be turned, it was ordered to conform with the flight of the hapless Second. There was huge congestion on the roads to the rear. Bridges were blown by panicky engineers before retreating units had reached them. Across the plains immense crowds of men and animals poured back towards the Tagliamento River where Cadorna intended to stand. Thousands of men from the Second Army were demobilising themselves, discarding arms, uniforms and equipment as they sought by any means to get away from the battle area and make their way home (a situation graphically depicted in Ernest Hemingway's *A Farewell to Arms*). The Third Army, however, retained its discipline and cohesion.

Senior French and British generals visited the front to assess the damage as soldiers of both nations arrived in Italy to buttress the line. Sir William Robertson, Chief of the Imperial General Staff, advised Cadorna to fight on and hold the river lines. Foch, never one to mince his words, told Cadorna that he 'had only lost one army!' and should fight on with the rest. The retreat went on and the Tagliamento Line was abandoned. The last-ditch stand had to be made on the line of the Piave, where the defenders dug in on 7 November. They were barely 20 miles from Venice as Cadorna issued his last Order of the Day, predictably exhorting his troops 'to die and not to yield' before he was replaced by General Armando Diaz, an equally capable but far more humane soldier. The line held and Diaz took stock. The Twelfth Isonzo, or Caporetto as it became known, had been a catastrophe. The Italians lost 10,000 killed, 30,000 wounded, a staggering 265,000 taken prisoner, and untold thousands of deserters. Losses of equipment were equally calamitous: over 3,000 guns, 3,000 machine guns, almost 2,000 mortars and vast quantities of stores and equipment.

This disaster had several surprising results. The Allies at last decided that a unified command was needed if Germany was to be brought low. An emergency summit held at Versailles created a Supreme War Council, leading at last to unified operational policies. Simultaneously, an astonishing spirit of national unity blazed in Italy; thanks to inspirational public speaking and writing by an oddly assorted pair, the poet and aviator Gabriele d'Annunzio and the socialist journalist Mussolini. A surge of patriotism drove hundreds of thousands to enlist and make good the losses at Caporetto. Prime Minister Orlando told his deputies that Italy would never surrender even if the army had to be withdrawn to Sicily. Diaz went quietly about the task of restoring his army, reinforced by French and British troops, guns and aircraft sent hurriedly from the Western Front. Morale rose again as the enemy, exhausted by their efforts and short of food, gave up trying to pierce the Allied line.

1917 had been a bad year for the Allies. The French Army had mutinied and the Russian Revolution continued to spread, freeing some of the Central Powers' armies for action elsewhere. But America had at last entered the war and the Germans knew that her vast resources would decide the outcome if Germany could not achieve the decisive breakthrough soon.

Throughout the spring and summer of 1918, as matters hung in the balance in France, the Italian front was quiet; Diaz, determined to give his army time to recover from Caporetto, declined to attack until ordered to do so by Orlando in October. By now the Italians had been augmented by significant French and British forces. Orlando believed an attack now was essential in order to gain bargaining power at the conference table – all the signs indicated that the Austro-Hungarian Empire was about to collapse. The offensive launched by Diaz on 24 October proved Orlando correct. As the Allied army attacked at Vittorio Veneto the Austrians broke and ran. A rout ensued, with mutiny and mass desertions by Serbian, Croatian, Czech and Polish troops. Mutiny also broke out in the Austrian Navy and on 3 November Austria signed armistice terms. The war in Italy was over.

Salonika and Macedonia

As the last Serbian troops were evacuated from Albania by sea in January 1916 the Allies realised they had missed a golden opportunity in failing to insist that the Greeks honoured their treaty obligation to go to Serbia's aid in the event of a Bulgarian invasion. The Serbs had outfought the Austrians, but the Bulgarian invasion proved too much. A combined Serbian and Greek army would have deterred Bulgarian ambitions and blocked passage from Germany to Constantinople over the Berlin–Baghdad railway.

French and British troops began to arrive at Salonika in the late summer of 1915, initially from Gallipoli where stalemate had set in after Hamilton's ill-starred August offensive. From October to December several abortive attempts were made to link up with the Serbs but the Bulgars drove the French back over the Greek border. At a conference held at Chantilly in December it was agreed that a Franco-British force would hold Salonika despite the defeat of Serbia. Meanwhile King Constantine of the Hellenes pledged his friendship to the Allies but declined to join them against the Central Powers.

By the end of 1915 construction of the 'Entrenched Camp' (or 'Birdcage' as its occupants called it) was almost complete. Its perimeter extended some 80 miles, much of it lakes and marshes presenting good obstacles. Despite Greek protests the Serbian Army was shipped to Corfu to recover. The French General, Maurice Sarrail, was appointed Joint Allied Commander at Salonika as further British reinforcements arrived from Gallipoli to join the 10th (Irish) Division in the 'Birdcage' and went to work on roads, docks, bridges and a railway. Sarrail's orders were to pin down German forces to prevent their transfer to Verdun on the Western Front. An advance out of the entrenched camp was planned for early March 1916 when the roads became passable. French and British accordingly pushed some 20 miles out of their positions towards the Bulgarian border. When Greek frontier troops handed over the key frontier fortress of Rupel to the Bulgarians in May without firing a shot in its defence the Allies realised that Greek neutrality was a negotiable commodity. Rising Greek dissent over the presence of Franco-British troops on the frontier was exacerbated by the arrival from Corfu of 118,000 Serbian troops, re-equipped and eager to avenge recent defeats. At this point the Allies almost fell out. Sarrail had been ordered by his government to advance beyond the Greek frontier, in anticipation

Russian troops arriving at Salonika before marching along the quay, headed by their colours, to music of a British Army band. Until the effects of the Russian revolution began to sap their morale and discipline, these troops fought well as part of the Allied command. (Mary Evans Picture Library)

that Romania was about to enter the war on the Allied side. The British local commander, General Milne, received contradictory orders from London: to consider himself under Sarrail's orders only for operations in and around the 'Birdcage', and to refrain from crossing the Greek frontier. After much discussion Sarrail was told to advance, if necessary with French and Serbian forces only. His command had swollen with the arrival of a Russian contingent to a strength of 250,000, and in August a large Italian force joined the Salonika Army. Further to the west, in Albania, an Italian corps faced the Austrians across the Voyusa River, where neither side took any action until the end of 1916.

In August 1916 Romania had at last decided, fatally as it happened, to enter the war, and the Bulgars advanced to forestall the Allies offering help to their new colleague. Sarrail was under orders from Paris to check the Bulgars and to launch a counter-offensive in September. Only the French and Serbs took part, and the British remained in their positions on the Struma front. After fierce fighting in which the Serbs distinguished themselves the Bulgarian line was broken and in November the Serbs renewed their attack, forcing the Bulgars to evacuate the battered town of Monastir before the bitter winter forced an end to serious campaigning.

Romania's decision to declare war on the Central Powers was calamitous. Falkenhayn, commanding the German Ninth Army, dealt a series of shattering blows to the Romanians, forcing them to retreat on Bucharest, and surrender early in the new year.

After the frictions of 1916 the Allies agreed on a defensive posture at Salonika. Sarrail's problems were increased by the Greeks, whose fully mobilised army was concentrated but static in Thessaly, even though Bulgarian troops had crossed into Greek territory. King Constantine had fallen out with his Prime Minister Venizelos who was dismissed, fleeing on 25 September 1916 to Crete where he set up his own Provisional Government. Early in October he arrived by invitation in Salonika where his government was immediately recognised by the Allies. The king was now isolated, but still enjoyed considerable support in and around Athens.

The Allies began to act energetically against the Greek royalist government, seizing ships of the Royal Hellenic Navy despite riots in Athens inspired by the king's supporters. As three Venizelist battalions joined the Allied army, Germany issued a formal warning to Greece, alleging 'infringements of neutrality'. The gloom was briefly lifted by the capture of Monastir, Sarrail claiming this to be 'the first French victory since the Marne', even though most of the fighting had been done by the Serbs, who showed their disgust by refusing to continue the advance when the campaign restarted in the spring of 1917.

The naval war in the Mediterranean

Problems of command, control and coordination afflicted the Allied naval staffs as much as their army colleagues. No Naval Staff, equating to the Army's General Staff, existed in the Royal Navy before 1912 and it would be 40 years before a truly Joint Central Staff was created in Whitehall. In 1914 the Admiralty was unaware that the army's staff had been conducting highly secret staff talks with their French opposite numbers for many years in order to ensure the rapid deployment of an Expeditionary Force to the continent in the event of war.

The presence of two, then (from 1915) three major Allied navies in the Mediterranean raised many problems. Prominent among these were those of national pride and the absence of any command structure or common doctrine. Even the language of command was a matter for acute debate. It got worse when a Japanese naval squadron joined the British, French and Italian fleets.

The Mediterranean had long been regarded as a 'British Lake' thanks to the Royal Navy's prestigious fleet based on Malta. It now had to be carefully partitioned to give the participating fleets their areas of operational responsibility. Four each were allotted to Britain and France and the Italian Navy was given three. The system was quite inflexible; if a valuable troopship under destroyer escort left one national zone it had to be picked up by a destroyer from another navy: U-boat commanders were not slow to acquire this intelligence and capitalised on it whenever a handover went amiss. Strong resistance by naval commanders to the institution of a convoy system led to appalling shipping losses as the U-boat campaign got under way.

Apart from the ex-German warships *Goeben* and *Breslau* the Ottoman Navy possessed few modern ships other than some torpedo boats; the old Turkish battleship *Messudieh* was sunk off Chanak in December 1914 by the British submarine B-11 and another pre-dreadnought, *Heiruddin Barbarossa* was torpedoed in the Sea of Marmara shortly after the Allied landings at Gallipoli. The saga of the *Goeben* remains an epic. Together with its escorting cruiser *Breslau* this modern battlecruiser had been very publicly on display at Constantinople in the summer of 1914 but slipped away for an unknown destination on the eve of the European war. It materialised off the French North African ports of Bone and Phillipeville to bombard them on 3 August 1914 before heading off to the east, impotently shadowed by the British Mediterranean fleet, which was unable to take action until Britain had formally declared war on Germany late on 4 August. Both ships evaded the pursuit and arrived off the Dardanelles to be given free passage up to Constantinople on the orders of Enver Pasha, in flagrant breach of an international convention denying passage to foreign warships in time of war. Following the confiscation of the two Turkish super-dreadnoughts nearing completion in Britain, the Germans presented *Goeben* and *Breslau* to the Ottoman Navy in a shrewd diplomatic move that did much to bring the Turks into the war on the side of the Central Powers. For much of the war they operated in the Black Sea, a considerable threat to the Russian fleet.

The combined Austro-Hungarian navy was based in the Adriatic, its capital ships securely bottled up there on Italy's entry into the war. These included several modern super-dreadnoughts of the *Viribus Unitis* class, each carrying 12 guns as main armament, more than a match for any of the pre-dreadnoughts of the Anglo-French fleet in the eastern Mediterranean. The Austrians were able to use a number of magnificent safe harbours and anchorages along their Adriatic coast, but the Italians had no safe naval bases on their east coast and it was easy for Austrian cruisers to carry out quick bombardment sorties against Italian coastal towns without fear of interception. The Italian Navy possessed some modern dreadnoughts, based on Taranto and Brindisi in the south, but there were to be no major fleet actions. The Austrian battle fleet stayed at home and the Adriatic saw a war of small ships and submarines. In May 1915 the German U-21 was the first to make the hazardous voyage from Germany to the Eastern Mediterranean; more followed, and soon flotillas of U-boats were based in Turkish and

Eastern Mediterranean and the heart of the Ottoman Empire 1914.

Austrian waters. Prefabricated parts of smaller submarines were sent from Germany overland for assembly at Cattaro, the main Austrian base, to play a significant part in the naval campaign.

By mid-May 1915, the arrival of German submarines in the Dardanelles area had tilted the balance dangerously. Following the loss of five elderly battleships – two to submarines, two to mines and one to a boldly handled torpedo boat – the remainder of the British fleet withdrew from close support of the troops ashore, reappearing off the beaches only for specific operations. An attempt was made to redress this deficiency later by sending out a number of monitors – shallow-draught ships carrying heavy-calibre guns, originally intended for operation in the shoal waters off the German coast and in the Baltic. Several of these were patrolling the entrance to the Dardanelles in 1918 when *Goeben* and *Breslau* made a final desperate sortie out into the Aegean; after blowing several of the monitors out of the water, both struck mines. *Breslau* sank with heavy loss of life and the damaged *Goeben* limped back to Constantinople where she remained for the rest of her long life as the flagship of a reconstituted Turkish Navy, and in later years as an accommodation and training ship, finally going to the breakers in the 1960s.

The U-boats operating out of Cattaro worried the Allies to such an extent that they constructed a barrage across the Straits of Otranto. By mid-1916 it was in place. Over 100 fishing drifters and 30 motor launches patrolled the buoyed anti-submarine nets stretching across the gulf, dropping explosive charges when a submarine was detected. In the event only two submarines

The former German battlecruiser *Goeben*, anchored in Constantinople, October 1914. With her escorting cruiser, *Breslau*, she had eluded the British Mediterranean fleet in August and made her way to Constantinople where they were (ostensibly) sold to the Ottoman government and embodied into the Turkish fleet. The German sailors, when ashore in Constantinople, wore the fez. Machine-gun detachments from both ships served on the Gallipoli peninsula, notably during the fierce fighting at Helles. (Topfoto)

were destroyed in many hundreds of successful passages by the Cattaro U-boats. The drifters and motor boats were lightly armed with 57mm guns; the captain of one gained the Victoria Cross when the Austrians made a rare sortie through the barrage, taking on a light cruiser at point blank range and miraculously surviving the loss of his boat, one of 14 lost on this occasion (before they sank them the Austrians chivalrously invited their crews to become prisoners of war). A scratch force of Allied destroyers vainly attempted to intercept the raiders and bring them to battle but skilful handling by their commander Captain Horthy (a future president of Hungary) enabled them to get home. Unlike the similar Dover Barrage whose destroyer guardships were permanently at sea, the Italian destroyers remained at anchor in harbour at Taranto. After the Austrian sortie the Italian admiral was sacked and the drifters were withdrawn from the barrage at night, enabling submarines to pass at will.

In the open Mediterranean, the Allied fleets struggled to ensure the free passage of merchant shipping essential to the war effort in the face of increasingly bold U-boat action. Under the terms of a convention signed by Britain, France and Italy, several combined fleets were created. There was still no agreed escort policy and casualties from U-boat action continued to rise. An ingenious ruse adopted by the Allies was to disguise harmless merchant ships as warships by adding wooden turrets, masts and funnels. One U-boat commander, believing he had torpedoed the British battle-cruiser *Tiger*, was astonished to see through his periscope that its guns, turrets and funnels were floating away as the ship went down.

The Austrian dreadnought *Szent Istvan* sinking after it had been torpedoed on 10 June 1918, 30 miles south of Pola. This was a particularly bold action on the part of a small Italian motor launch which got within 400 yards of its target before firing two torpedoes. Hit in the engine room, the battleship was left dead in the water and unable to use its pumps. As it heeled over, most of the crew managed to escape by walking over the keel as the ship turned turtle. (Mary Evans Picture Library)

In April 1917 the U-boat campaign in the Mediterranean reached a climax as 278,038 tons of Allied shipping went to the bottom with a further 113,000 tons severely damaged. It was decided to encourage merchant ships to sail by night, and to introduce a partial convoy system. Where appropriate, merchant shipping bound for the eastern Mediterranean from the United Kingdom was advised to use the Cape route, and intensified use of the Italian railway system was recommended. Twenty-eight U-boats were known to be based at Cattaro and Pola with the Kaiser's personal instructions to attack unescorted Allied hospital ships, a move foiled by attaching Spanish naval officers to their crews, thus granting neutral status.

The Allied fleets maintained a programme of shore bombardment against Austrian and Turkish installations, and the Italians developed the use of small motor torpedo boats to attack enemy ships in harbour. A notable success was achieved in December 1917 when two motor boats penetrated the defences at Trieste to sink the Austrian battleship *Wien*. In the following year this success was spectacularly repeated when motor boats torpedoed the super-dreadnought *Szent Istvan*, forcing the Austrians to cancel a planned sortie against the Otranto barrage. Further successful attacks were made against Austrian capital ships in the final weeks of the war, by which time the Emperor's navy was in a ferment of mutiny, but a gallant attempt to torpedo the former *Goeben* led to the loss of the British submarine E-14 and the death of her captain, who was given a posthumous VC.

For the Allied navies the Mediterranean campaign had been one of steady application rather than dramatic fleet actions. But despite the difficulties of divided command and the lack of standardisation, the Austrian fleet that had been the chief threat was effectively prevented from exercising its power, and that of Turkey was neutralised from the start.

PORTRAIT OF A SOLDIER: CECIL, HAROLD AND NOEL WRIGHT

The Great World War of 1914–1918 affected entire populations. Few families were spared the impact of the casualty lists publishing the dead, wounded and missing. One family in Christleton, a Cheshire village far from the battlefields, was typical.

Frederick Wright, a joiner, married Frances Tushingham in the 1880s, and they moved into a cottage in Quarry Lane. A large family duly arrived. The eldest, Fred, was followed by Marshall (Marsh), Harold, Hylton, Cecil, Noel and finally three daughters: Effie, Amy and Eva. All the children attended the village school until their 14th year, when the boys sought work. The Wright boys found employment in Chester, 3 miles' walk away.

In 1907 a major overhaul of the British Army and its reserve forces created the Territorial Force, which included the Earl of Chester's Yeomanry, originally raised in the 18th century for home defence. By the summer of 1914 Cecil was riding as a trumpeter with the regiment for its summer camp at Llangollen. Weeks later, on mobilisation, the yeomanry went to Northumberland to defend the coastline. They were still there a year later. Cecil wrote to his sister Eva from Morpeth Common camp in October 1915 describing the primitive conditions and appalling weather (spelling throughout the letters remains uncorrected):

> It has rained for 28 hours without a stop, things are in a fine mess if it is only catching hold of the dirty wet headropes, it is rotten. I have finished transport driving and gone to the troop again. We do very little drill here, it is all road work, every other day we go between 40 and 50 miles we are seeing the countryside and a very nice country it is … on Thursday we started at 6.30 am and landed back at 7.15 pm just before dark, it was a lovely day and the Cheviot Hills looked fine … PS the Scotchish Horse that was here before us went to the Front some at home may have been in the papers where they have been cut up.

In 1917 the Wright brothers meet near Gaza: (left to right) Harold, Noel, Cecil. They never met again. Cecil became an infantryman when the Cheshire Yeomanry were unhorsed in Palestine to compensate for the loss of infantry battalions sent to the Western Front. He was also bound for France, on transfer to the King's Shropshire Light Infantry and died there of Spanish Influenza in November 1918, two days before the Armistice. (Courtesy of Michael Hickey)

(The Scottish Horse had been sent via Egypt to Gallipoli where they had to fight as infantry.)

On one postcard dated 15 October 1915 Cecil added a message telling her that he had been promoted to corporal:

> I believe we are going to the first line in a month or two. We have had a big week. The ground was covered with frost at 11 am so you can see what it is like sleeping in the open …

Cecil's subsequent letters are all from Egypt and Palestine. Three of the Wright brothers served in that theatre. Noel transferred to the Royal Flying Corps as ground crew and Harold served in the Royal Garrison Artillery (RGA). By May 1917 General Murray's Egyptian Expeditionary Force had slowly advanced up the Mediterranean coast into Palestine but had been repulsed in two attempts to take the town of Gaza. Harold wrote to his sister shortly after the second battle:

> … don't think we are having a bad time here although there is a war on, for speaking the truth we are having a jolly good time at present … I hope they forget us and leave us here for the duration. We get nothing else but sunshine from morning till night, we have blue glasses and short pants. The lanes are 3 inches deep in dust so when we were marching we got smothered and choked and we were not allowed to have a drink out of our water bottles and when we halted we dared not drink for it is a bad practice to drink water out here we just rinced our mouths out. We rise in the morning and go on parade at 6 and have an hour on Swedish drill, then we have breakfast, oatmeal porridge, bacon and bread and good stuff it is and we wash it down with a pint of tea with plenty of sugar – the only thing we go short of is milk for cows are very scarce here. We go on parade again at 9 until 11.30 on the guns, a bit tiring owing to the heat. Then we go to the guns again from 3 to 4.30, getting cooler than, and we have finished the day.

Shortly after this, by a happy coincidence, the three brothers managed to meet on Whit Sunday 1917 on the battlefield, an event celebrated with a photograph. It was the last time they would all be together.

Meanwhile, Cecil continued fighting and marching with the dismounted yeomanry. On the eve of the third battle of Gaza he sent a card to Eva:

> Well, I have not got much time as we are on the move tonight. All the movements are done at night, it's a lot better for marching in the cool. We are looking forward to the rainy season starting. You can take this for granted

> an infantryman out here never as a good time. We are starting tonight on this mobile stunt that means iron rations …

In a letter dated 22 November 1917 Harold described the recent battle of Gaza, although he also took the opportunity to complain that none of his sisters had written to him for weeks – 'how would you like it all my pals receiving letters from home and me having none you don't seem to realise what a letter means on a shell-riddled desert'. He then goes on to describe the battle:

> Now before the great advance I had a letter from Cecil to say he was ready, that meant to meet the Turkish Army so you could tell what my feelings were when the great guns roaring and the Turkish shells flying not far from me, then to see the lights going up and lighting the earth for miles. Our artillery forming the barrage to clear the way for our infantry that were firing their rifles and charging with there bayonets. You at home don't seem to realise what a horrible clash it all is and me thinking how poor Cecil was going on. I knew he was in front but what part I did not know but I afterward found out that he was in the attack on Beersheba, that is where the Cheshire Yeo made there debut and they were received with a strong force of the Turkish Army but they did not fail to do so for they put him on the run with there bayonets … we have had some very hard strugles and our infantry must have had very hard times for we have had very hot weather considering it is well on in November and we have had some very wet days, marching in this country with a full pack is above all jokes but the scarcest thing of all is water but in spite of all these drawbacks we have chased him for miles, we are well past Jerusalem and Bethlehem …

After the third battle of Gaza the campaign slowed down. While Cecil was in a Cairo hospital with fever in April 1918, Harold met Noel in Alexandria where they lived in luxury for a couple of days:

> Fancy me and Noel in Alex with bags of cash and Cecil stony in Cairo, me and Noel had a royal time, we did live, he only had two half days off but was out by 5.30 every night and we had supper together every day, it's a true saying that there's corn in Egypt but not only corn. To give you some idea, for breakfast, 4 eggs, bread, butter, and tea as much as I wanted for one shilling, for dinner which I had at the finest café in Alex, Chip potatoes, beef steak, two vegetables, and tea … After tea we went for a stroll or the pictures, then for Supper we went to a Posh café for coffee … then I sent Noel home like some Lord going from his club in our open carriage and if that's not going the swank I don't know what is …

The crew of a 60-pounder gun of the Royal Garrison Artillery, Palestine, during the third battle of Gaza. (Courtesy of Michael Hickey)

However, despite this luxury, Harold was still homesick:

> … but Eva, a leave here seeing all these sights is nothing, I would give you my word, I would rather have come to dear old Blighty and as cold as it is to stand in the food queues all day just to get amongst a little bit of civilisation and to here the Old English language spoken once more …

Back in the desert conditions were harsh again:

> Today there is a terrible sand storm so when we go out we have to wear sand goggles to protect our eyes or otherwise we would get nearly blinded and the flies are terrible while I am writing these lines they are in bunches on my hands and face I believe they are watching what I am writing about …

When Allenby resumed the offensive Harold's battery was in constant action. His letters increasingly reflect his homesickness and the soldier's eternal complaint about mail from home. In July, from 'Somewhere in Judaea' he writes at length:

> You never wrote me a single line telling how you enjoyed yourself at 'Whit' Monday. I was wondering Eva when I shall have that great pleasure of rowing on the Dee and listening to the band … it's Saturday night 9 pm and I am on duty till Monday night on the telephone at the guns and we have just finished firing for Johnny [Turk] as given us a very rough time in our section today. He has done a deal of damage the shrapnel as been falling like rain and flashing like lightning but I am pleased to say they were falling ½ mile short of me. It's a fine sight watching them but not very pleasant stopping it according to what I could see Harry Culham and Frank Rowlands were having their full share I am anxiously waiting to hear all they have to say about it for we go visiting each other when things are quiet. (PS Harry as been over tonight, Monday, he's alright.)

Cecil had been posted from the Yeomanry to the Kings Shropshire Light Infantry on the Western Front. After home leave he saw much action until October 1918 when he fell sick with the virulent Spanish influenza sweeping Europe. Taken to a military hospital at Etaples near Le Havre he died on 9 November, two days before the Armistice. The telegram notifying his death was delivered to the family cottage at Christleton on the 11th, casting the Wrights into deep mourning as the rest of the village rejoiced.

In August Harold, his long epistles failing to draw a response, wrote to Eva calling her an 'ungrateful hussy' but as the Egyptian Expeditionary Force's campaign ended he wrote in mellower mood on 5 November:

> Just a few lines to tell you I am still in Ismailia Egypt but returning to Palestine in a few days but I am pleased to say as you know I am not returning to fight. That is one great consolation for the scrapping finished last week so it only means going back to Ludd to rejoin my battery … I don't think I will ever see any more fighting and a good thing too …

Two days later Harold wrote again:

> Dear Eva, a few lines to let you know whilst I was commencing to write in the 'Chester Hut' Ismailia, YMCA, it has been announced that Germany has signed an Armistice. With Loud Cheers and everybody sang (praise God from whom all blessings flow) … and I am now longing for the day when I embark on the boat to sail for Good Old Blighty and be with you all at home and to remain … get plenty of music ready for that happy day.

A week later, from Palestine, and unaware of Cecil's death, he described the celebrations of the previous week:

> How did you all receive the news. I hope you are not all suffering from shell shock. We got the great news at 5.30 pm on the 11th you see how quickly good news travels and it is approaching 4000 miles from home. It was received here as you can guess with loud cheers we nearly all went mad, they all sang songs, beat tins, and made bon-fires. The big guns fired blank cartridges and gun cotton but the anti-aircraft fired shrapnel so you can imagine what a time we had that night. But Eva that will be the night when we get safely home, we will have a jubilee, what do you say. The next time we meet will be in Good Old Chester. So keep smiling Eva, you will have a good time running to the station to meet us all in our turns. That will be great sport, what do you think …

For the Wrights of Christleton at least, the war was over.

THE WORLD AROUND WAR: THE LOOSE ENDS OF WAR

The years following the Armistice of 1918 brought to all the nations involved a host of new problems. The Allied blockade of the Central Powers had not been entirely effective, because Germany and the Austro-Hungarian Empire had both received much help (as had the Allies) from neutrals. Although geography had prevented a full blockade of the Ottoman Empire, its creaking infrastructure was unequal to the logistic loads placed upon it and this, combined with the closure of the Dardanelles and the elimination of the Turkish merchant fleet, contributed to its economic as well as military decline, and eventual defeat.

The causes of the Austro-Hungarian military defeat are not hard to find: the ethnic, religious and political diversities faced by the Habsburgs combined to overwhelm them by 1918. These problems distracted the government in Vienna whilst their armies were trying to cope with war on several fronts. The civilian population found its living conditions steadily eroding and starvation set in. Resistance to infection declined and when the influenza pandemic got under way in 1918 it decimated whole populations in central and eastern Europe. Food riots became commonplace in the cities of the empire and civil unrest spread to the armies, sapping their will to fight.

The outbreak of war in 1914 had been greeted enthusiastically on both sides; mobilisation of the huge continental armies took place in a euphoric atmosphere of bands, flowers stuck in rifle barrels and patriotic songs. Poets saw the war in romantic terms. The better ones still spared a thought for the young men who would not return, but some produced doggerel of appalling quality, celebrating 'men going forth to die in martial ecstasy upon the bayonets'. In Germany the most popular theme was that of God's presence in support of fleets and armies; every German soldier bore the motto '*Gott mit Uns*' – God with us – on his belt buckle, and even Rupert Brooke felt moved to thank God for 'matching us to His Hour'. In the darkest hours of 1915 a note of elevated optimism is still evident in poems flooding back from the fronts. The Royal Naval Division at Gallipoli numbered several outstanding poets in its ranks, although Brooke had died of sickness in the Aegean on the eve of the April landings. Most had received rigorous classical educations and their works reflected a romantic attachment to the idea of fighting within sight of ancient Troy. Patrick Shaw-Stewart, himself to die on the Western Front in 1917, was a typical product of what must have seemed a coming golden age; educated at Eton and Balliol College Oxford, his friend Rupert Brooke thought him 'the most brilliant man they've had at Oxford for ten years'.

The early optimism and patriotism of the war poets evaporated forever after the bloodbaths of Loos and Gallipoli in 1915 and the Somme in the following year. Sassoon, Graves and, above all, Wilfred Owen, display a growing sense of futility, especially among the front-line soldiers and their officers. Even Rudyard Kipling, whose rousing words did much to stimulate recruiting in the first year of the war, changed his tone after his beloved only son, a subaltern in the Irish Guards, was lost at Loos. Thereafter, his works convey an elegiac sense of realisation that it is always the youth of a nation that pays the price for its politicians' ineptitude and pride.

Culture survived despite all else throughout Europe. Paradoxically the arts thrive in times of war, as people seek escape from grisly reality. England's leading composer Edward Elgar set numerous patriotic works to music; his occasional music for Imperial events like coronations and jubilees had already become widely known, and his adaptation of the First Pomp and Circumstance March to

Hygiene enters modern warfare. Major John Claypool MC, Assistant Division Surgeon for the 80th Division, is shown here breaking a tube of chlorine into a cup of water. The advances in hygiene and medical care throughout the war were remarkable. (NARA)

words by A. C. Benson gave the nation an alternative anthem: *Land of Hope and Glory*. For the first time, the government appointed well-established artists to record all aspects of the war; the results of this imaginative enterprise, deposited at the Imperial War Museum in London, comprise one of the most comprehensive collections of 20th-century British art to be found anywhere. The outstanding wartime work of Stanley Spencer, conceived when he was serving as a medical orderly in Macedonia, can be seen in mural form at a memorial chapel near Newbury.

Wars invariably lead to remarkable advances in technology, whether for destructive or benevolent purpose. In the latter case, medicine stands to benefit above all else, for it is a nation's interest to maintain the health of its people as well as to ensure that the maximum number of fighting men wounded in battle are returned to the firing line. The Great War of 1914–1918 was probably the first in which deaths in battle exceeded those resulting from disease, but the Spanish influenza that devastated the world after 1918 probably killed more than all the battles put together. In the South African war of 1899–1902 over 60 per cent of the British dead had been from sickness, prompting the War Office to conduct searching examination of its medical services. Improved medical research in the first decade of the century resulted in greatly improved preventive measures in sanitation, control of infections, better education in personal hygiene and inoculation against some of the most dangerous diseases including typhoid. In the first year of the war half of Britain's doctors were mobilised, depriving many hospitals of their key personnel but ensuring that the armed forces received the best possible medical attention. Whether serving in uniform or in the teaching hospitals and research departments of universities, doctors were able to benefit from an explosion of innovation and discovery in medical science. Developments in radiology, anaesthesia, pathology, orthopaedics, plastic surgery and the psychiatric treatment of what became known as 'shell shock' led not only to vastly improved chances of survival for battle casualties, but in the longer term to improved standards of national health. Although the discovery of antibiotics lay years ahead, great advances were being made in the effective treatment of wounds using new antiseptic solutions that, unlike phenol or carbolic acid, would not damage human tissue.

If advances were being made by all the combatants in the treatment of battle wounds, the fight against disease went in parallel. At Salonika the Anglo-French forces were stricken by virulent strains of malaria, at Gallipoli dysentery and typhoid claimed thousands of victims and in Mesopotamia the Indian troops were victims of a deficiency disease as a result of an inadequate diet. This brought about an urgent examination of the roles of the newly discovered vitamins. Before 1912 many doctors believed that beri-beri was caused by bacteria. Until it was found that vitamin B1, present in yeast, would arrest scurvy, the sepoys of the Indian Army in Mesopotamia were prostrated by this ailment. The deficiency in their rations made good by doses of Marmite, they rapidly recovered.

Inevitably, as the advances made in life-saving medical techniques were taken up by all the warring nations, so too was there rapid progress in military technology. Before 1914 Britain had relied on its navy as the sure shield of the nation; the army was regarded as an imperial gendarmerie, trained and equipped accordingly. Thus, when it was forced to take part in a gigantic war of attrition on the Western Front, it was out-gunned by a German Army with superior artillery and vastly greater manpower. The advent of trench warfare presented the British and French general staffs with a seemingly intractable problem: how to break through the immensely strong German trench systems, protected as they were by wide belts of barbed wire covered by machine guns. The answer was the tank, developed in England and initially launched on the Somme in penny packets and over totally unsuitable terrain. Not until 1917 when several hundred broke through the German lines at Cambrai was it possible to see that a new era in land warfare had begun. Even so, the insistence of the high command that horsed cavalry should be used to exploit the success of the tanks – which it signally failed to do – reflects the conservatism of many generals at even this late stage of the war. Cavalry, the *Arme Blanche* whose role was shock action against infantry, had become obsolete overnight in the Franco-Prussian war of 1870–1871 when it was mown down by a deadly combination of machine gun, quick-firing field artillery and the magazine rifle.

Battlefield tactics underwent a transformation after 1914. The British had attempted to apply mid-19th-century battle drills against Boer marksmen on the South African veldt in 1899 and paid a dreadful price. In 1914 the Germans made the same mistake, pitting their massed columns against a British regular army that had learned its South African lesson and could bring controlled and highly accurate rifle fire to bear with devastating effect. Lethal in defence, the magazine rifle also enabled infantry to fight in extended order when in the attack, instead of in close order. Unhappily, this improvement was neutralised on 1 July 1916 when the British Army left its trenches on the Somme and trudged towards the uncut German wire and machine guns.

Sea warfare had been changed forever by the launch of the world's first all-big-gun battleship, HMS *Dreadnought,* in 1906. Her arrival triggered a race between Britain and Germany to equip their main battle fleets with ships of this power. In the event the long-expected clash, when it took place in the North Sea in June 1916, was inconclusive. What it did prove was that German technology had produced battleships well suited to such a slogging match; their gunnery was superb and their ships better protected against

Three American divisions served alongside British troops, two of which were issued with British weapons and, in some cases, British uniforms with American buttons. The soldiers here, from the 111th Infantry, 28th Division, have just been issued their Lee-Enfield Mk III rifles, which were used throughout the war with devastating effect. (NARA)

plunging fire. The craft that actually influenced the war at sea more than any other was the formerly despised submarine. The Germans, effectively bottled up in their bases by the Allied blockade, sought to destroy their enemies' seaborne commerce and very nearly succeeded. While the great battle fleets of both sides spent the war in almost total idleness it was the destroyers and other anti-submarine ships that finally obtained the decision, and then only with the belated aid of the convoy system.

The innovations playing a part in the operations of all fleets were those for which Admiral Fisher had fought so relentlessly against deeply entrenched conservatism in the Royal Navy and Admiralty: oil fuel, steam turbine propulsion, submarines, tethered mines, torpedoes, naval aviation, wireless telegraphy and radical new methods of officer selection and training. Few serving officers in any navy in 1918 would have dared to prophesy that of all these, it would be naval aviation and the aircraft carrier that would win decisive naval campaigns of the next war in the distant Pacific.

The Wright brothers had made their first unsteady flight at Kittyhawk a bare 11 years before the Archduke Franz Ferdinand met his untimely end at

Sarajevo. All major armies in Europe had set up air wings before 1914 but the initiative rested with the Germans until 1916, when the Allies at last developed the essential device enabling machine guns to be mounted to fire forward through the propeller. In the opening months of the war, aircraft were limited to the reconnaissance and spotting roles but air-to-air combat soon ensued, demanding ever-heavier armament and higher performance from the combat aircraft. The British Expeditionary Force went to France in August 1914 with fewer than 100 machines. By April 1918 when the RFC and Royal Naval Air Service were merged to form the Royal Air Force, thousands of aircraft and no less than 30,000 spare engines had been constructed. Heavy bombers were being used by both sides to bomb their opponents' homelands; the dawn of the strategic bomber offensive. Proponents of air power – Trenchard in Britain, Emilio Douhet in Italy and Brigadier-General Billy Mitchell in the United States – confidently forecast that in any future war navies and armies would be subordinate to the air arm and that 'the bomber would always get through'.

As boulders hurled into still waters generate ever-widening ripples, the fighting on the Western and Eastern fronts between 1914 and 1918 can be seen as the biggest stones; but the campaigns around the shores of the Mediterranean and its hinterlands may be seen as lesser pebbles whose ripples interacted on each other, in ways that significantly affected the outcome of the main contest, bringing down the German and Austro-Hungarian Empires, and with them, that of the Ottomans. The peace secured at Versailles was illusory, as it failed to extinguish the embers of nationalism that would plunge Western Europe into a yet more bloody war. America's failure to join the League of Nations helped to ensure the rise of Fascism, for none of the member states was prepared to act against Mussolini and Hitler as they launched their respective aggressions in the 1930s. The rise of Arab nationalism would lead to seemingly insoluble problems in the Middle East. Even decisive wars create as many new problems as they solve old ones.

PORTRAIT OF A CIVILIAN: THE VILLAGE OF CHRISTLETON

The Great War was a watershed in British society, affecting every family and home in the United Kingdom, as in all the combatant nations. In the village of Christleton most able-bodied men were serving by the end of 1915 in far-flung theatres of war. Three of the Wright brothers were in the Near East. On the strength of the meagre training in his school cadet corps Brian Hickey, the parson's son, was given a commission in the county regiment and was posted to the 11th Cheshires in France in midsummer 1916. Families at home had to come to terms with not only the absence of breadwinners but also the need to generate income. Men found medically unfit for the armed forces were directed into work supporting the war effort. Frederick Wright senior and his eldest son, as skilled workers, worked on the construction of the huge hutted camps springing up in every district; in their case around Wrexham just across the county border. Their womenfolk had to get on with running the family home despite growing shortages of foodstuffs. These shortages were caused by the German U-boats, which in April 1917 sank 25 per cent of all ships leaving British ports, a total of a million tons. Domestic food supplies were affected and in that summer huge queues formed outside Chester's butchers and grocers. In the early spring the national reserve of grain had been down to six weeks. The vital supply of pit props from neutral Scandinavia was also affected, causing the government to set up the Forestry Commission with a remit to grow the timber needed for the mines. Faced with continuing shipping losses the Admiralty was forced to adopt the convoy system, which immediately stabilised the crisis in the Atlantic – but not in the Mediterranean where it was not fully implemented.

It was clear by the end of 1917 that food distribution in the UK was haphazard, producing great inequalities, especially in the industrial towns of the Midlands and north. Bread had already risen to a price of 10 pence a loaf, depriving the very poor of a basic foodstuff. The government ordered higher wheat extraction rates to give more flour but the resultant 'national' loaf, being off-white, proved unpopular. Trades unionists staged demonstrations in Hyde Park against rising food prices and early in 1918 a rationing scheme was introduced under the auspices of Lord Rhondda at the new Ministry of Food. Each citizen was issued with a book of coupons, to be handed over the counter when paying for a given quantity of sugar, meat or butter. Additional foodstuffs were placed on the ration as necessary. Margarine, on ration, went on general sale as an unpalatable butter substitute. The scheme was accepted by the people as an equitable way of ensuring that all got their fair share, even though little or no attempt was made by the authorities to audit the huge piles of coupons handed over to local food offices by grocers and butchers. Legislation enabling the government to introduce and enforce such measures stemmed from the notorious Defence of the Realm Act, known as DORA, hurriedly enacted by Parliament in August 1914 and thereafter employed as the catch-all giving powers of requisition of property, the enforcement of conscription for military and industrial service, and the arrest and detention of anyone suspected of unpatriotic activities. It was held by many to be a denial of basic civil liberties. As the war went on it was used to impose food controls and public house licensing hours (to counter the wave of drunkenness among workers in the war industries). The rector of Christleton, as secretary of the Chester Diocesan Temperance Association, considered it his patriotic duty to enrol the youth of the parish into its ranks, issuing Eva Wright and her sisters with certificates pledging themselves to lives of total abstinence.

The impact of war on a village like Christleton came gradually. Fields had to be tilled and as the war continued, county agricultural committees, usually chaired by the big landowners and squirearchy, endeavoured to increase yields; they and the government were all too aware that a national farmers' strike would bring the nation to its knees, once the U-boat campaign had begun to bite. By 1916, women were working on the land, tackling jobs hitherto performed only by men. As in the factories, where the productivity of women workers consistently exceeded that of men, they were initially treated with ridicule, soon changing to grudging admiration.

The early battles involved only the regular army, but with the arrival of the Territorials and Yeomanry at the front, familiar names began to appear on casualty lists and almost every Sunday the rector announced from the pulpit that another local man had been killed or gone missing. In October 1916 his

Opposite:
Trumpeter Cecil Wright, Cheshire Yeomanry, at the regiment's summer camp in North Wales, 1913. He would have been mounted on one of the hundreds of working horses 'impressed' under the terms of the Army Act from firms and farms all over Cheshire in order to equip the regiment for camp. During the war a comprehensive remounts service, run by retired army officers, went into action all over the United Kingdom and Ireland to select and purchase the thousands of additional animals needed to provide chargers, gun teams and draught horses. (Courtesy of Michael Hickey)

own son's name joined the lists. Second Lieutenant Hickey had been severely wounded on the eve of his 19th birthday when a shell burst in the trench where he and his men were preparing for a major assault. Although church leaders repeatedly urged the nation to turn to God, the blurring of class distinctions that took place during the war years had begun to erode the influence of the churches. The relaxation of time-honoured social taboos led to huge increases in illegitimacy and in the incidence of prostitution and venereal disease, especially in garrison towns, and in the areas where huge hutted training camps had been set up. When peace came, the whole social structure had changed beyond recall. There had been a time when village girls had little choice but to enter domestic service on low pay and with little chance of bettering themselves. As the school-leaving age was raised to 14, a better-educated generation of young women raised their expectations too. Eva Wright and her sisters could not wait to apply for jobs as shop assistants in Chester as soon as they were 18. Although the militant and often violent campaign of the pre-war Suffragette movement led by Mrs Pankhurst had alienated much of the population, she and her supporters had given their wholehearted support to the war effort, in particular the use of women in industry, agriculture, transport and in the new uniformed auxiliary services. The enthusiastic response of the nation's women to the war, described by Mrs Pankhurst as 'God's vengeance on the people (i.e. men) who held women in subjection' was to gain the vote in 1918 for those over 30 and eventually for all over 21.

Enemy air action against England during the first three years of the war was almost entirely limited to raids by Zeppelin airships. These caused some damage in London and in the east coast towns, but on occasion one or two reached the Manchester and Liverpool areas, leading to the imposition of domestic and industrial black-out measures. Mrs Wright and her daughters sewed their own thick curtains, purchased in the sales at Brown's, Chester's main department store. Prudently set aside in 1918 they were to see service again in 1939. Writing from the Somme two weeks before he was wounded, the rector's son, not without a touch of irony, expressed his pleasure that 'the Zeppelins didn't bomb the house or the tennis courts', adding that 'I am as lousy as it is almost possible to get and would be very pleased if you could send me a tin of Boots's "Vermin in the Trenches", which I am told is a good thing to have about one'.

After almost four years, and despite the efforts of the government to keep up the nation's spirits, war weariness set in. Civilians were urged in 1918 to observe one meatless day a week (the army capitalised on this with recruiting posters offering recruits 'Meat every Day!'). The civilian ration had been reduced by then to 1lb of sugar, 1½lb meat and a few ounces of fat, margarine or butter a week. This was sufficient to maintain reasonable health levels, unlike in the blockaded states of the Central Powers where many starved, and disease due to poor nutrition prepared the way for the influenza pandemic that was about to sweep Europe. The influenza killed Cecil Wright, whose family received the dreaded telegram announcing his death in France as Christleton church bells rang out for victory on the 11th day of November.

All through the war years the Wrights had sustained their spirits by home-made entertainment round the parlour piano; one of the songs they sang was the great hit *Keep the Home Fires Burning*, written by one Ivor Novello, an officer in the Royal Naval Air Service who, as Ivor Davies, had been a chorister with Brian Hickey at Magdalen College Oxford in the reign of King Edward VII. The cinema had begun to capture audiences that had formerly packed the galleries – the 'Gods' – of the music halls, whose days were numbered. Chester enjoyed a thriving cultural life throughout the war, based on its choral societies, its amateur orchestra and its operatic society. Visiting theatre and opera companies – notably the Carl Rosa – performed the stock repertoire and the Wright sisters long remembered Mascagni's *Cavaliera Rusticana* in a particularly dire rendition that reduced the audience in the 'Gods' to helpless laughter. The people of Christleton thought nothing of walking the 3 miles into town and back for these treats.

With peace came the homecoming of the men who had survived four years of fighting in places they would never see again; indeed, most of the men from Christleton who served in the ranks had never been beyond the county boundaries before 1914. Their service had broadened their perspectives but all were adamant that they would never undergo the experience again. The Wright brothers settled down into their civilian jobs. Employment was still high, and in any case they were skilled men, capable of holding down jobs in a booming building trade. In December 1918 women over 30 voted for the first time in a general election called immediately after the Armistice by the wily Lloyd George, who asked the electorate to vote for his list of Liberal and Conservative candidates bearing what former Prime Minister Asquith (who lost his seat) caustically called the 'coupon of approval'. Lloyd George swept back into power with 479 MPs against an opposition of 229 and promptly reneged on virtually all his election promises; the 'Land fit for Heroes' did not materialise and the stage was set for years of industrial and economic unrest as a Britain in decline became a debtor nation. The landowners and industrial magnates who had lived in the larger houses in and around Christleton had lost their sons, and Brian Hickey his closest friends, on the battlefields of France and Flanders, Gallipoli and Palestine. The domestic staff who had serviced these families were no longer available, and in a harsher economic climate the formerly wealthy families decayed and departed.

HOW THE WAR ON THE MEDITERRANEAN FRONT ENDED: END OF THE TRAGEDY

The death of the aged Austrian Emperor on 21 November 1916 was the end of an era. His long reign had been punctuated by personal tragedy and the Vienna of his youth, enriched by a gaiety and culture unmatched elsewhere in Europe, was no more. Austrian national morale was sinking and the Allied blockade had brought the empire to the brink of starvation. The new Emperor Charles inherited an unhappy situation.

Fighting broke out in Athens at the beginning of December 1916 between troops still loyal to the king, and Allied sailors and marines. Allied ambassadors called on the king and delivered a 24-hour ultimatum to the royalist government. Reluctantly, the Greek Army began to pull out of Thessaly under Anglo-French supervision. In reply, a royal warrant was issued for the arrest of Venizelos who for good measure was anathematised by the Patriarch Archbishop of Athens. A vicious campaign of assassination was directed against the prime minister's supporters. 'Between me and the King', commented Venizelos, 'there is now a lake of blood'. More Allied troops arrived at Salonika, where Sarrail planned to renew the offensive as soon as the roads were passable. The results were not encouraging. Two British divisions failed to break into the German–Bulgar positions at the end of April but Sarrail went ahead with his offensive on 5 May. A British night attack on the Doiran front failed due to the Bulgars' skilful use of searchlights, and the Serbs' refusal to advance after suffering over 14,000 casualties for little gain brought the offensive to a halt.

The struggle for power in Greece came to a head. King Constantine abdicated following the Allied ultimatum and was succeeded by his second son Alexander. Venizelos returned as prime minister, his first act being to declare war on the Central Powers.

The summer heat of 1917 brought thousands of casualties from disease at Salonika. The Struma valley was notorious for a particularly lethal strain of malaria and the British had to pull back to higher ground in an attempt to reduce the numbers of the sick, which by October had reached 21,000. Disease and lack of leave triggered mutinies in the French contingent. After months of complaints from the other Allies, Sarrail was finally replaced in December by General Marie Louis Guillaumat, who succeeded within weeks in repairing all the damage wrought by the slippery Sarrail by visiting all units under his command and re-invigorating the jaded Allied force. His opportunity to show his skills as a field commander was denied when, in June 1918, he was summarily recalled to Paris by his government without reference to the other Allies, and replaced by General Louis Franchet d'Esperey. The great German offensive on the Western Front drained the

Salonika force of troops. As more Greek troops went into the line at Salonika it was possible to send 20,000 French and British troops to France.

Sporadic fighting had been in progress throughout 1917 in Albania where Italian troops, sent there without reference to the other Allies, had established a coastal bridgehead. In the summer of 1918, supported by the Royal Air Force, they attacked the Austrians north of Valona. A counter-attack in August drove them back, the last military success enjoyed by the Austro-Hungarian Empire.

In Macedonia the final Allied offensive got under way in September across the River Vardar. The Bulgarian Chief of Staff, General Lukov, suggested to Tsar Boris that he sue for peace, to be told to 'go out and die in your present positions'. By 17 September the Bulgarian Army that had fought hard and well for three years began to disintegrate as whole units mutinied and made for home. The Anglo-French attack on the Doiran, however, met furious resistance, the British suffering heavily. In the 65th Brigade of the 22nd Division only 200 men survived. The attack was renewed on the following day, failing again when 'friendly fire' halted the British advance. General Milne informed General d'Esperey that his men could do no more; in any case no more was required, as the Bulgars were broken. RAF aircraft reported on 21 September that huge columns were heading home in disarray, and a week later the Bulgarian Government sought armistice terms, signing them on the 29th.

There was one last act. On 7 October the Allied Supreme War Council directed Milne to lead the Salonika Army eastward through Thrace and on to Constantinople. The Turks had already decided to seek an armistice, and this was duly signed on 30 October as the other Central Powers crumbled into defeat.

CONCLUSION AND CONSEQUENCES: AFTERMATHS

The precise cost of the First World War, in terms of human lives, will probably never be known. German losses numbered at least 1,808,545 dead and 4,247,143 wounded, while French casualties have been estimated at nearly 5,000,000, of whom 1,385,300 were dead or missing. The Americans lost 115,660, with an overall casualty figure of 325,876. The total losses of the British Empire were 3,260,581, including 947,023 dead and missing. On the Western Front alone, British and Dominion casualties were 2,690,054.

A little over 12 per cent of the total number of British soldiers who served in France and Belgium were killed or died and almost 38 per cent were wounded. Thus about half of the BEF's soldiers on the Western Front would expect to become casualties, some more than once. Approximately one in eight would be killed. The BEF's non-battle casualties, from sickness and accidental injuries, amounted to 3,528,468 officers and men. Of these 32,098 died from a variety of causes, including pneumonia, frostbite and meningitis. It is a tribute to the BEF's medical services, however, that around 80 per cent of wounded soldiers who passed through their hands not only recovered but even returned to some form of duty. One should also note that world-wide mortalities from the Spanish influenza pandemic of 1918–1919 may have reached 50 million – more than were killed in the war.

Estimates of Russian war dead range between half a million and two million, and like the figures for deaths, those for Russian prisoners of war and missing vary considerably. The most authoritative post-war study gave 3,409,433 captured and 228,838 missing. When the figures for captured or missing are placed alongside the figures of dead, the Russian Army differs markedly from the other major belligerents. For every 100 dead in 1914–1918 Russia had 251 captured or missing, Austria-Hungary 150, Italy 92, Germany 65, France 46 and British/British Empire forces 21. In other words, Russian soldiers were far more often than others either led into situations where capture was inevitable, or were very much readier to surrender than others.

Austria-Hungary lost 905,299 dead, 60 per cent of them on the Eastern Front, and 837,483 missing. The latter figure was revised to 181,000 after the war, since most of the missing turned out to be Slav troops who had surrendered or defected. During 1917–1918 many Russian units dissolved spontaneously because peasant soldiers went home to ensure they did not miss out on land redistribution resulting from break-up of the landlords' estates. Others left because they saw no point in staying, illustrating the difficulty in a very large country of obtaining national unity. In the 1904–1905 war with Japan, Russian observers complained that only soldiers

Crowds gathered outside Buckingham Palace on Armistice Day, 11 November 1918. (IWM Q47852)

from east of Lake Baikal took the war seriously; conversely, in 1917–1918 the Siberian regiments were the first to leave the front, on the grounds that 'the Germans won't be coming to Siberia'.

The consequences of the First World War in the East included the restoration of an independent Poland, the severance of East Prussia from the rest of Germany by the Polish Corridor, independence of the three Baltic States and Finland and dismembering of the Russian, Habsburg and Ottoman Empires. The settlement would in due course prove to have created more problems than it solved, because the new states mostly contained ethnic minorities and/or territories that could be subjects of irredentist claims by Germany or the Soviet Union.

Ukraine, Georgia, Eastern Poland, Estonia, Latvia, Lithuania, some Finnish territory, Bessarabia and part of Bukovina (from Romania) and Ruthenia (from Czechoslovakia) all came under Soviet rule under Stalin, whose revolutionary rhetoric covered an ambition to restore and even extend the frontiers of the former Russian Empire as much as possible. In post-Second World War negotiations he revived, though he did not pursue, Nicholas' claim for control of the Turkish Straits, and sought the return of Kars and Ardahan.

Probably the major consequence was the creation of the Soviet Union. A bitter civil war resulted in the replacement of a self-proclaimed autocracy by an autocracy, then an oligarchy, that both claimed to be democratic and socialist, and of a self-proclaimed empire by an empire that claimed to be the arch-enemy of empires. Stalin's autocracy would prove far more oppressive than that of Nicholas II, but also much more efficient at harnessing the nation's resources and industrialising its economy. In 1941–1945 the Soviet Union would experience losses of people and territory far greater than those that brought down Tsarism. But it would emerge a victorious superpower, form a bloc of satellite states, and remain a superpower until in 1991 the empire collapsed yet again, leaving post-Soviet Russia with western frontiers closely resembling those imposed by the Treaty of Brest-Litovsk.

Of 7.8 million men mobilised in the Habsburg Empire no fewer than 90 per cent were killed, died of sickness, were wounded or taken prisoner or went missing in battle (by comparison, Britain's losses came to just under 39 per cent of those in uniform). Political disintegration was already evident in Vienna months before the Armistice. Reluctant recognition of a Czech Republic had been granted in April 1918 and the promise of independence for other Habsburg minority nations by the Allies had further undermined the Austrian position. The proclamation of the Austrian Republic on 13 November 1918 spelt the end for the Habsburgs and was immediately followed by the proclamations of the Hungarian Republic and the United

Kingdom of Serbs, Croats and Slovenes. With the drastic curtailment of her borders Austria became a landlocked German state. Cut off from its previous sources of raw materials and hedged by vengeful tariff barriers imposed by the victors, the young republic was no longer a sound economic entity and unrest soon spread. Unification with Germany, the obvious solution, was prohibited by the Allies; social and political instability prevailed and a failed Nazi coup in 1934 served only to hasten the inevitable German invasion of 1938, which was overwhelmingly endorsed by a plebiscite.

In the Balkans, old scores remained to be settled. The Serbs soon revived their efforts to bring Yugoslavia under their control, despite the ferocious resistance of Croats and Slovenes. Desperately trying to bring a measure of stability, King Alexander imposed a dictatorship in 1929; it brought temporary relief but still left the Serbs in a powerful position and he was assassinated at Marseilles in 1934 by a member of one of the dissident minorities. Even worse chaos prevailed in Albania through the 1920s until President Ahmed Bey Zogu proclaimed himself king as Zog I. Trying to modernise his primitive realm, he was making reasonable progress until April 1939 when an Italian invasion forced him into exile.

The political infighting in Greece between King George II and premier Venizelos continued for years. Following its defeat in its ill-starred war with Turkey Greece agreed to a massive exchange of populations; over 1.25 million Greeks left Asia Minor as Turks returned from the former Ottoman provinces in Greece. The hapless Armenians of eastern Anatolia paid a dreadful price for their support of Russia and the Western Allies during the Great War and at least a million died in uncontrolled massacres. Greece lurched unsteadily from kingship to republicanism, an uneasy truce prevailing between Venizelos the dedicated nationalist and his king. The prime minister was not finally ousted until 1928 after an unexpected electoral rout, and he died in exile in 1936, following the return of George II to the throne.

Italy had suffered losses in battle of 600,000 dead and had high hopes of reward from the Allies. These were soon dashed; apart from a grudging grant of some Austrian territory there were to be no gifts of ex-German colonies. Britain and France did not feel generous toward Italy. They regarded Italy's conduct in sending troops over to Albania at the height of the war, and an expeditionary force to southern Turkey in 1919 before any treaties had been ratified as irresponsible. Political chaos took over in Italy as socialists, smarting under national humiliation and faced by the forces of conservatism and the Church, split into new factions. The new man was Benito Mussolini, who took advantage of the situation to launch his Fascist party, which took power in Milan in 1922, then marched on Rome where King Victor Emmanuel invited Mussolini to form a government.

In 1918 it had seemed that the Hashemite dynasty, staunch allies of Lawrence in the Desert war of the Hedjaz, would reap their just reward and become rulers of much of Arabia and Transjordan. History decreed otherwise. Emerging from Kuwait in 1925 the al-Saud family and their followers seized the holy places of Islam, the cities of Mecca and Medina, and also the port of Jeddah, establishing a firm grip over the Muslim pilgrimage trade, and enforcing adherence to the principles (if not always the strict practice) of puritanical Wahhabi Islam. The careful and often cynical planning of French and British agents in the war years had turned to dust and the future shape of Arabia rested with the Saudis.

Britain's influence in Egypt dated back to 1882 and was tolerated by the majority of the population for 30 years; although nominally still part of the Ottoman Empire in 1914 the country prospered as a British protectorate and had been formally declared such in December 1914. Since 1882 great steps had been made in irrigation, provision of an infrastructure of roads and railways and education. The British had scrupulously respected the Muslim faith and the educated classes were mostly compliant. But during the war years, when the British had resorted to mass conscription for ill-paid labour and had requisitioned vast quantities of useful material, a nationalist movement had burgeoned. Its political party was the *Wafd* and its programme was independence. Deportations of its leaders led to serious insurrection, put down vigorously by the British Army under Field Marshal Allenby who was appointed High Commissioner in 1919. As the result of a Commission headed by Lord Milner, independence was proposed, subject to guarantees for British interests, principally those concerned with the Suez Canal. Britain terminated the protectorate in 1922 but kept a military presence. Discussions between the two countries continued intermittently, resulting in a treaty of 1936 in which Britain reserved the right to maintain a garrison in the Canal Zone.

In Britain the post-war years were troubled. The nation was tired and bankrupt. The men returned to anything but the 'Land fit for Heroes' promised by that most glib of politicians Lloyd George.

The various campaigns around the Mediterranean failed in the end to divert much attention from the Western Front where the final decisions were fought out, and where the British Army under Haig would win the greatest victory in its long history. Yet very little was truly solved by the peace settlement imposed by the Treaty of Versailles of 28 June 1919. Professor Ian Beckett describes the Treaty as being, in some respects, 'an unhappy compromise between the French desire for a punitive settlement, the British desire for stability and the American desire to create a better world based on principles of internationalism, democracy and self-determination'. It did not fail, as has so often been argued, because its terms were too severe. Germany had to return Alsace-Lorraine to France and give up conquered territories inhabited primarily by non-German peoples, while the Rhineland was divided into three zones which were to be occupied respectively by Allied forces for five, ten and 15 years. Germany was also called upon to pay reparations – principally to France and Britain – though the amounts to be found were not specified until the early 1920s. In the event, by the time the reparations were terminated in 1932, Germany had paid less than half the sum set a decade or so earlier, the victors of Versailles having lacked the political will or military muscle to extract the full amount. Moreover, if Germany was forbidden by the Versailles settlement to maintain a large conscript army or possess offensive weapons such as submarines, battleships and aircraft, the Treaty did not dismember the country nor did it deprive Germany of the industrial complex upon which her war machine had hitherto been based. On the other hand, reparations almost certainly helped to undermine the post-war German economy and, together with the attribution of 'war guilt' to Germany under Article 231 of the Treaty, sowed the seeds of resentment which were only too eagerly exploited by Hitler and the Nazis in the 1920s and early 1930s. The latter chose to ignore the inconvenient detail that the German Army was essentially beaten in the field by November 1918 and would have unquestionably suffered an even more humiliating defeat the following year. Indeed, they used the fact that the German Army was still in action on the Western Front when the Armistice was signed as an excuse to nurture the myth that domestic collapse had constituted a 'stab in the back' and betrayed the country's fighting men.

International stability was not enhanced by the creation of new states – such as Czechoslovakia and Yugoslavia – in central, eastern and southern Europe which would themselves contain frustrated national or ethnic minorities. The establishment of a League of Nations represented a laudable effort to ensure that international disputes would henceforth be settled without recourse to war. Unfortunately, the attempt failed, largely because of the non-participation of its main proponent – the United States Senate having declined to ratify the settlement on the grounds that it would infringe national sovereignty. In Britain and France, war-weariness, emphasised by the literature of disillusionment in the late 1920s and early 1930s and intensified by economic slump and mass unemployment, encouraged appeasement and weakened national resolve to resist Hitler's ambitions until it was too late to prevent another cataclysmic conflict.

BIBLIOGRAPHY

Aspinall-Oglander, C. F., *Military Operations: Gallipoli*, 2 vols (London, 1929–1932).

Asprey, R., *The German High Command at War: Hindenburg and Ludendorff and the First World War* (London, 1991).

Bean, C. E. W., *Official History of Australia in the War of 1914–1918: The Australian Imperial Force in France (1916–1918)*, vols III–IV (Sydney, 1929–1942).

Beckett, I. F. W., *The Great War 1914–1918* (London, 2001).

Blaxland, G., *Amiens 1918* (London, 1968).

Bond, B. and N. Cave (eds), *Haig: A Reappraisal 70 Years On* (Barnsley, 1999).

Brusilov, A., *A Soldier's Notebook* (London, 1930).

Churchill, W. S., *The World Crisis*, 4 vols (London, 1927).

Cowles, V., *The Kaiser* (New York, 1963).

Crutwell, C. M. R. F., *A History of the Great War* (Oxford, 1936).

DeGroot, G., *Blighty: British Society in the Era of the Great War* (London, 1996).

Edmonds, J. E. and H. R. Davies, *Official Histories of the War: Military Operations 1915–1919* (London, 1919).

Falls, C., *Armageddon 1918* (London, 1964).

Falls, C., *Caporetto* (London, 1966).

Falls, C., *Military Operations: Macedonia*, 4 vols (London, 1935).

Falls, C., *Military Operations: Egypt and Palestine*, 2 vols (London, 1928).

Feldman, G., *Army, Industry and Labour in Germany 1914–1918* (New Jersey, 1966).

French, D., *British Strategy and War Aims 1914–1916* (London, 1986).

Golovine, N., *The Russian Army in the World War* (Oxford, 1931).

Griffith, P., *Battle Tactics of the Western Front: The British Army's Art of Attack, 1916–1918* (London, 1994).

Gudmundsson, B., *Stormtroop Tactics: Innovation in the German Army 1914–1918* (New York, 1989).

Harris, J. P. and N. Barr, *Amiens to the Armistice: The BEF in the Hundred Days' Campaign, 8 August–11 November 1918* (London, 1998).

History of the First World War (London, 1969–71).

Holmes, R., *The Little Field Marshal: Sir John French* (London, 1981).

Horne, A., *The Price of Glory: Verdun 1916* (London, 1962).

James, R. Rhodes, *Gallipoli* (London, 1965).

Keegan, J., *The First World War* (London, 1988).

Knox, A., *With the Russian Army* (New York, 1921).

Lawrence, T. E., *Revolt in the Desert* (London, 1927).

Ludendorff, E., *My War Memories* (London, 1919).

Massie, R. K., *Nicholas and Alexandra* (London, 1968).

Middlebrook, M., *The First Day on the Somme: 1 July 1916* (London, 1971).

Moberley, F. J., *The Campaign in Mesopotamia*, 4 vols (London, 1923–27).

Nicholls, J., *Cheerful Sacrifice: The Battle of Arras 1917* (London, 1990).

Palmer, A., *The Gardeners of Salonika* (London, 1966).

Passingham, I., *Pillars of Fire: The Battle of Messines Ridge, June 1917* (Stroud, 1998).

Pedersen, P., *Monash as Military Commander* (Melbourne, 1985).

Philpott, W., *Anglo-French Relations and Strategy on the Western Front 1914–1918* (London, 1996).

Prior, R. and T. Wilson, *Passchendaele: The Untold Story* (London, 1996).

Rawlings, B., *Surviving Trench Warfare: Technology and the Canadian Corps, 1914–1918* (Toronto, 1992).

von Sanders, L., *Five Years in Turkey* (London, 1928).

Schreiber, S., *Shock Army of the British Empire: The Canadian Corps in the Last 100 Days of the Great War* (Westport, 1997).

Sheffield, G., *Forgotten Victory: The First World War, Myths and Realities* (London, 2001).

Simkins, P., *Kitchener's Army: The Raising of the New Armies 1914–1916* (Manchester, 1988).

Smith, L., *Between Mutiny and Obedience: The Case of the French Fifth Infantry Division during World War I* (New Jersey, 1994).

Strachan, H., *The First World I: Volume 1, To Arms* (Oxford, 2001).

Terraine, J., *To Win a War; 1918, the Year of Victory* (London, 1978).

Travers, T., *How the War was Won: Command and Technology in the British Army on the Western Front, 1917–1918* (London, 1992).

Walker, J., *The Blood Tub: General Gough and the Battle of Bullecourt, 1917* (Staplehurst, 1998).

Wavell, A. P., *The Palestine Campaign* (London, 1928).

Williams, J., *The Home Fronts: Britain, France and Germany 1914–1918* (London, 1972).

INDEX

B

G

H

I

J

K

L

M

N

O

P

Q

R